FULL METAL PANIC. 04

Original Author **SHOUJI GATOU**
Art **RETSU TATEO**
Character Creation **SHIKIDOUJI**

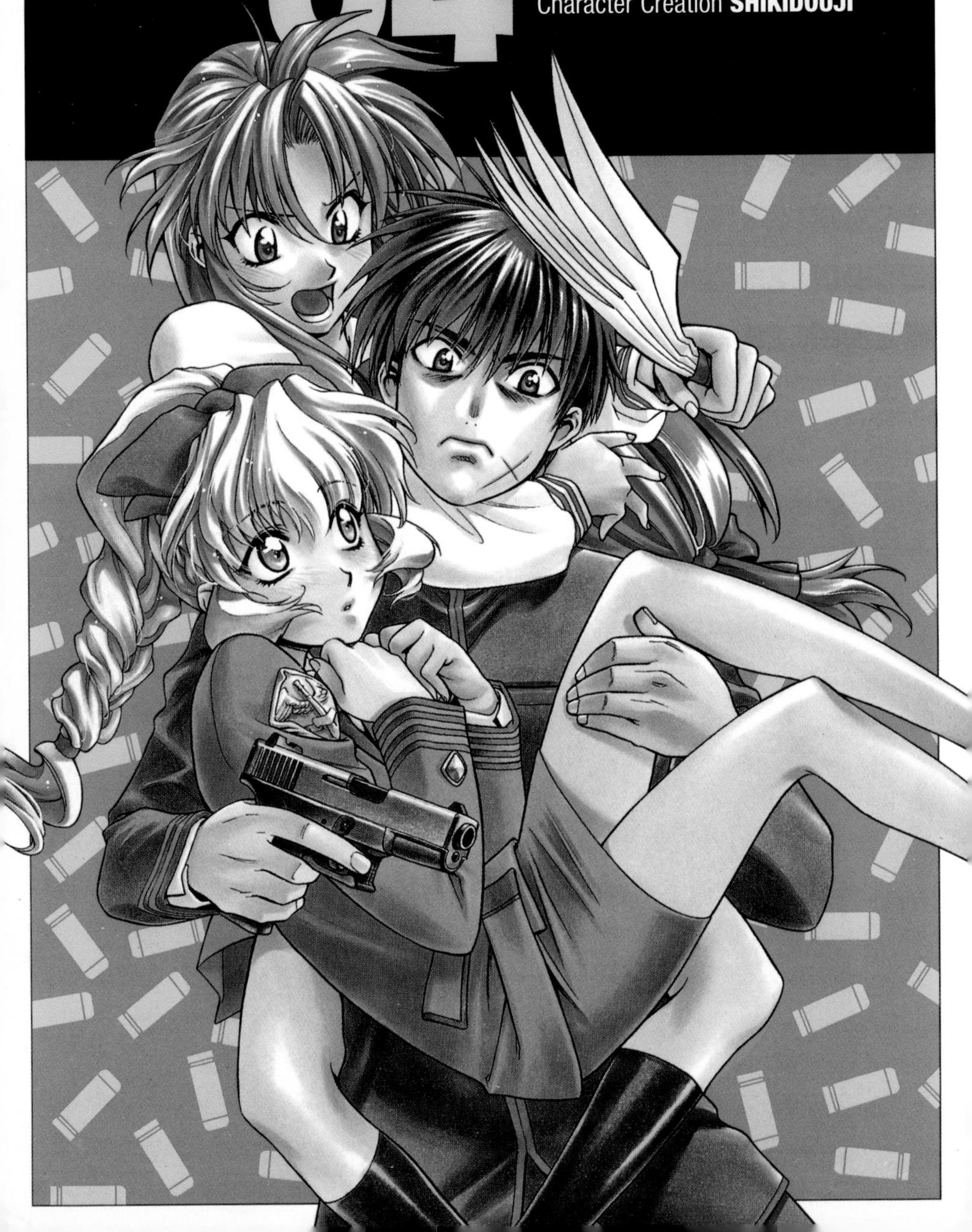

FULL METAL PANIC!

CONTENTS

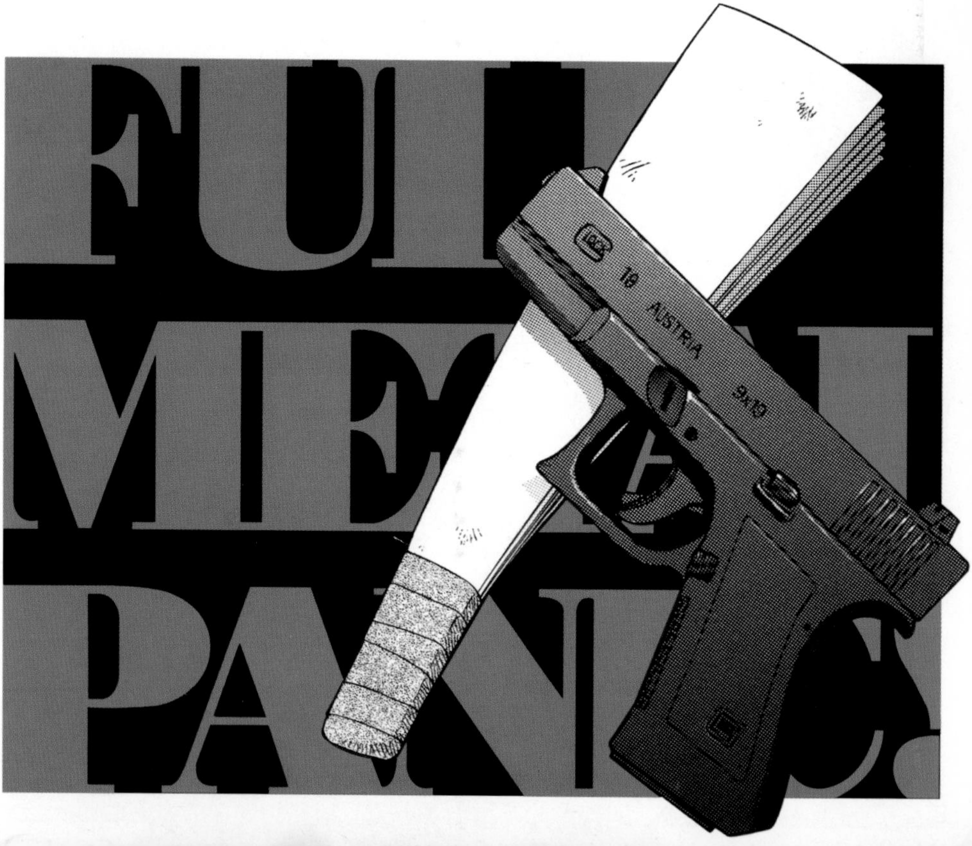

19
AUSTRIA
9x19

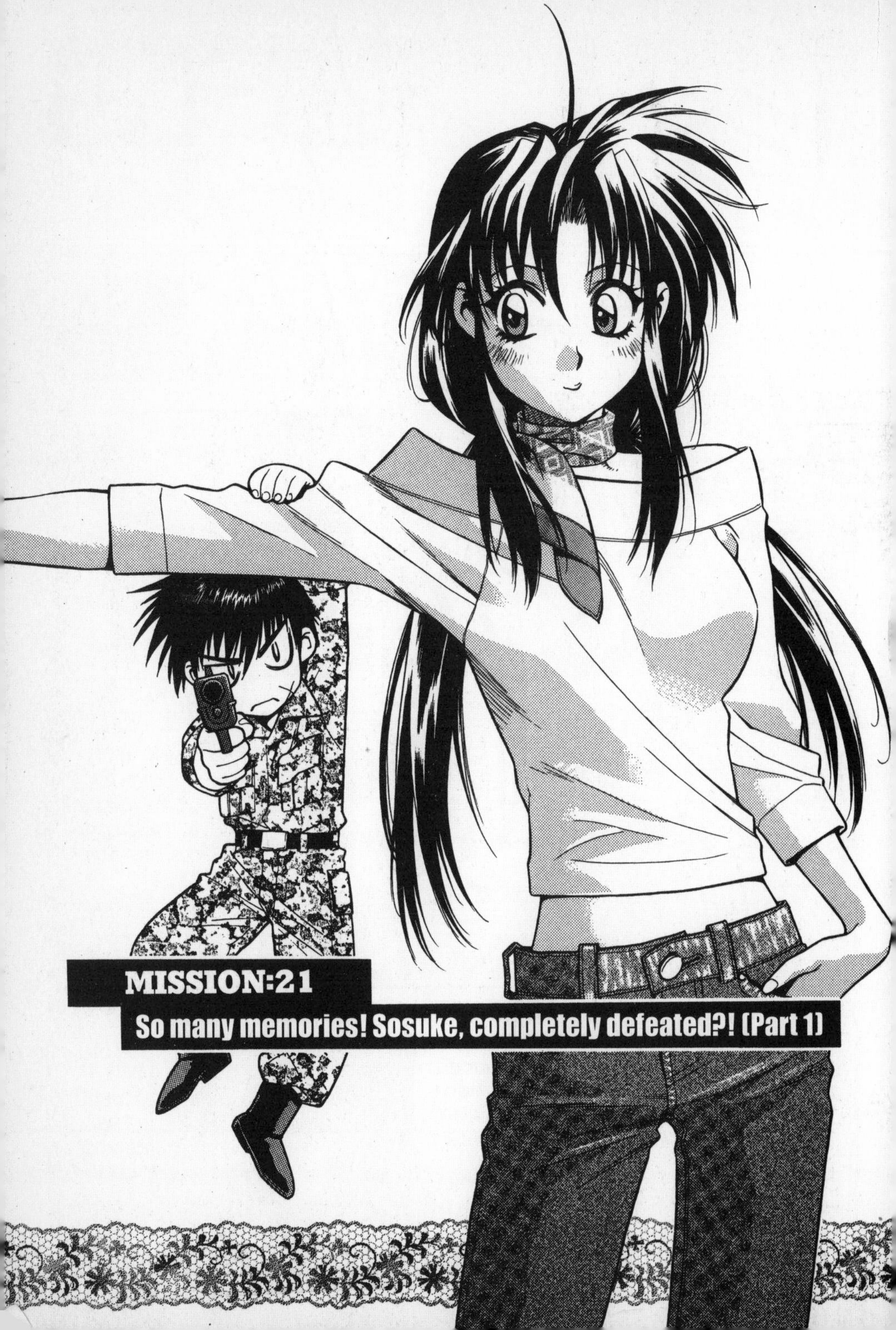
MISSION:21
So many memories! Sosuke, completely defeated?! (Part 1)

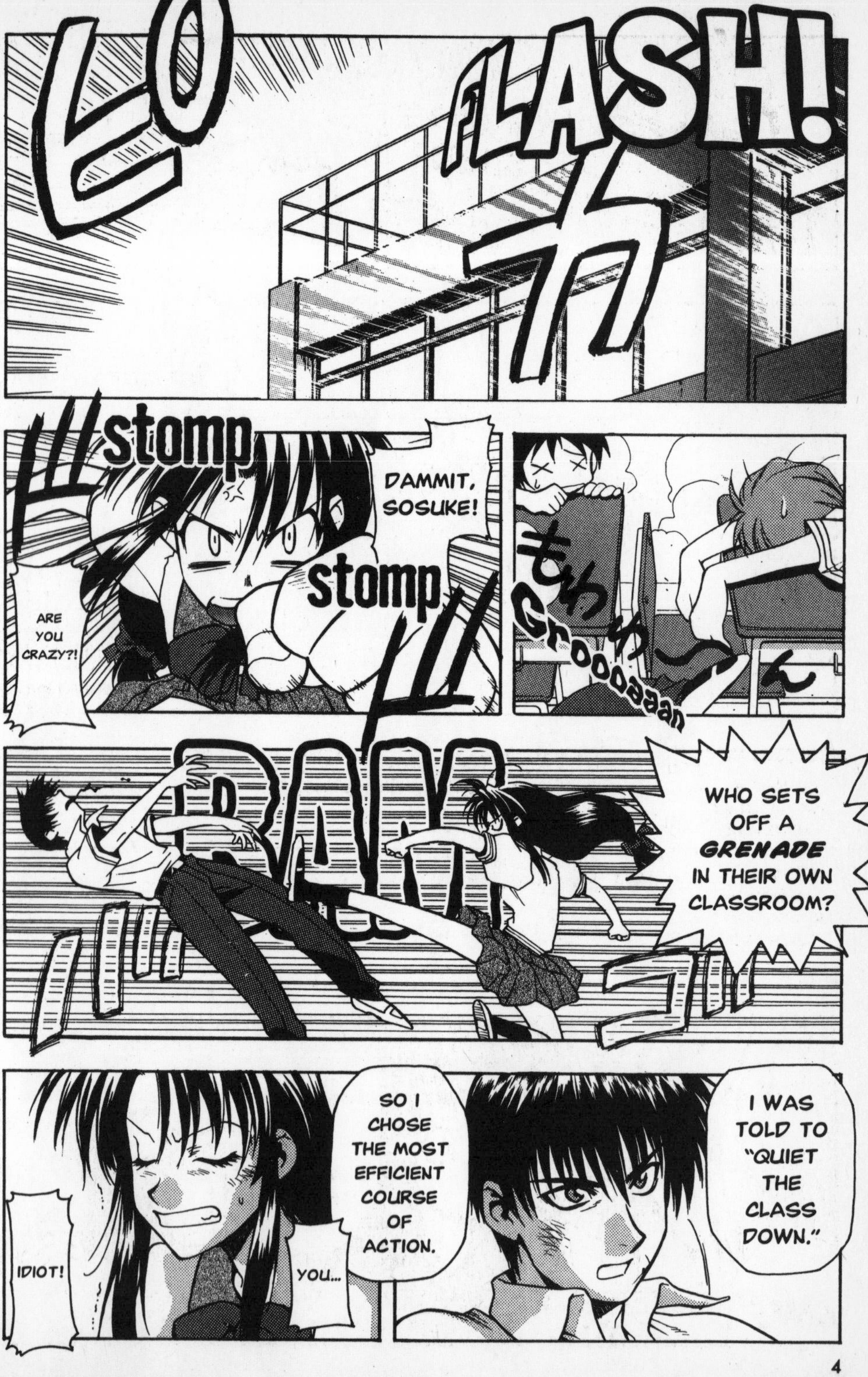
FLASH!
Groooaaaan
DAMMIT, SOSUKE!
stomp
stomp
ARE YOU CRAZY?!
WHO SETS OFF A ***GRENADE*** IN THEIR OWN CLASSROOM?
I WAS TOLD TO "QUIET THE CLASS DOWN."
SO I CHOSE THE MOST EFFICIENT COURSE OF ACTION.
YOU...
IDIOT!

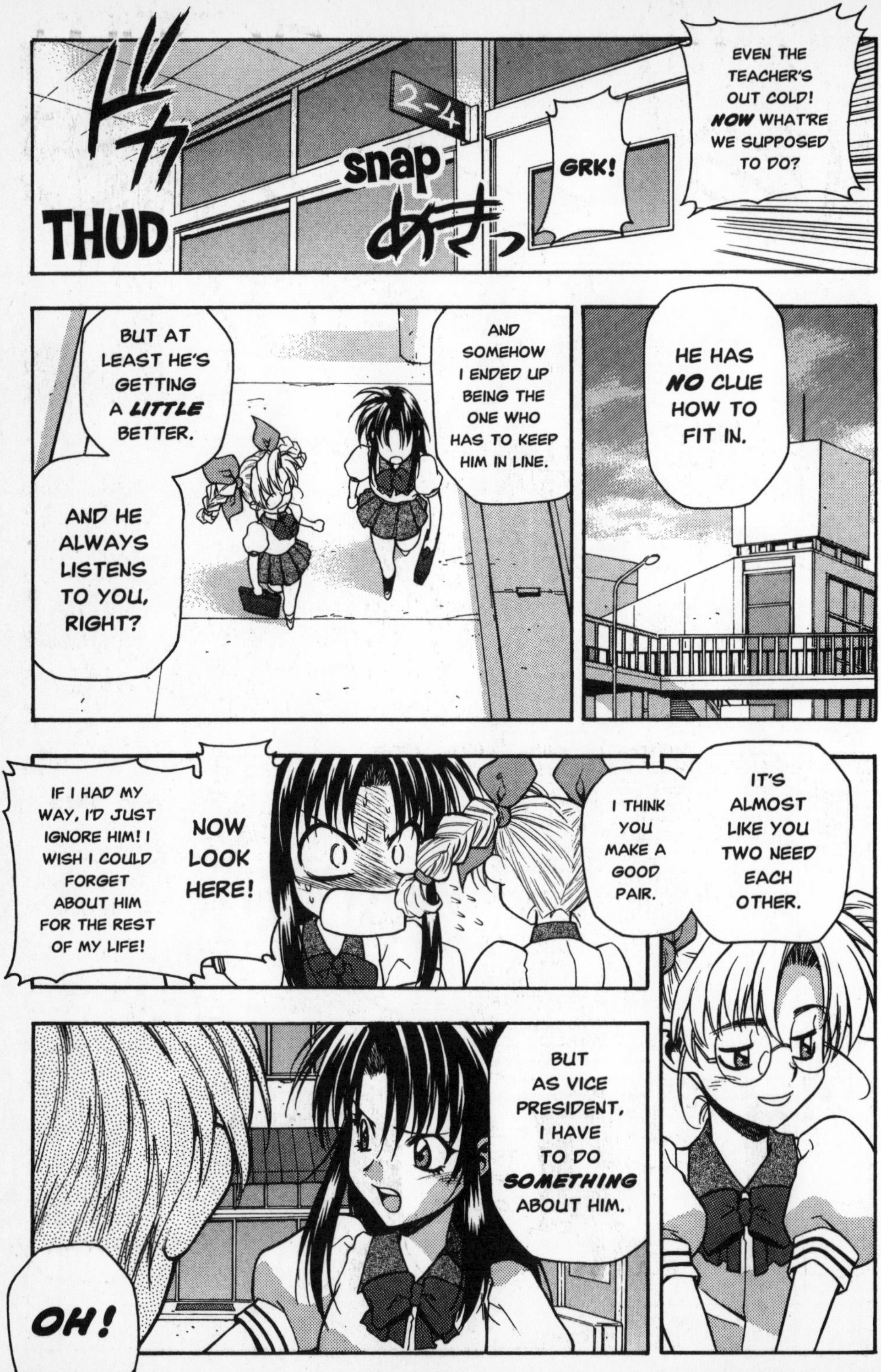

EVEN THE TEACHER'S OUT COLD! ***NOW*** WHAT'RE WE SUPPOSED TO DO?
GRK!
2-4
snap
あきっ
ドカ
THUD
HE HAS ***NO*** CLUE HOW TO FIT IN.
AND SOMEHOW I ENDED UP BEING THE ONE WHO HAS TO KEEP HIM IN LINE.
BUT AT LEAST HE'S GETTING A ***LITTLE*** BETTER.
AND HE ALWAYS LISTENS TO YOU, RIGHT?
IT'S ALMOST LIKE YOU TWO NEED EACH OTHER.
I THINK YOU MAKE A GOOD PAIR.
NOW LOOK HERE!
IF I HAD MY WAY, I'D JUST IGNORE HIM! I WISH I COULD FORGET ABOUT HIM FOR THE REST OF MY LIFE!
BUT AS VICE PRESIDENT, I HAVE TO DO ***SOMETHING*** ABOUT HIM.
OH!

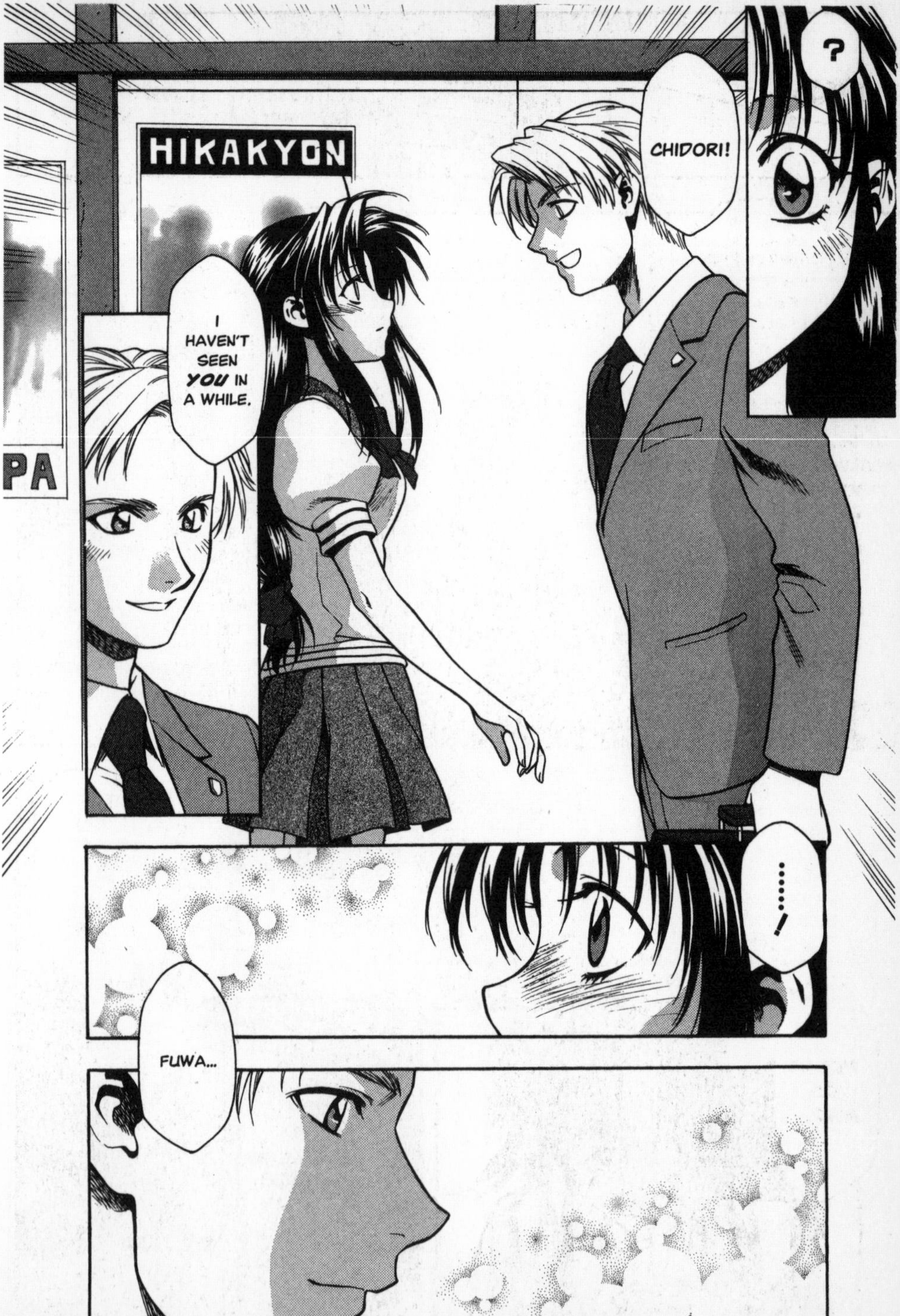
?
CHIDORI!
HIKAKYON
PA
I HAVEN'T SEEN *YOU* IN A WHILE.
......!
FUWA...

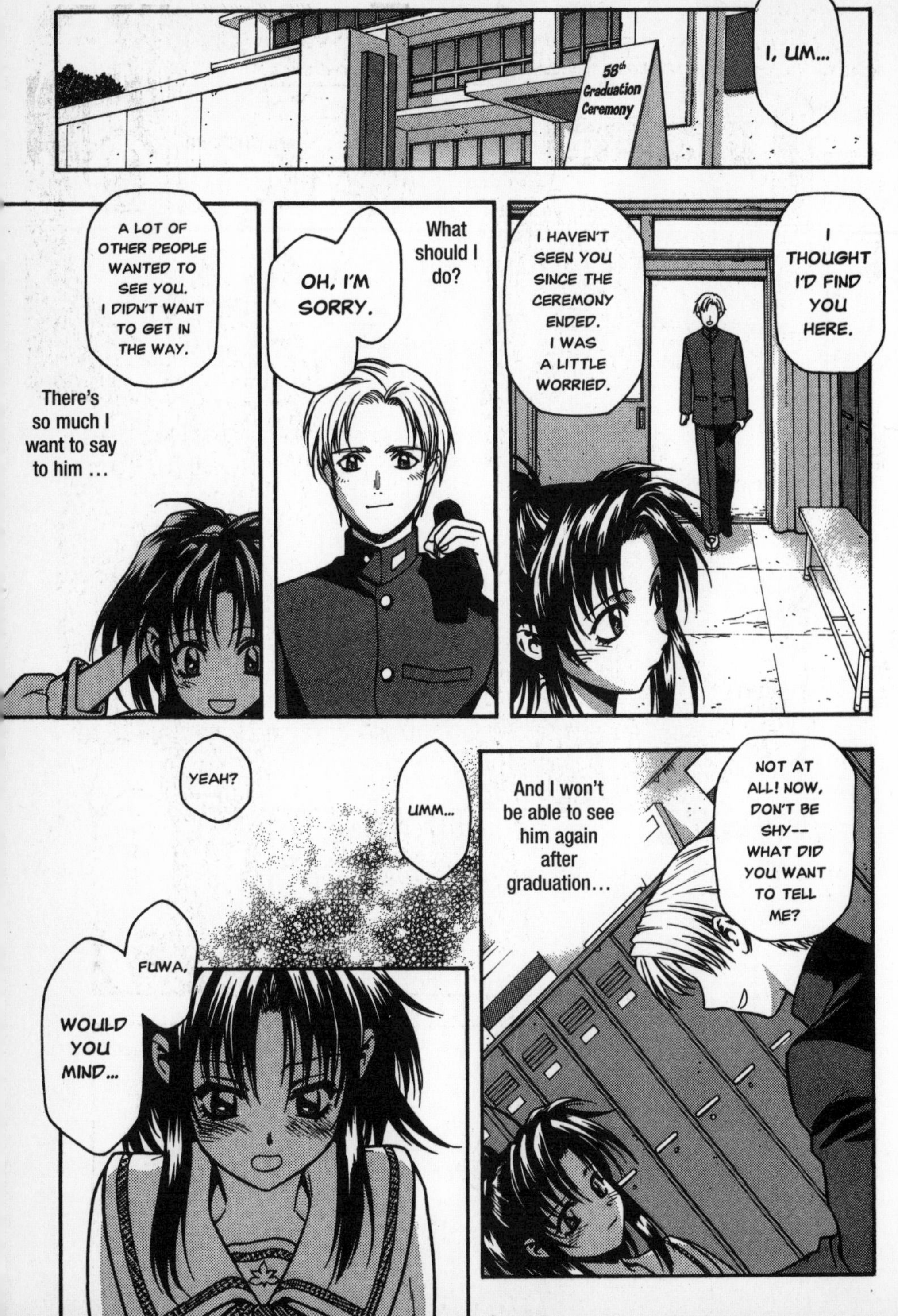
I, UM...
58th Graduation Ceremony
I THOUGHT I'D FIND YOU HERE.
I HAVEN'T SEEN YOU SINCE THE CEREMONY ENDED. I WAS A LITTLE WORRIED.
What should I do?
OH, I'M SORRY.
A LOT OF OTHER PEOPLE WANTED TO SEE YOU. I DIDN'T WANT TO GET IN THE WAY.
There's so much I want to say to him …
NOT AT ALL! NOW, DON'T BE SHY-- WHAT DID YOU WANT TO TELL ME?
And I won't be able to see him again after graduation…
UMM...
YEAH?
FUWA,
WOULD YOU MIND...

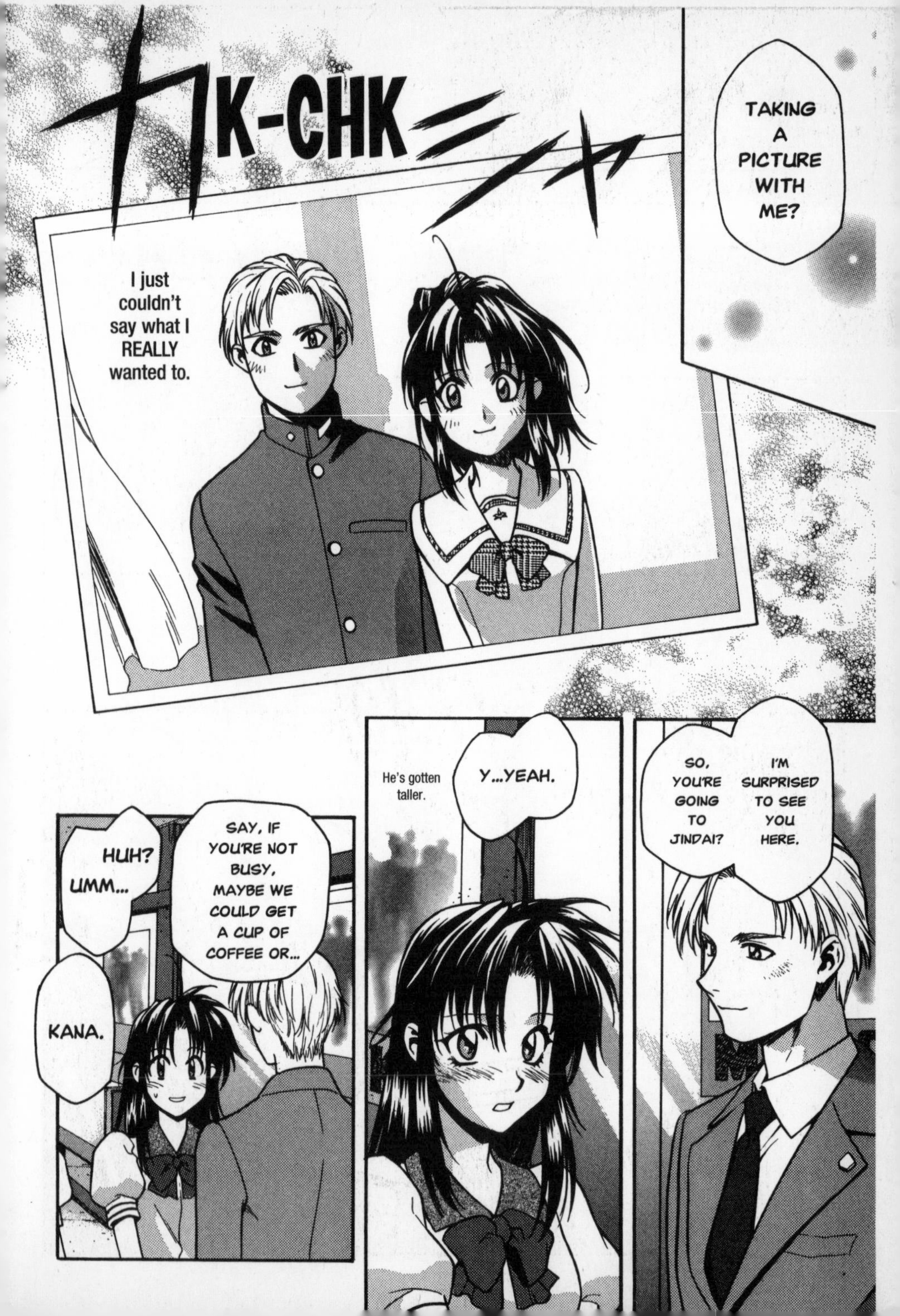
TAKING A PICTURE WITH ME?
K-CHK
I just couldn't say what I REALLY wanted to.
I'M SURPRISED TO SEE YOU HERE.
SO, YOU'RE GOING TO JINDAI?
Y...YEAH.
He's gotten taller.
SAY, IF YOU'RE NOT BUSY, MAYBE WE COULD GET A CUP OF COFFEE OR...
HUH? UMM...
KANA.

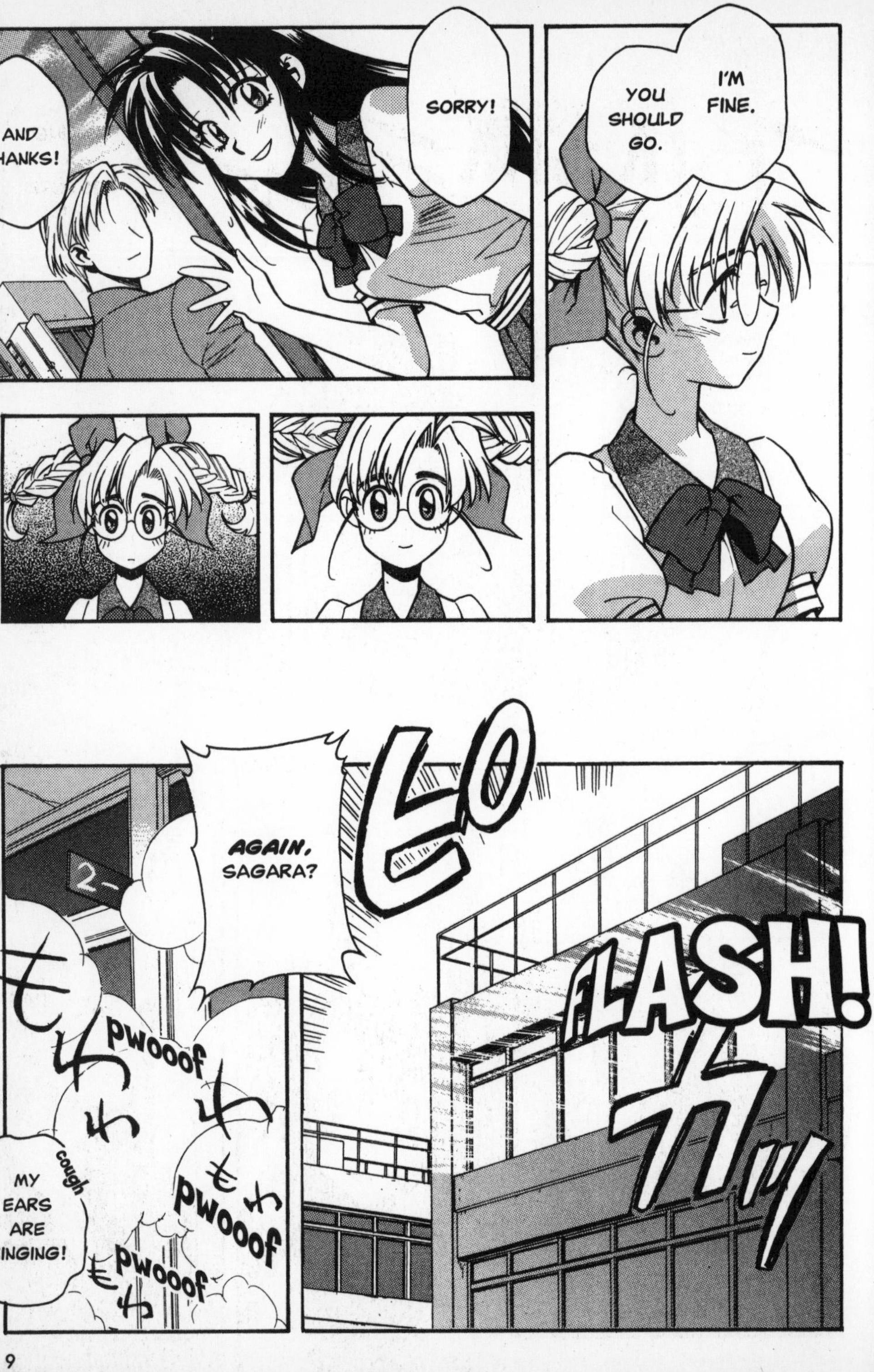
I'M FINE.
YOU SHOULD GO.
SORRY!
AND THANKS!
FLASH!
AGAIN, SAGARA?
pwooof
pwooof
pwooof
cough
MY EARS ARE RINGING!

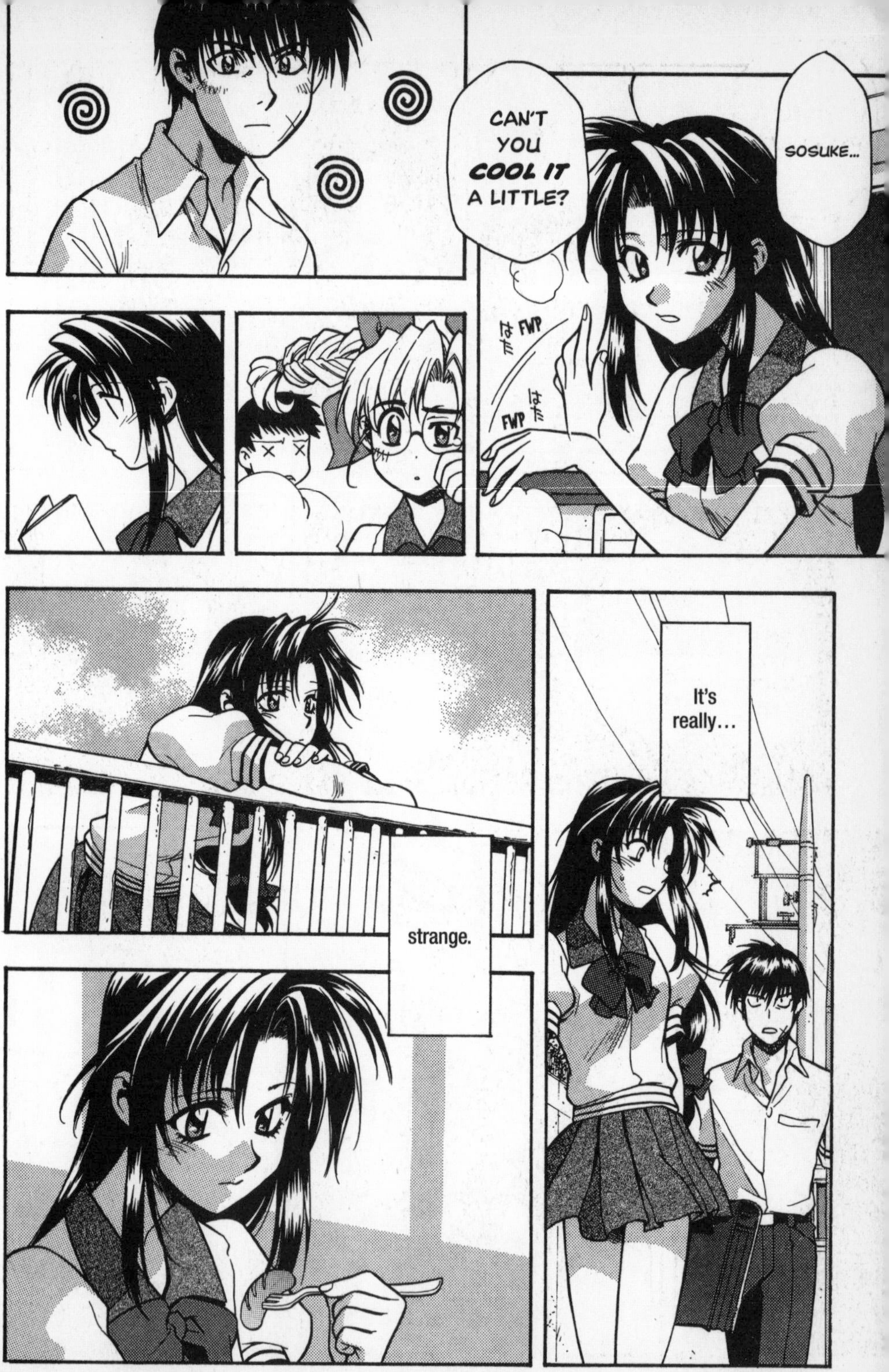
SOSUKE...
CAN'T YOU COOL IT A LITTLE?
はた FWP
はた FWP
It's really…
strange.

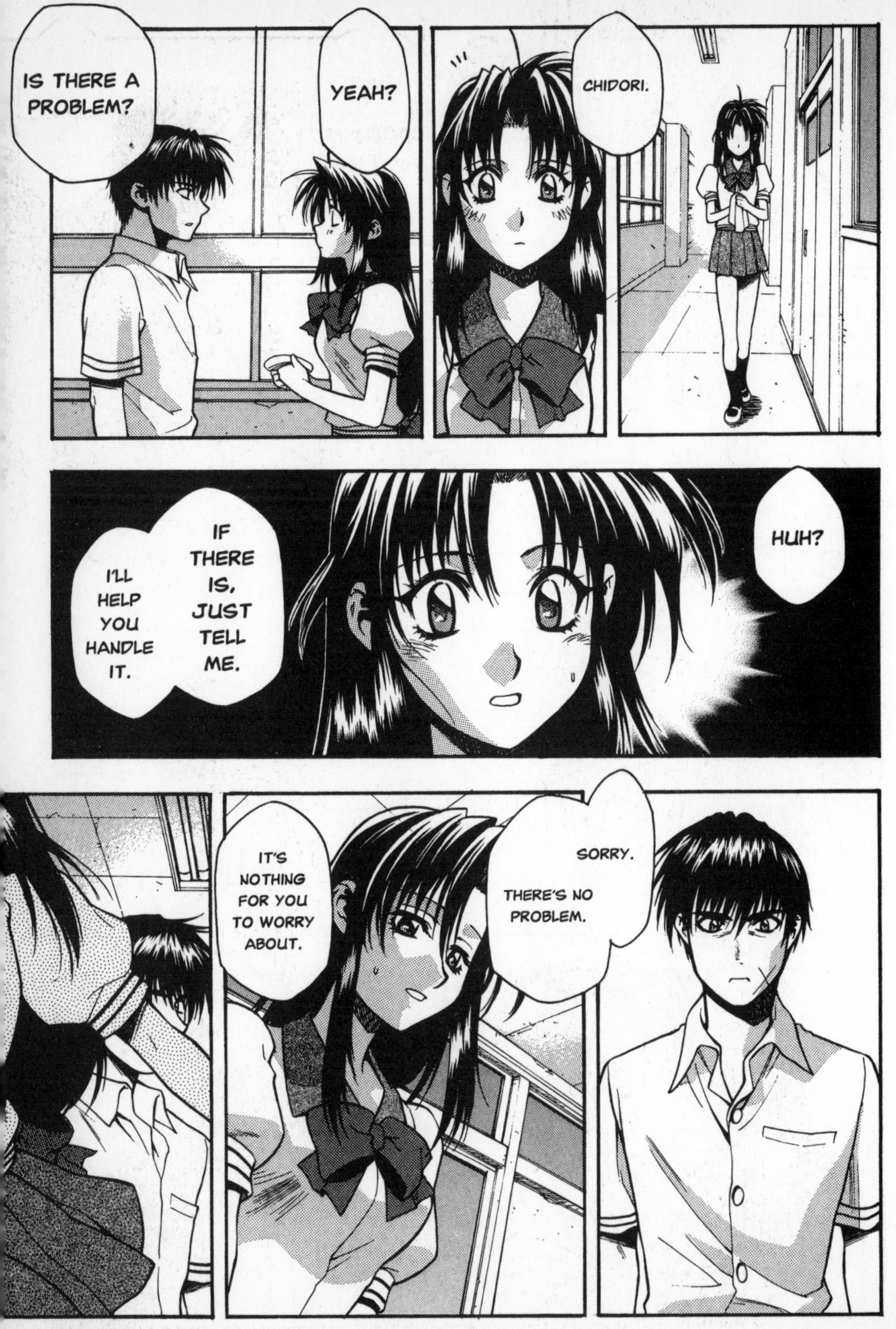
CHIDORI.
YEAH?
IS THERE A PROBLEM?
HUH?
IF THERE IS, JUST TELL ME.
I'LL HELP YOU HANDLE IT.
SORRY.
THERE'S NO PROBLEM.
IT'S NOTHING FOR YOU TO WORRY ABOUT.

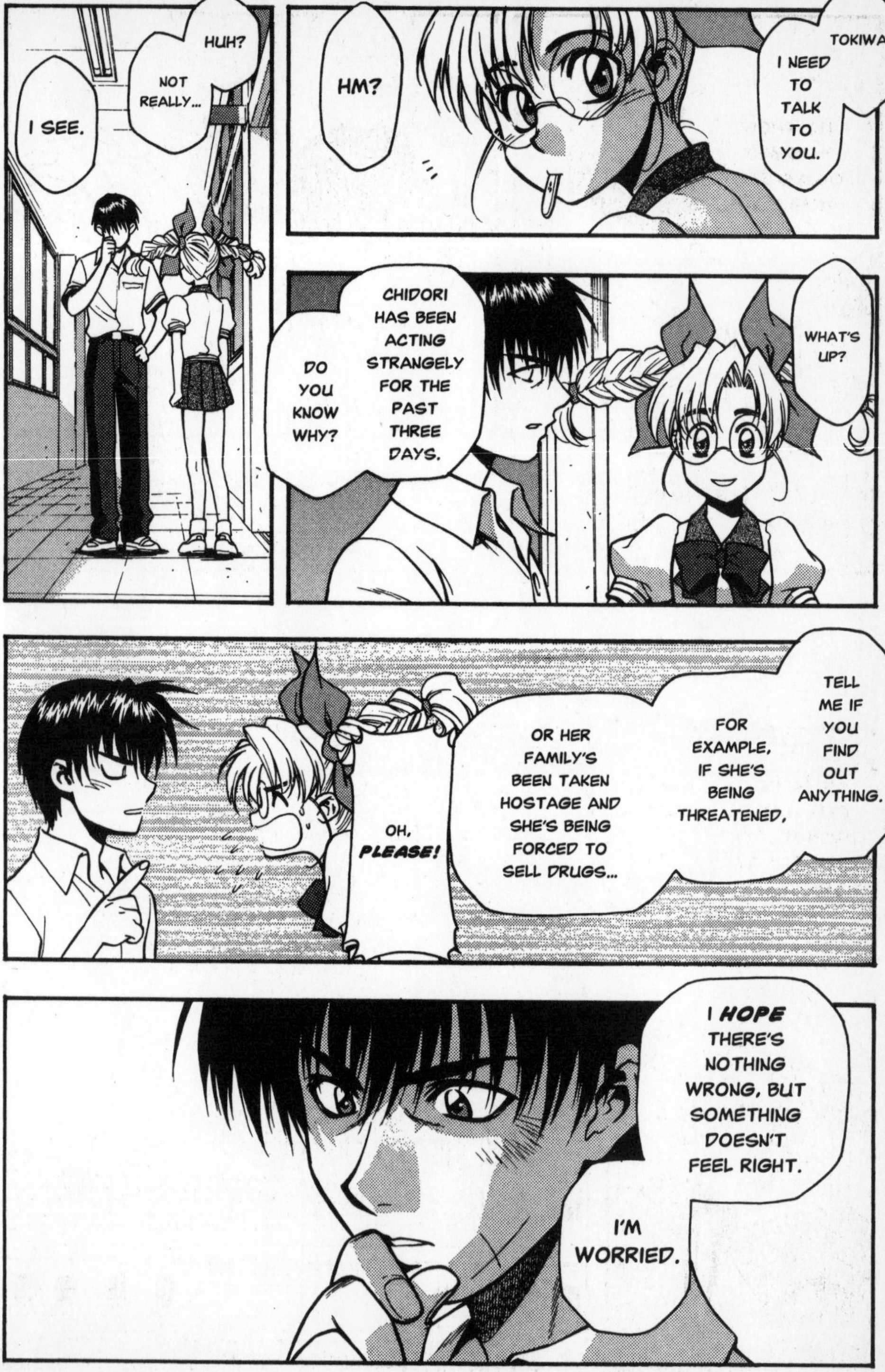
TOKIWA. I NEED TO TALK TO YOU.
HM?
WHAT'S UP?
CHIDORI HAS BEEN ACTING STRANGELY FOR THE PAST THREE DAYS.
DO YOU KNOW WHY?
HUH? NOT REALLY...
I SEE.
TELL ME IF YOU FIND OUT ANYTHING.
FOR EXAMPLE, IF SHE'S BEING THREATENED,
OR HER FAMILY'S BEEN TAKEN HOSTAGE AND SHE'S BEING FORCED TO SELL DRUGS...
OH, *PLEASE!*
I *HOPE* THERE'S NOTHING WRONG, BUT SOMETHING DOESN'T FEEL RIGHT.
I'M WORRIED.

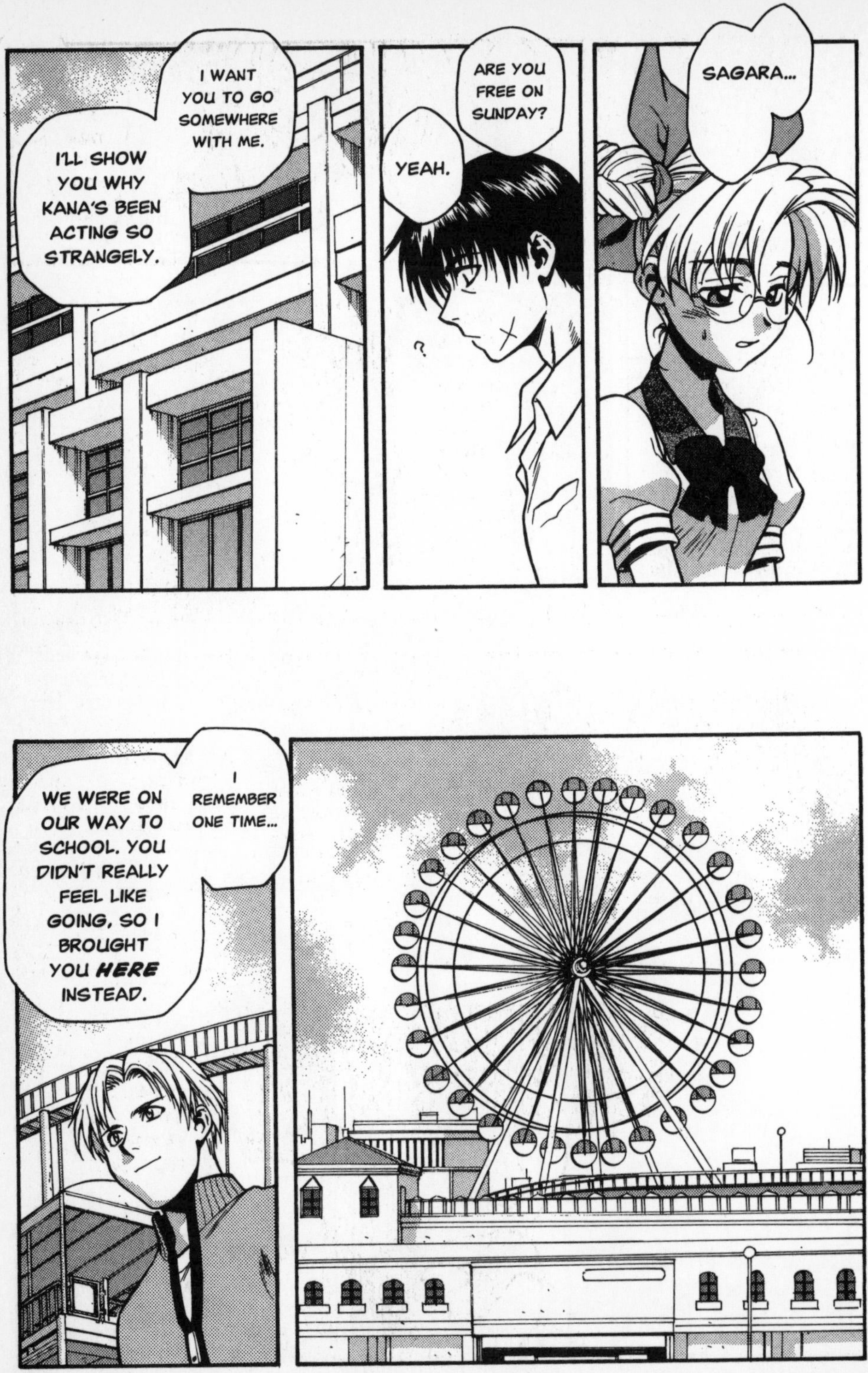
SAGARA...
ARE YOU FREE ON SUNDAY?
YEAH.
I WANT YOU TO GO SOMEWHERE WITH ME.
I'LL SHOW YOU WHY KANA'S BEEN ACTING SO STRANGELY.
I REMEMBER ONE TIME...
WE WERE ON OUR WAY TO SCHOOL. YOU DIDN'T REALLY FEEL LIKE GOING, SO I BROUGHT YOU ***HERE*** INSTEAD.

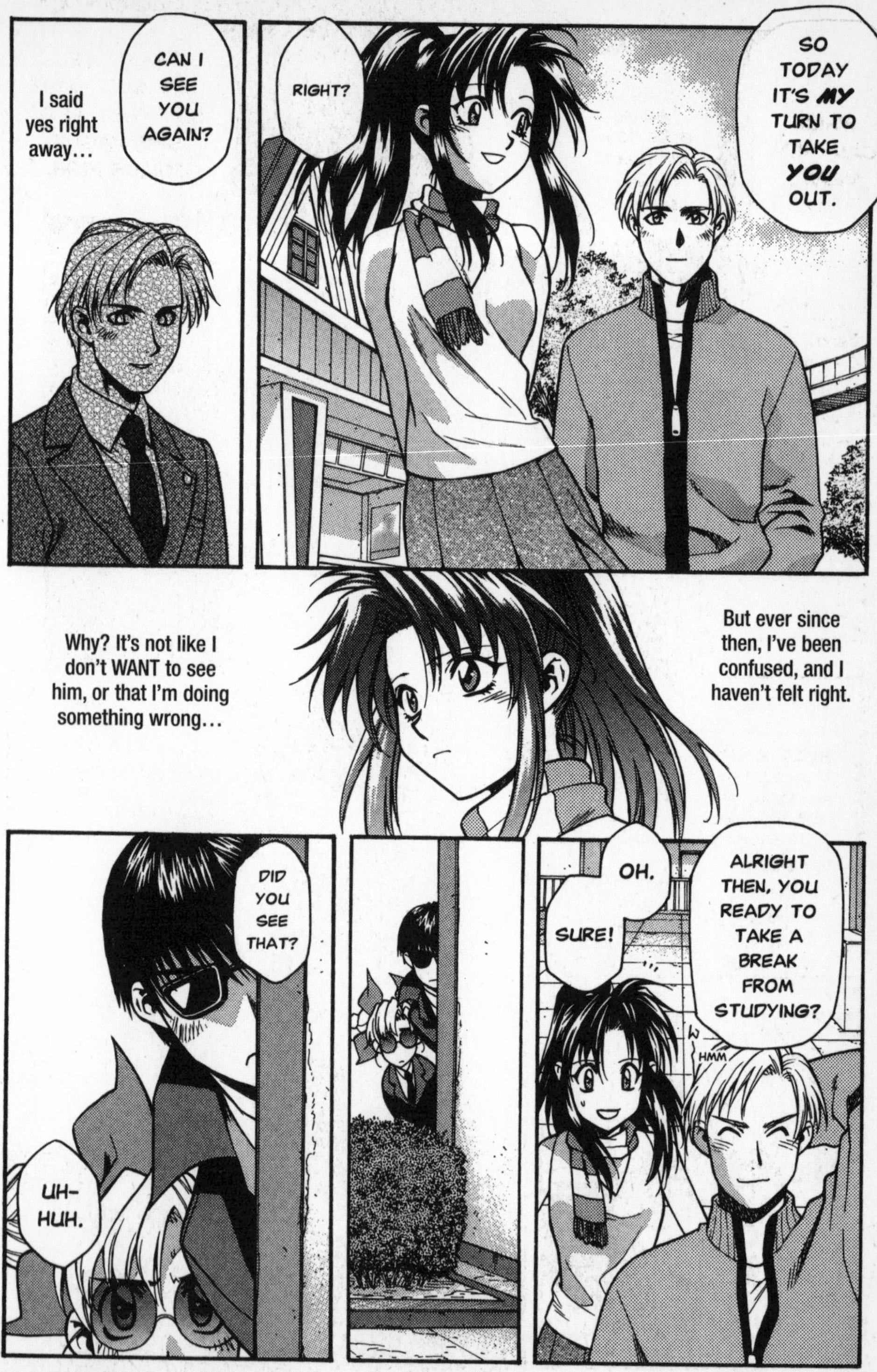
SO TODAY IT'S MY TURN TO TAKE YOU OUT.
RIGHT?
CAN I SEE YOU AGAIN?
I said yes right away…
But ever since then, I've been confused, and I haven't felt right.
Why? It's not like I don't WANT to see him, or that I'm doing something wrong…
ALRIGHT THEN, YOU READY TO TAKE A BREAK FROM STUDYING?
OH.
SURE!
HMM
DID YOU SEE THAT?
UH-HUH.

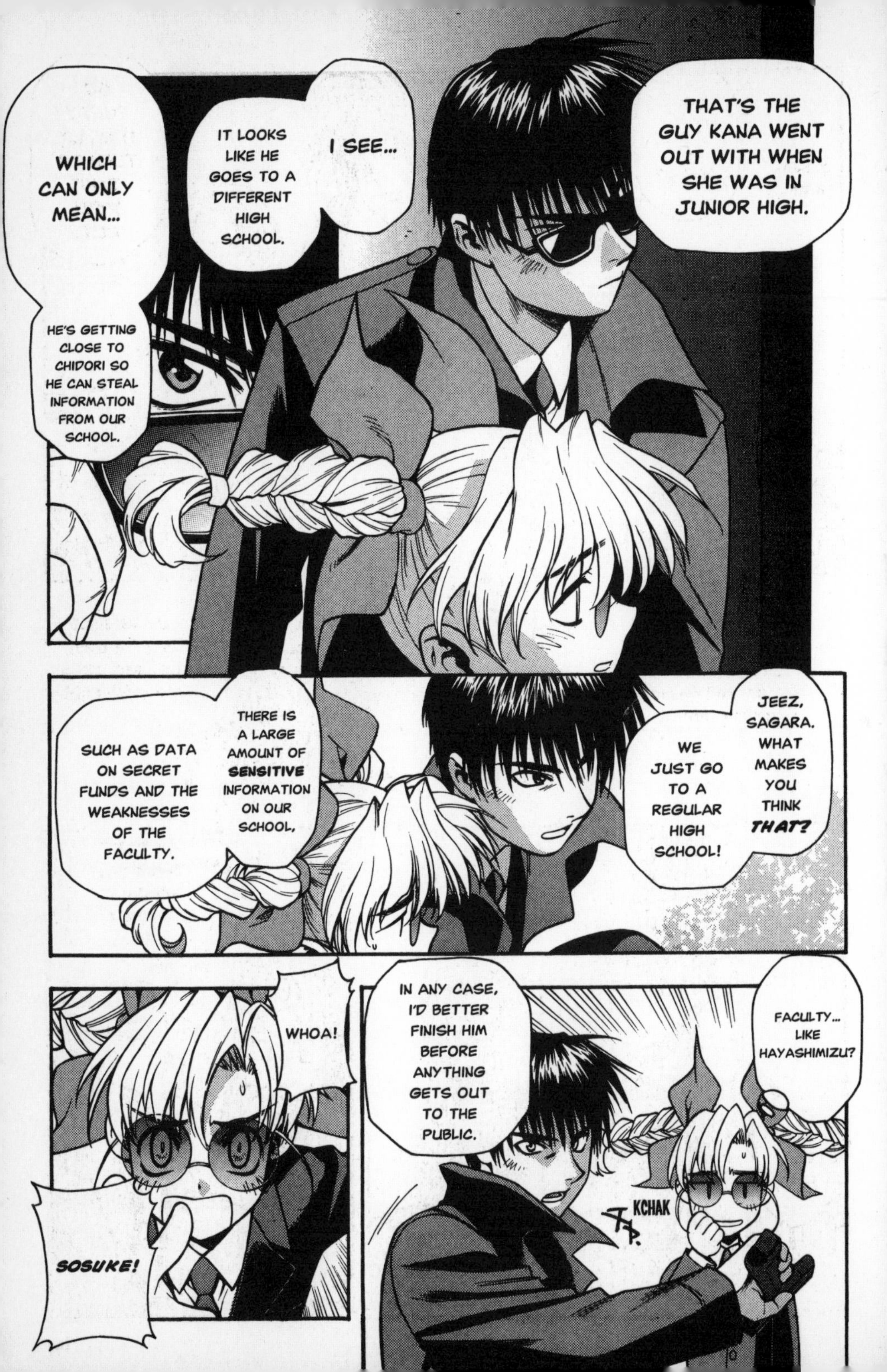
THAT'S THE GUY KANA WENT OUT WITH WHEN SHE WAS IN JUNIOR HIGH.
I SEE...
IT LOOKS LIKE HE GOES TO A DIFFERENT HIGH SCHOOL.
WHICH CAN ONLY MEAN...
HE'S GETTING CLOSE TO CHIDORI SO HE CAN STEAL INFORMATION FROM OUR SCHOOL.
JEEZ, SAGARA. WHAT MAKES YOU THINK THAT?
WE JUST GO TO A REGULAR HIGH SCHOOL!
THERE IS A LARGE AMOUNT OF SENSITIVE INFORMATION ON OUR SCHOOL,
SUCH AS DATA ON SECRET FUNDS AND THE WEAKNESSES OF THE FACULTY.
FACULTY... LIKE HAYASHIMIZU?
IN ANY CASE, I'D BETTER FINISH HIM BEFORE ANYTHING GETS OUT TO THE PUBLIC.
KCHAK
WHOA!
SOSUKE!

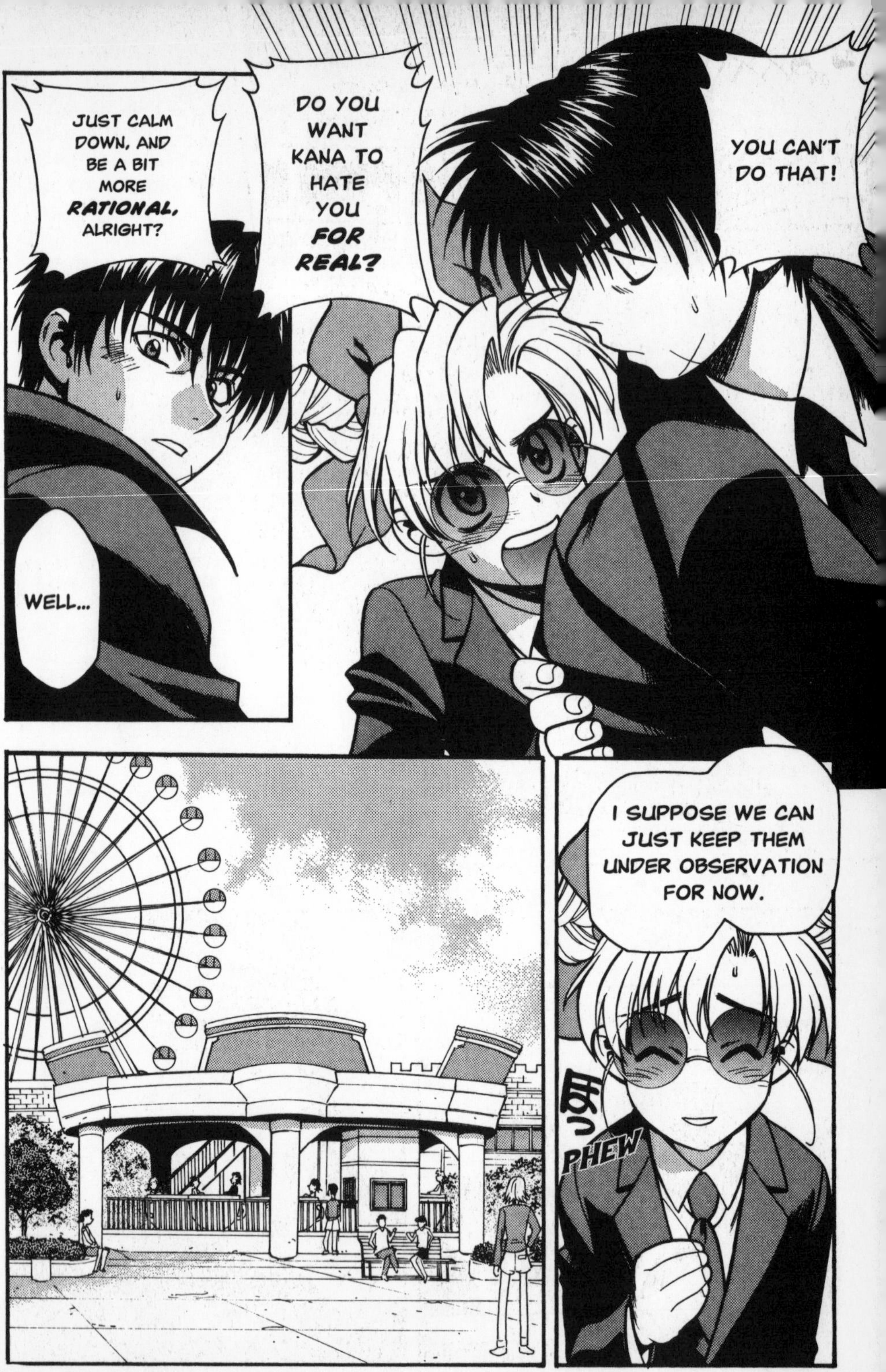
YOU CAN'T DO THAT!
DO YOU WANT KANA TO HATE YOU FOR REAL?
JUST CALM DOWN, AND BE A BIT MORE RATIONAL, ALRIGHT?
WELL...
I SUPPOSE WE CAN JUST KEEP THEM UNDER OBSERVATION FOR NOW.
ほっ
PHEW

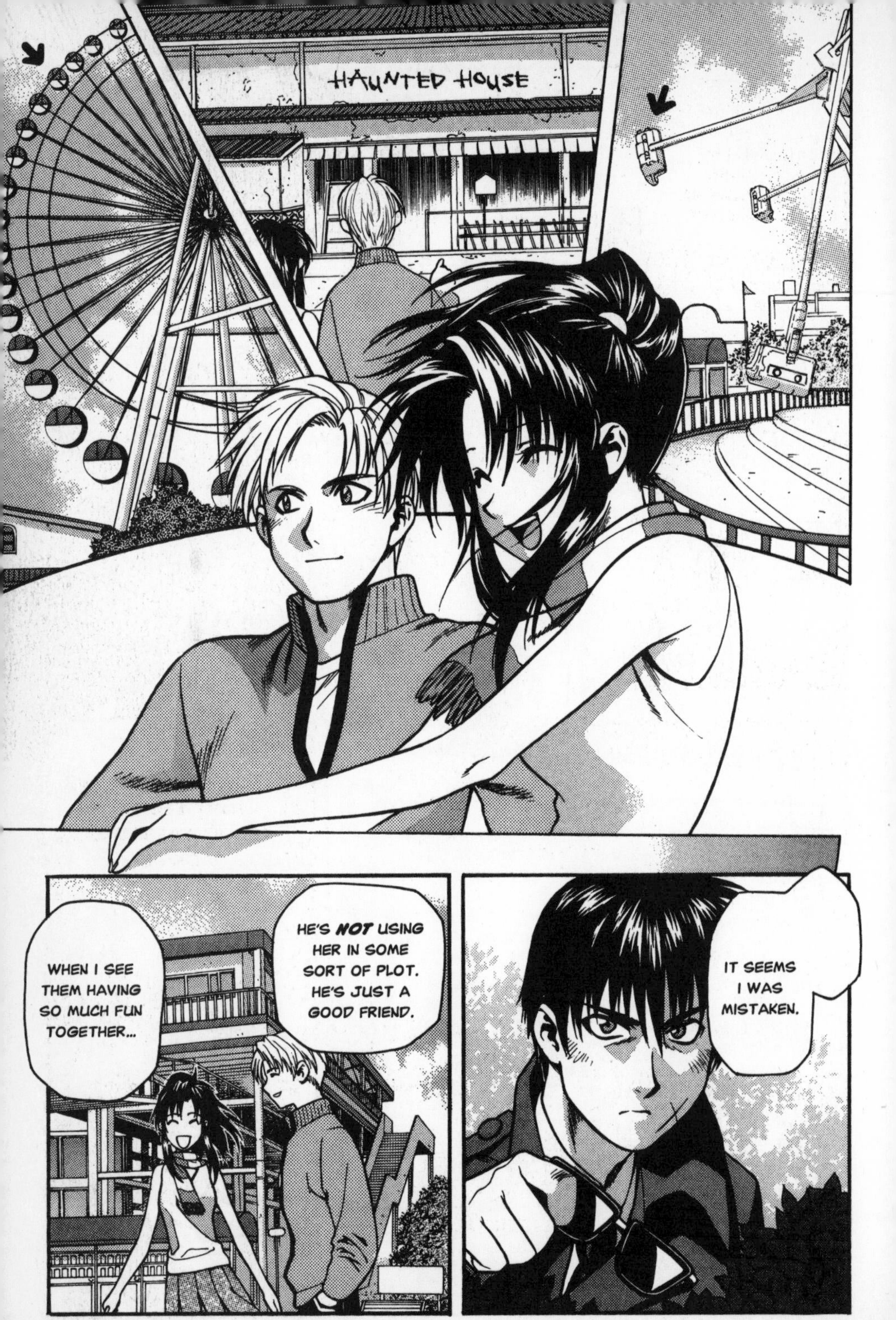
HAUNTED HOUSE
IT SEEMS I WAS MISTAKEN.
HE'S **NOT** USING HER IN SOME SORT OF PLOT. HE'S JUST A GOOD FRIEND.
WHEN I SEE THEM HAVING SO MUCH FUN TOGETHER...

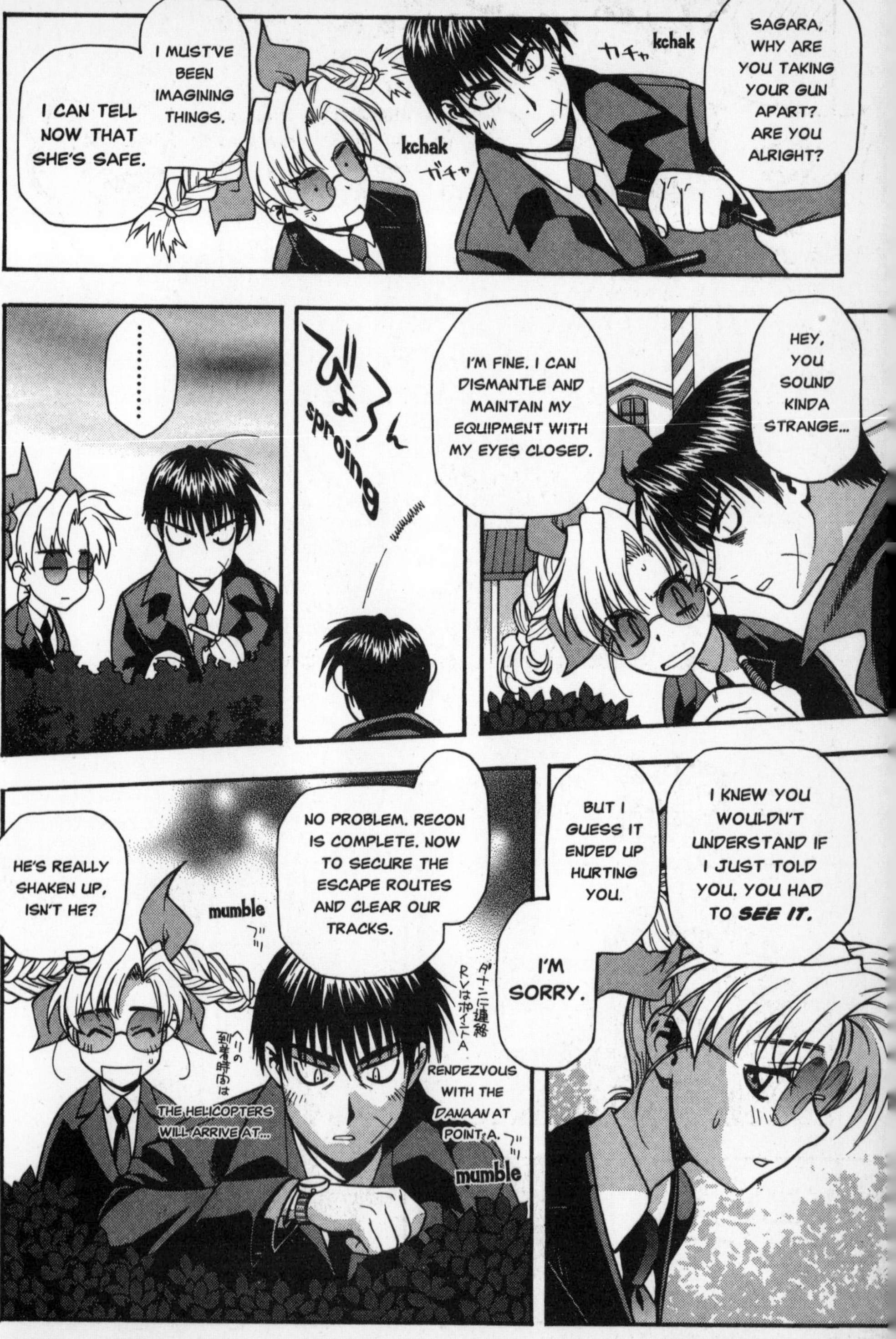
SAGARA, WHY ARE YOU TAKING YOUR GUN APART? ARE YOU ALRIGHT?
カチャ kchak
kchak ガチャ
I MUST'VE BEEN IMAGINING THINGS.
I CAN TELL NOW THAT SHE'S SAFE.
HEY, YOU SOUND KINDA STRANGE...
I'M FINE. I CAN DISMANTLE AND MAINTAIN MY EQUIPMENT WITH MY EYES CLOSED.
びよ〜ん
sproing
......
I KNEW YOU WOULDN'T UNDERSTAND IF I JUST TOLD YOU. YOU HAD TO *SEE IT.*
BUT I GUESS IT ENDED UP HURTING YOU.
I'M SORRY.
NO PROBLEM. RECON IS COMPLETE. NOW TO SECURE THE ESCAPE ROUTES AND CLEAR OUR TRACKS.
mumble ブツ
ダナンに連絡 RVはポイントA
RENDEZVOUS WITH THE DANAAN AT POINT A.
ブツ mumble
ヘリの到着時間は
THE HELICOPTERS WILL ARRIVE AT...
HE'S REALLY SHAKEN UP, ISN'T HE?

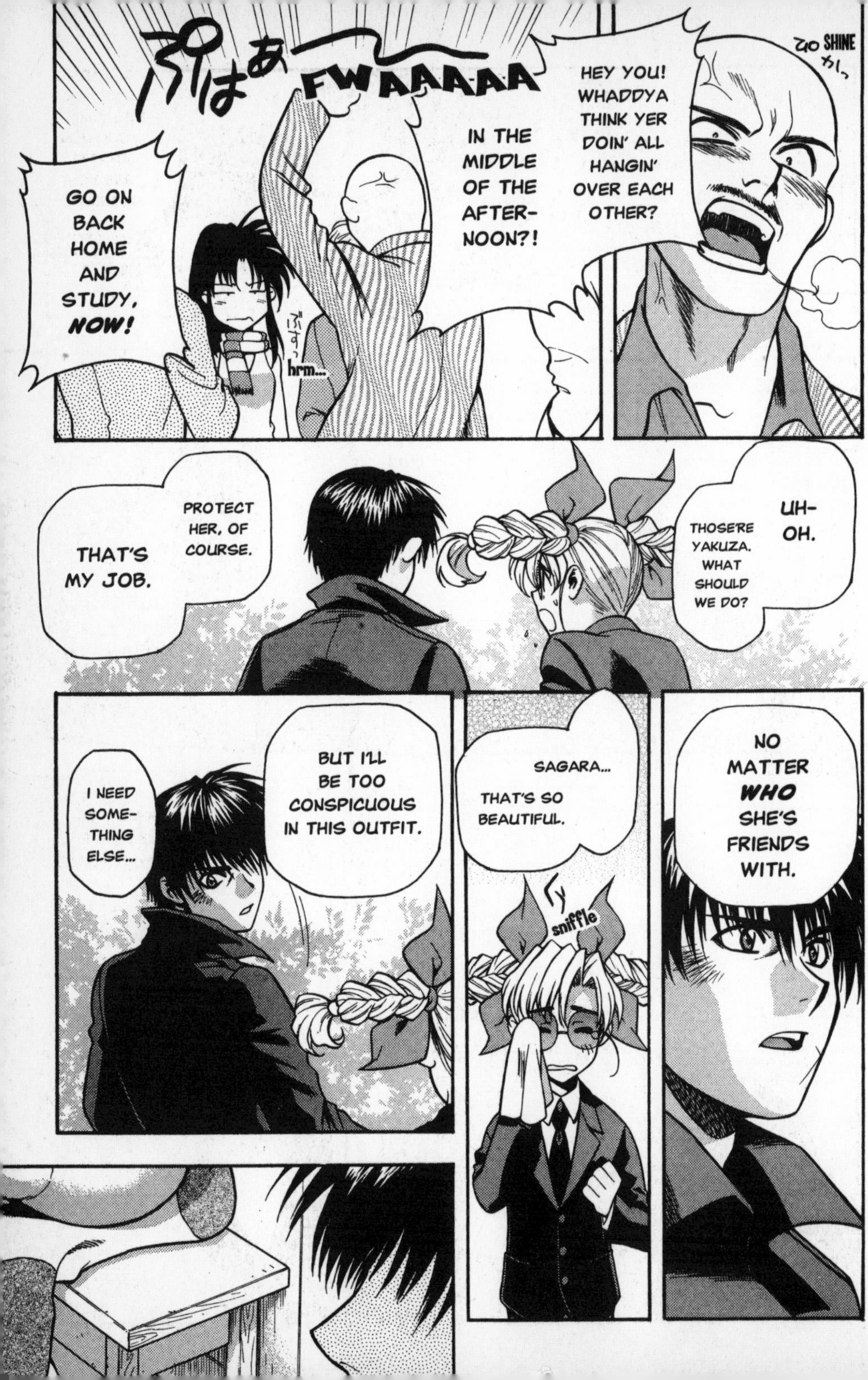
SHINE
HEY YOU! WHADDYA THINK YER DOIN' ALL HANGIN' OVER EACH OTHER?
ぷはあ〜
FWAAAAA
IN THE MIDDLE OF THE AFTER-NOON?!
GO ON BACK HOME AND STUDY, **NOW!**
ぶすっ
hrm...
UH-OH.
THOSE'RE YAKUZA. WHAT SHOULD WE DO?
PROTECT HER, OF COURSE.
THAT'S MY JOB.
NO MATTER ***WHO*** SHE'S FRIENDS WITH.
SAGARA...
THAT'S SO BEAUTIFUL.
sniffle
BUT I'LL BE TOO CONSPICUOUS IN THIS OUTFIT.
I NEED SOME-THING ELSE...

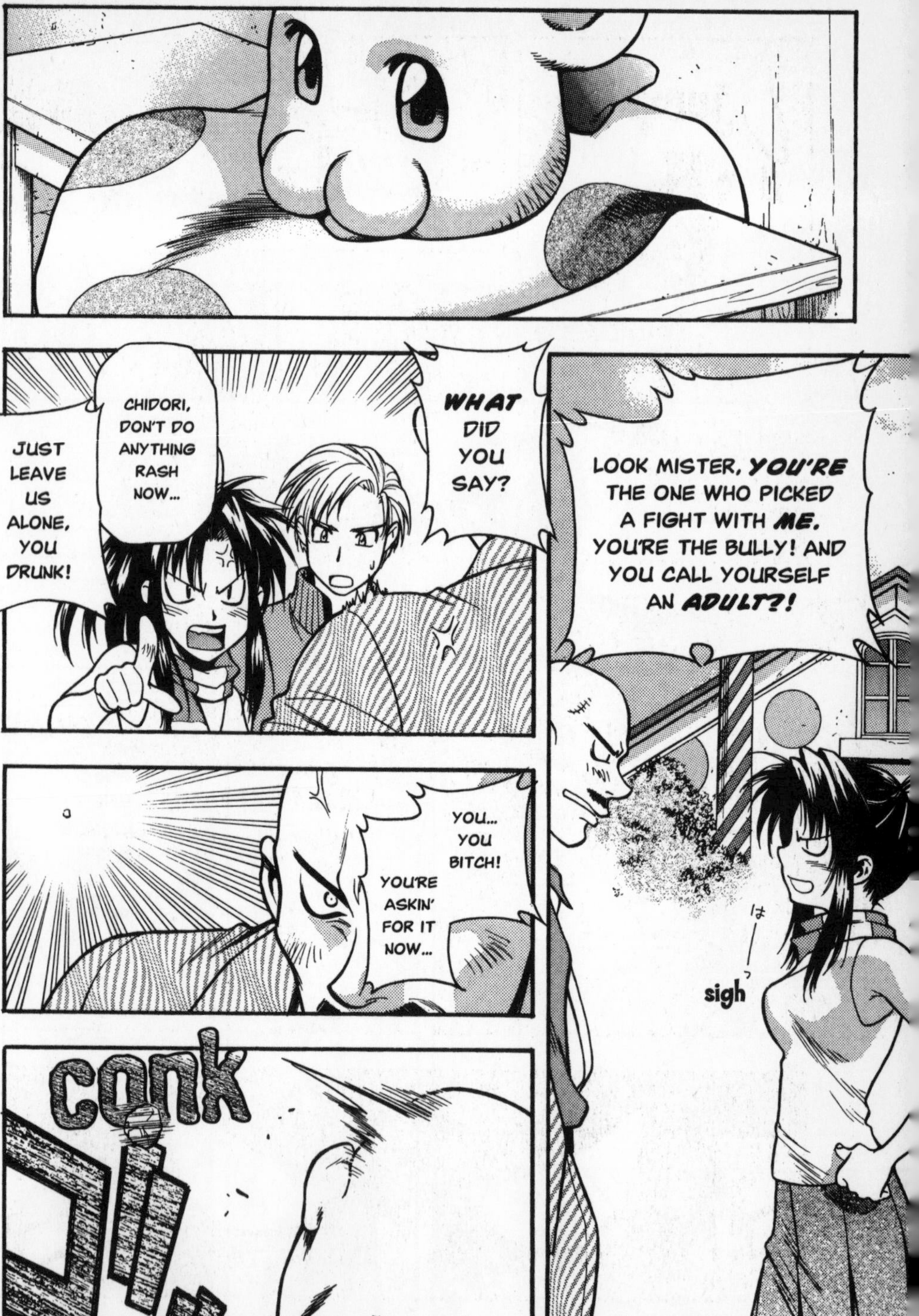
LOOK MISTER, ***YOU'RE*** THE ONE WHO PICKED A FIGHT WITH ***ME.*** YOU'RE THE BULLY! AND YOU CALL YOURSELF AN ***ADULT?!***
は—っ
sigh
WHAT DID YOU SAY?
CHIDORI, DON'T DO ANYTHING RASH NOW...
JUST LEAVE US ALONE, YOU DRUNK!
YOU... YOU BITCH!
YOU'RE ASKIN' FOR IT NOW...
conk

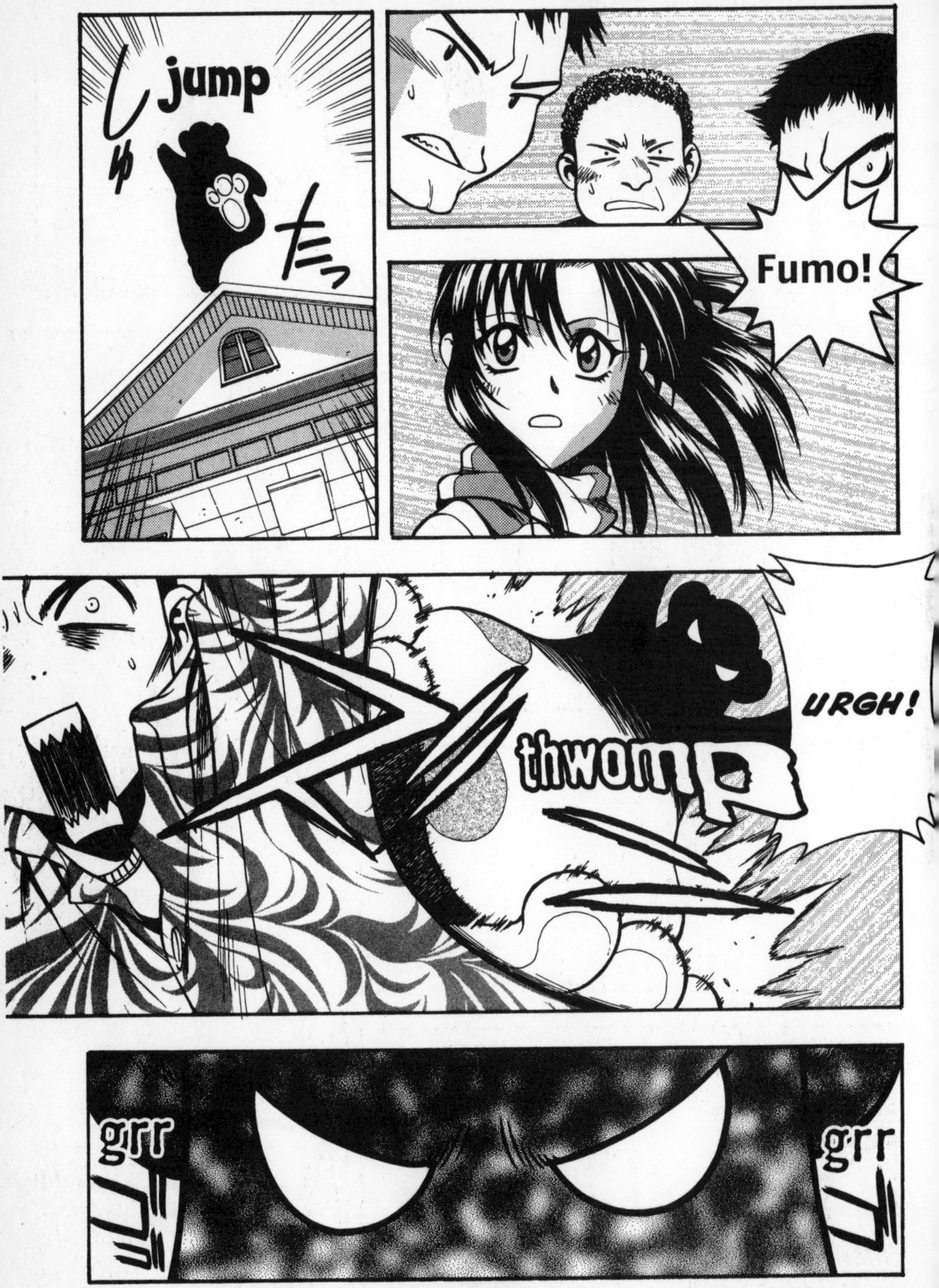

Fumo!
jump
しゅ
たっ
URGH!
thwomp
grr
grr

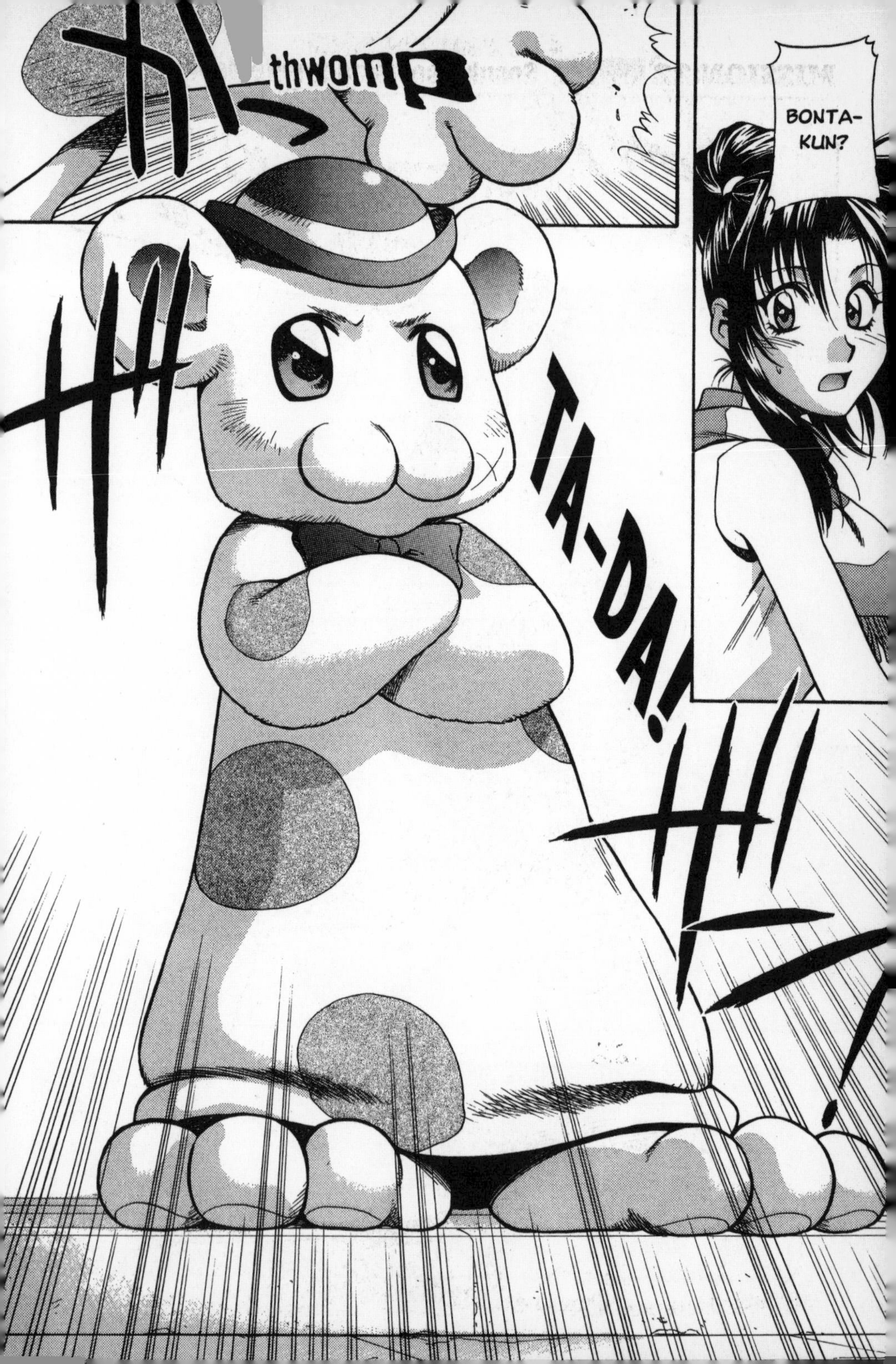
BONTA-KUN?
thwomp
TA-DA!

MISSION:22 [redacted] So many memories! Sosuke, completely defeated?! (Part 2)

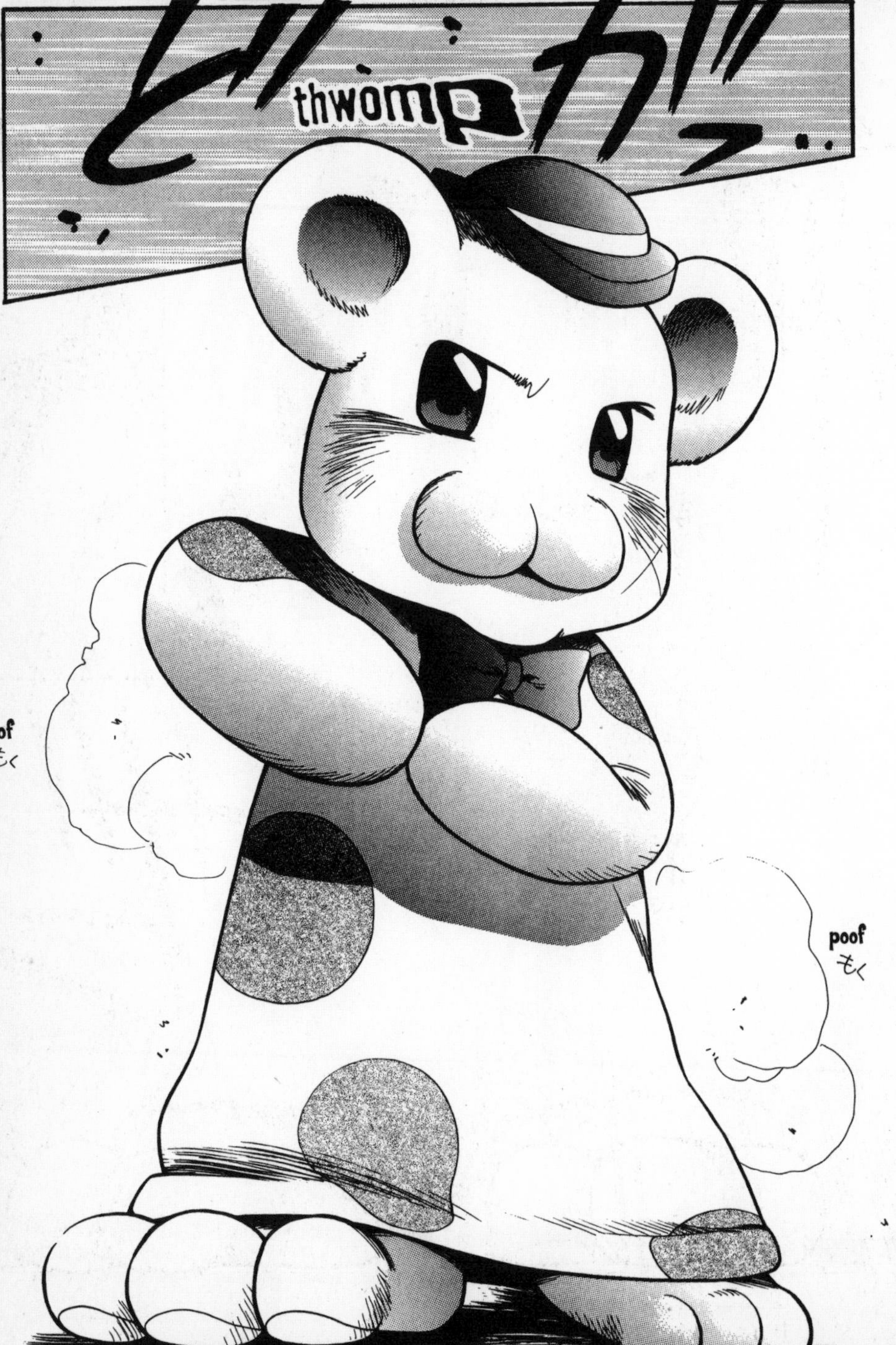

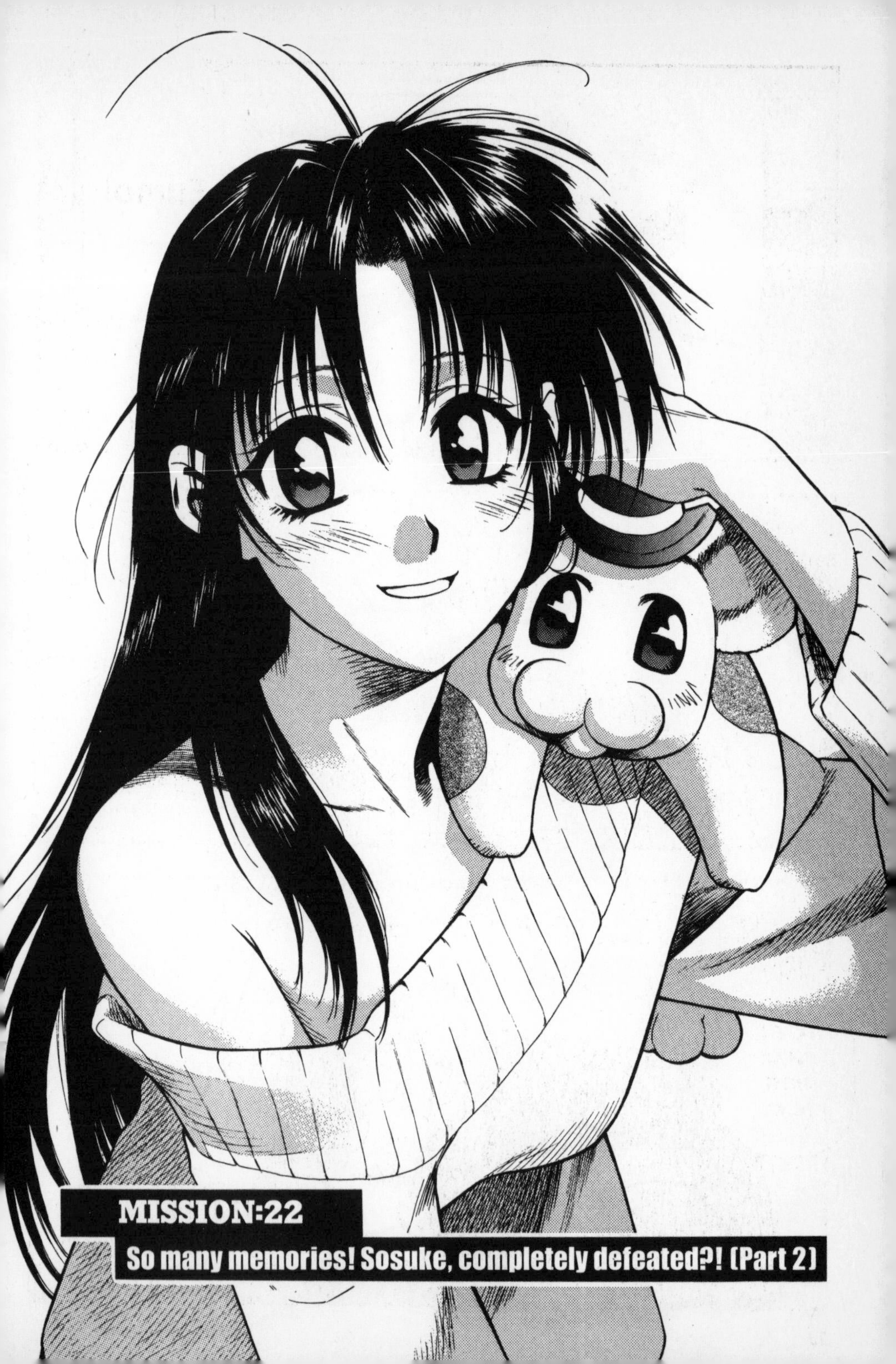

MISSION:22

So many memories! Sosuke, completely defeated?! (Part 2)

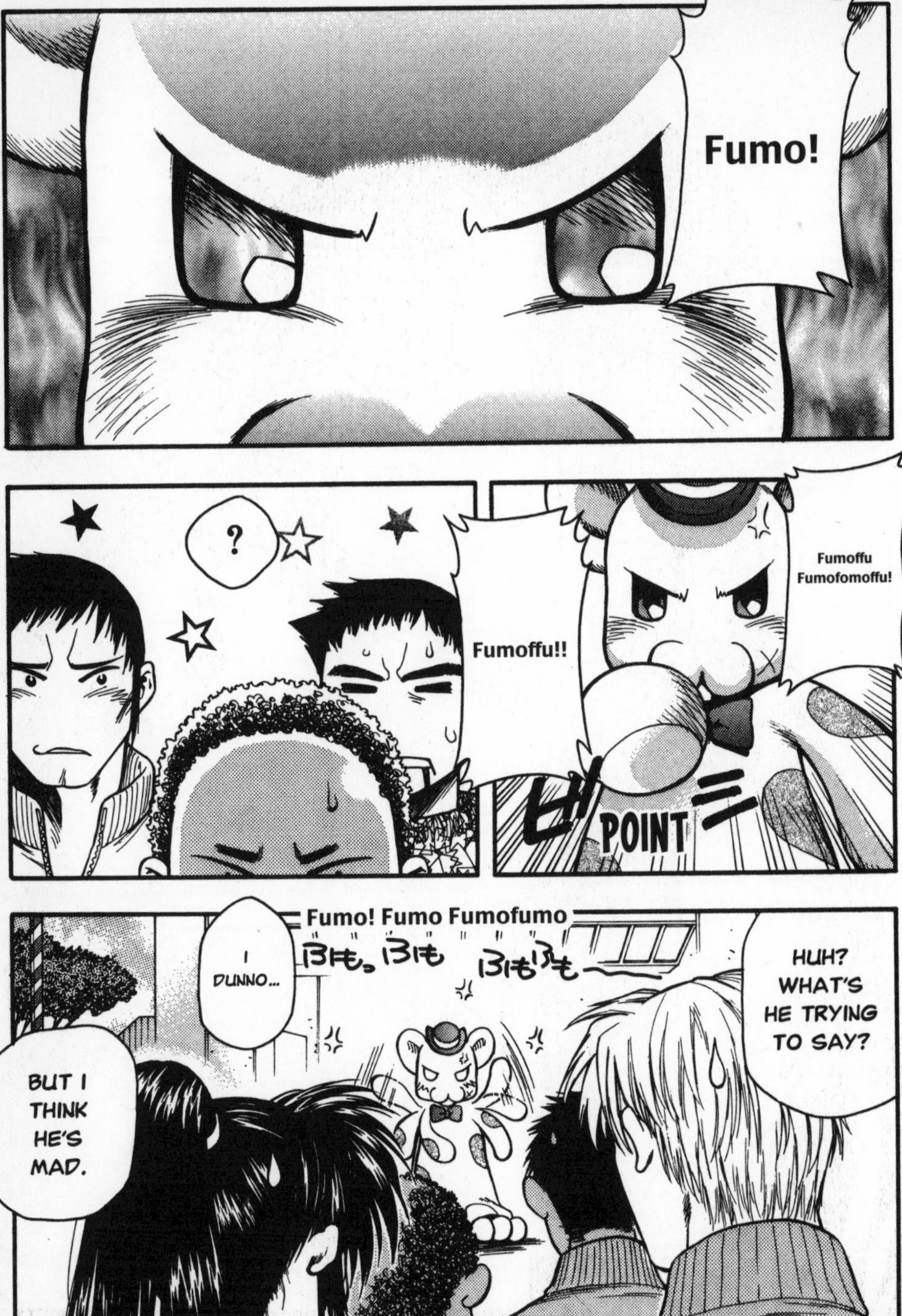
Fumo!
Fumoffu Fumofomoffu!
Fumoffu!!
POINT
?
HUH? WHAT'S HE TRYING TO SAY?
Fumo! Fumo Fumofumo
I DUNNO...
BUT I THINK HE'S MAD.

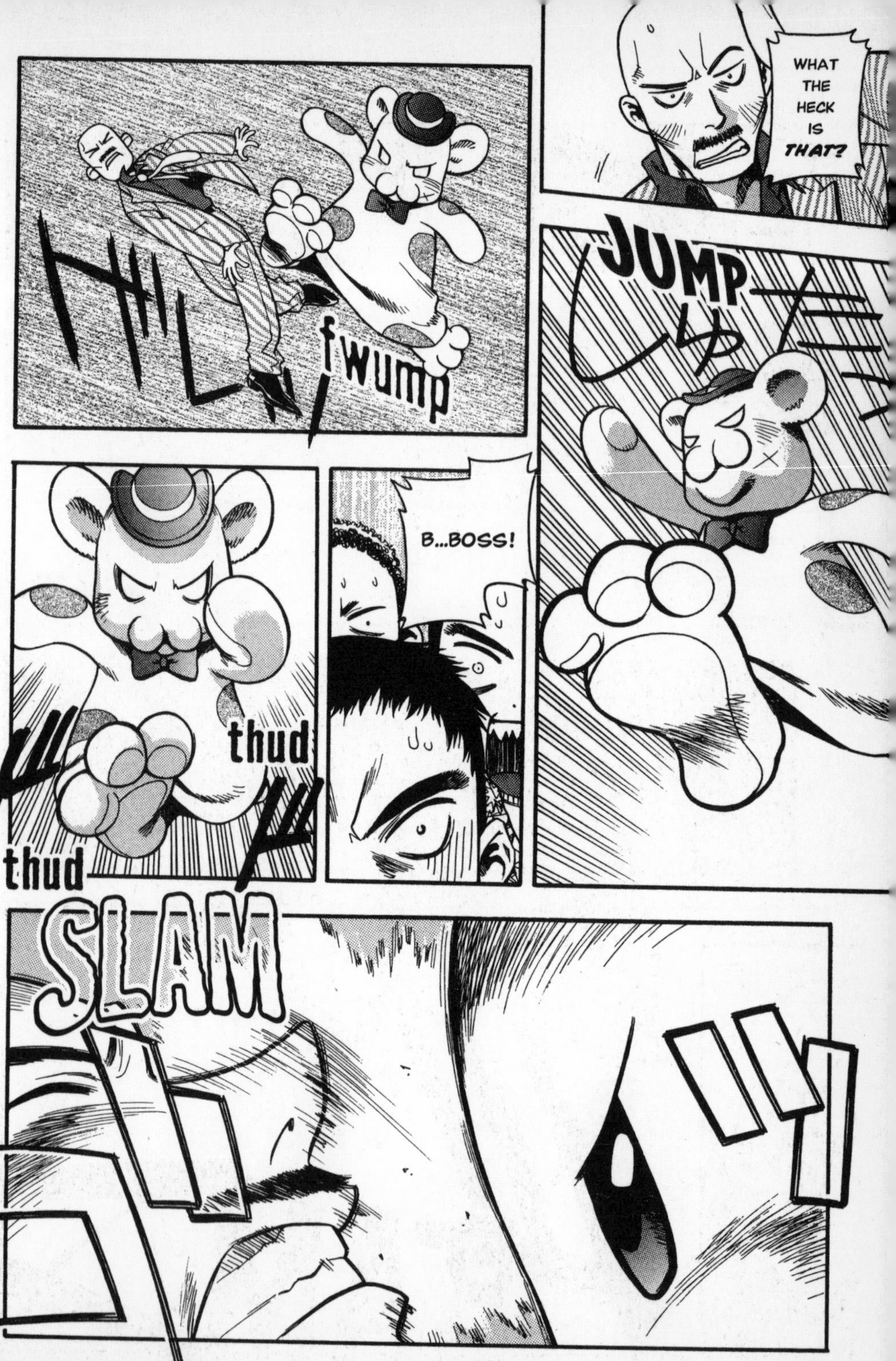
WHAT THE HECK IS *THAT?*
fwump
JUMP
B...BOSS!
thud
thud
SLAM

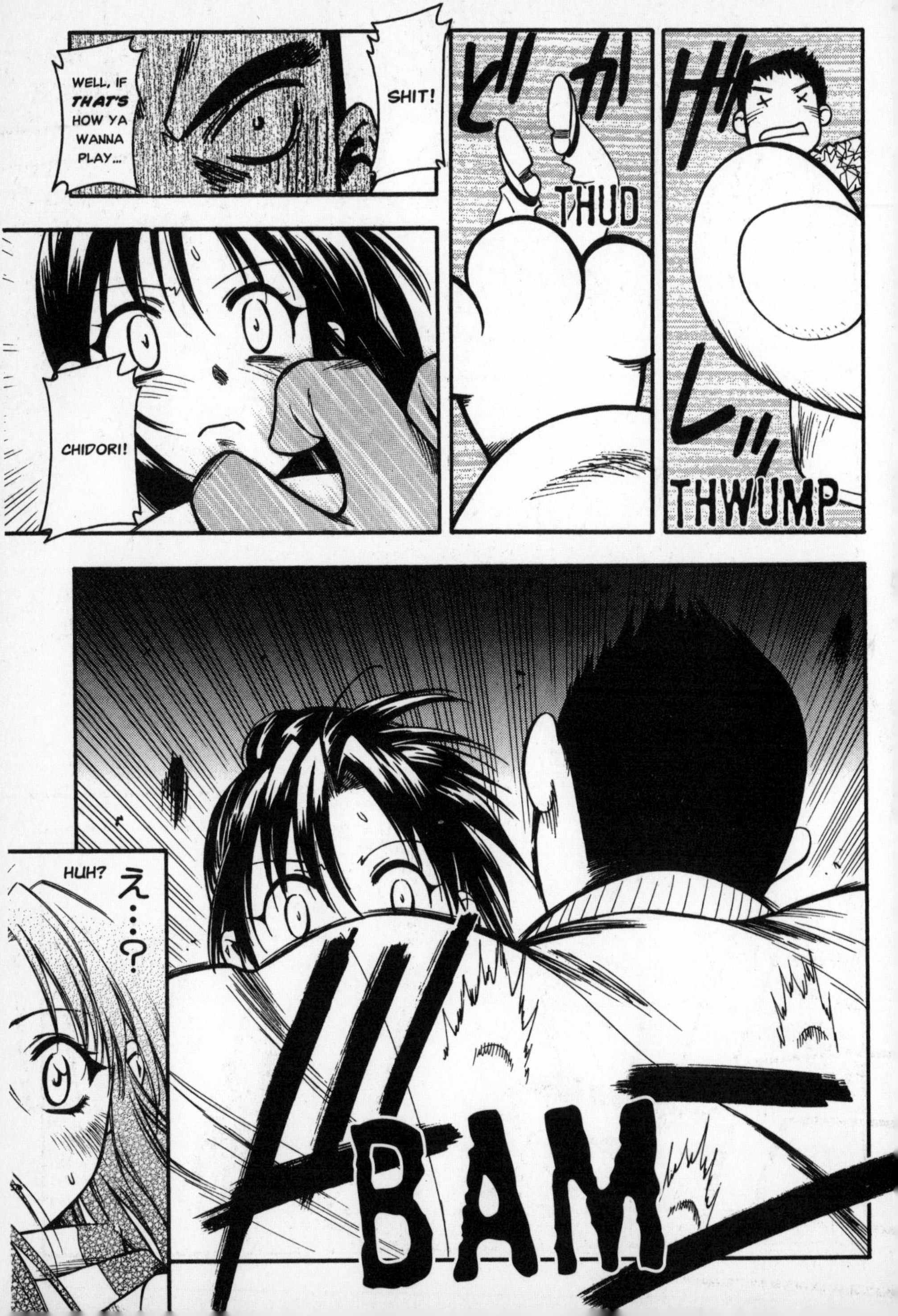
THWUMP
THUD
SHIT!
WELL, IF *THAT'S* HOW YA WANNA PLAY...
CHIDORI!
HUH?
え…？
BAM

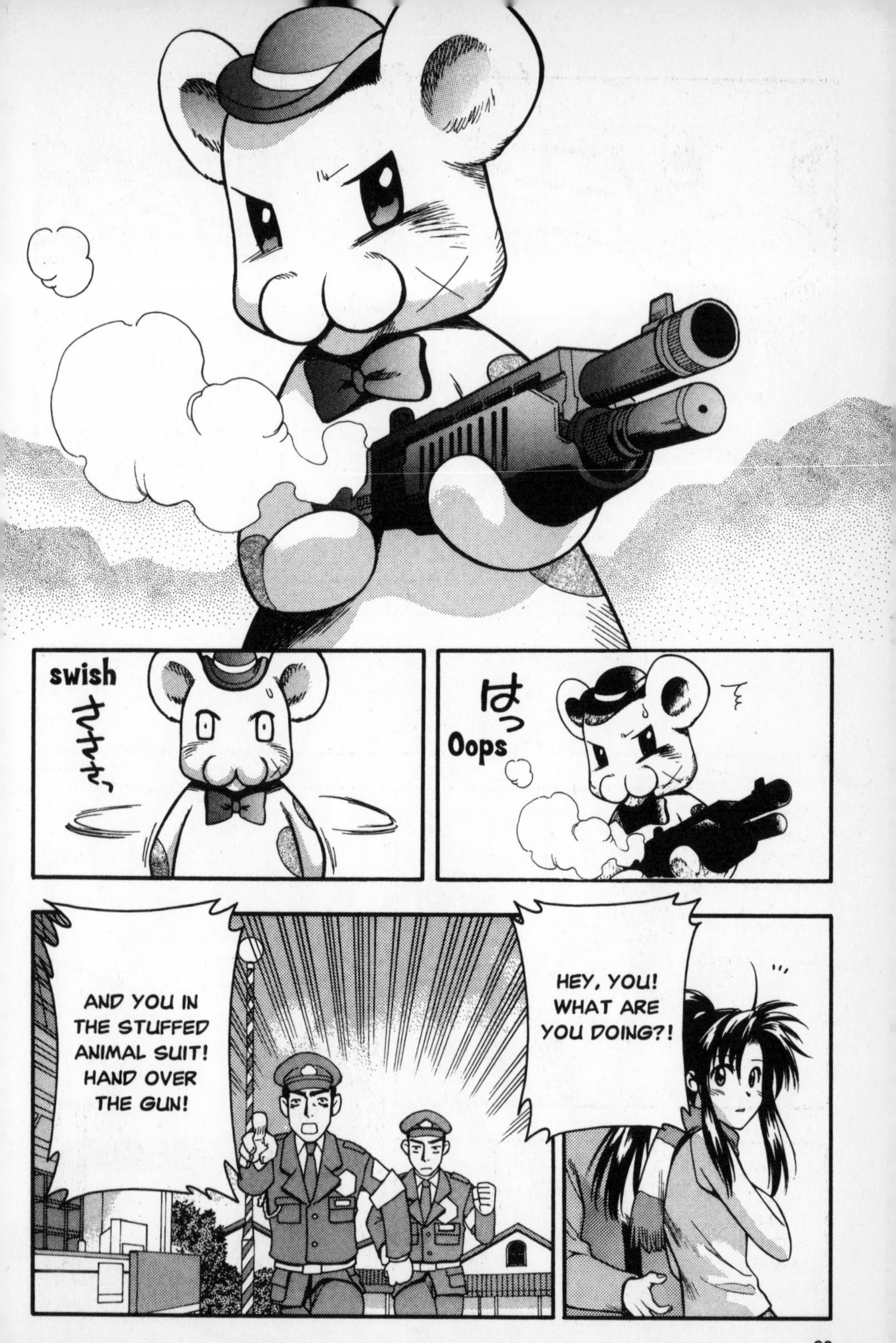

はっ
Oops
swish
HEY, YOU! WHAT ARE YOU DOING?!
AND YOU IN THE STUFFED ANIMAL SUIT! HAND OVER THE GUN!

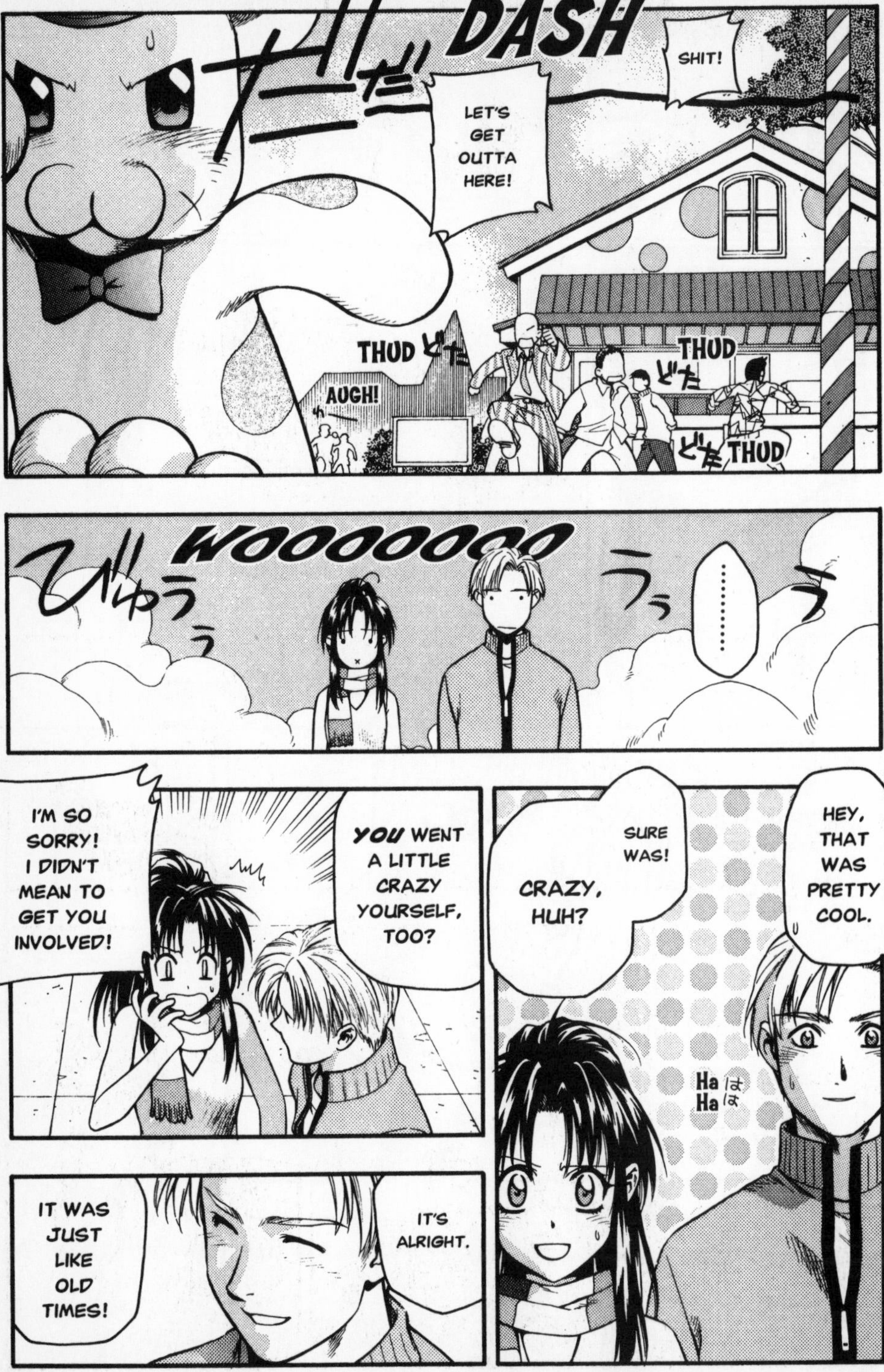
SHIT!
DASH
LET'S GET OUTTA HERE!
THUD
THUD どた
THUD
AUGH!
WOOOOOO
……
HEY, THAT WAS PRETTY COOL.
SURE WAS!
CRAZY, HUH?
Ha Ha はは
YOU WENT A LITTLE CRAZY YOURSELF, TOO?
I'M SO SORRY! I DIDN'T MEAN TO GET YOU INVOLVED!
IT'S ALRIGHT.
IT WAS JUST LIKE OLD TIMES!

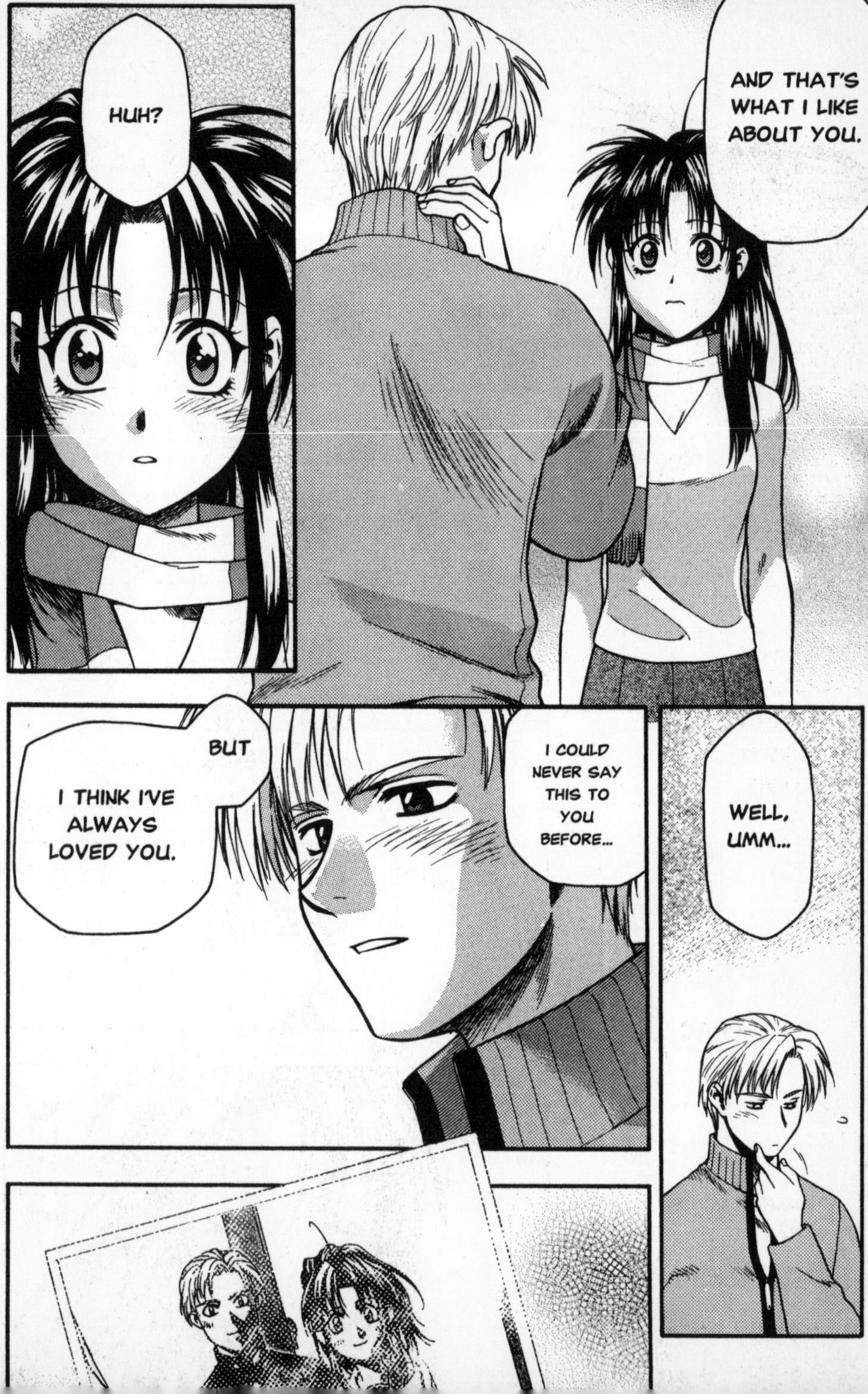
AND THAT'S WHAT I LIKE ABOUT YOU.
HUH?
WELL, UMM...
I COULD NEVER SAY THIS TO YOU BEFORE...
BUT
I THINK I'VE ALWAYS LOVED YOU.

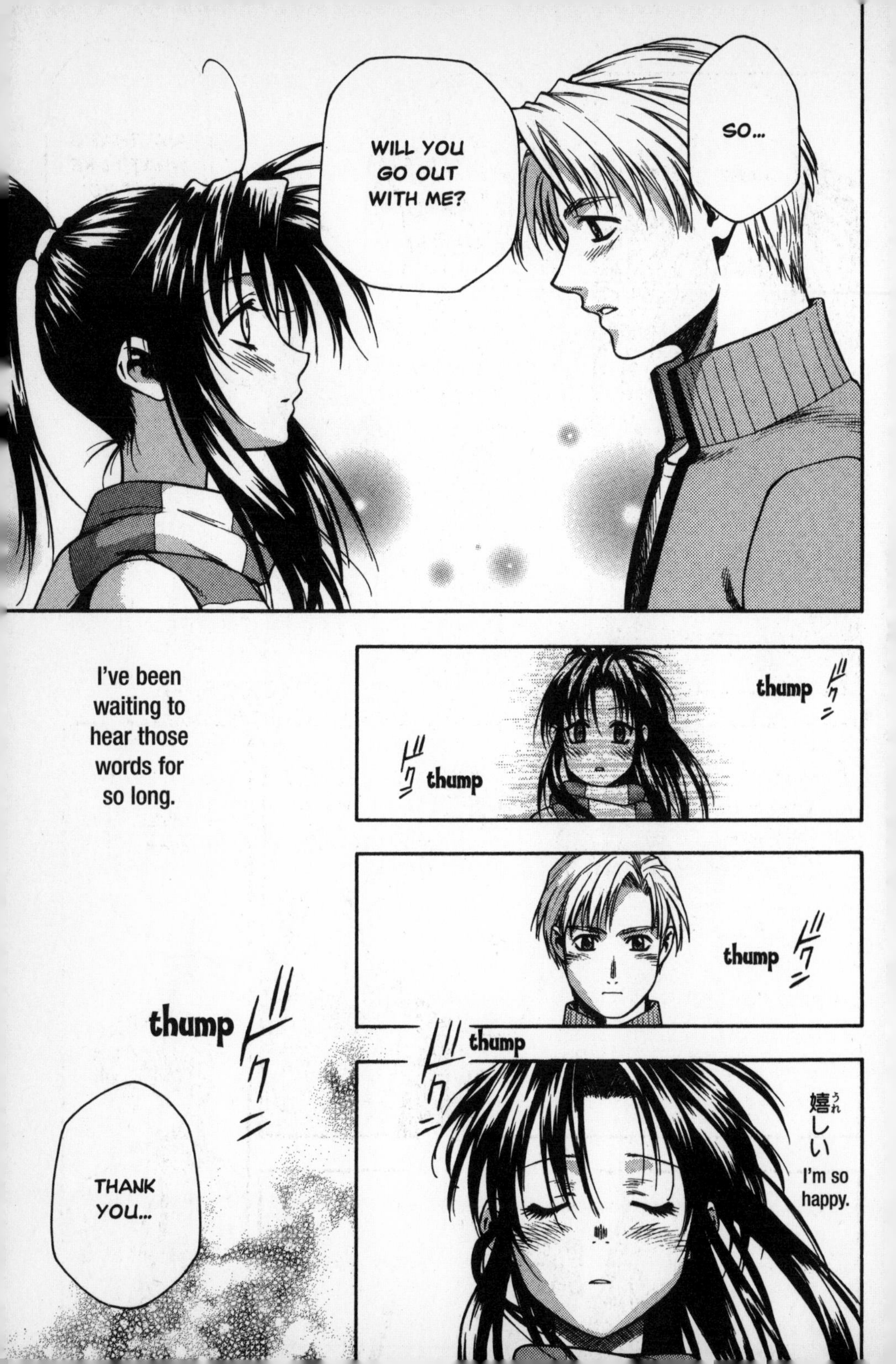
SO...
WILL YOU GO OUT WITH ME?
thump
thump
I've been waiting to hear those words for so long.
thump
嬉しい
I'm so happy.
thump
thump
THANK YOU...

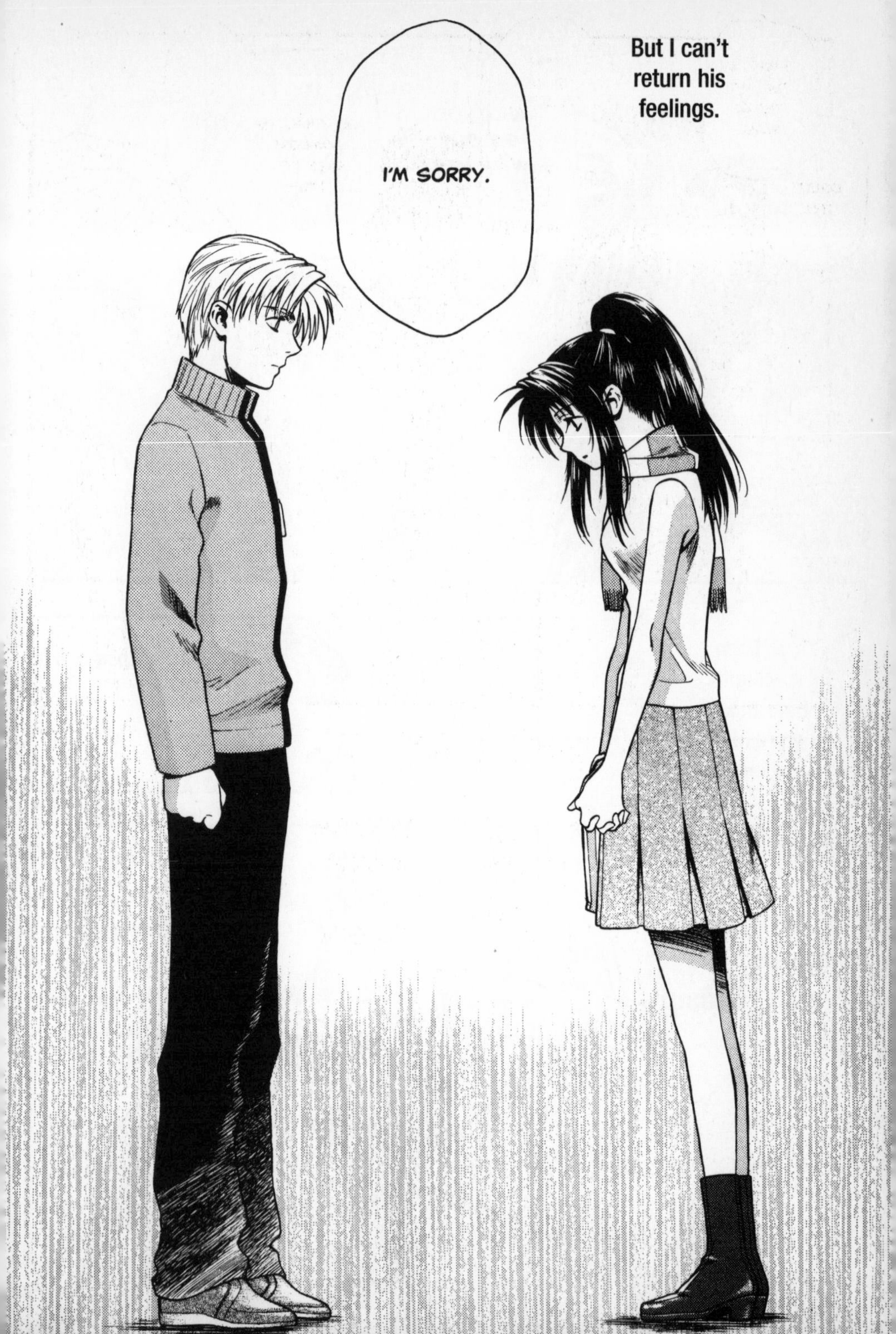
But I can't return his feelings.
I'M SORRY.

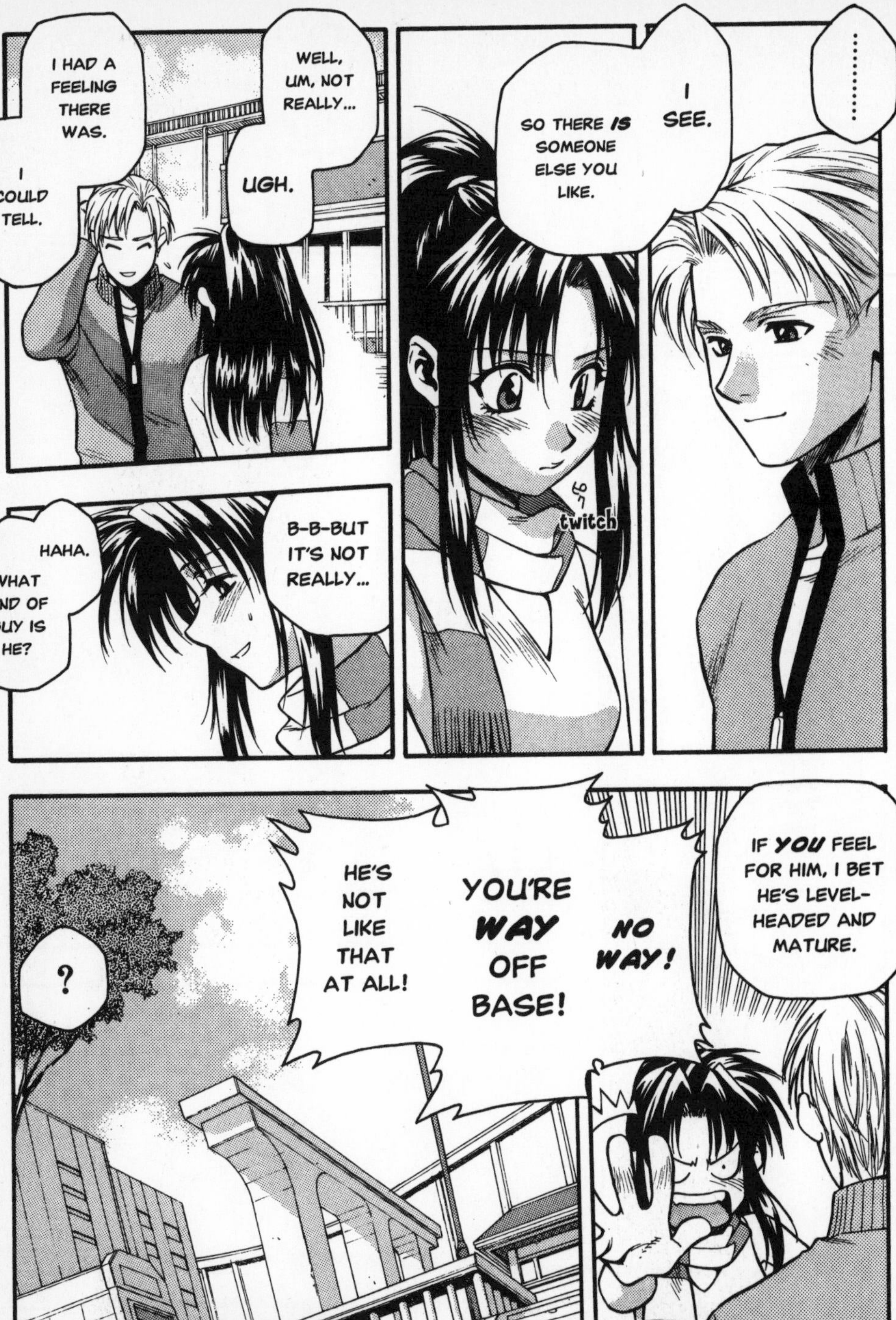
......
I SEE.
SO THERE IS SOMEONE ELSE YOU LIKE.
twitch
WELL, UM, NOT REALLY...
UGH.
I HAD A FEELING THERE WAS.
I COULD TELL.
B-B-BUT IT'S NOT REALLY...
HAHA.
WHAT KIND OF GUY IS HE?
IF YOU FEEL FOR HIM, I BET HE'S LEVEL-HEADED AND MATURE.
NO WAY!
YOU'RE WAY OFF BASE!
HE'S NOT LIKE THAT AT ALL!
?

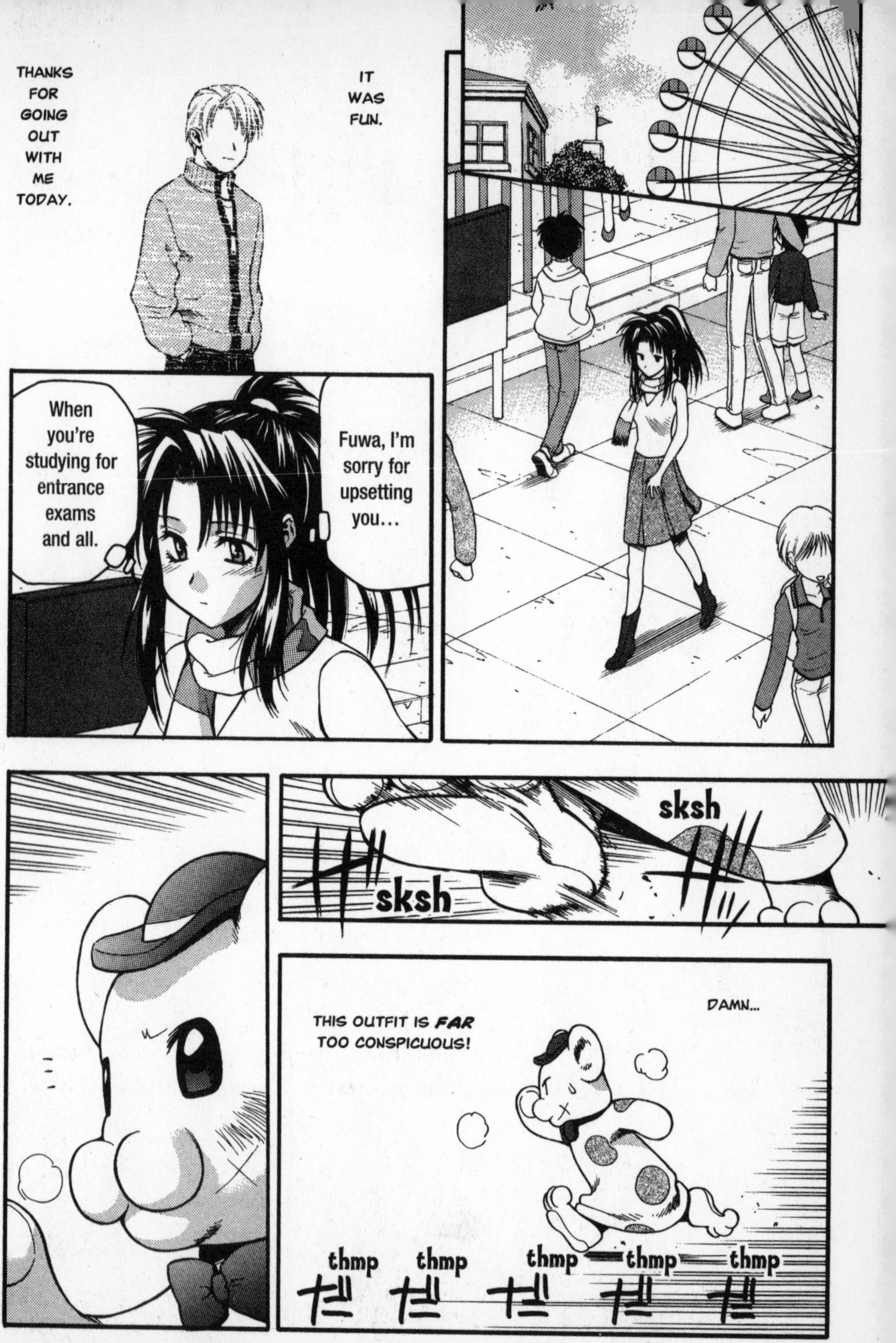
IT WAS FUN.
THANKS FOR GOING OUT WITH ME TODAY.
Fuwa, I'm sorry for upsetting you…
When you're studying for entrance exams and all.
sksh
sksh
DAMN...
THIS OUTFIT IS **FAR** TOO CONSPICUOUS!
thmp
だ
thmp
だ
thmp
だ
thmp
だ
thmp
だ

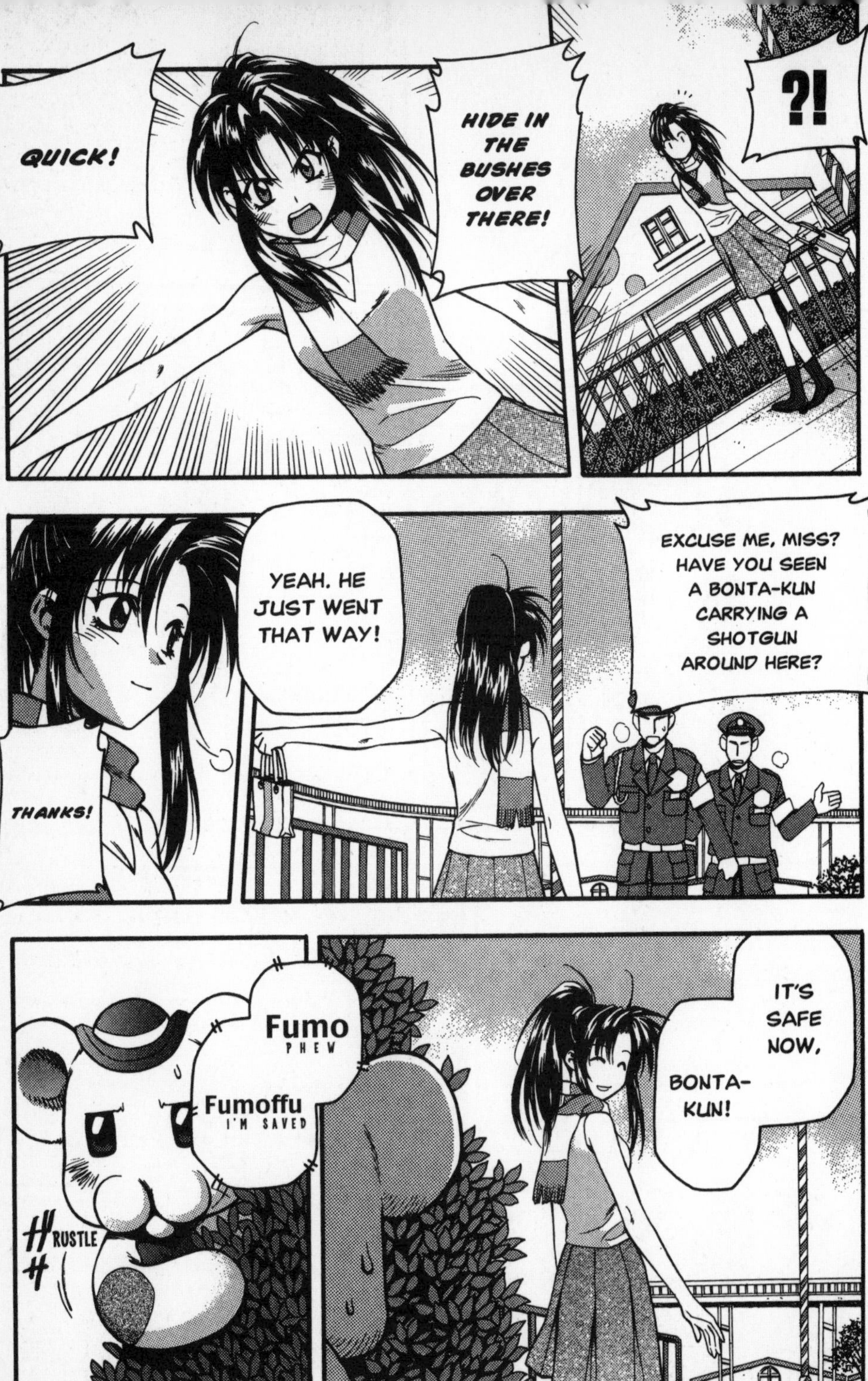
?!
HIDE IN THE BUSHES OVER THERE!
QUICK!
EXCUSE ME, MISS? HAVE YOU SEEN A BONTA-KUN CARRYING A SHOTGUN AROUND HERE?
YEAH. HE JUST WENT THAT WAY!
THANKS!
IT'S SAFE NOW,
BONTA-KUN!
Fumo
PHEW
Fumoffu
I'M SAVED
RUSTLE

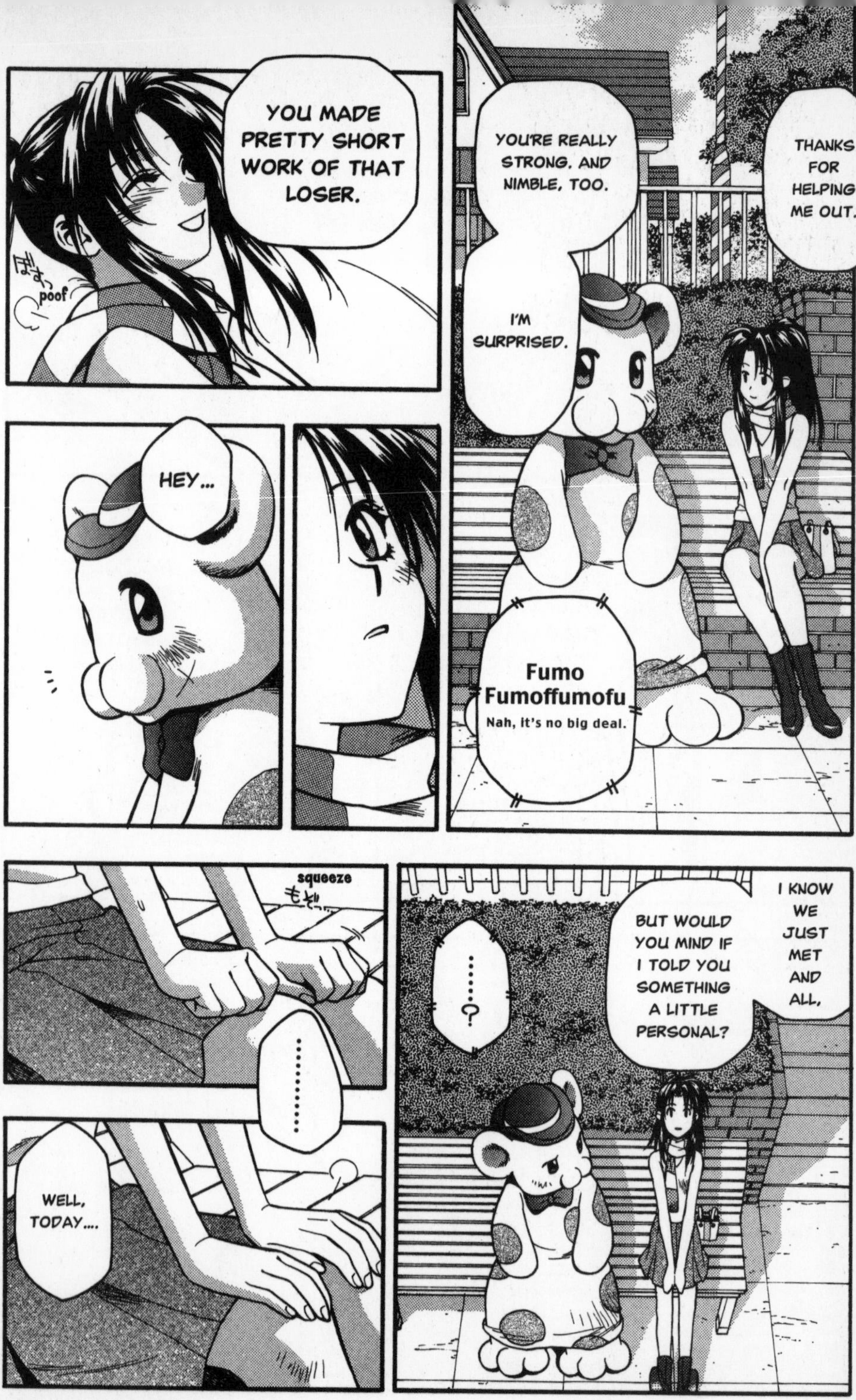

THANKS FOR HELPING ME OUT.
YOU'RE REALLY STRONG. AND NIMBLE, TOO.
I'M SURPRISED.
Fumo Fumoffumofu
Nah, it's no big deal.
YOU MADE PRETTY SHORT WORK OF THAT LOSER.
ぽすっ
poof
HEY...
I KNOW WE JUST MET AND ALL,
BUT WOULD YOU MIND IF I TOLD YOU SOMETHING A LITTLE PERSONAL?
......?
squeeze
もぞ...
....
WELL, TODAY....

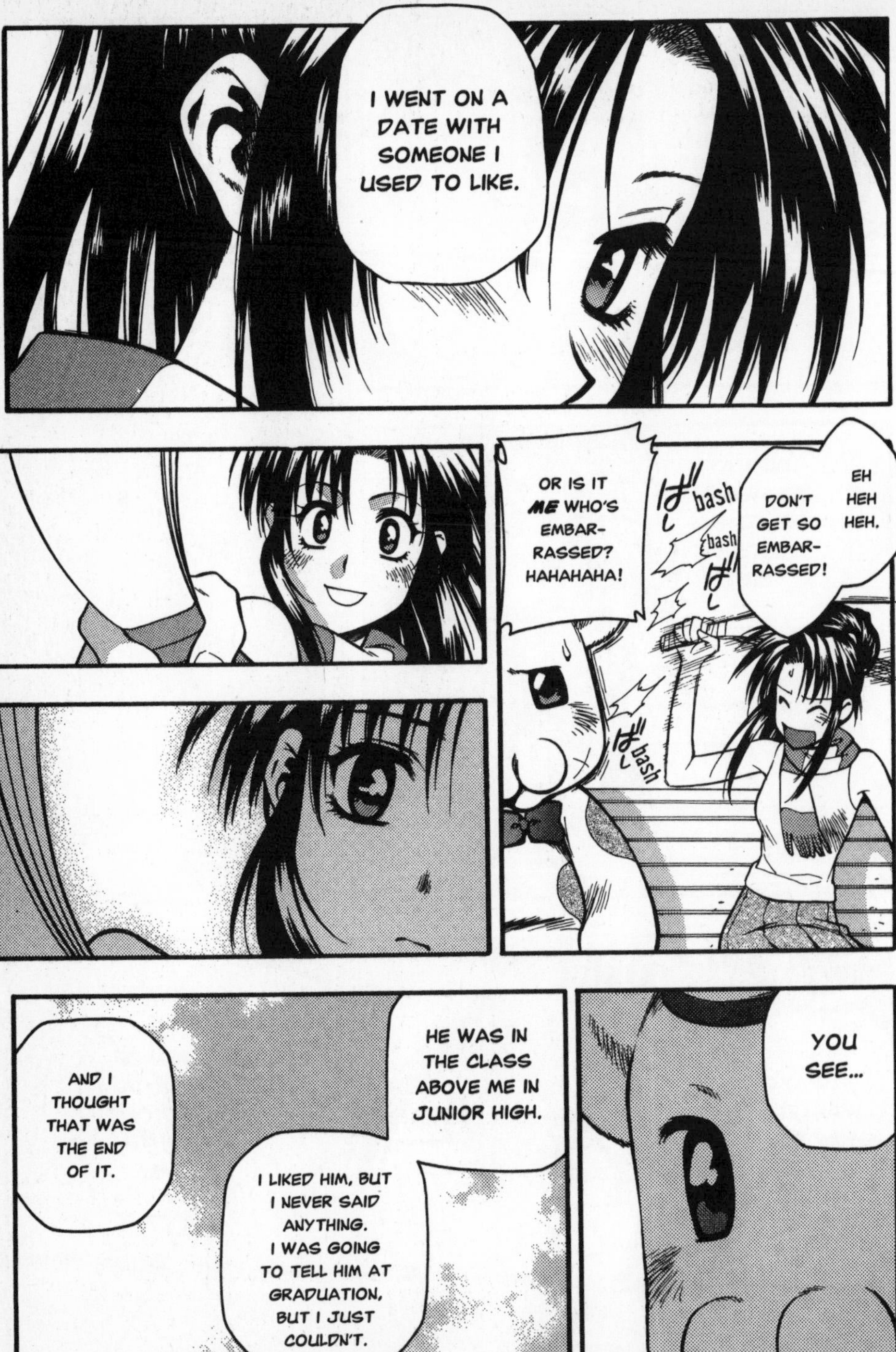
I WENT ON A DATE WITH SOMEONE I USED TO LIKE.
EH HEH HEH.
DON'T GET SO EMBAR-RASSED!
ばし bash
ばし bash
ばし bash
OR IS IT *ME* WHO'S EMBAR-RASSED? HAHAHAHA!
YOU SEE...
HE WAS IN THE CLASS ABOVE ME IN JUNIOR HIGH.
I LIKED HIM, BUT I NEVER SAID ANYTHING. I WAS GOING TO TELL HIM AT GRADUATION, BUT I JUST COULDN'T.
AND I THOUGHT THAT WAS THE END OF IT.

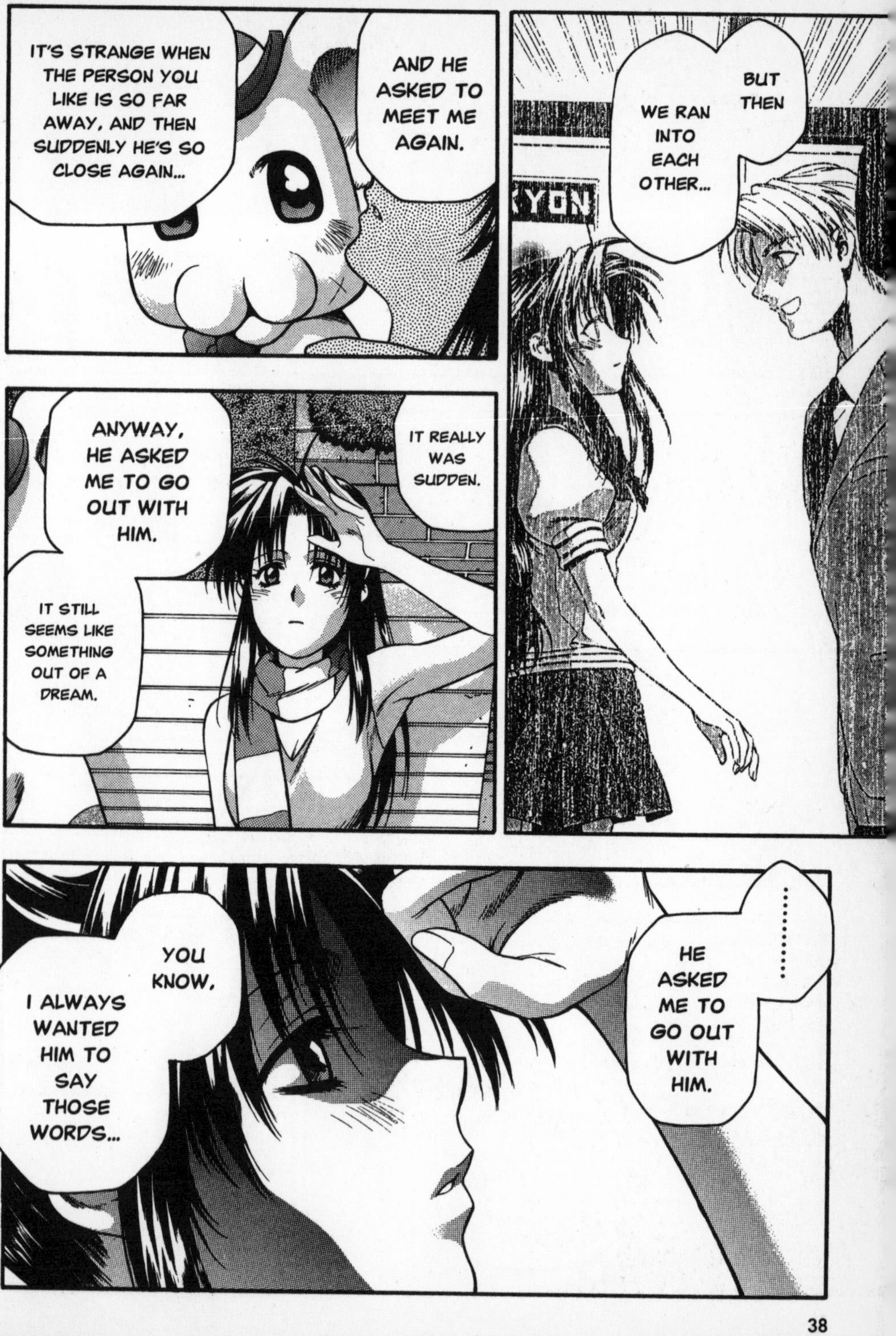
BUT THEN
WE RAN INTO EACH OTHER...
KYON
AND HE ASKED TO MEET ME AGAIN.
IT'S STRANGE WHEN THE PERSON YOU LIKE IS SO FAR AWAY, AND THEN SUDDENLY HE'S SO CLOSE AGAIN...
IT REALLY WAS SUDDEN.
ANYWAY, HE ASKED ME TO GO OUT WITH HIM.
IT STILL SEEMS LIKE SOMETHING OUT OF A DREAM.
......
HE ASKED ME TO GO OUT WITH HIM.
YOU KNOW,
I ALWAYS WANTED HIM TO SAY THOSE WORDS...

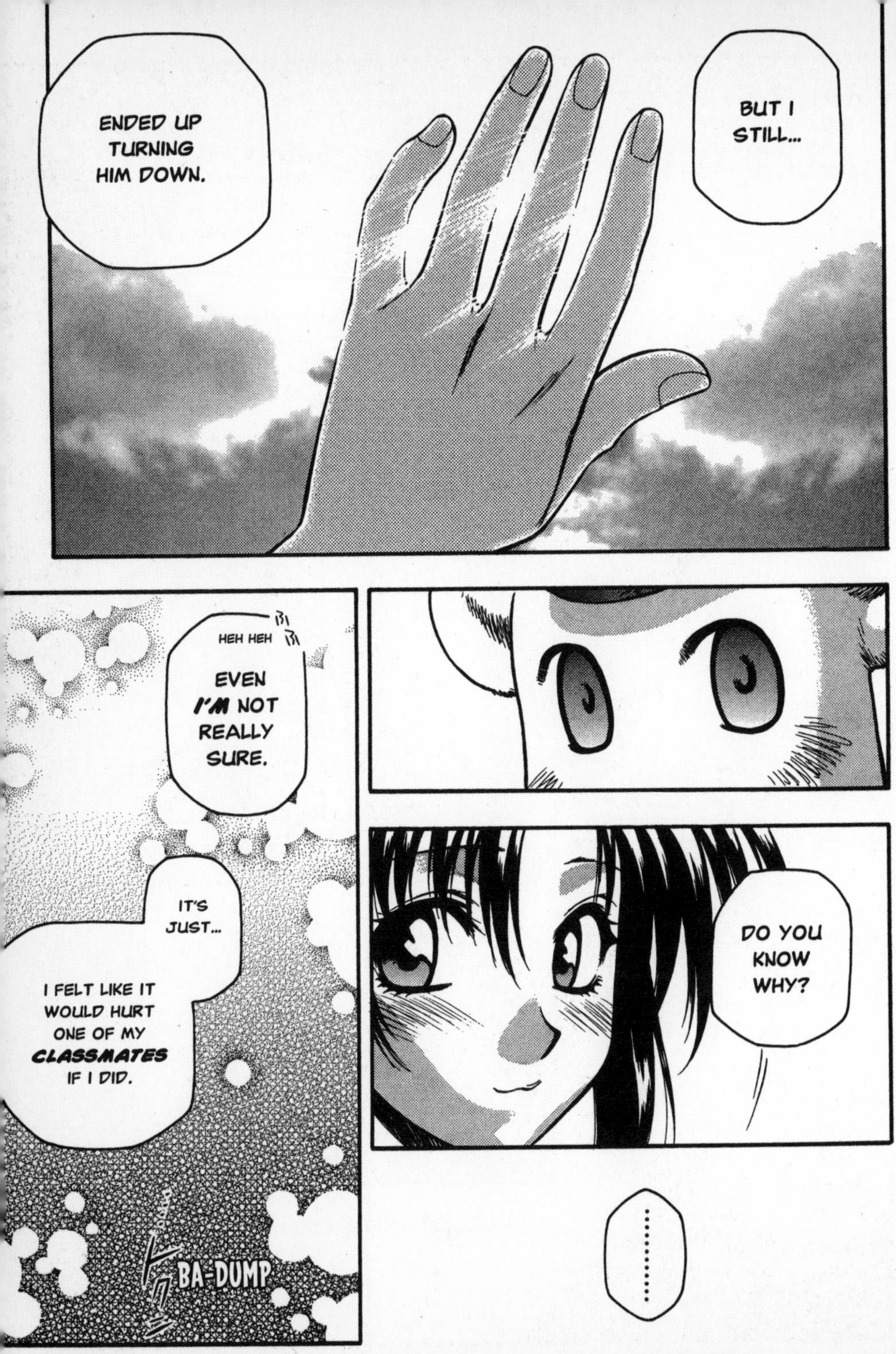
BUT I STILL...
ENDED UP TURNING HIM DOWN.
DO YOU KNOW WHY?
......
HEH HEH
EVEN I'M NOT REALLY SURE.
IT'S JUST...
I FELT LIKE IT WOULD HURT ONE OF MY CLASSMATES IF I DID.
BA-DUMP

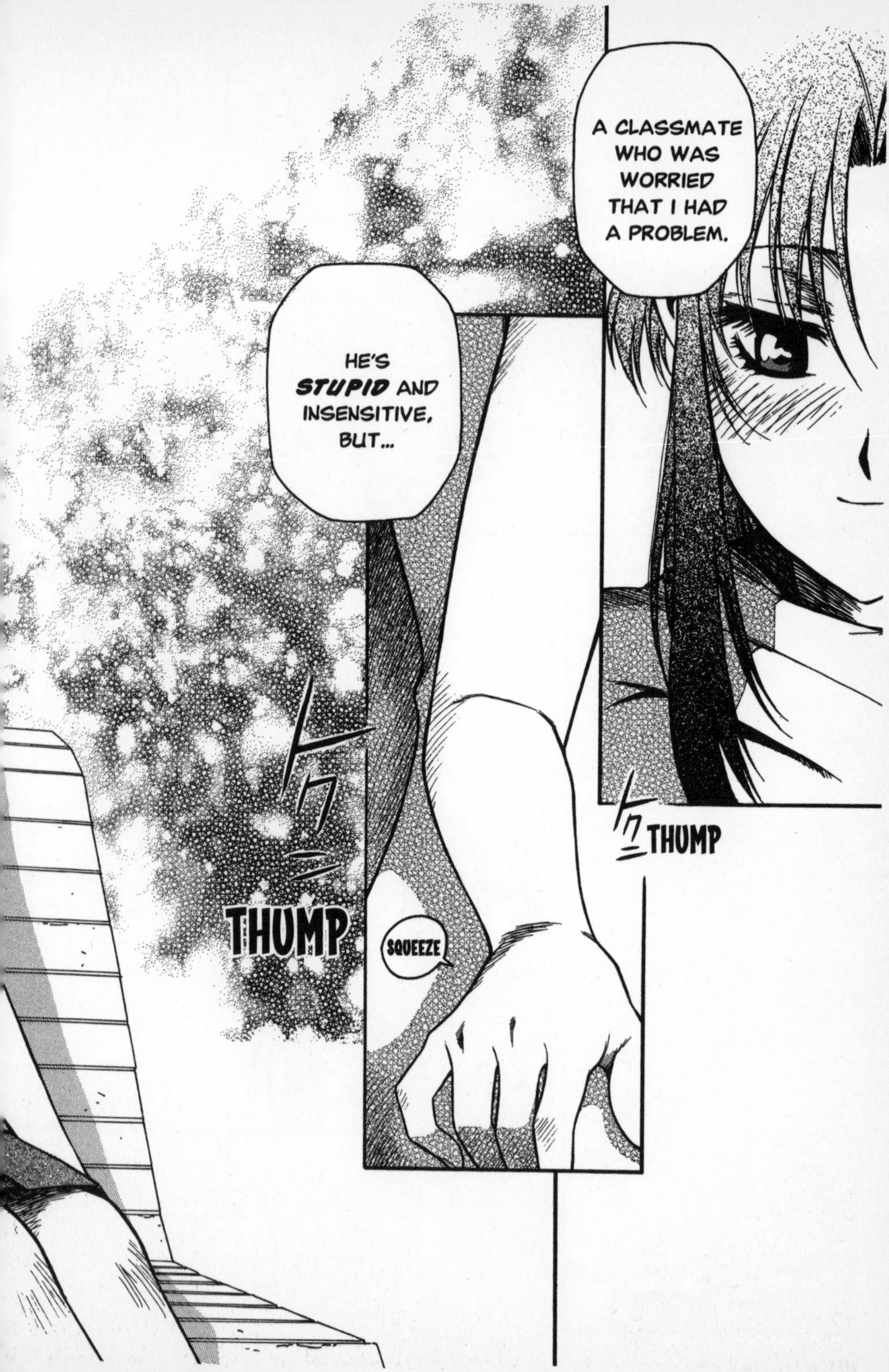
A CLASSMATE WHO WAS WORRIED THAT I HAD A PROBLEM.
THUMP
HE'S STUPID AND INSENSITIVE, BUT...
SQUEEZE
THUMP

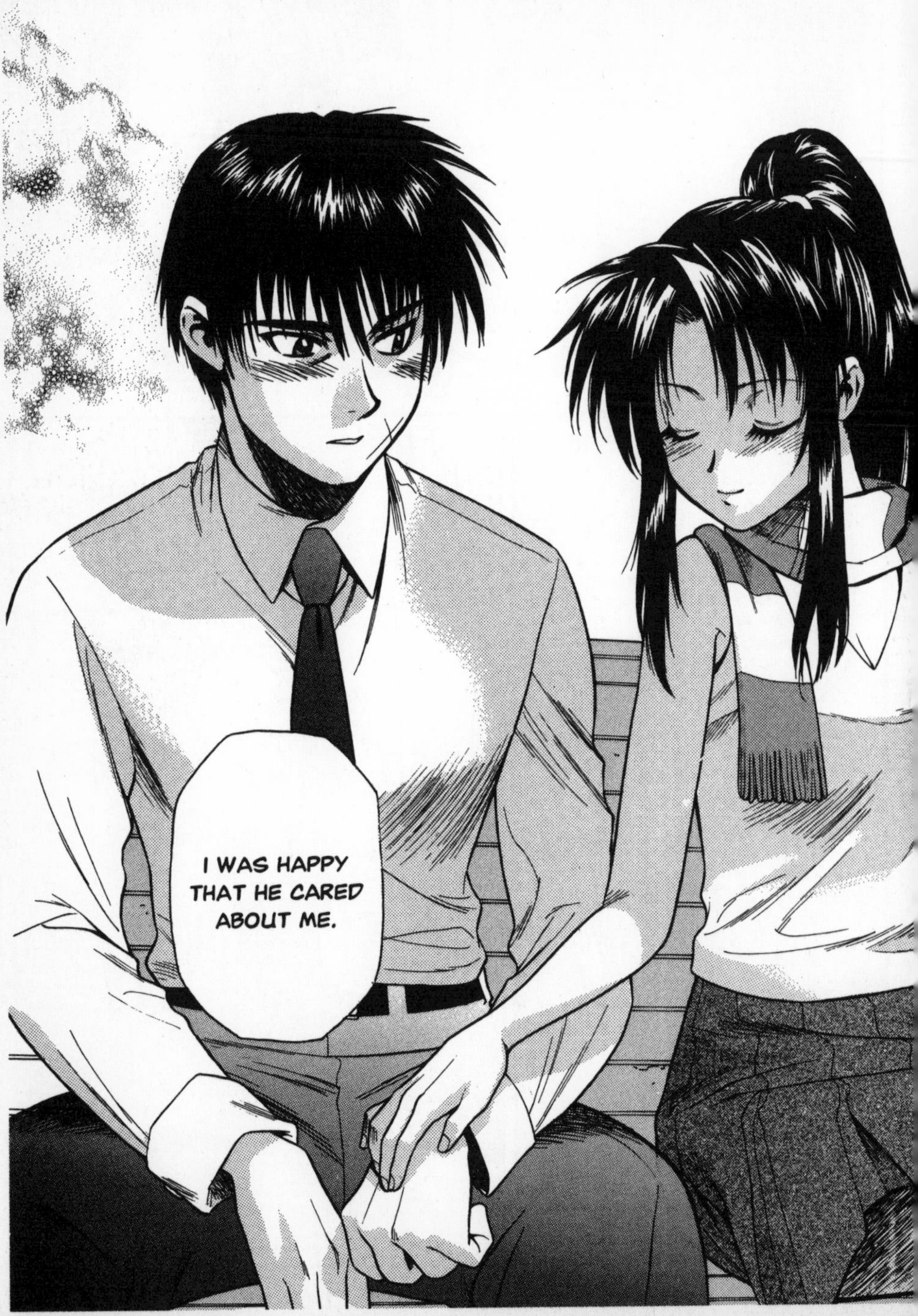
I WAS HAPPY THAT HE CARED ABOUT ME.

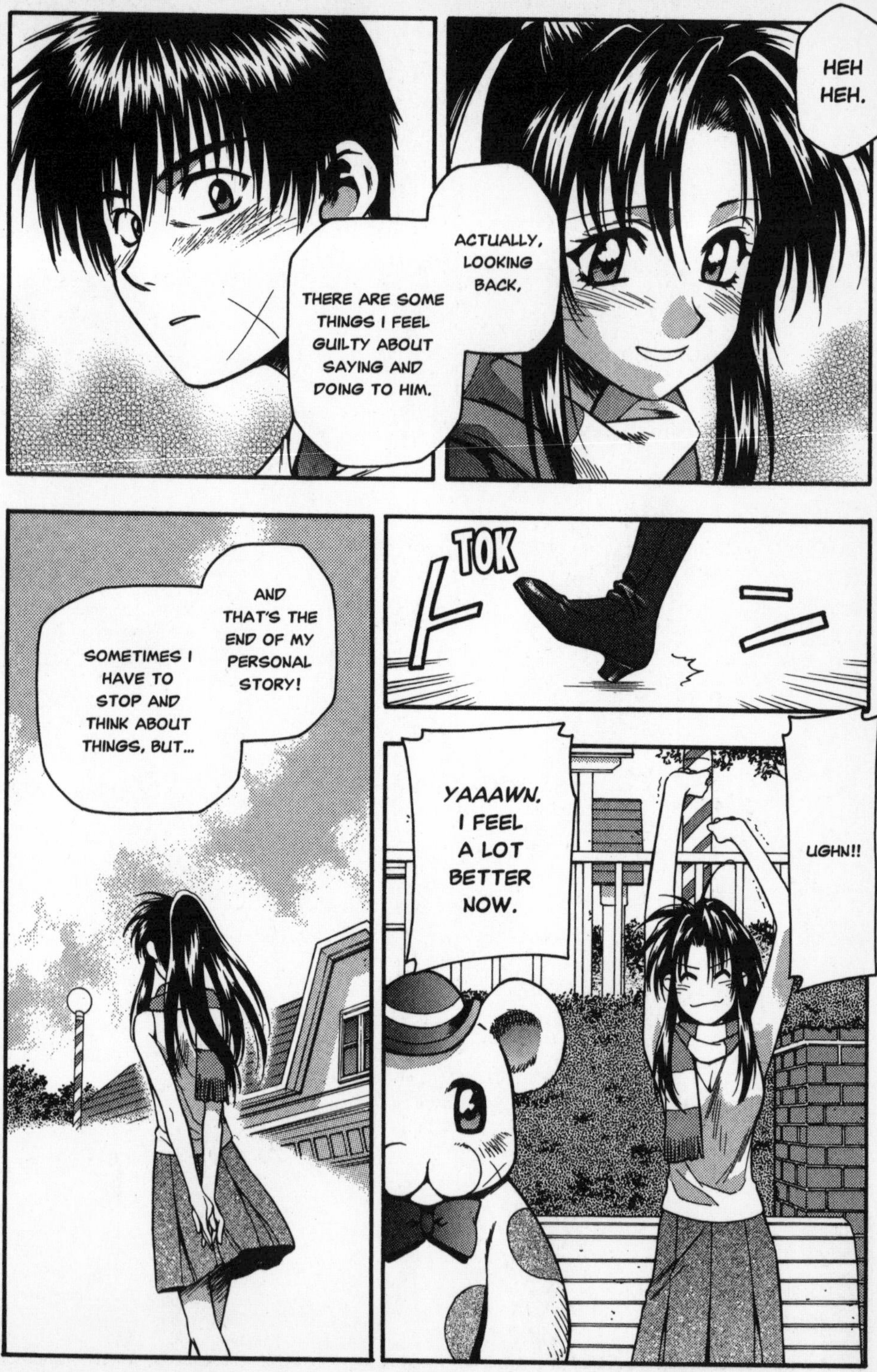
HEH HEH.
ACTUALLY, LOOKING BACK,
THERE ARE SOME THINGS I FEEL GUILTY ABOUT SAYING AND DOING TO HIM.
TOK
UGHN!!
YAAAWN. I FEEL A LOT BETTER NOW.
AND THAT'S THE END OF MY PERSONAL STORY!
SOMETIMES I HAVE TO STOP AND THINK ABOUT THINGS, BUT...

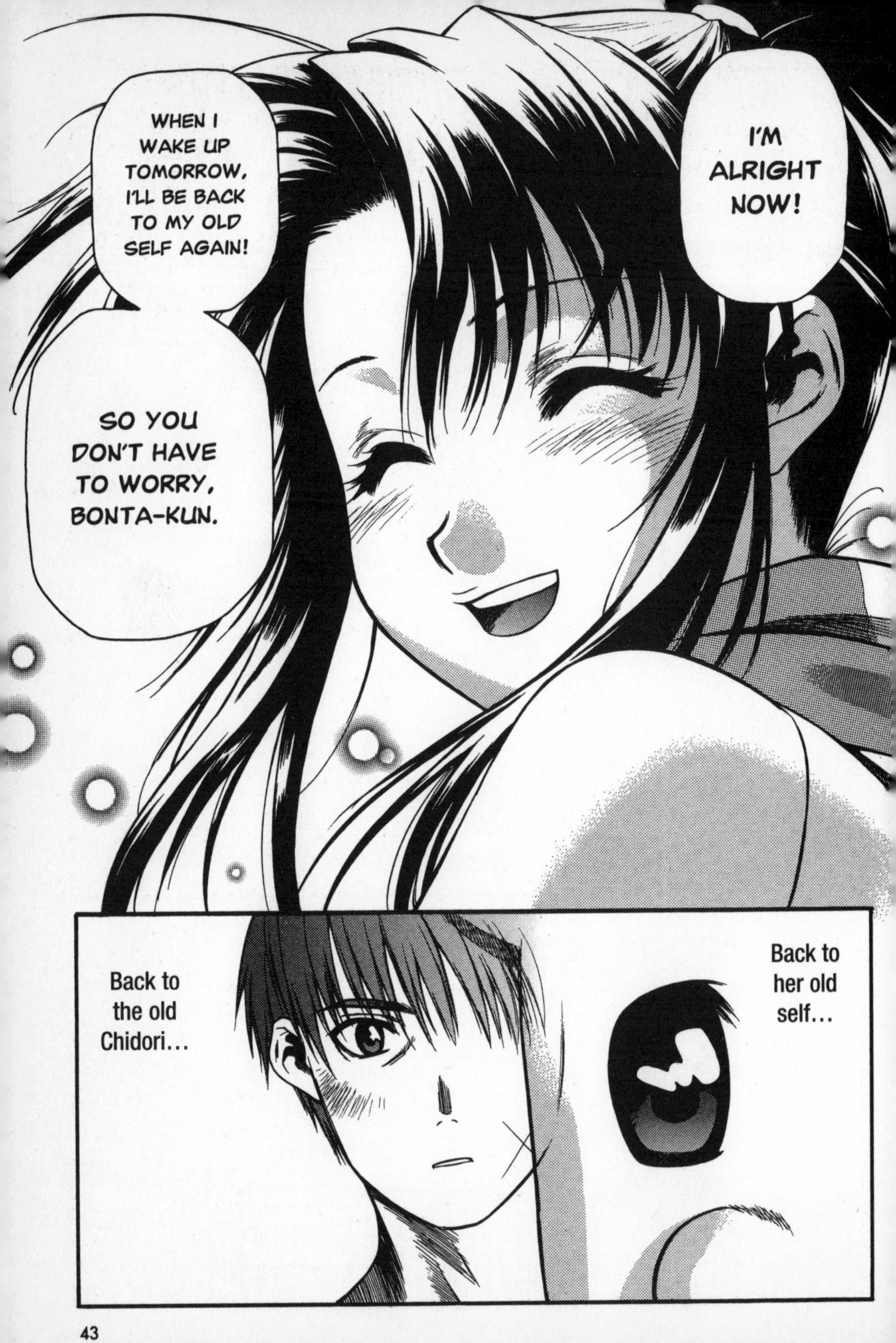
I'M ALRIGHT NOW!
WHEN I WAKE UP TOMORROW, I'LL BE BACK TO MY OLD SELF AGAIN!
SO YOU DON'T HAVE TO WORRY, BONTA-KUN.
Back to her old self…
Back to the old Chidori…

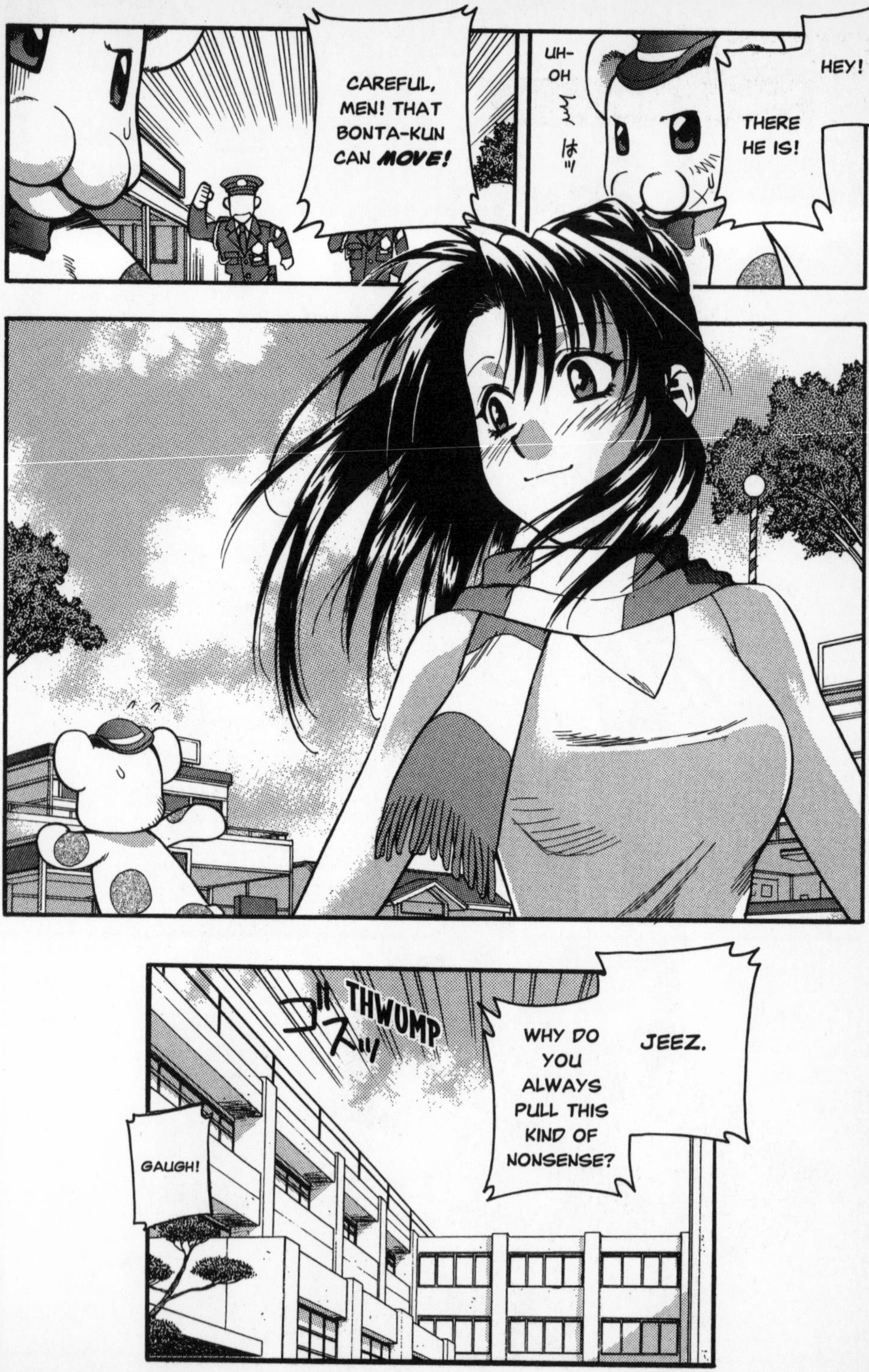
HEY!
THERE HE IS!
UH-OH
CAREFUL, MEN! THAT BONTA-KUN CAN **MOVE!**
JEEZ.
WHY DO YOU ALWAYS PULL THIS KIND OF NONSENSE?
THWUMP
GAUGH!

MISSION:23

Surprise! Who are you?

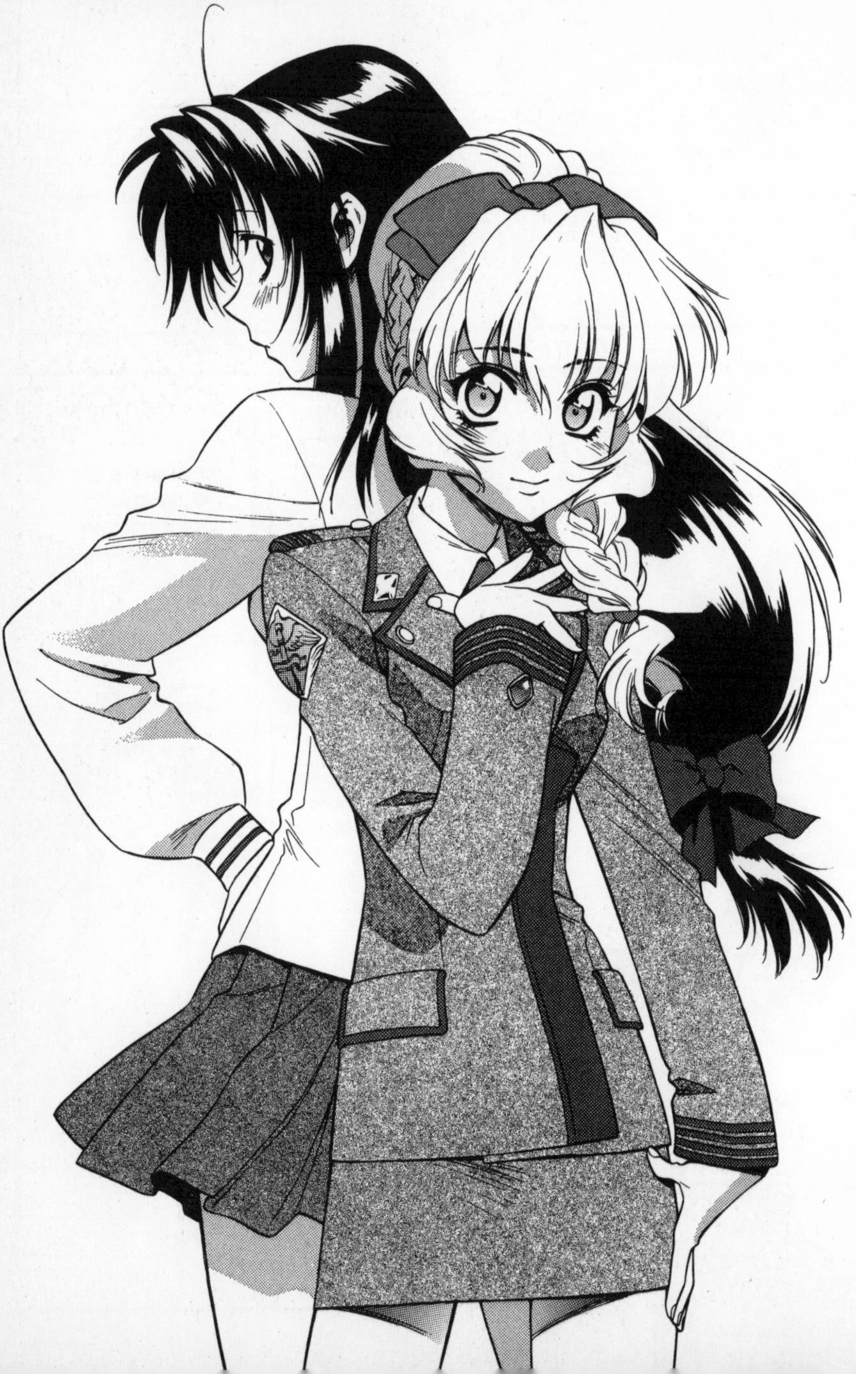

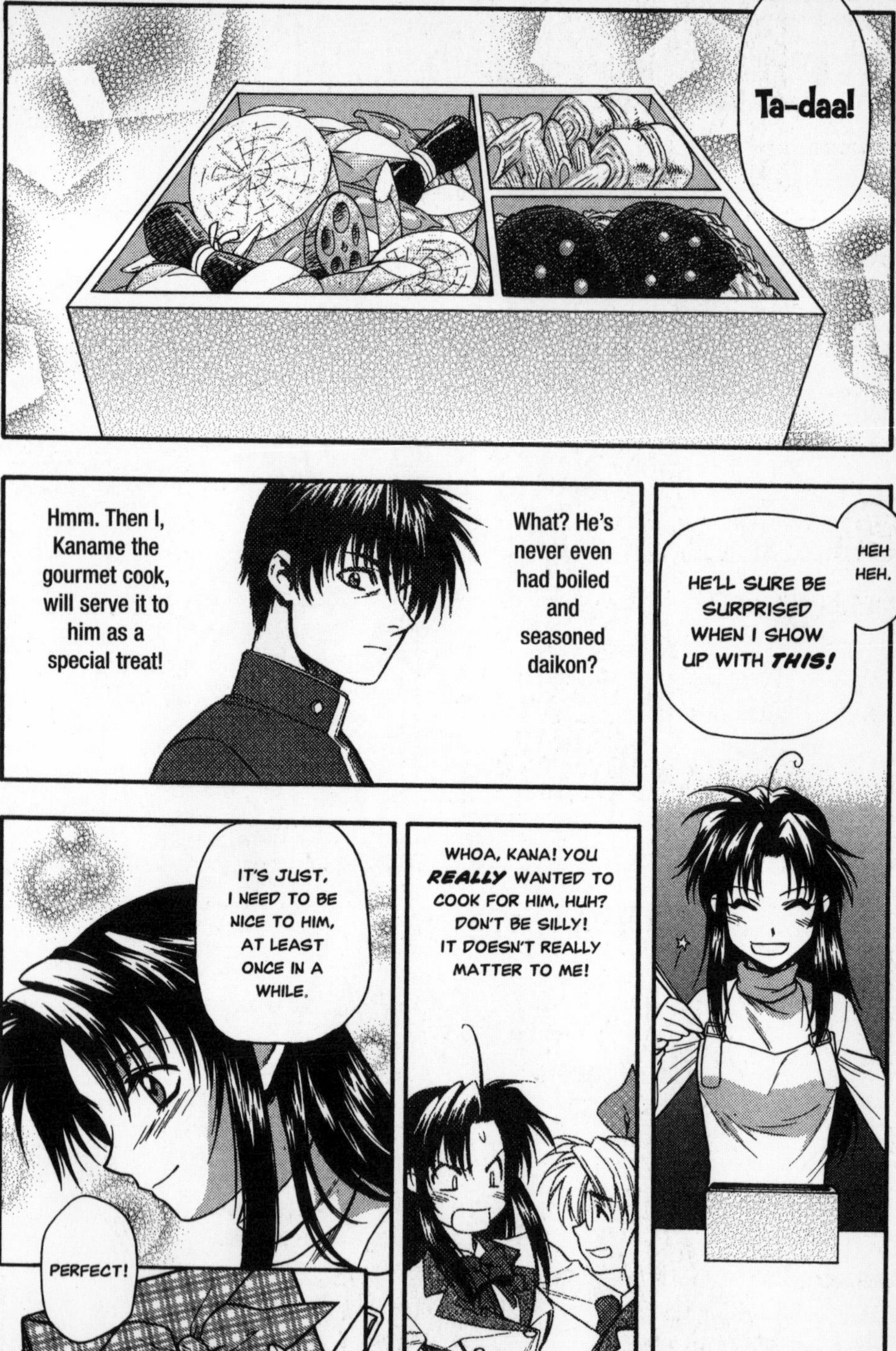
Ta-daa!
HEH HEH.
HE'LL SURE BE SURPRISED WHEN I SHOW UP WITH *THIS!*
What? He's never even had boiled and seasoned daikon?
Hmm. Then I, Kaname the gourmet cook, will serve it to him as a special treat!
WHOA, KANA! YOU *REALLY* WANTED TO COOK FOR HIM, HUH?
DON'T BE SILLY! IT DOESN'T REALLY MATTER TO ME!
IT'S JUST, I NEED TO BE NICE TO HIM, AT LEAST ONCE IN A WHILE.
PERFECT!

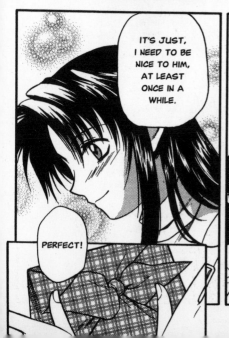

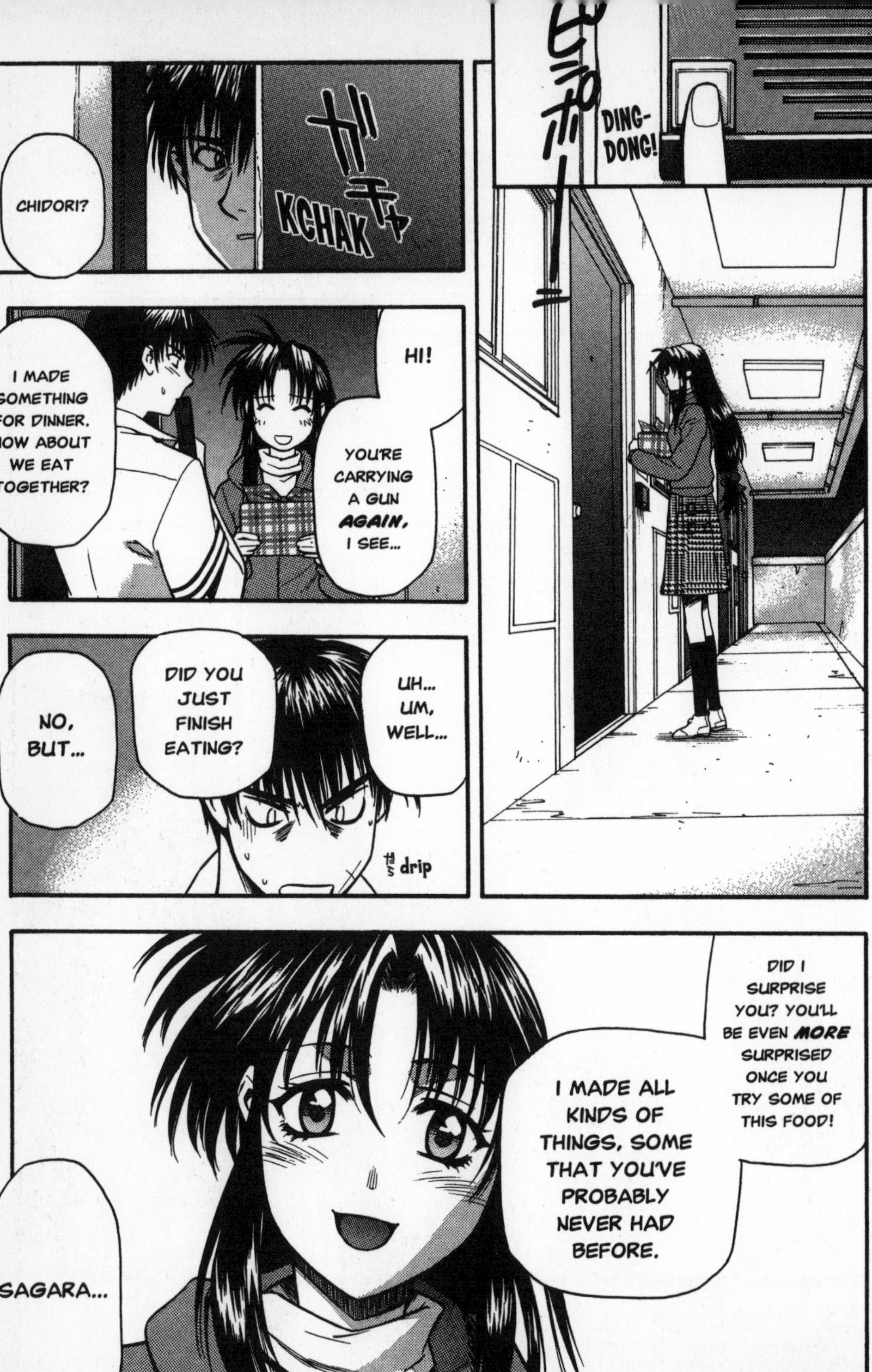
DING-DONG!
CHIDORI?
KCHAK
HI!
YOU'RE CARRYING A GUN *AGAIN,* I SEE...
I MADE SOMETHING FOR DINNER. HOW ABOUT WE EAT TOGETHER?
UH... UM, WELL...
DID YOU JUST FINISH EATING?
NO, BUT...
drip
DID I SURPRISE YOU? YOU'LL BE EVEN *MORE* SURPRISED ONCE YOU TRY SOME OF THIS FOOD!
I MADE ALL KINDS OF THINGS, SOME THAT YOU'VE PROBABLY NEVER HAD BEFORE.
SAGARA...

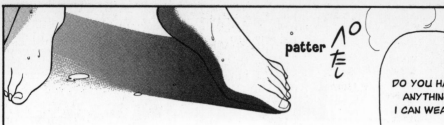

patter パ
        た

DO YOU HAVE
ANYTHING
I CAN WEAR?

OH
DEAR...

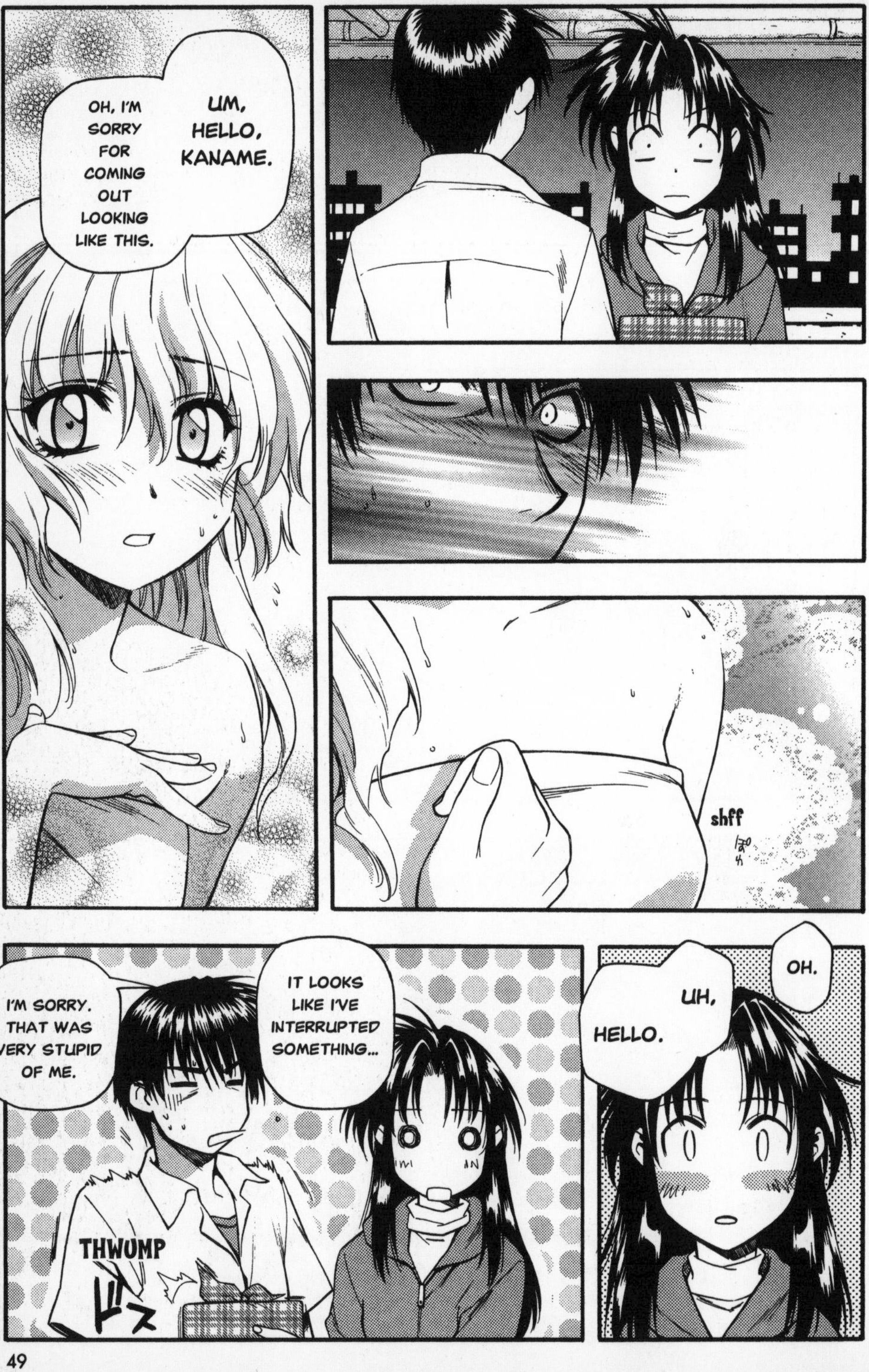
shff
UM, HELLO, KANAME.
OH, I'M SORRY FOR COMING OUT LOOKING LIKE THIS.
OH.
UH, HELLO.
IT LOOKS LIKE I'VE INTERRUPTED SOMETHING...
I'M SORRY. THAT WAS VERY STUPID OF ME.
THWUMP
ドス

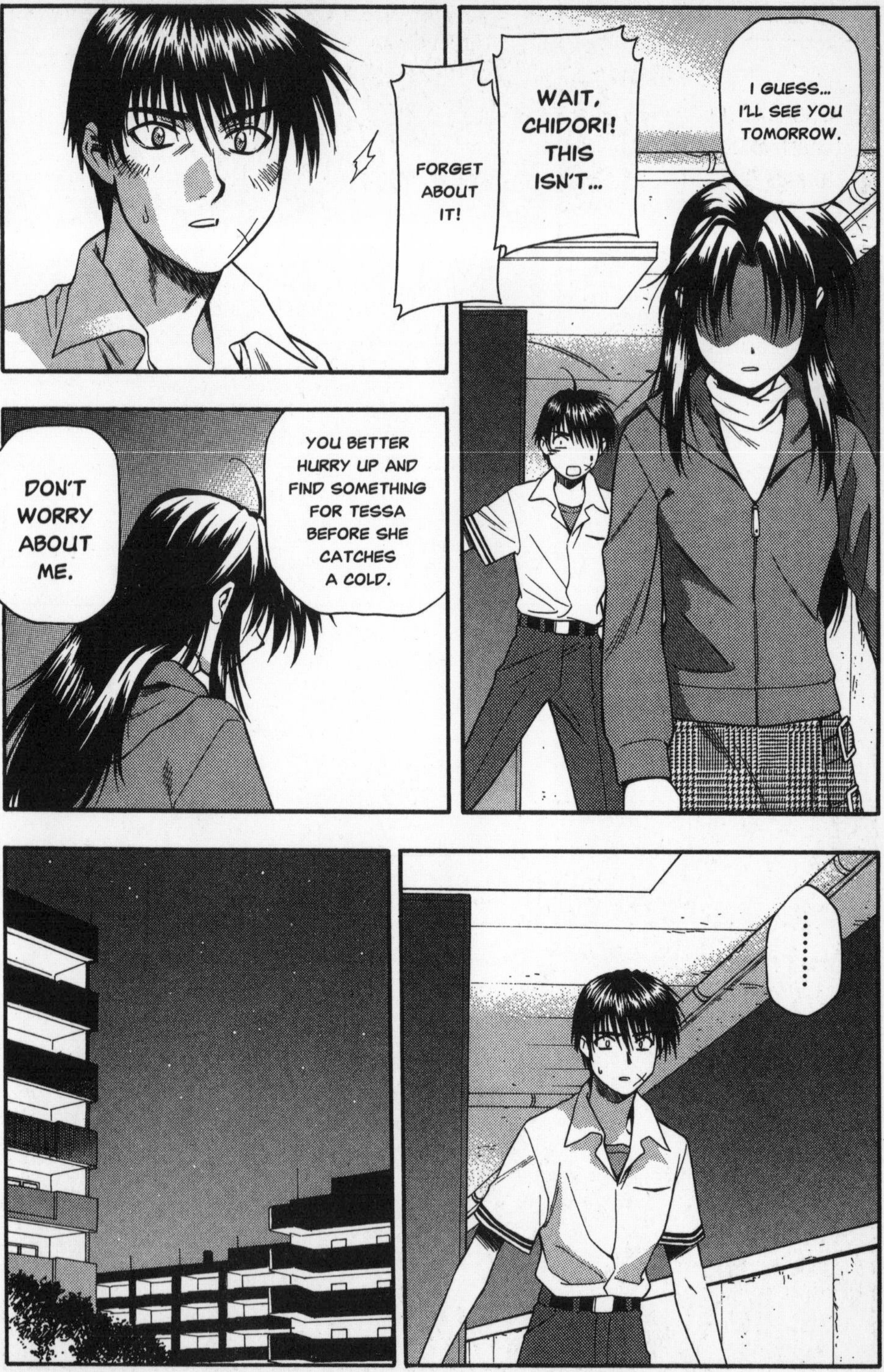
I GUESS... I'LL SEE YOU TOMORROW.
WAIT, CHIDORI! THIS ISN'T...
FORGET ABOUT IT!
YOU BETTER HURRY UP AND FIND SOMETHING FOR TESSA BEFORE SHE CATCHES A COLD.
DON'T WORRY ABOUT ME.
......

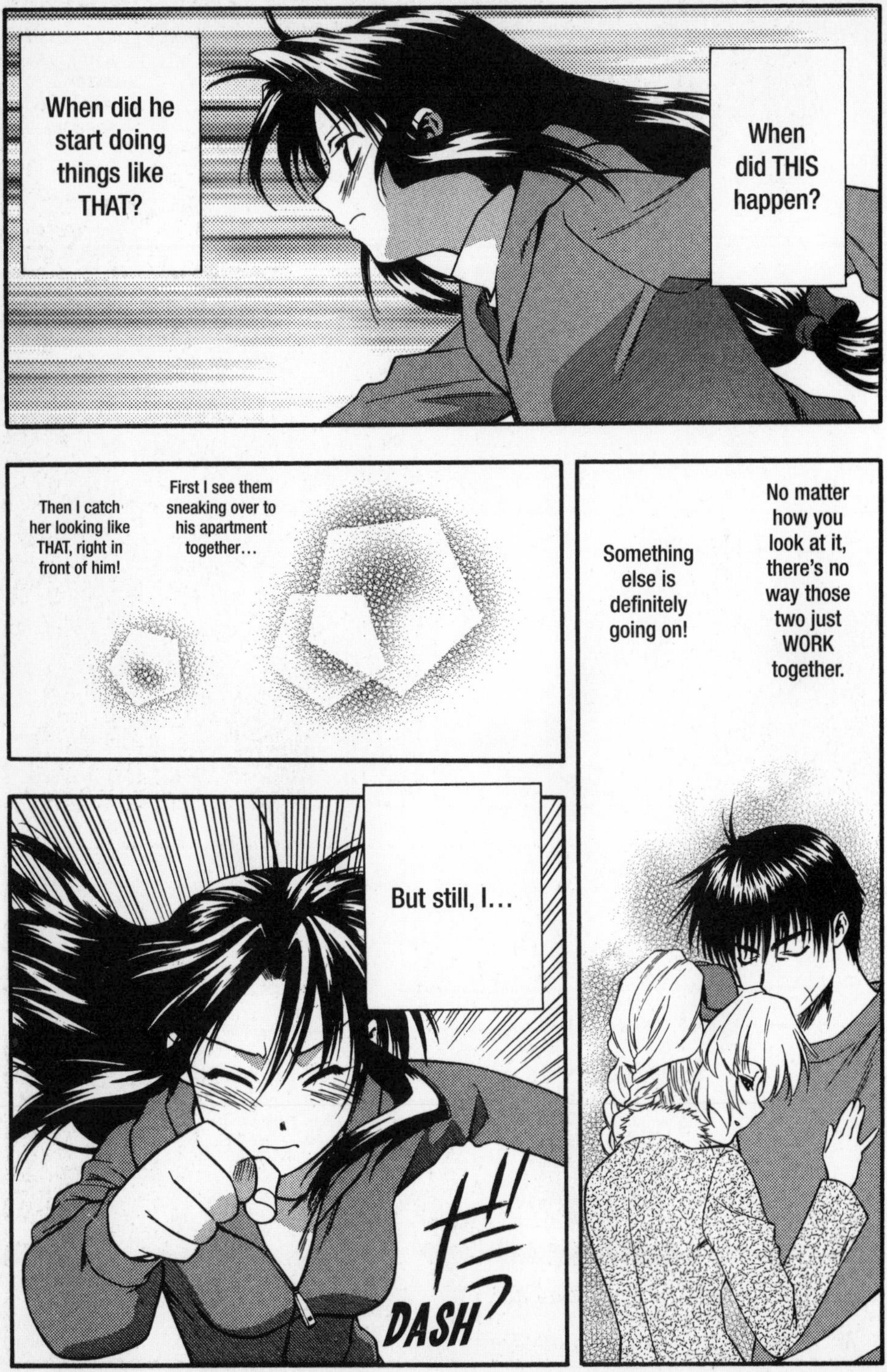
When did THIS happen?
When did he start doing things like THAT?
No matter how you look at it, there's no way those two just WORK together.
Something else is definitely going on!
First I see them sneaking over to his apartment together…
Then I catch her looking like THAT, right in front of him!
But still, I…
DASH

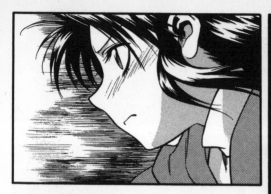

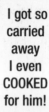

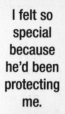

I felt so special because he'd been protecting me.
I got so carried away I even COOKED for him!
I am…
SUCH an idiot.
DO YOU THINK SHE'S ALRIGHT?
HUH?

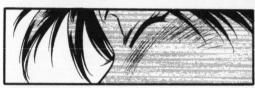

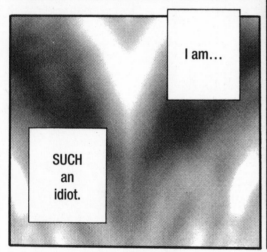

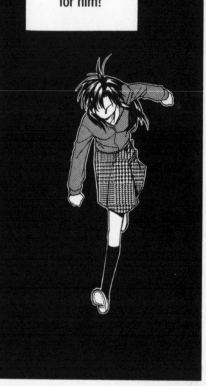

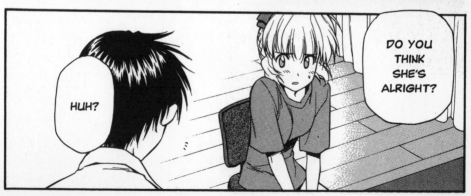

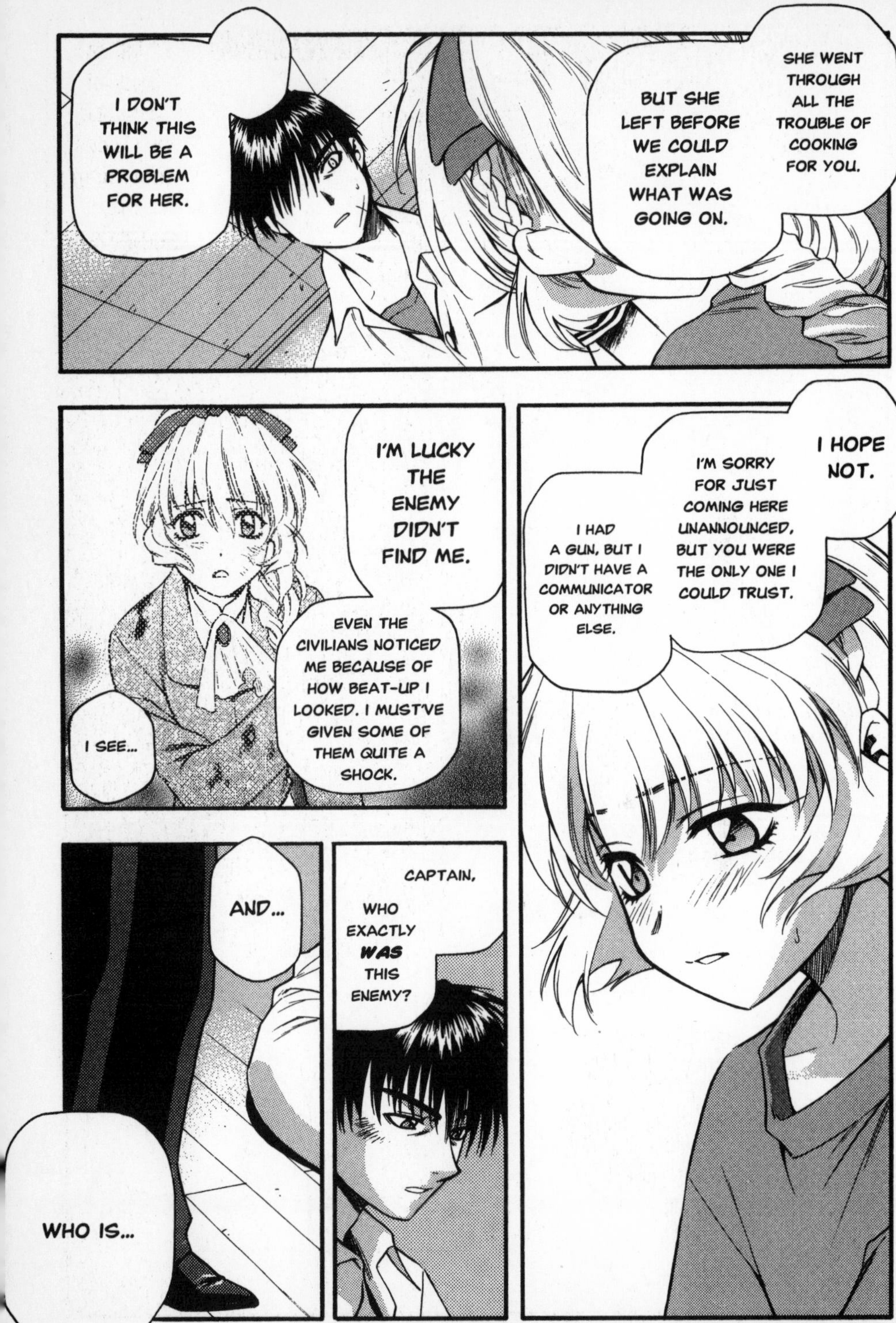
SHE WENT THROUGH ALL THE TROUBLE OF COOKING FOR YOU.
BUT SHE LEFT BEFORE WE COULD EXPLAIN WHAT WAS GOING ON.
I DON'T THINK THIS WILL BE A PROBLEM FOR HER.
I HOPE NOT.
I'M SORRY FOR JUST COMING HERE UNANNOUNCED, BUT YOU WERE THE ONLY ONE I COULD TRUST.
I HAD A GUN, BUT I DIDN'T HAVE A COMMUNICATOR OR ANYTHING ELSE.
I'M LUCKY THE ENEMY DIDN'T FIND ME.
EVEN THE CIVILIANS NOTICED ME BECAUSE OF HOW BEAT-UP I LOOKED. I MUST'VE GIVEN SOME OF THEM QUITE A SHOCK.
I SEE...
CAPTAIN,
WHO EXACTLY WAS THIS ENEMY?
AND...
WHO IS...

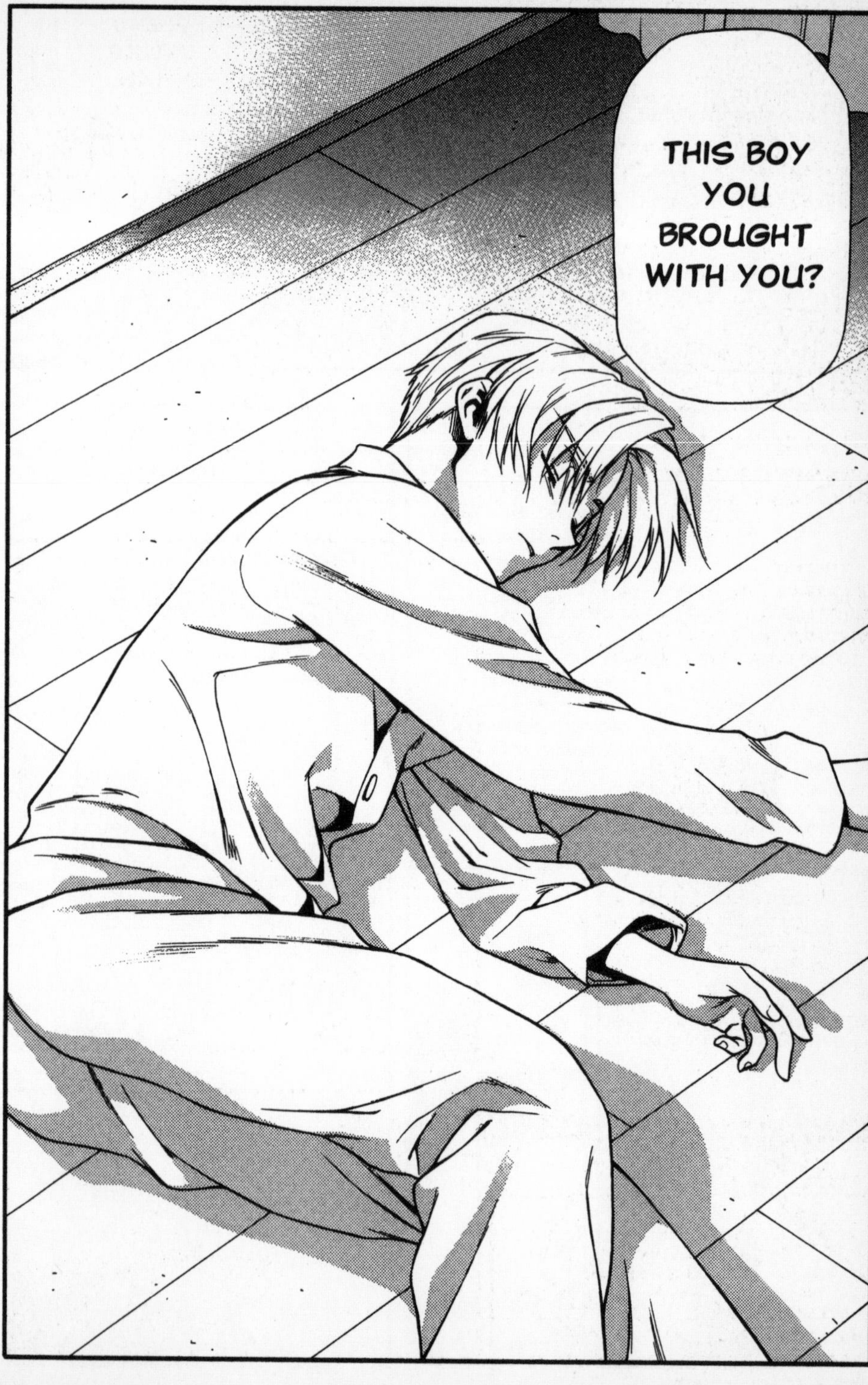
THIS BOY YOU BROUGHT WITH YOU?

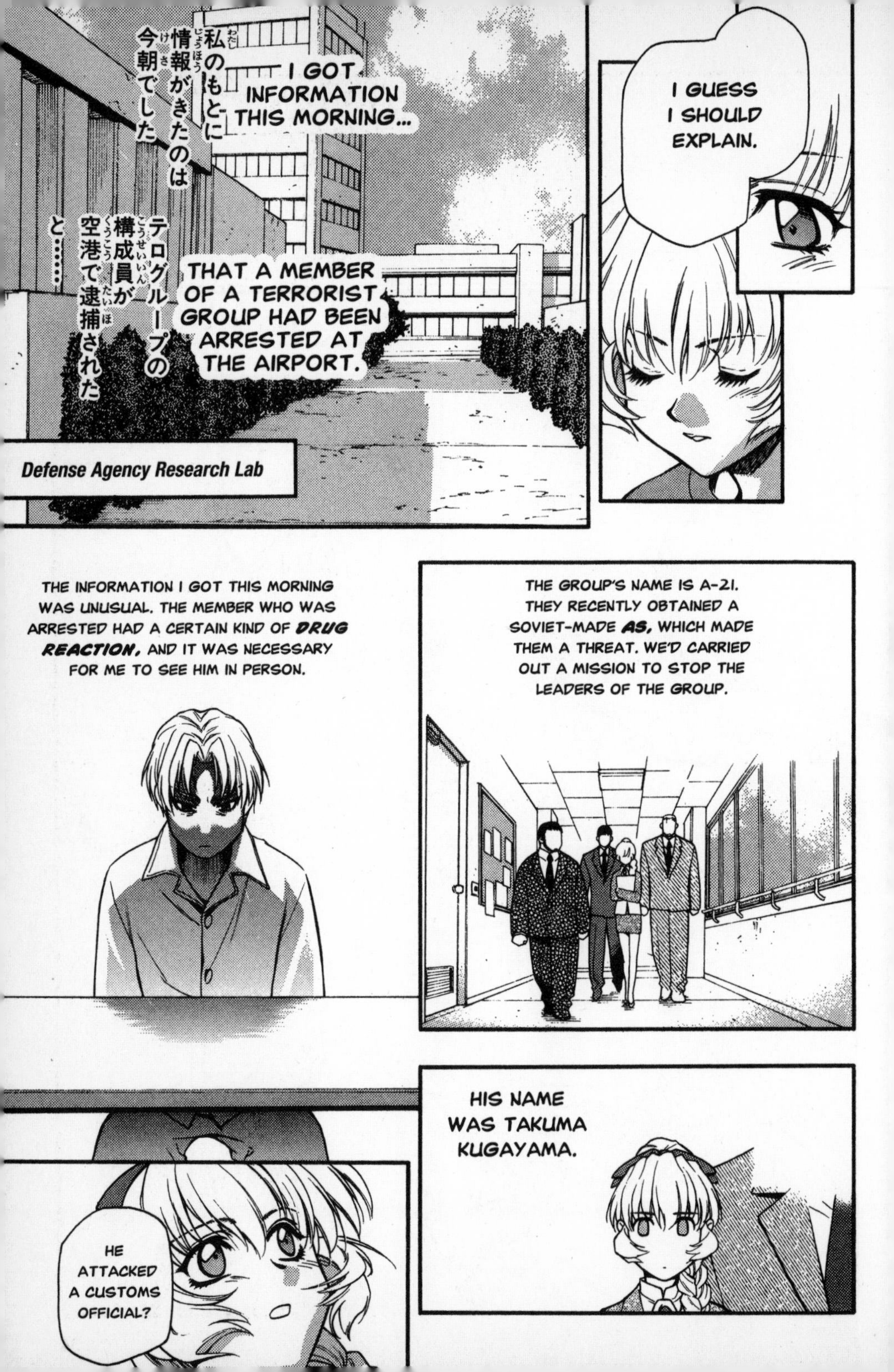
I GUESS I SHOULD EXPLAIN.
私のもとに情報がきたのは今朝でした
I GOT INFORMATION THIS MORNING...
テログループの構成員が空港で逮捕されたと……
THAT A MEMBER OF A TERRORIST GROUP HAD BEEN ARRESTED AT THE AIRPORT.
Defense Agency Research Lab
THE GROUP'S NAME IS A-21. THEY RECENTLY OBTAINED A SOVIET-MADE AS, WHICH MADE THEM A THREAT. WE'D CARRIED OUT A MISSION TO STOP THE LEADERS OF THE GROUP.
THE INFORMATION I GOT THIS MORNING WAS UNUSUAL. THE MEMBER WHO WAS ARRESTED HAD A CERTAIN KIND OF DRUG REACTION, AND IT WAS NECESSARY FOR ME TO SEE HIM IN PERSON.
HIS NAME WAS TAKUMA KUGAYAMA.
HE ATTACKED A CUSTOMS OFFICIAL?

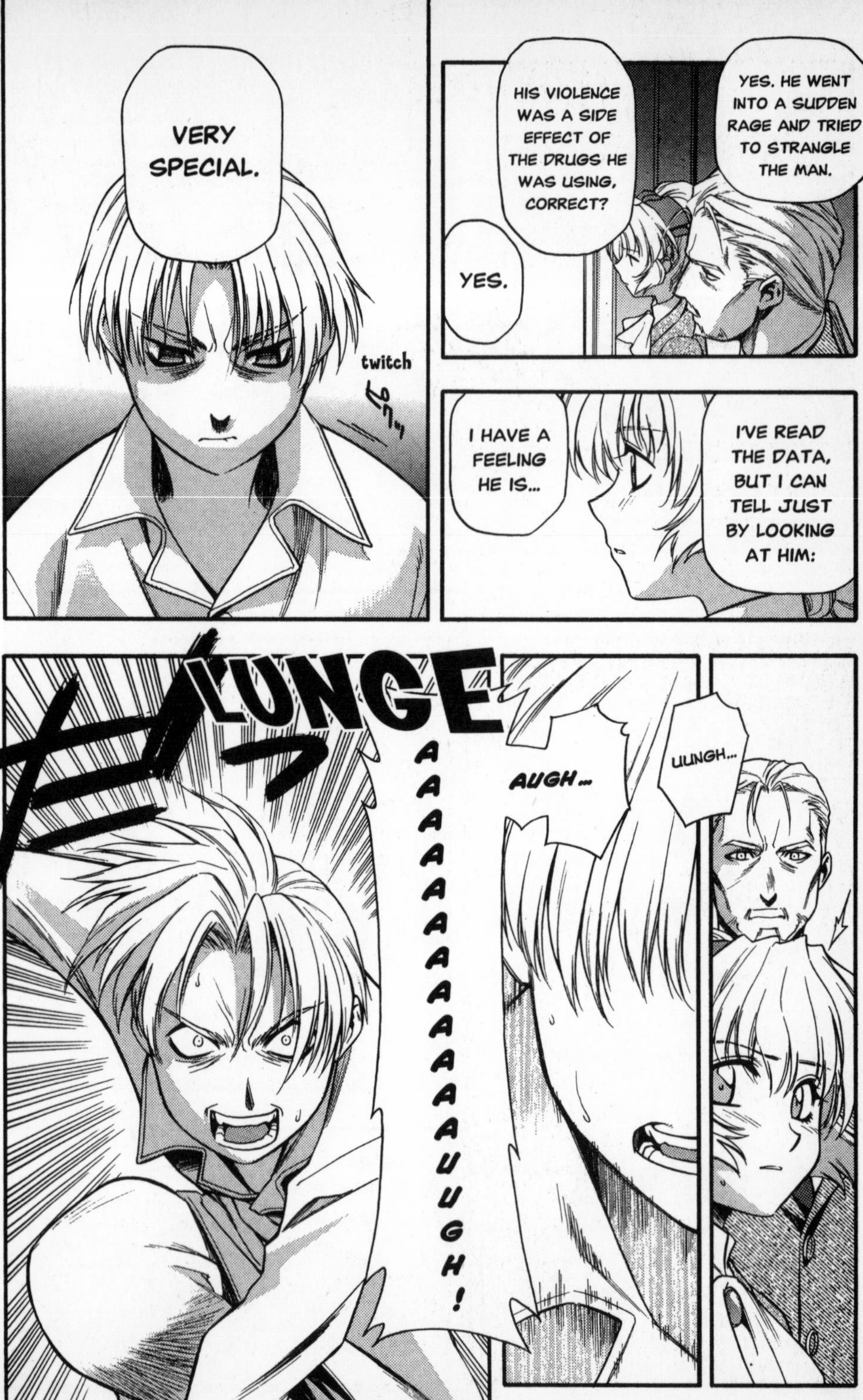

YES. HE WENT INTO A SUDDEN RAGE AND TRIED TO STRANGLE THE MAN.
HIS VIOLENCE WAS A SIDE EFFECT OF THE DRUGS HE WAS USING, CORRECT?
YES.
I'VE READ THE DATA, BUT I CAN TELL JUST BY LOOKING AT HIM:
I HAVE A FEELING HE IS...
VERY SPECIAL.
twitch
UUNGH...
AUGH...
LUNGE
AAAAAAAAAAAAAAAUUGH!

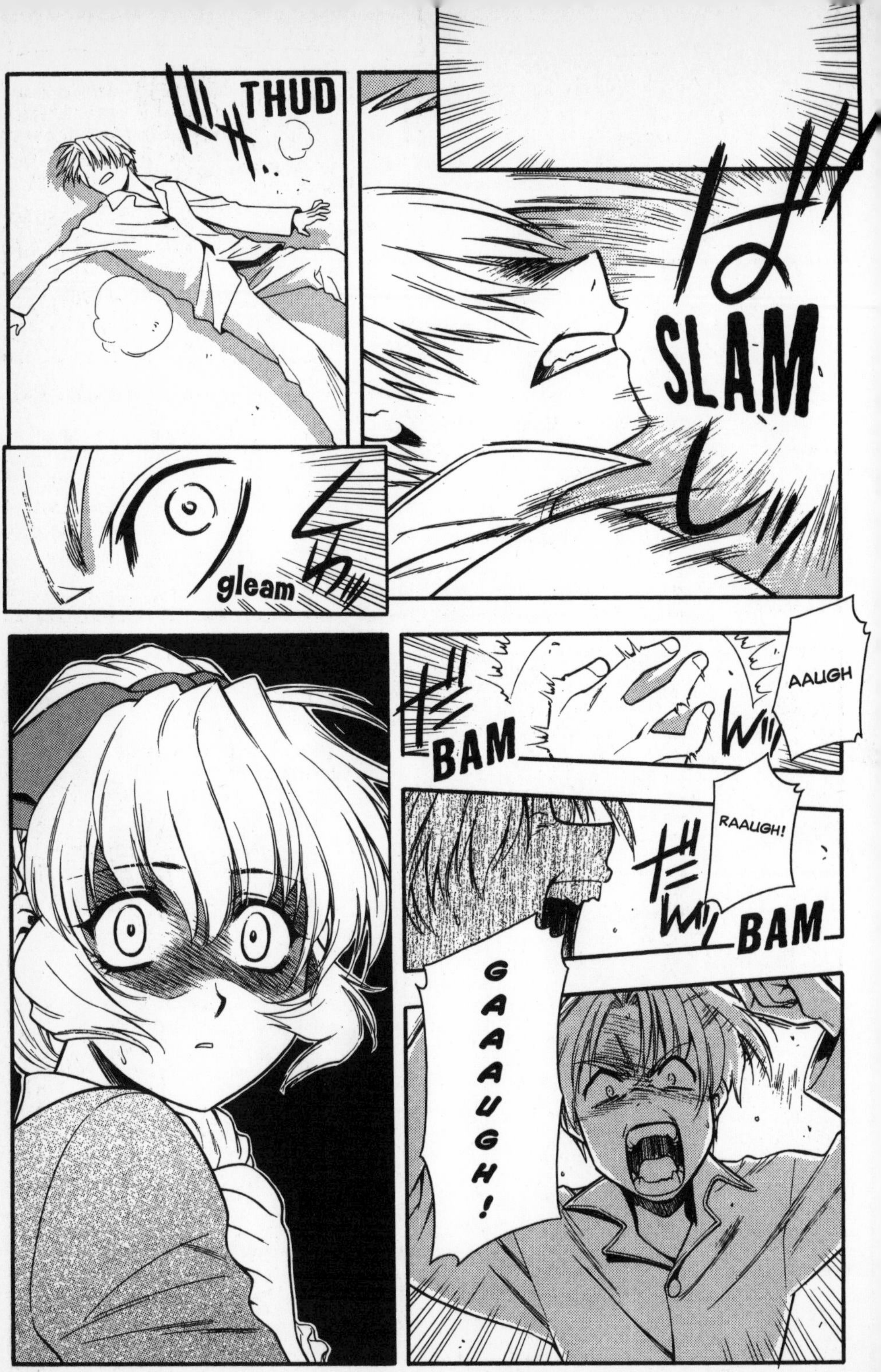
SLAM
THUD
gleam
AAUGH
BAM
RAAUGH!
BAM
GAAAAUGH!

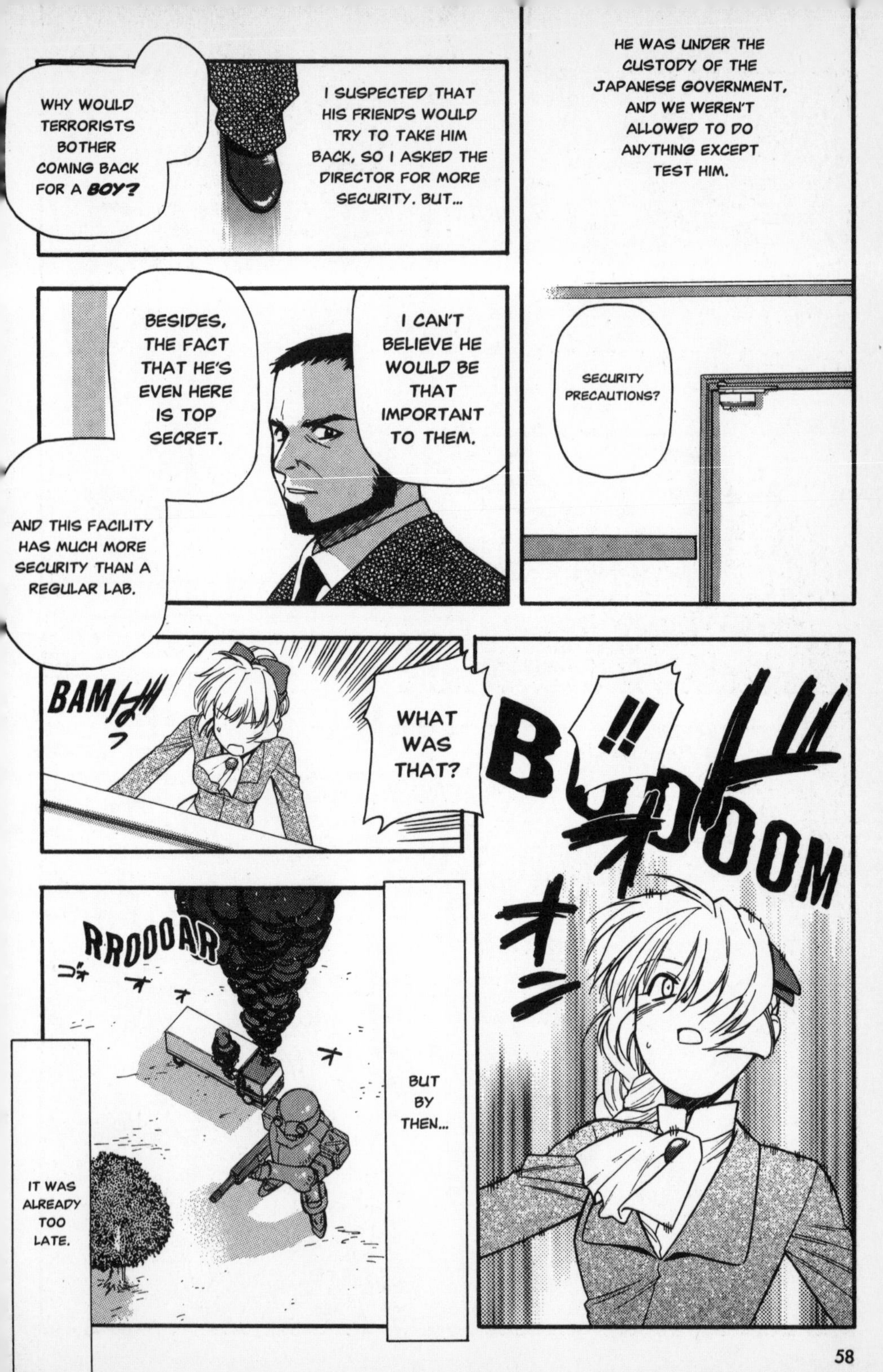
HE WAS UNDER THE CUSTODY OF THE JAPANESE GOVERNMENT, AND WE WEREN'T ALLOWED TO DO ANYTHING EXCEPT TEST HIM.
SECURITY PRECAUTIONS?
I SUSPECTED THAT HIS FRIENDS WOULD TRY TO TAKE HIM BACK, SO I ASKED THE DIRECTOR FOR MORE SECURITY. BUT...
WHY WOULD TERRORISTS BOTHER COMING BACK FOR A BOY?
I CAN'T BELIEVE HE WOULD BE THAT IMPORTANT TO THEM.
BESIDES, THE FACT THAT HE'S EVEN HERE IS TOP SECRET.
AND THIS FACILITY HAS MUCH MORE SECURITY THAN A REGULAR LAB.
!!
BUDOOM
WHAT WAS THAT?
BAM
BUT BY THEN...
RRROOOAR
IT WAS ALREADY TOO LATE.

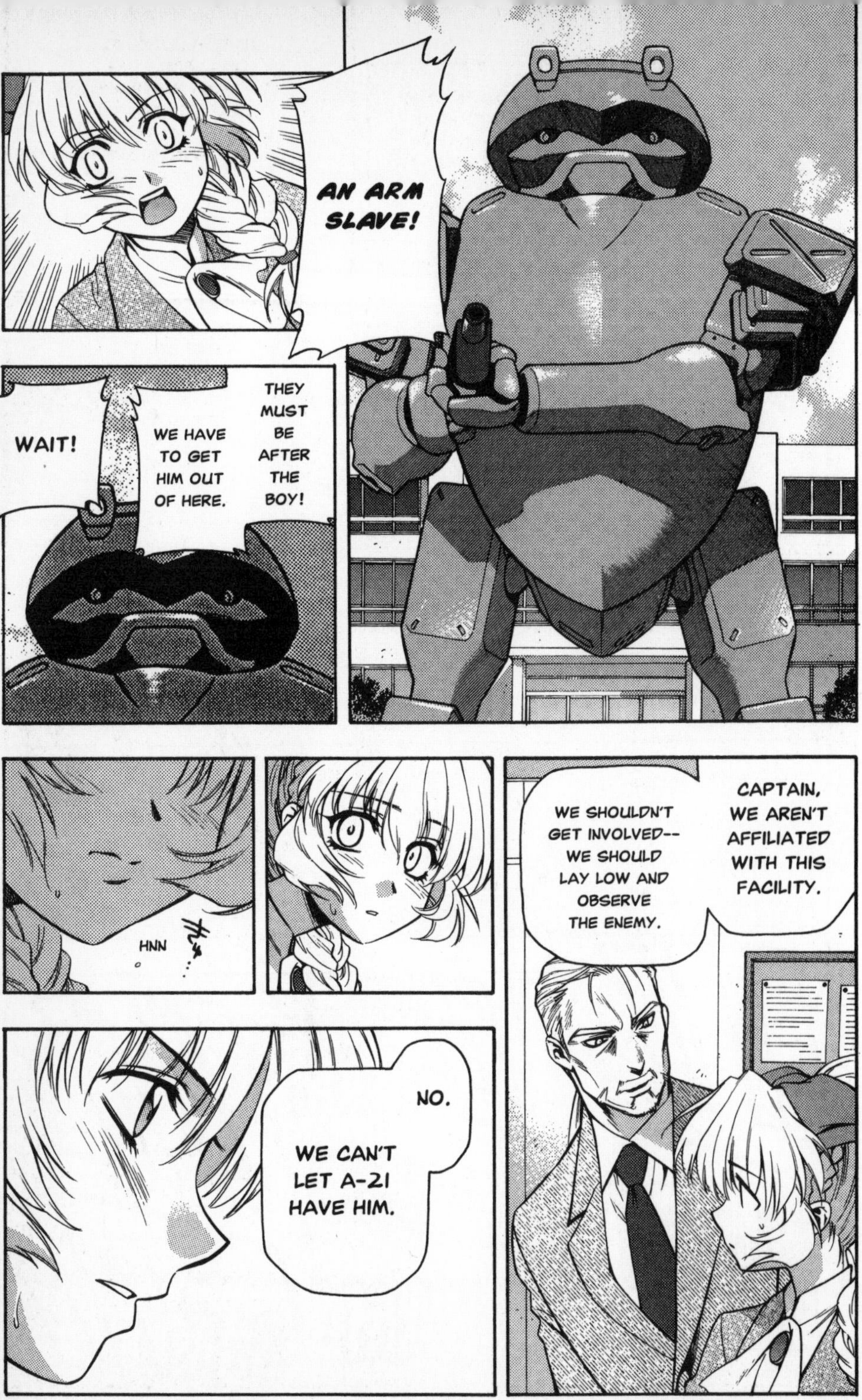
AN ARM SLAVE!
THEY MUST BE AFTER THE BOY!
WE HAVE TO GET HIM OUT OF HERE.
WAIT!
CAPTAIN, WE AREN'T AFFILIATED WITH THIS FACILITY.
WE SHOULDN'T GET INVOLVED-- WE SHOULD LAY LOW AND OBSERVE THE ENEMY.
HNN
NO.
WE CAN'T LET A-21 HAVE HIM.

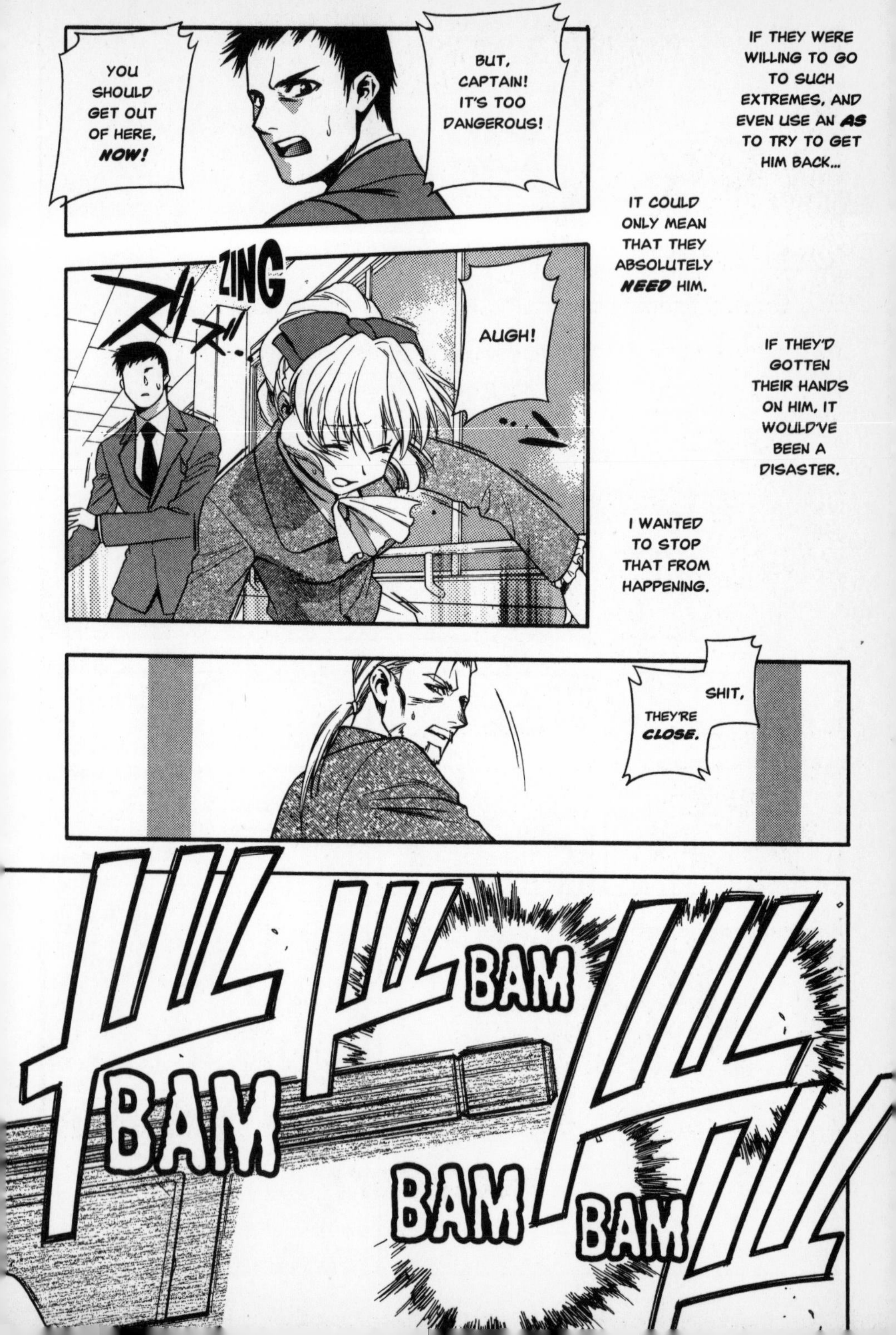
IF THEY WERE WILLING TO GO TO SUCH EXTREMES, AND EVEN USE AN AS TO TRY TO GET HIM BACK...
BUT, CAPTAIN! IT'S TOO DANGEROUS!
YOU SHOULD GET OUT OF HERE, NOW!
IT COULD ONLY MEAN THAT THEY ABSOLUTELY NEED HIM.
IF THEY'D GOTTEN THEIR HANDS ON HIM, IT WOULD'VE BEEN A DISASTER.
AUGH!
ZING
I WANTED TO STOP THAT FROM HAPPENING.
SHIT, THEY'RE CLOSE.
BAM
BAM
BAM
BAM

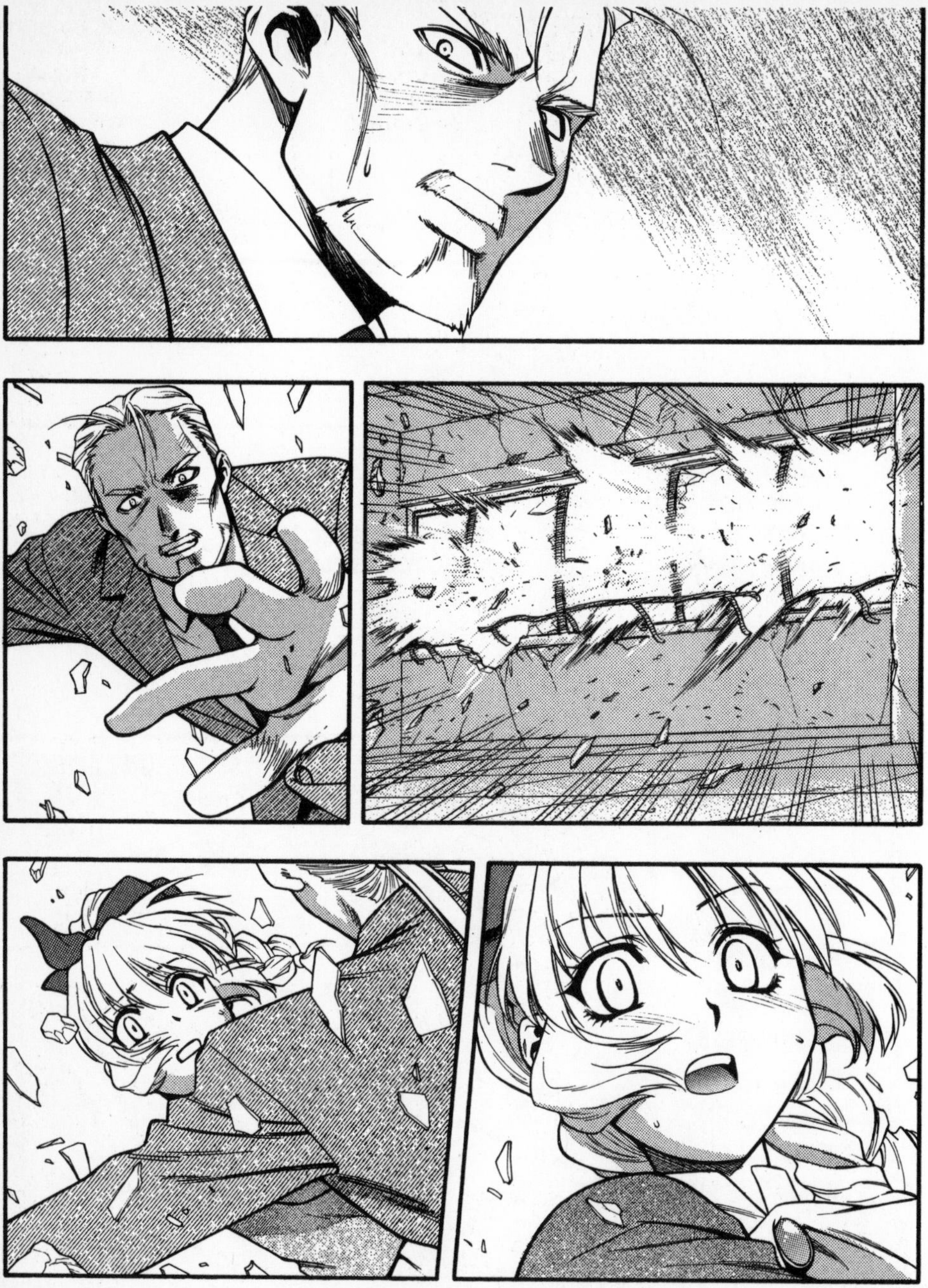
KALININ!

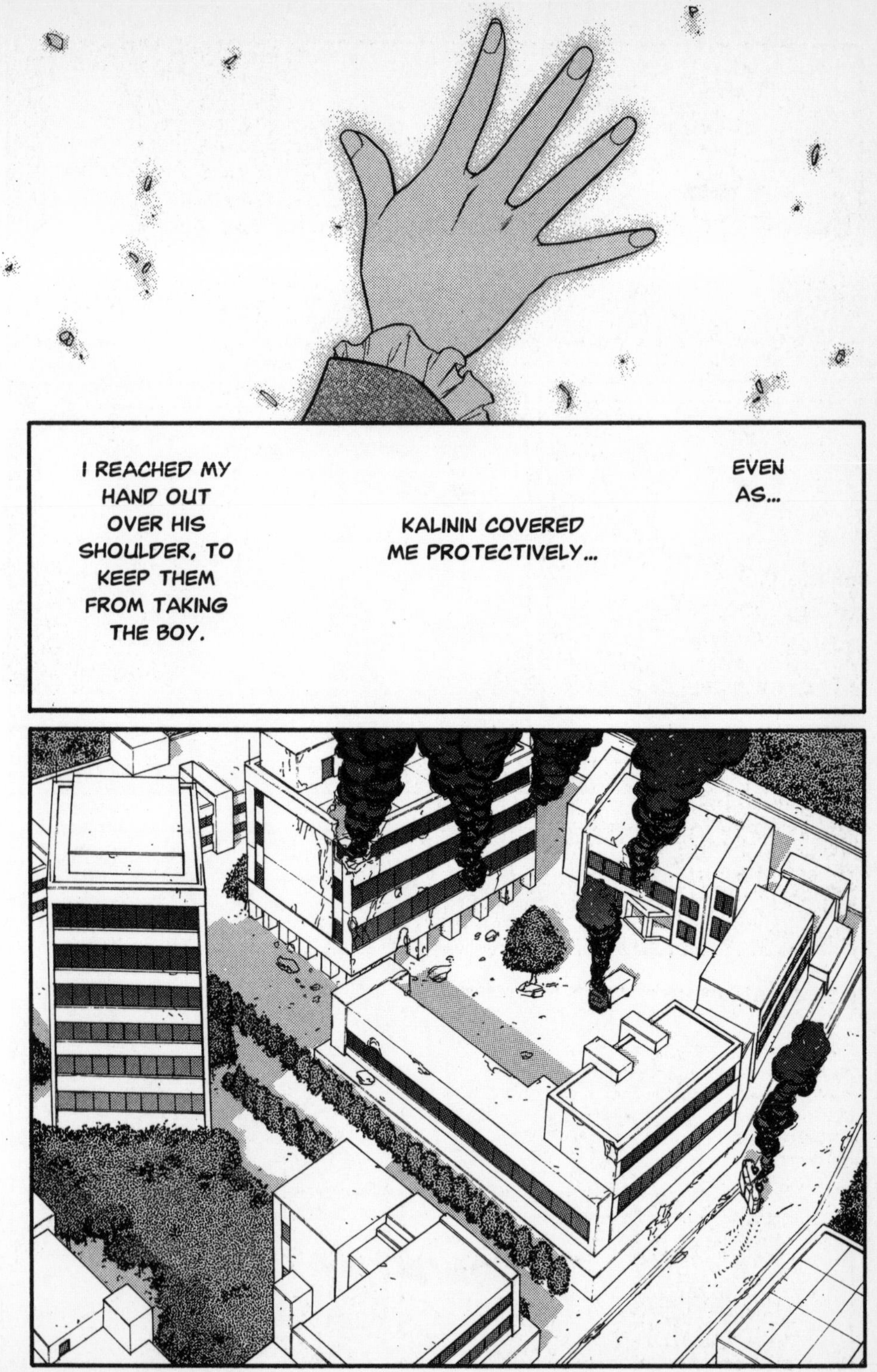
EVEN AS...
KALININ COVERED ME PROTECTIVELY...
I REACHED MY HAND OUT OVER HIS SHOULDER, TO KEEP THEM FROM TAKING THE BOY.

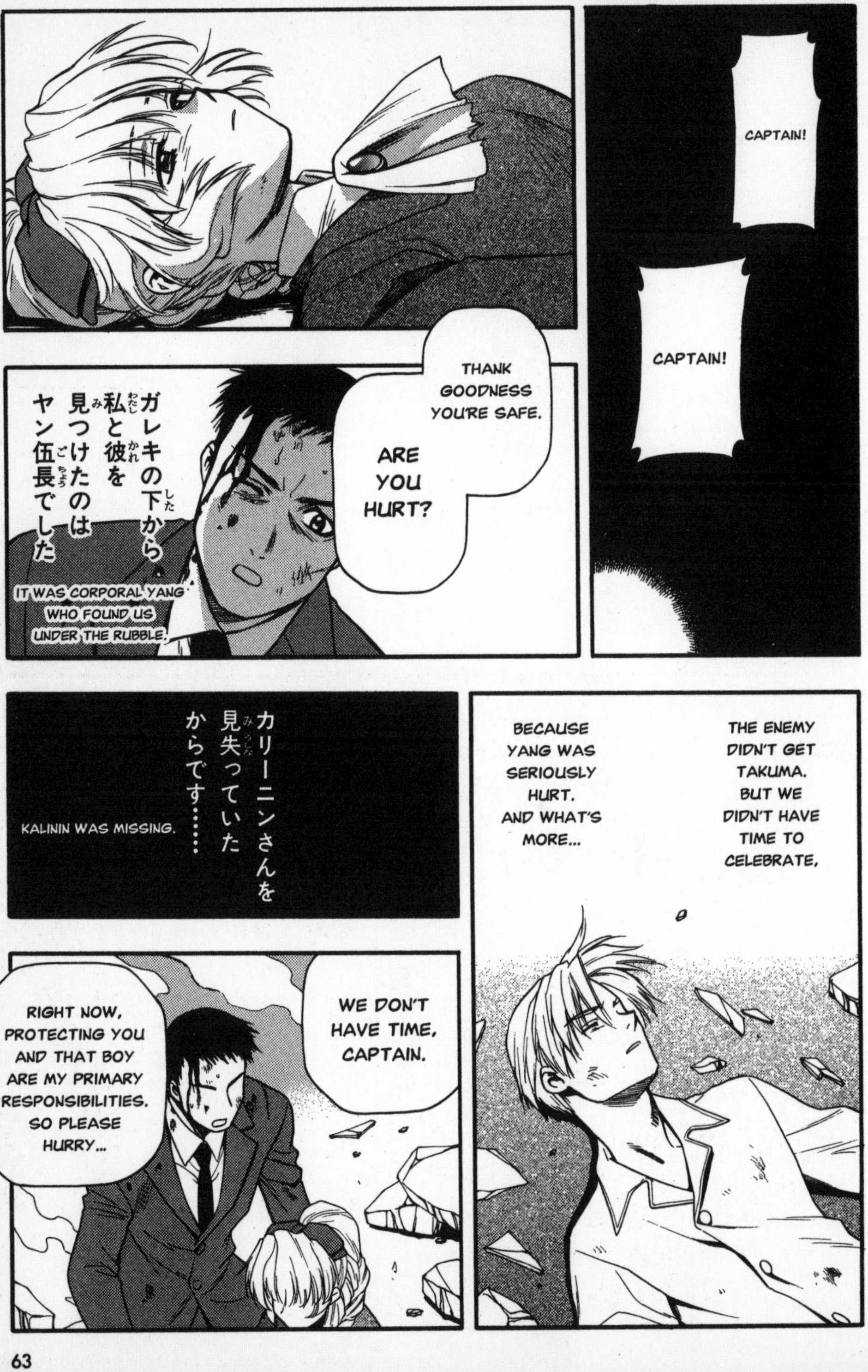

CAPTAIN!
CAPTAIN!
THANK GOODNESS YOU'RE SAFE.
ARE YOU HURT?
ガレキの下から私と彼を見つけたのはヤン伍長でした
IT WAS CORPORAL YANG WHO FOUND US UNDER THE RUBBLE.
THE ENEMY DIDN'T GET TAKUMA. BUT WE DIDN'T HAVE TIME TO CELEBRATE,
BECAUSE YANG WAS SERIOUSLY HURT. AND WHAT'S MORE...
カリーニンさんを見失っていたからです……
KALININ WAS MISSING.
WE DON'T HAVE TIME, CAPTAIN.
RIGHT NOW, PROTECTING YOU AND THAT BOY ARE MY PRIMARY RESPONSIBILITIES. SO PLEASE HURRY...

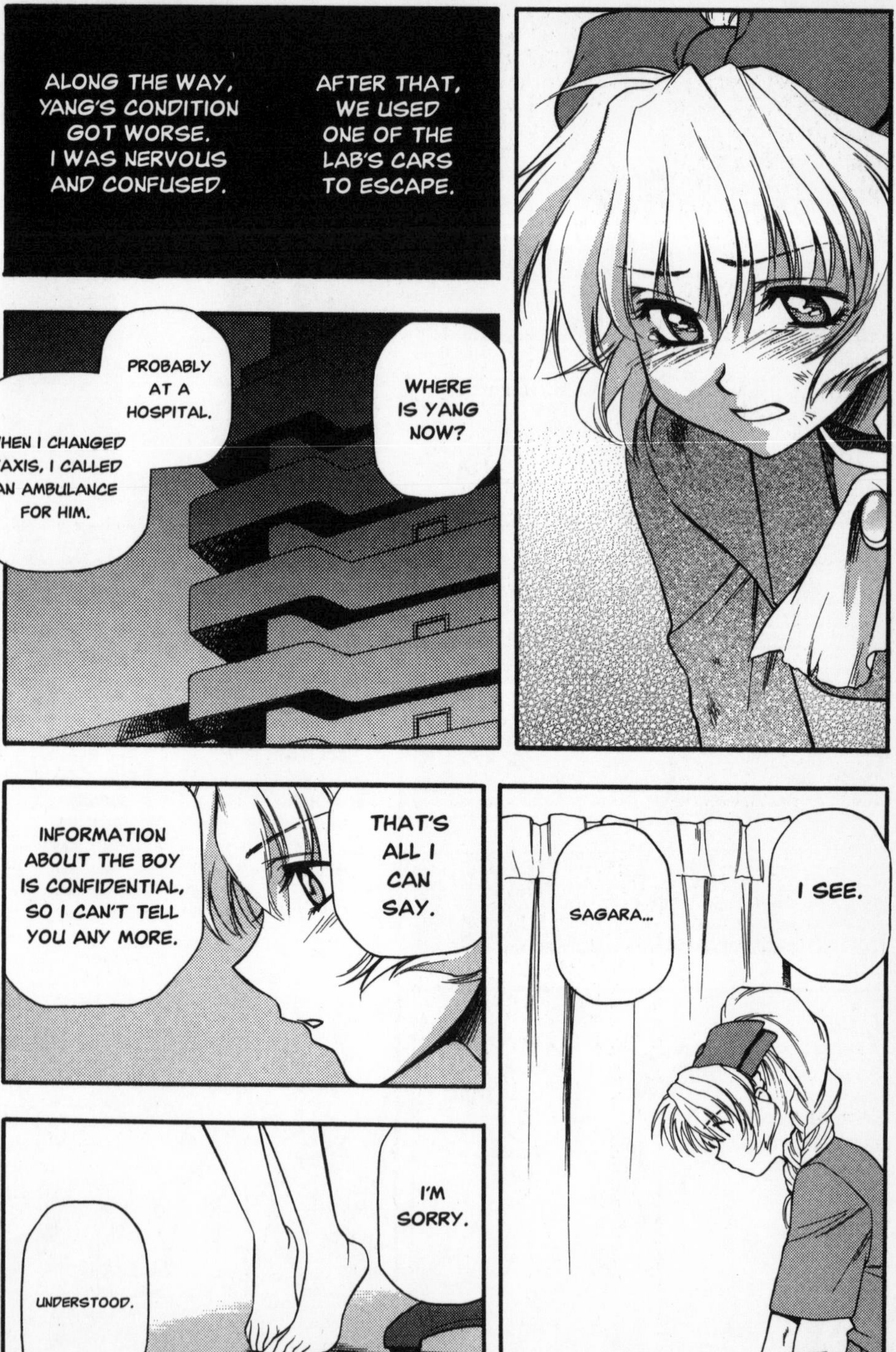
AFTER THAT, WE USED ONE OF THE LAB'S CARS TO ESCAPE.
ALONG THE WAY, YANG'S CONDITION GOT WORSE. I WAS NERVOUS AND CONFUSED.
WHERE IS YANG NOW?
PROBABLY AT A HOSPITAL.
WHEN I CHANGED TAXIS, I CALLED AN AMBULANCE FOR HIM.
I SEE.
SAGARA...
THAT'S ALL I CAN SAY.
INFORMATION ABOUT THE BOY IS CONFIDENTIAL, SO I CAN'T TELL YOU ANY MORE.
I'M SORRY.
UNDERSTOOD.

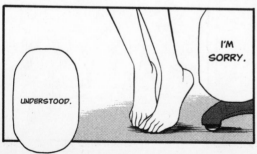

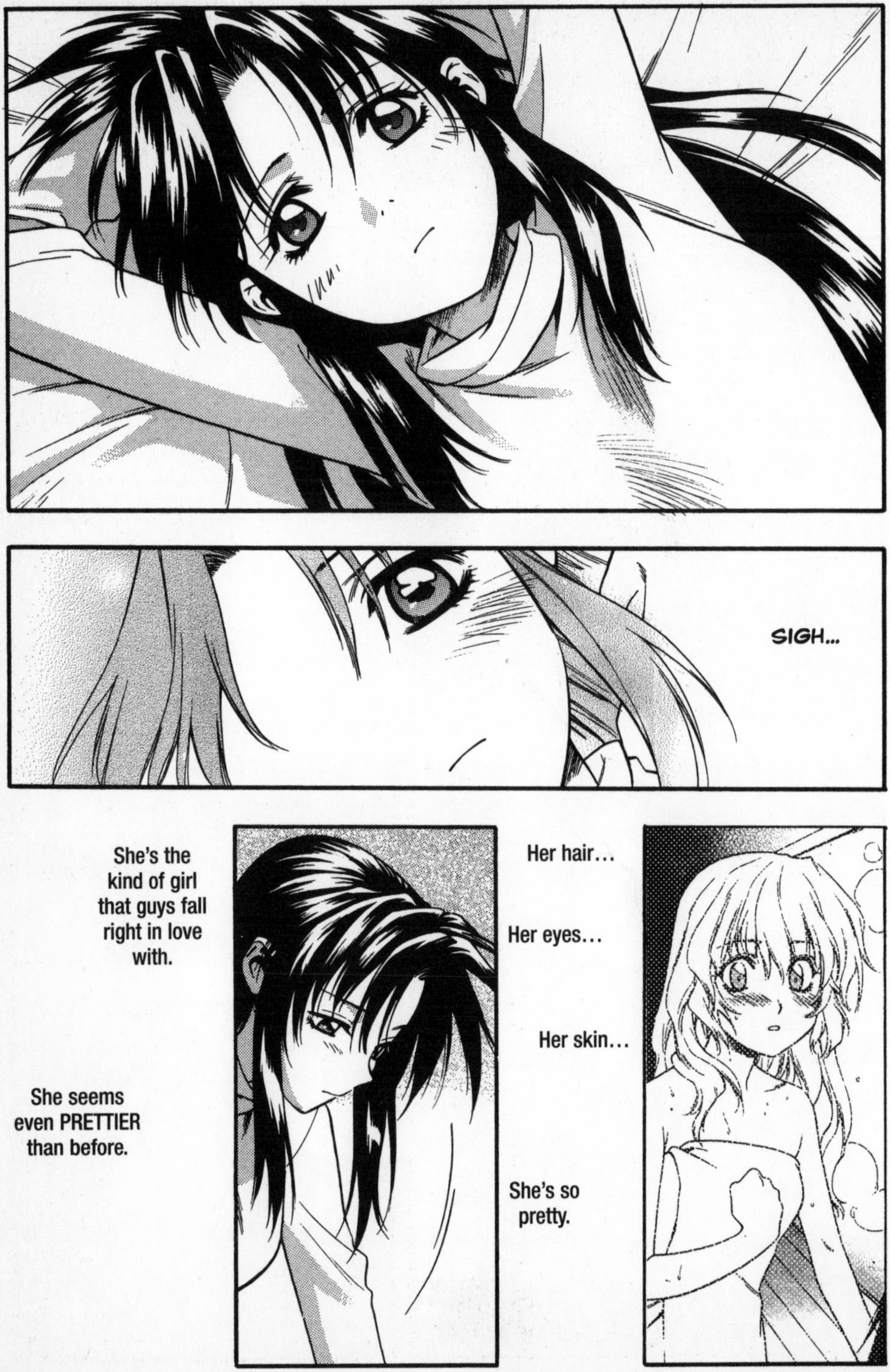
SIGH...
Her hair…
Her eyes…
Her skin…
She's so pretty.
She's the kind of girl that guys fall right in love with.
She seems even PRETTIER than before.

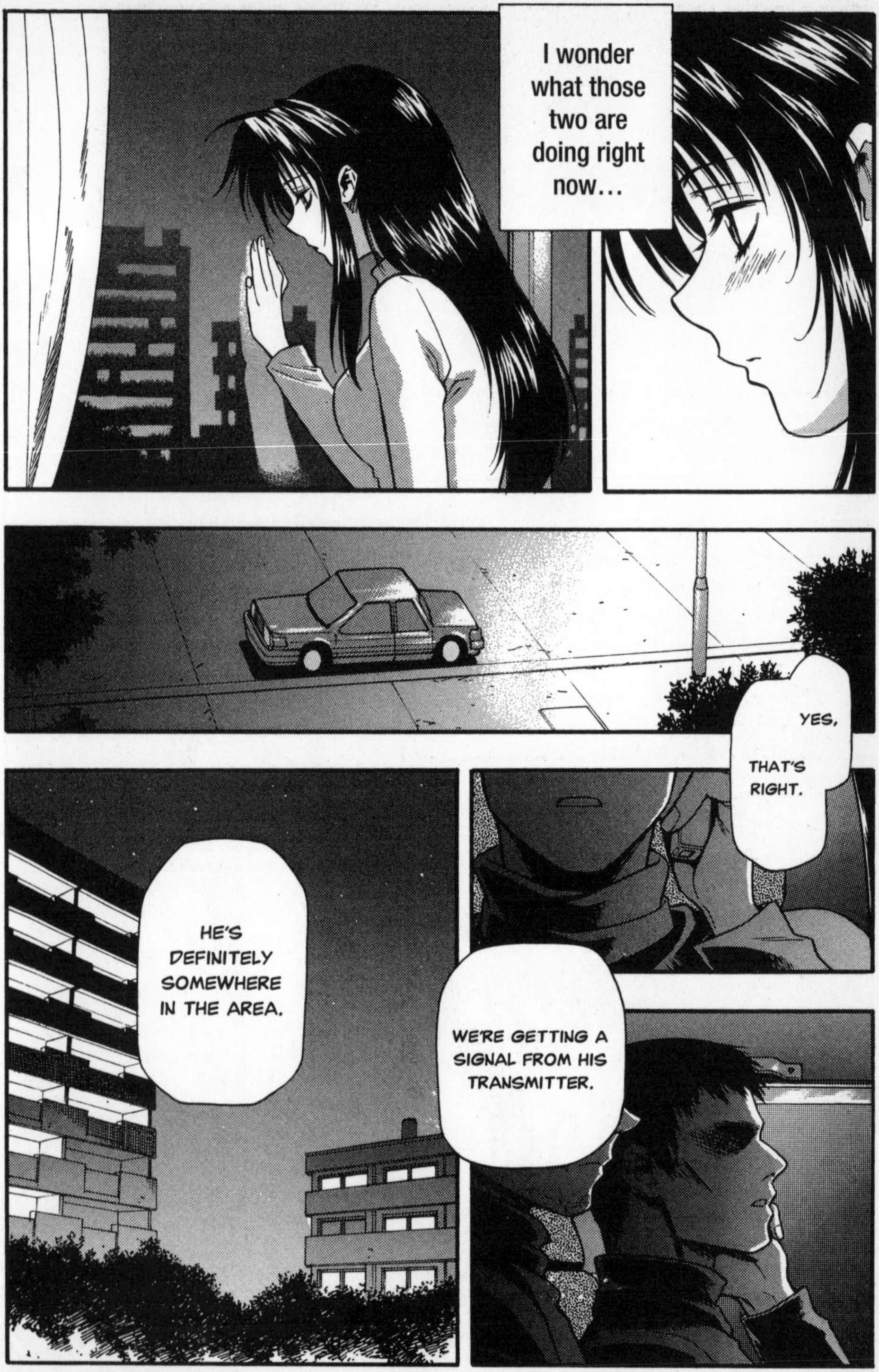
I wonder what those two are doing right now…
YES, THAT'S RIGHT.
WE'RE GETTING A SIGNAL FROM HIS TRANSMITTER.
HE'S DEFINITELY SOMEWHERE IN THE AREA.

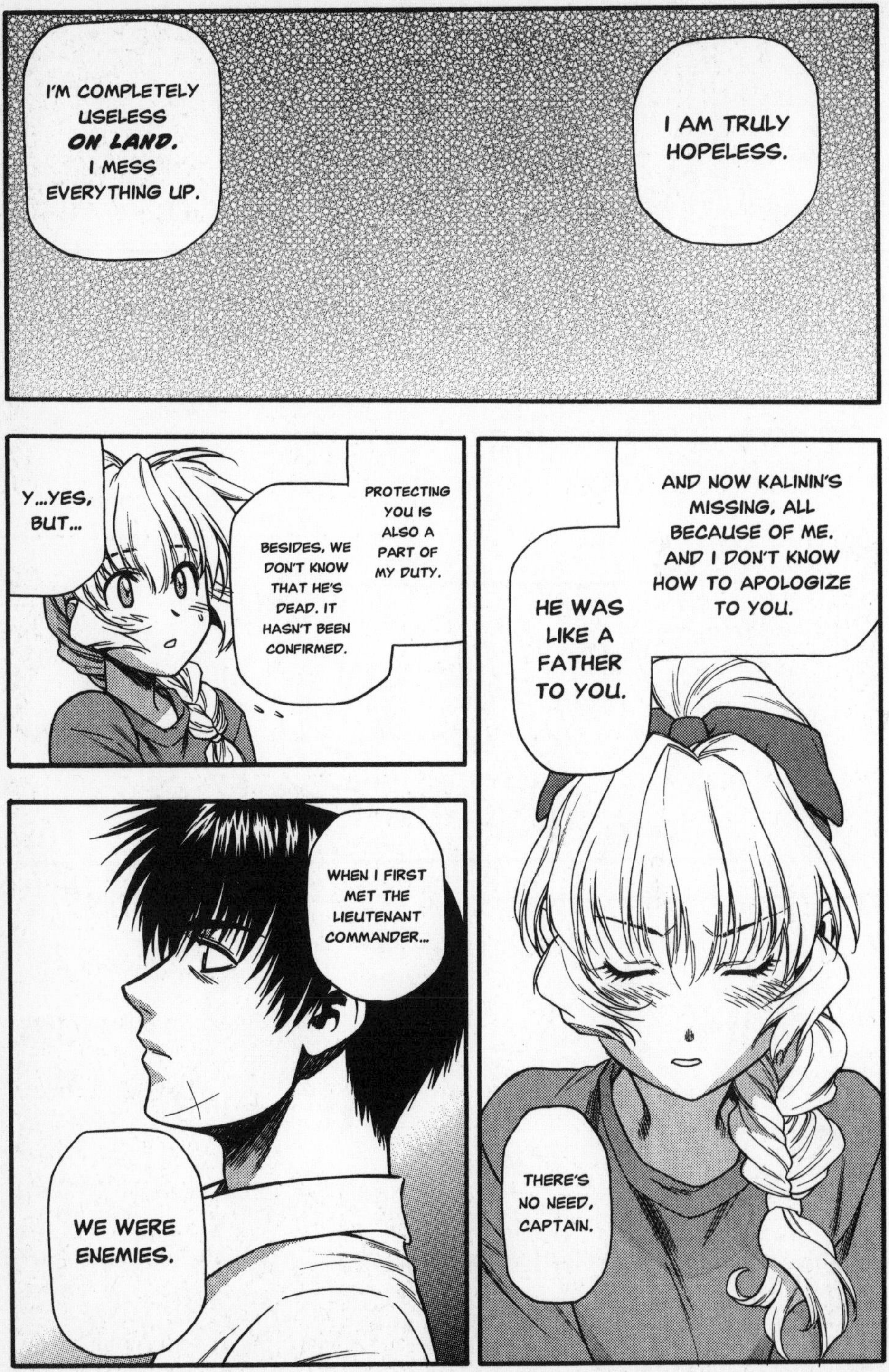
I AM TRULY HOPELESS.
I'M COMPLETELY USELESS ***ON LAND.*** I MESS EVERYTHING UP.
AND NOW KALININ'S MISSING, ALL BECAUSE OF ME. AND I DON'T KNOW HOW TO APOLOGIZE TO YOU.
HE WAS LIKE A FATHER TO YOU.
THERE'S NO NEED, CAPTAIN.
PROTECTING YOU IS ALSO A PART OF MY DUTY.
BESIDES, WE DON'T KNOW THAT HE'S DEAD. IT HASN'T BEEN CONFIRMED.
Y...YES, BUT...
WHEN I FIRST MET THE LIEUTENANT COMMANDER...
WE WERE ENEMIES.

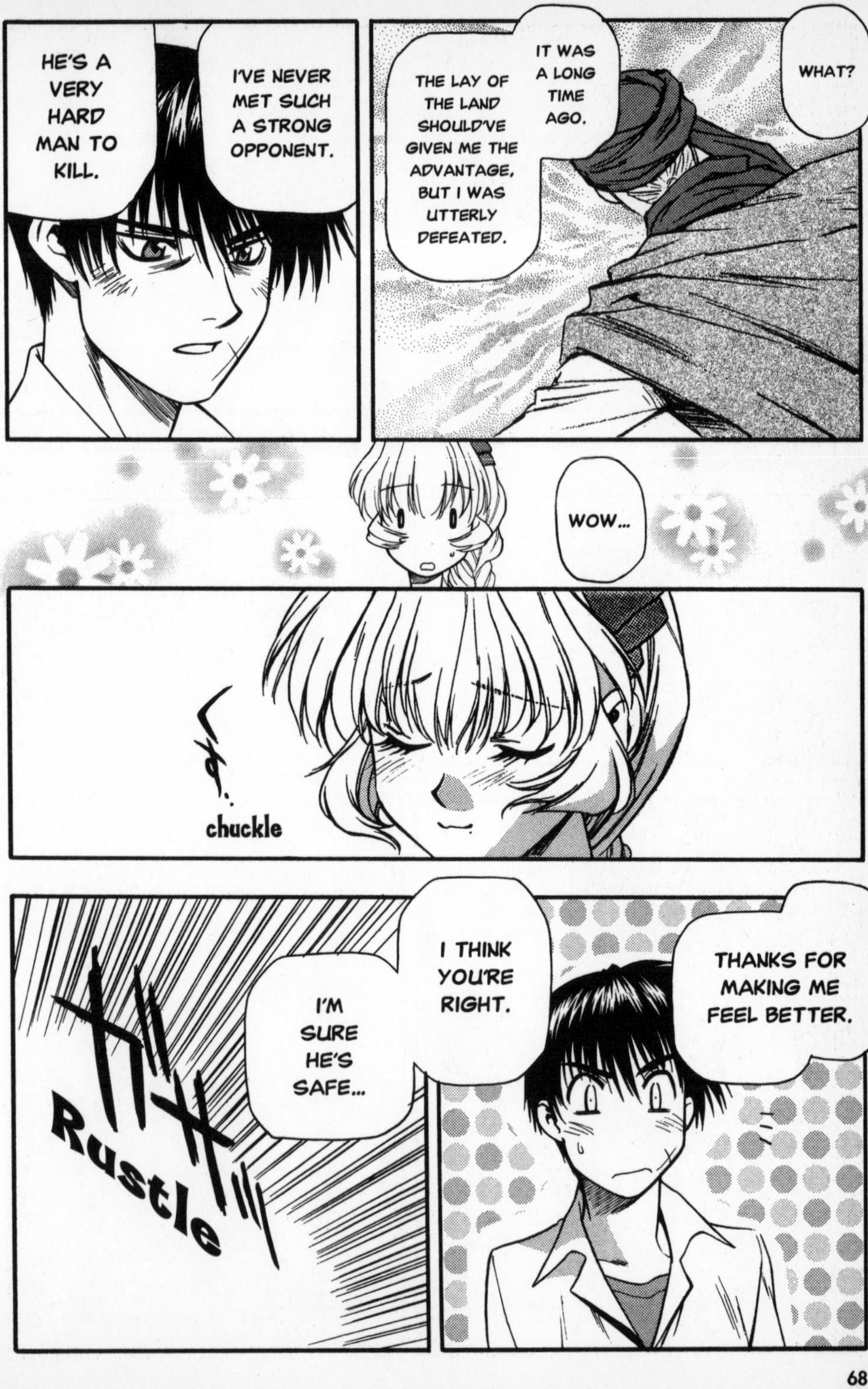
WHAT?
IT WAS A LONG TIME AGO.
THE LAY OF THE LAND SHOULD'VE GIVEN ME THE ADVANTAGE, BUT I WAS UTTERLY DEFEATED.
I'VE NEVER MET SUCH A STRONG OPPONENT.
HE'S A VERY HARD MAN TO KILL.
WOW...
chuckle
THANKS FOR MAKING ME FEEL BETTER.
I THINK YOU'RE RIGHT.
I'M SURE HE'S SAFE...
Rustle

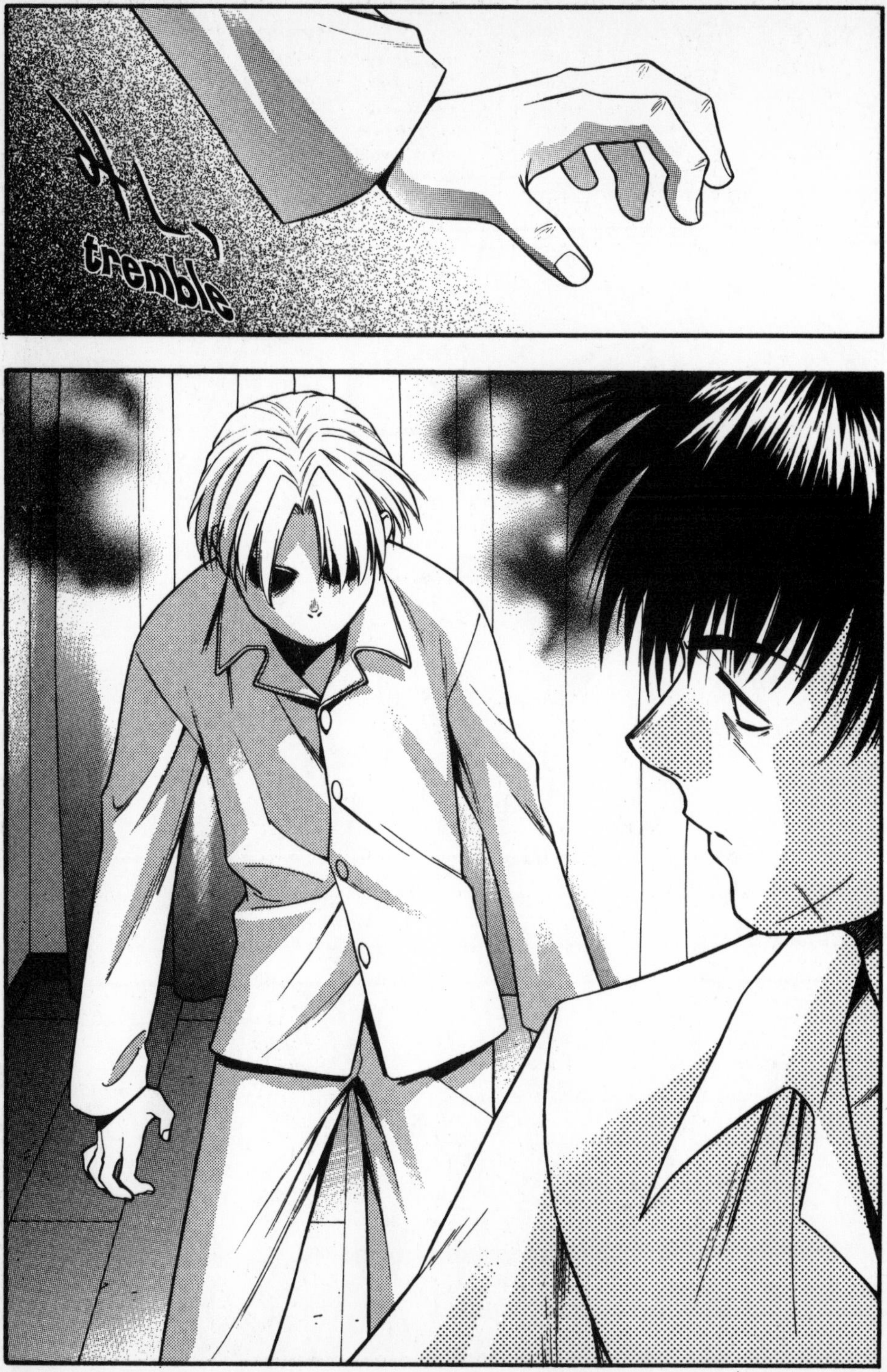
tremble

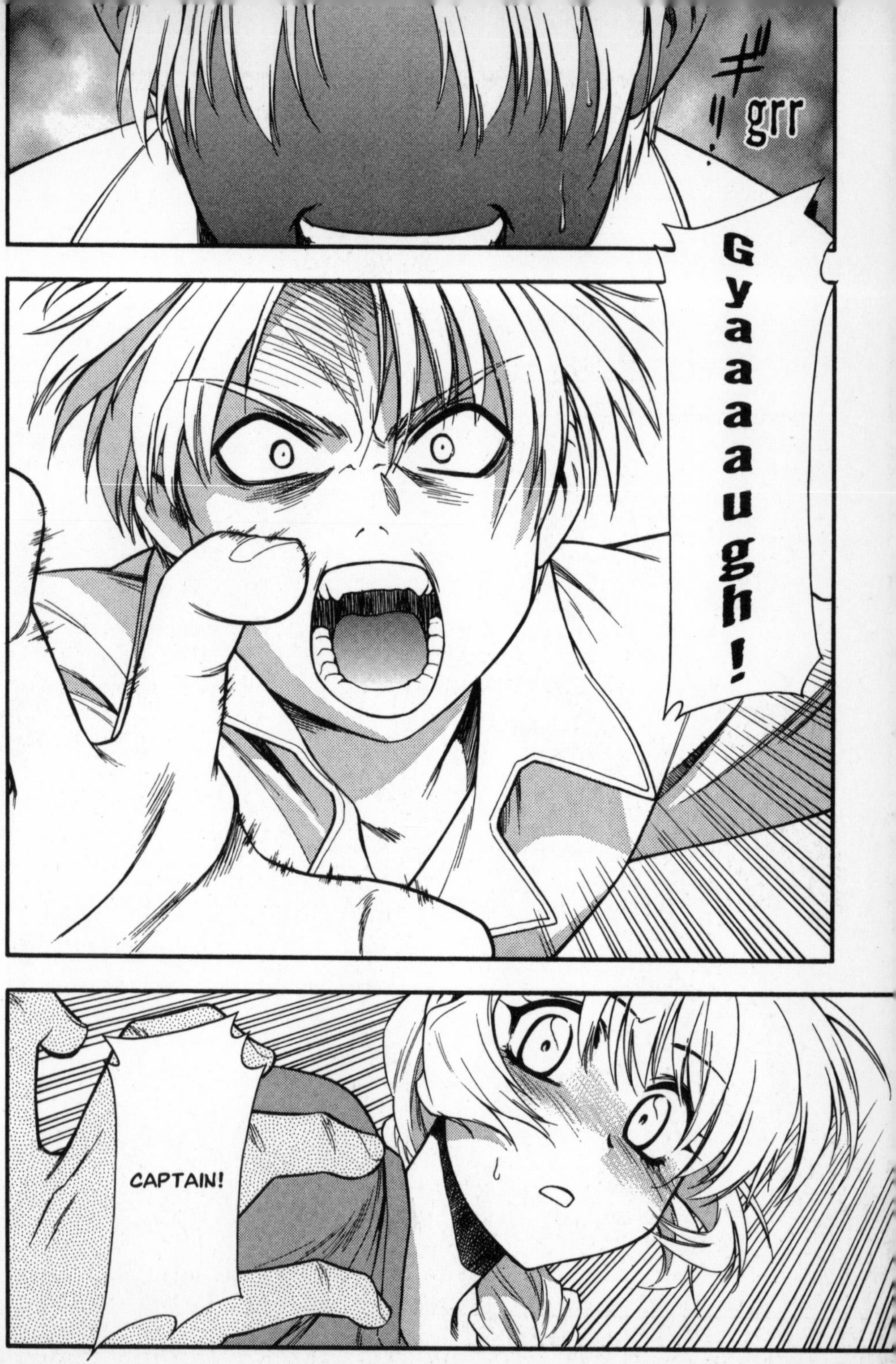
ギリ
grr
Gyaaaaugh!
CAPTAIN!

MISSION:24 Nothing to counter the captain's tears?!

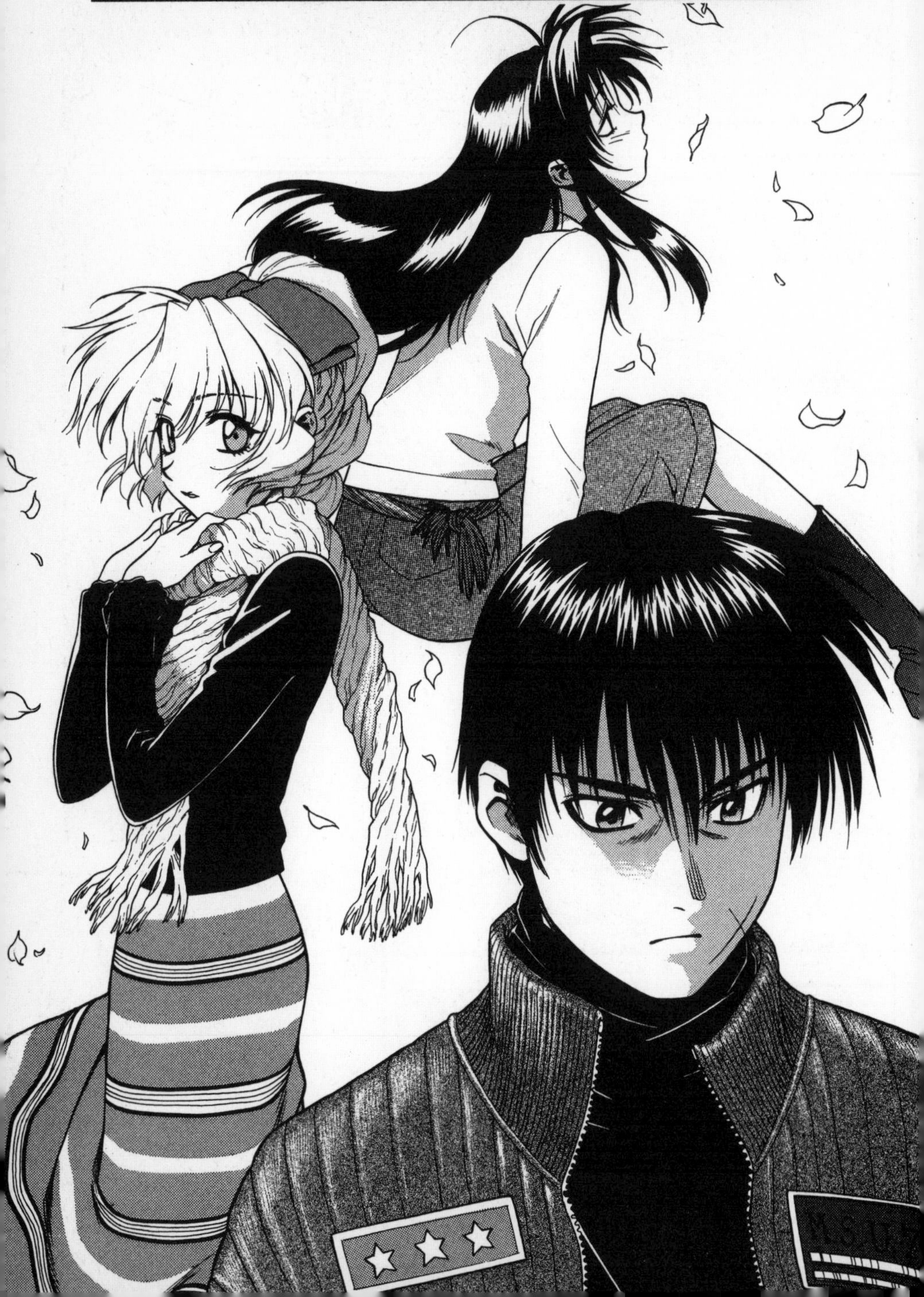

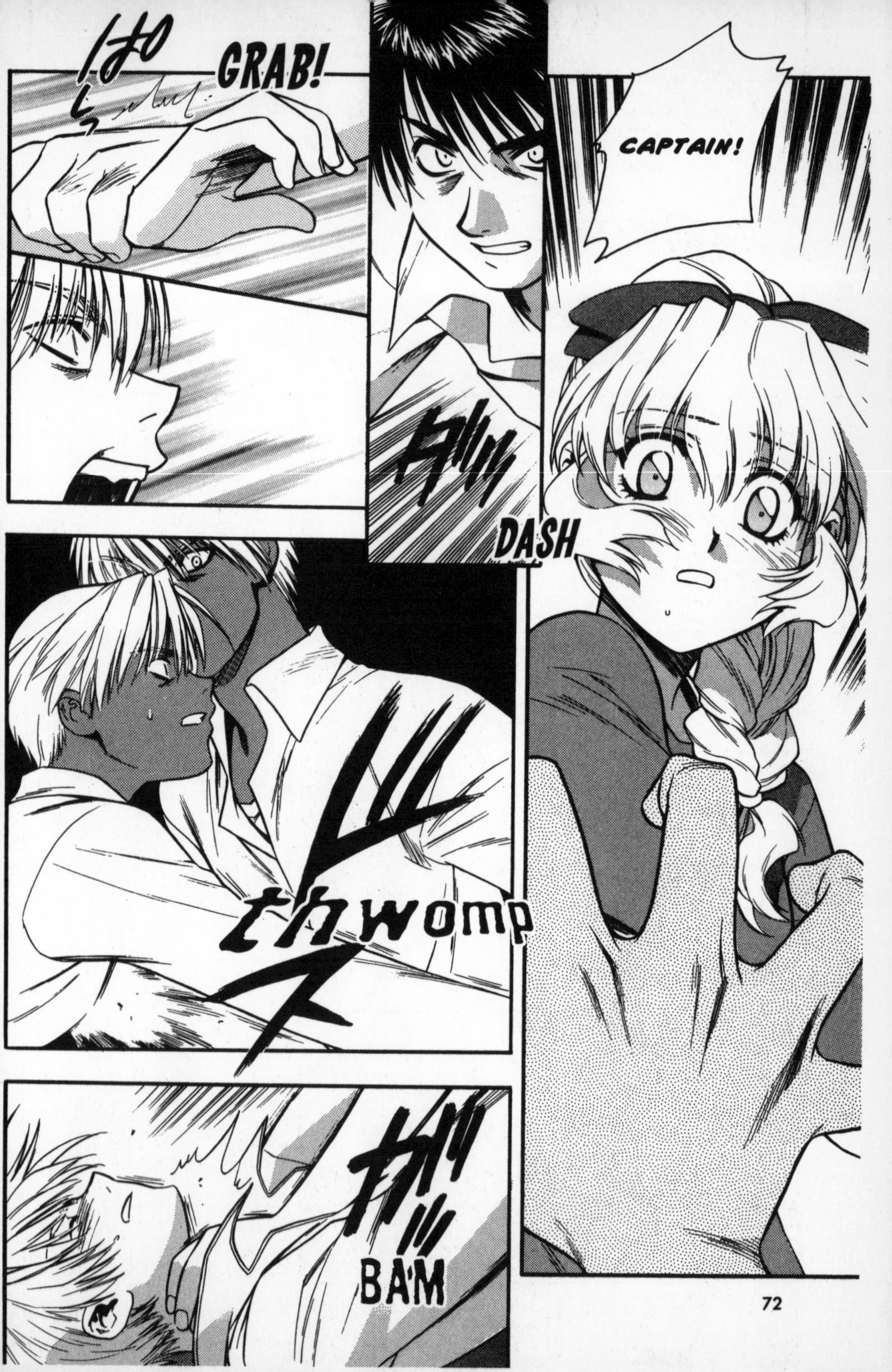
CAPTAIN!
DASH
GRAB!
thwomp
BAM

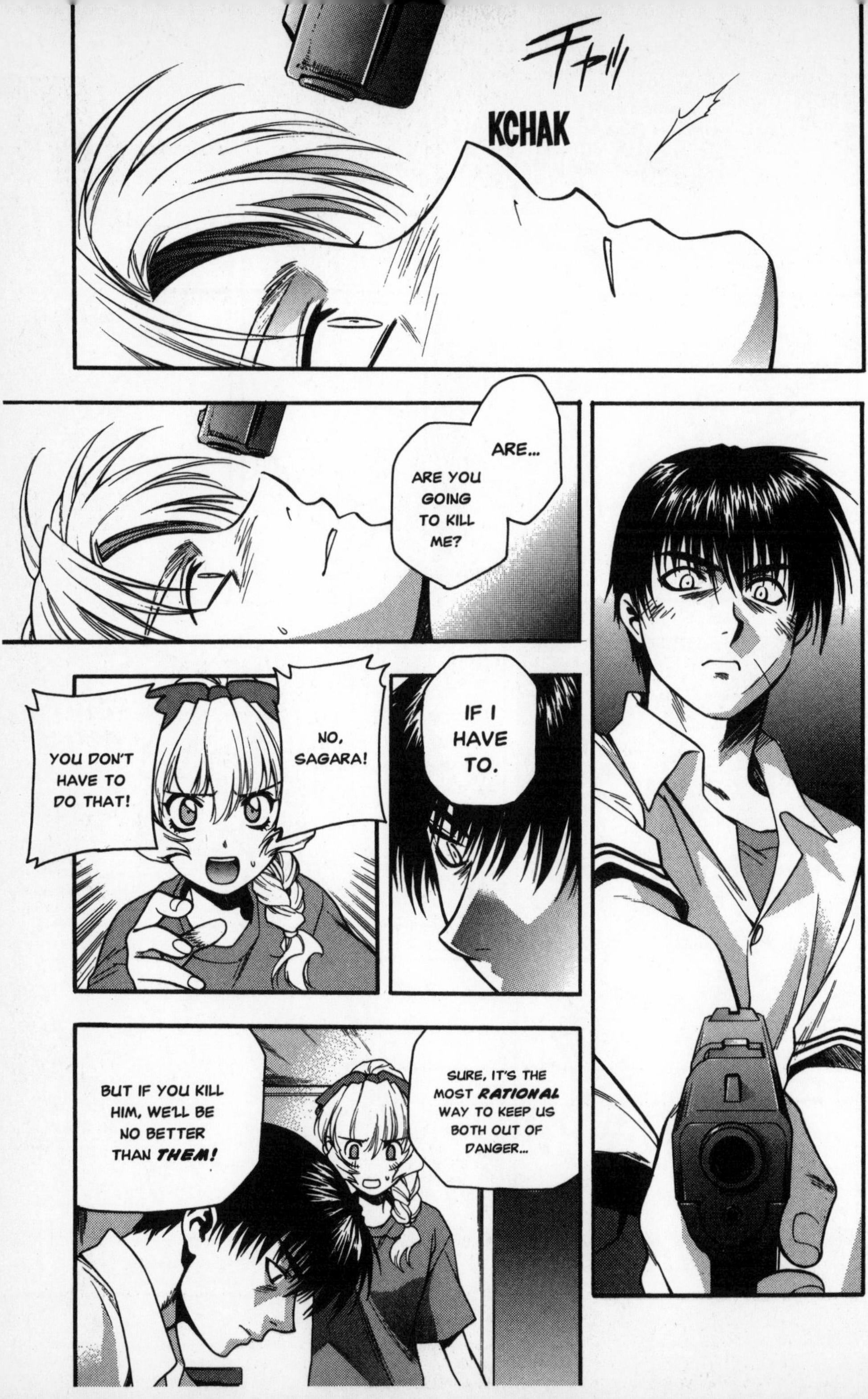
KCHAK
ARE...
ARE YOU GOING TO KILL ME?
IF I HAVE TO.
NO, SAGARA!
YOU DON'T HAVE TO DO THAT!
SURE, IT'S THE MOST ***RATIONAL*** WAY TO KEEP US BOTH OUT OF DANGER...
BUT IF YOU KILL HIM, WE'LL BE NO BETTER THAN ***THEM!***

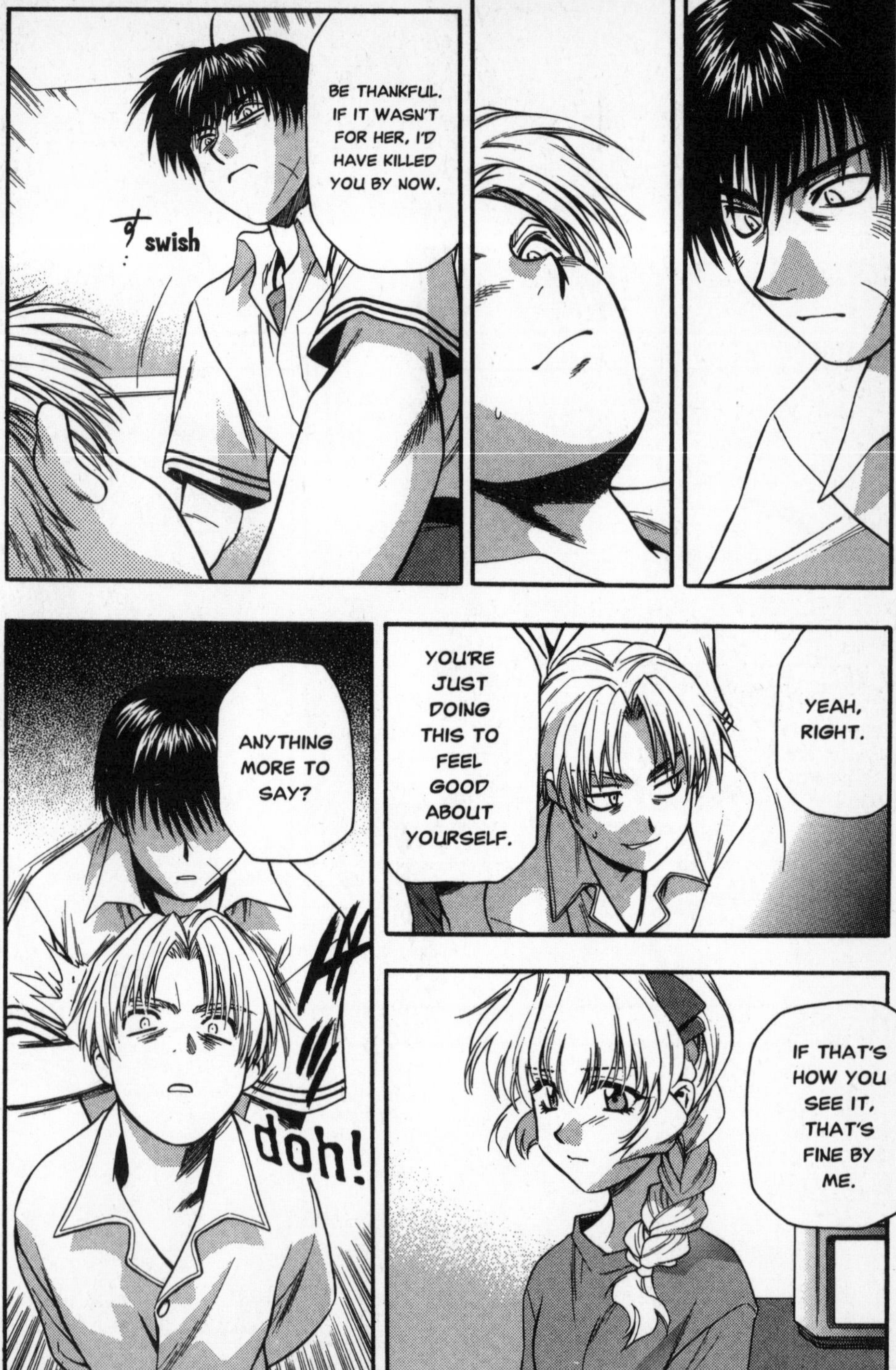
BE THANKFUL. IF IT WASN'T FOR HER, I'D HAVE KILLED YOU BY NOW.
す swish
YOU'RE JUST DOING THIS TO FEEL GOOD ABOUT YOURSELF.
YEAH, RIGHT.
IF THAT'S HOW YOU SEE IT, THAT'S FINE BY ME.
ANYTHING MORE TO SAY?
doh!

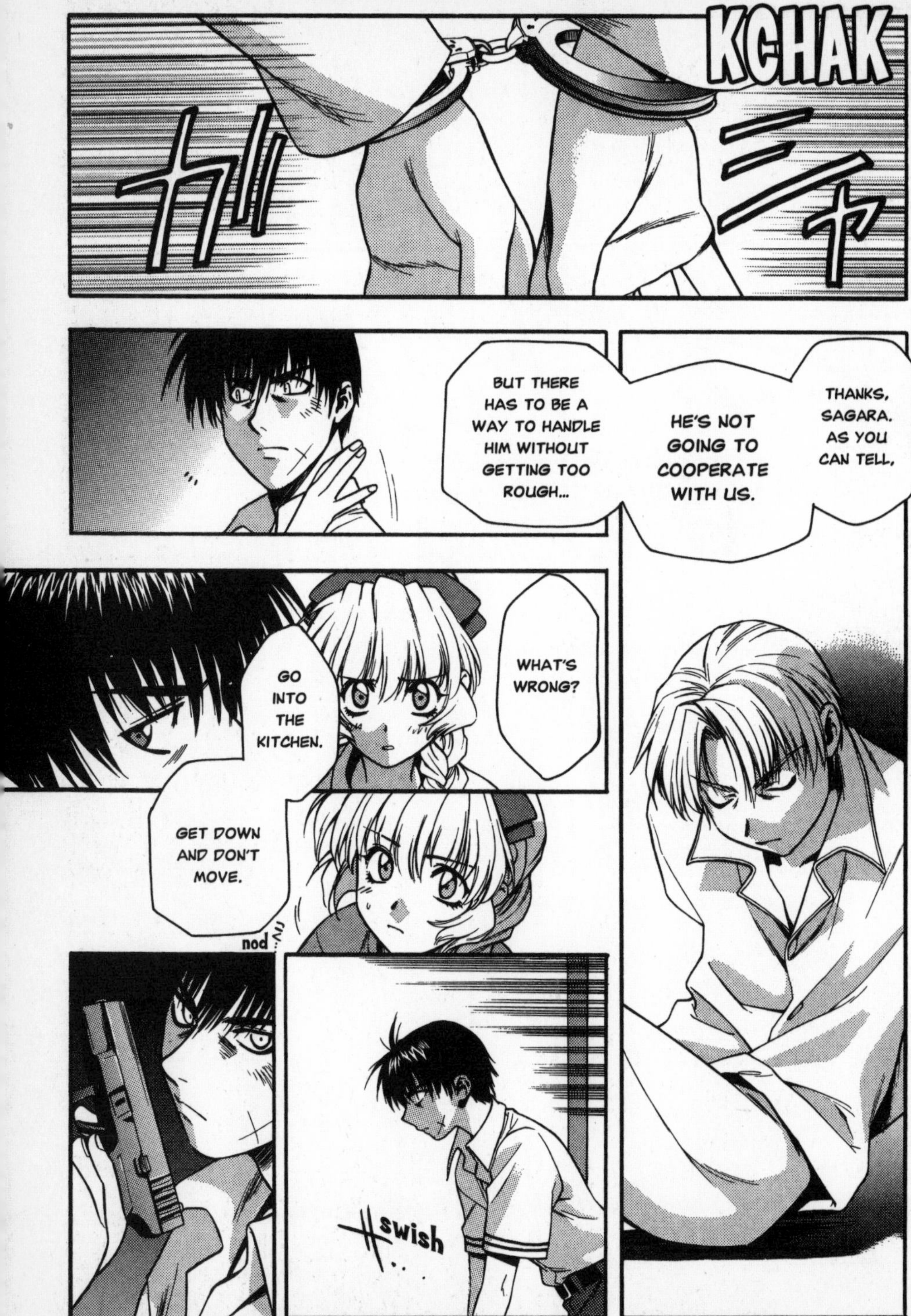
KCHAK
THANKS, SAGARA. AS YOU CAN TELL,
HE'S NOT GOING TO COOPERATE WITH US.
BUT THERE HAS TO BE A WAY TO HANDLE HIM WITHOUT GETTING TOO ROUGH...
WHAT'S WRONG?
GO INTO THE KITCHEN.
GET DOWN AND DON'T MOVE.
nod...
swish

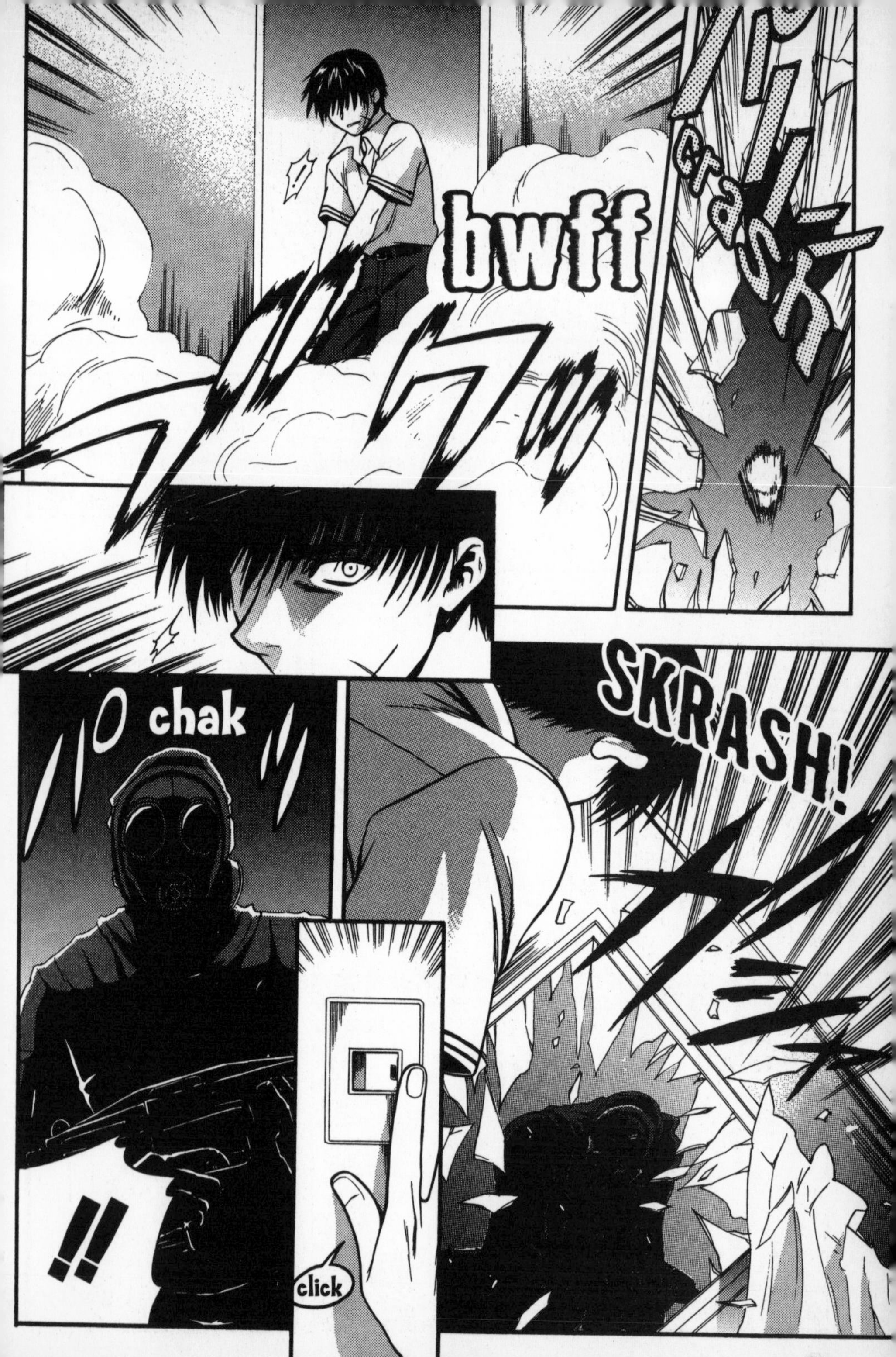
crash
bwff
!
SKRASH!
click
chak
!!

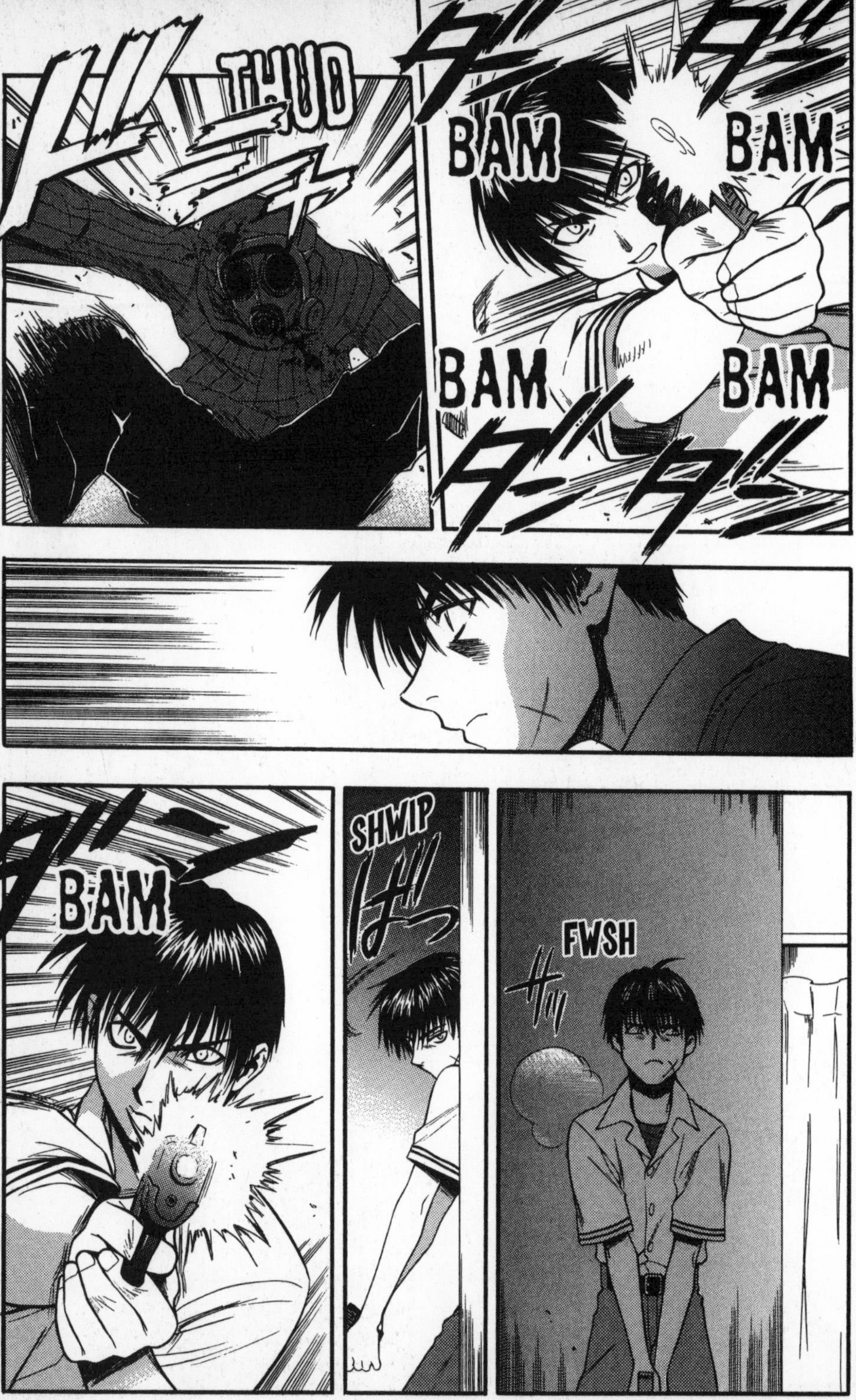

ダン
BAM
ダン
BAM
BAM
BAM
ダン
ダン
THUD
FWSH
SHWIP
ばっ
ダー
BAM

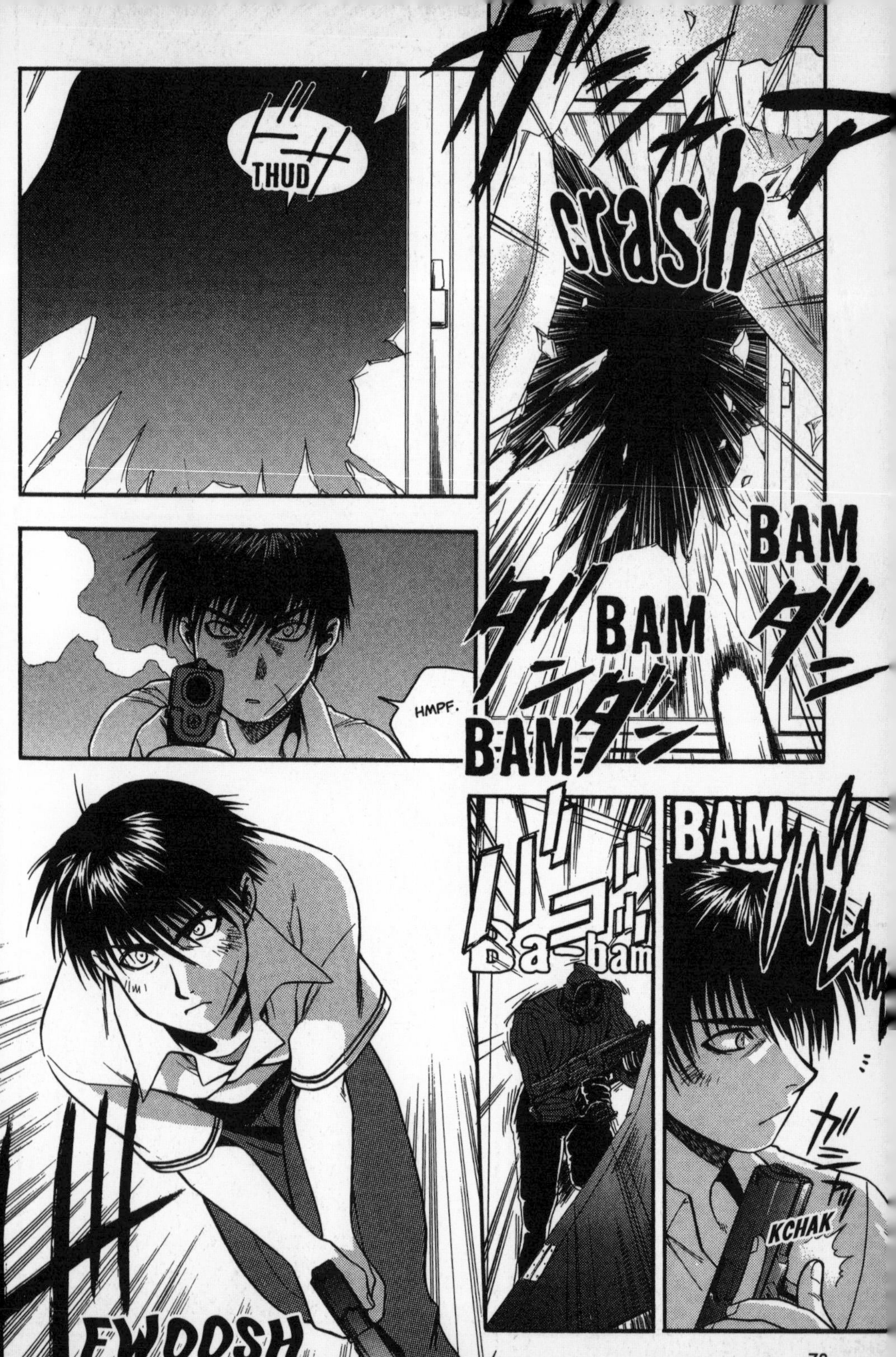
crash
BAM
BAM
BAM
THUD
HMPF.
BAM
KCHAK
Ba-bam
FWOOSH

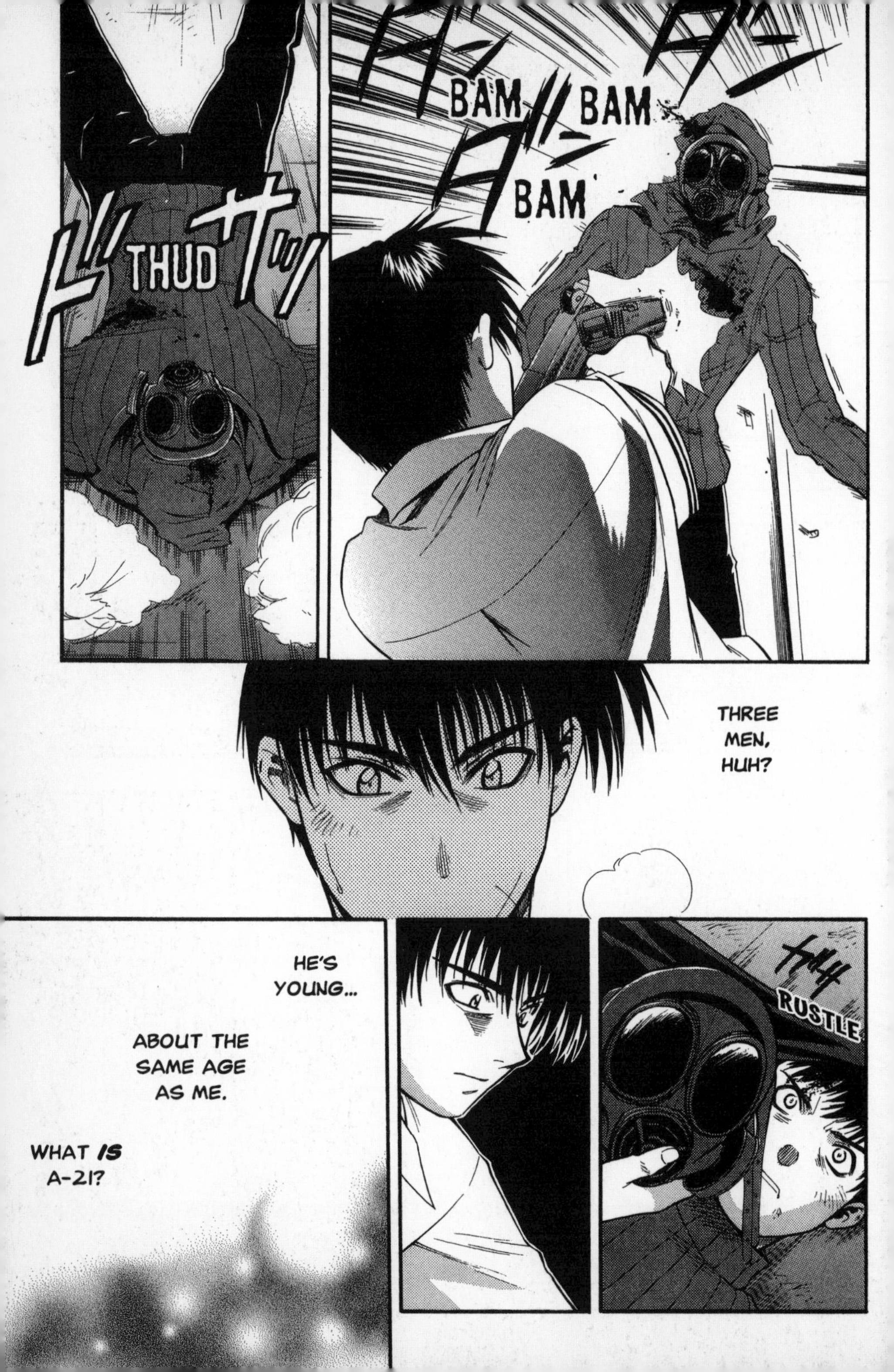

BAM
BAM
BAM
THUD
THREE MEN, HUH?
RUSTLE
HE'S YOUNG...
ABOUT THE SAME AGE AS ME.
WHAT *IS* A-21?

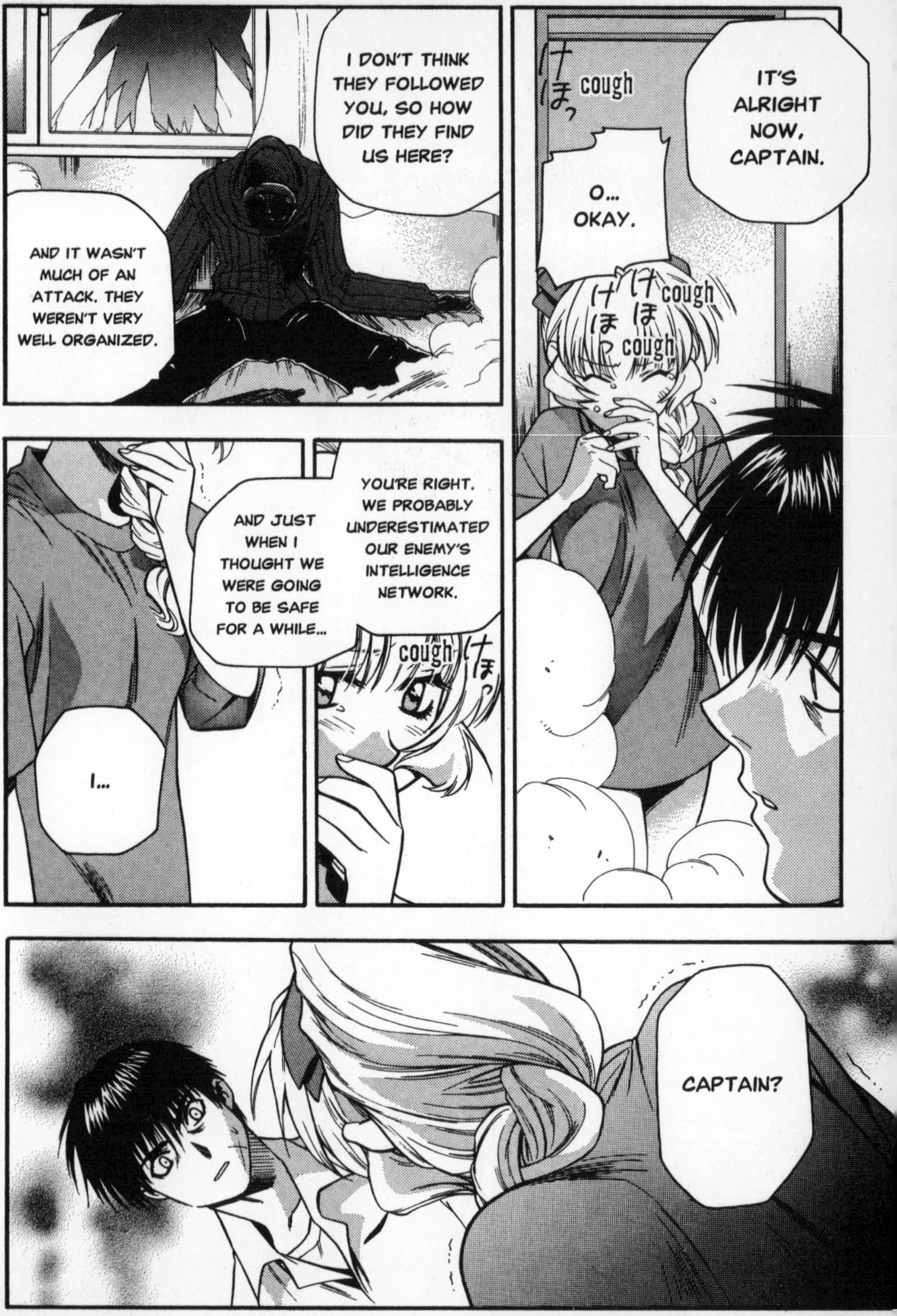
IT'S ALRIGHT NOW, CAPTAIN.
けほっ cough
O... OKAY.
けほけほっ cough cough
I DON'T THINK THEY FOLLOWED YOU, SO HOW DID THEY FIND US HERE?
AND IT WASN'T MUCH OF AN ATTACK. THEY WEREN'T VERY WELL ORGANIZED.
YOU'RE RIGHT. WE PROBABLY UNDERESTIMATED OUR ENEMY'S INTELLIGENCE NETWORK.
cough けほっ
AND JUST WHEN I THOUGHT WE WERE GOING TO BE SAFE FOR A WHILE...
I...
CAPTAIN?

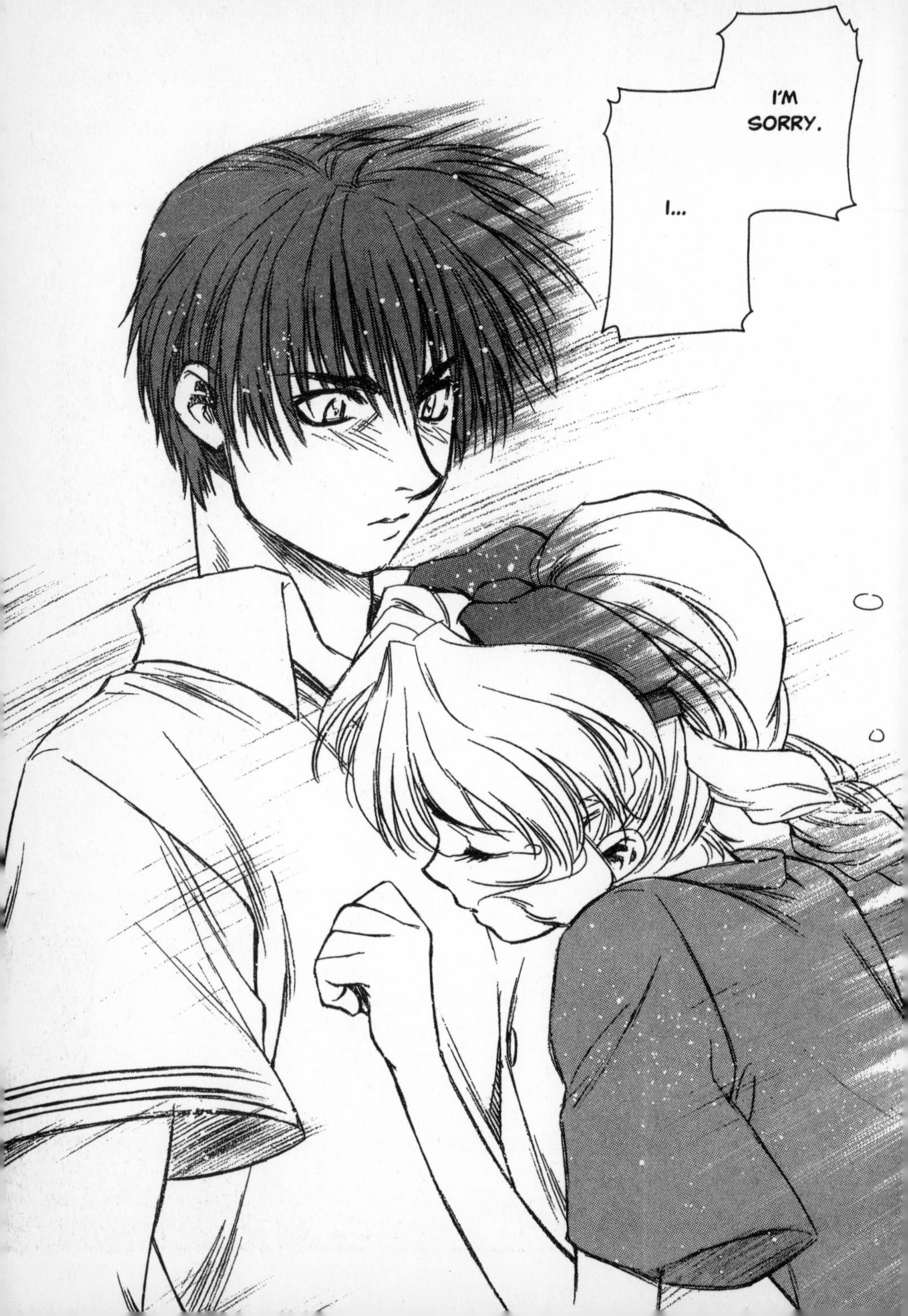

I'M SORRY.
I...

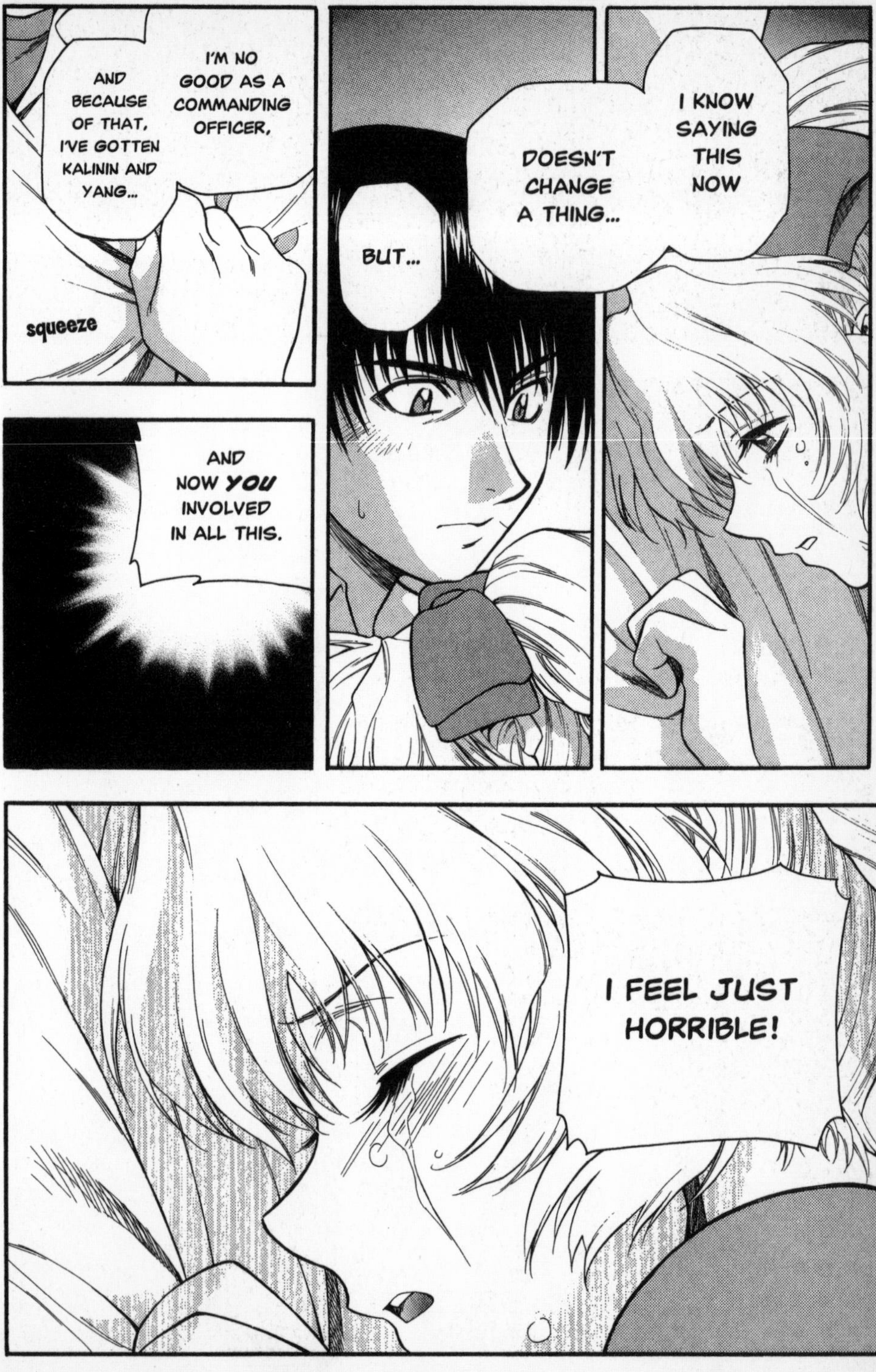
I KNOW SAYING THIS NOW
DOESN'T CHANGE A THING...
BUT...
I'M NO GOOD AS A COMMANDING OFFICER,
AND BECAUSE OF THAT, I'VE GOTTEN KALININ AND YANG...
squeeze
AND NOW *YOU* INVOLVED IN ALL THIS.
I FEEL JUST HORRIBLE!

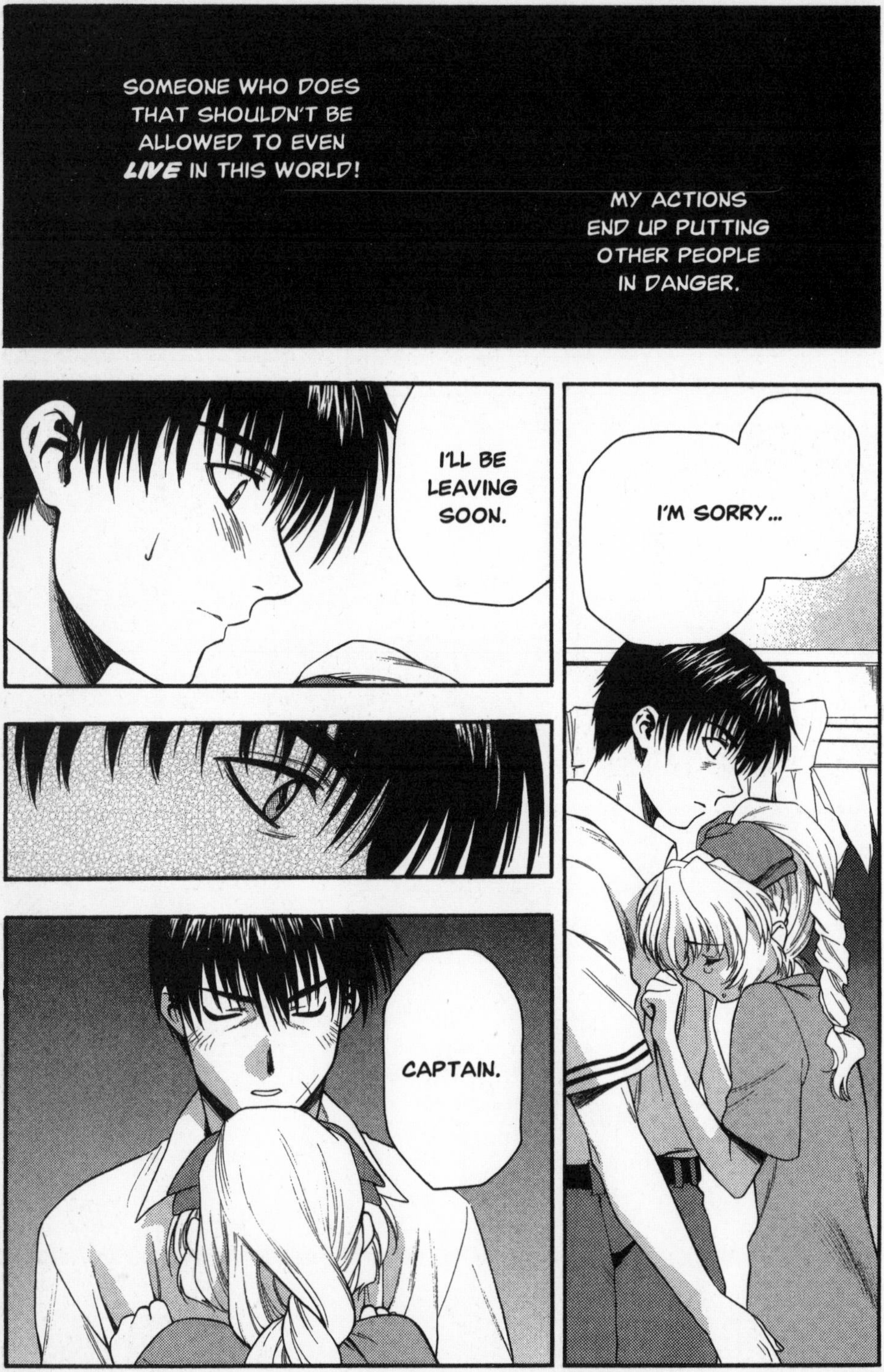
SOMEONE WHO DOES THAT SHOULDN'T BE ALLOWED TO EVEN *LIVE* IN THIS WORLD!
MY ACTIONS END UP PUTTING OTHER PEOPLE IN DANGER.
I'M SORRY...
I'LL BE LEAVING SOON.
CAPTAIN.

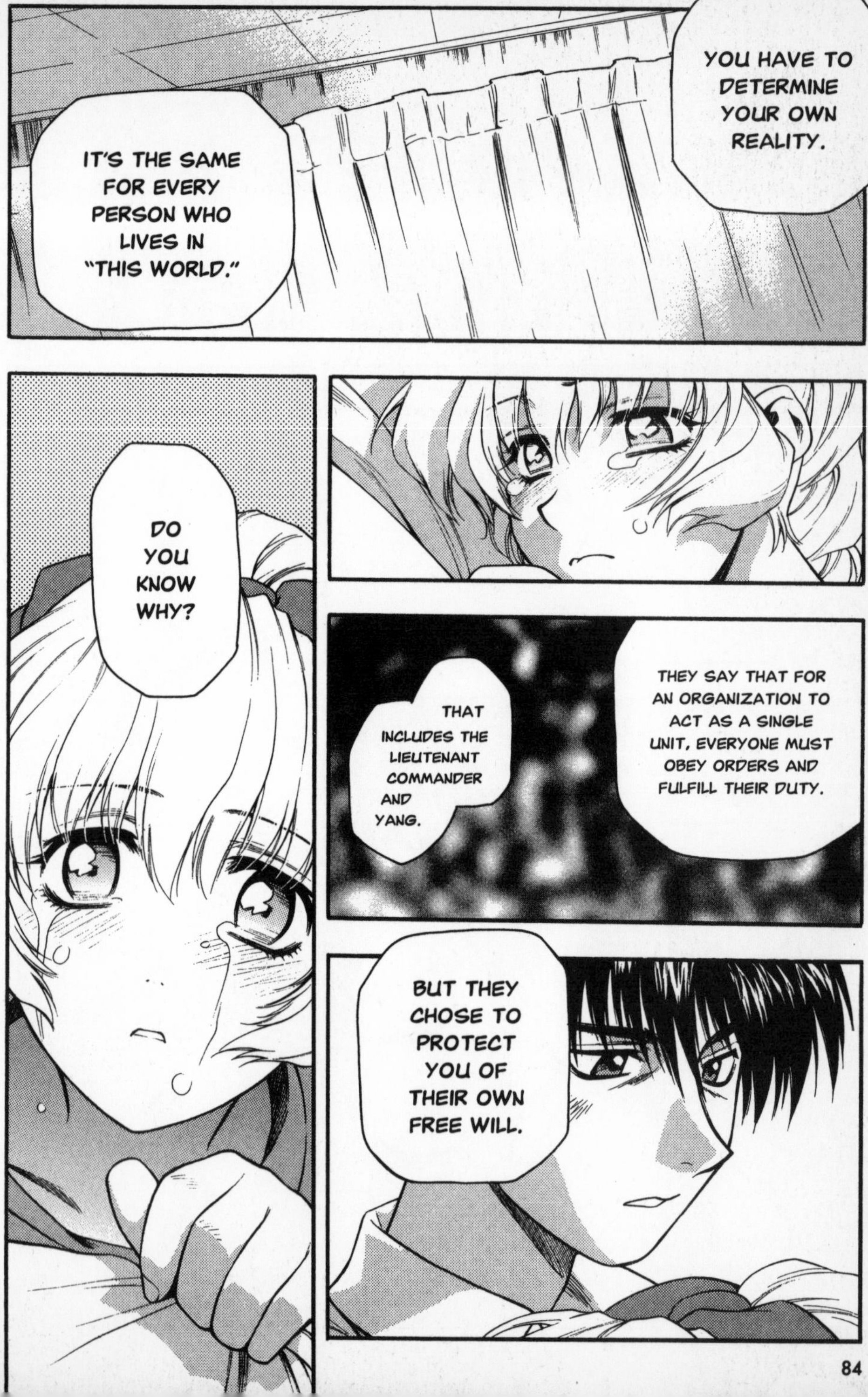
YOU HAVE TO DETERMINE YOUR OWN REALITY.
IT'S THE SAME FOR EVERY PERSON WHO LIVES IN "THIS WORLD."
THEY SAY THAT FOR AN ORGANIZATION TO ACT AS A SINGLE UNIT, EVERYONE MUST OBEY ORDERS AND FULFILL THEIR DUTY.
THAT INCLUDES THE LIEUTENANT COMMANDER AND YANG.
BUT THEY CHOSE TO PROTECT YOU OF THEIR OWN FREE WILL.
DO YOU KNOW WHY?

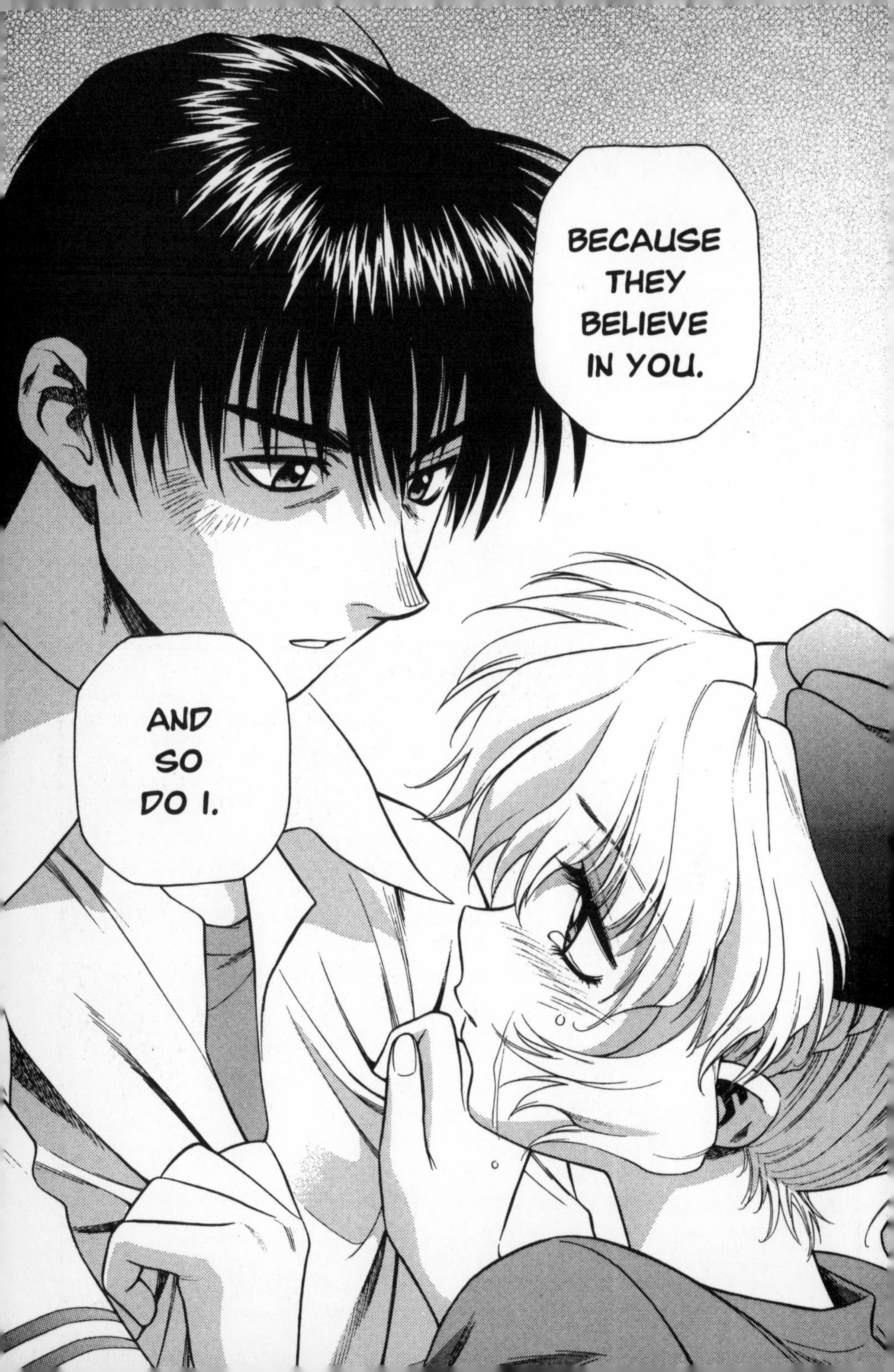
BECAUSE THEY BELIEVE IN YOU.
AND SO DO I.

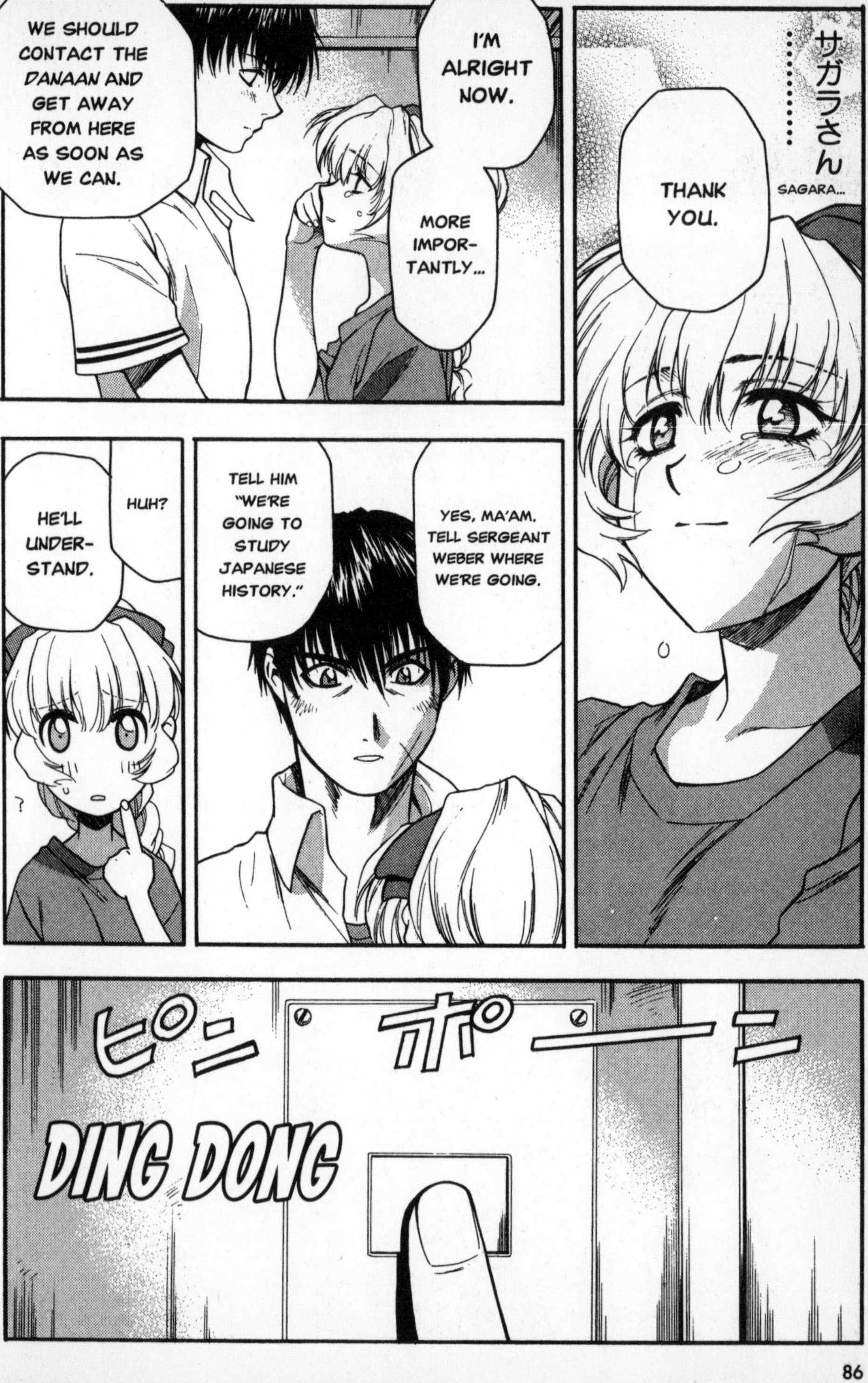
サガラさん……
SAGARA...
THANK YOU.
I'M ALRIGHT NOW.
MORE IMPORTANTLY...
WE SHOULD CONTACT THE DANAAN AND GET AWAY FROM HERE AS SOON AS WE CAN.
YES, MA'AM. TELL SERGEANT WEBER WHERE WE'RE GOING.
TELL HIM "WE'RE GOING TO STUDY JAPANESE HISTORY."
HUH?
HE'LL UNDERSTAND.
?
ピンポーン
DING DONG

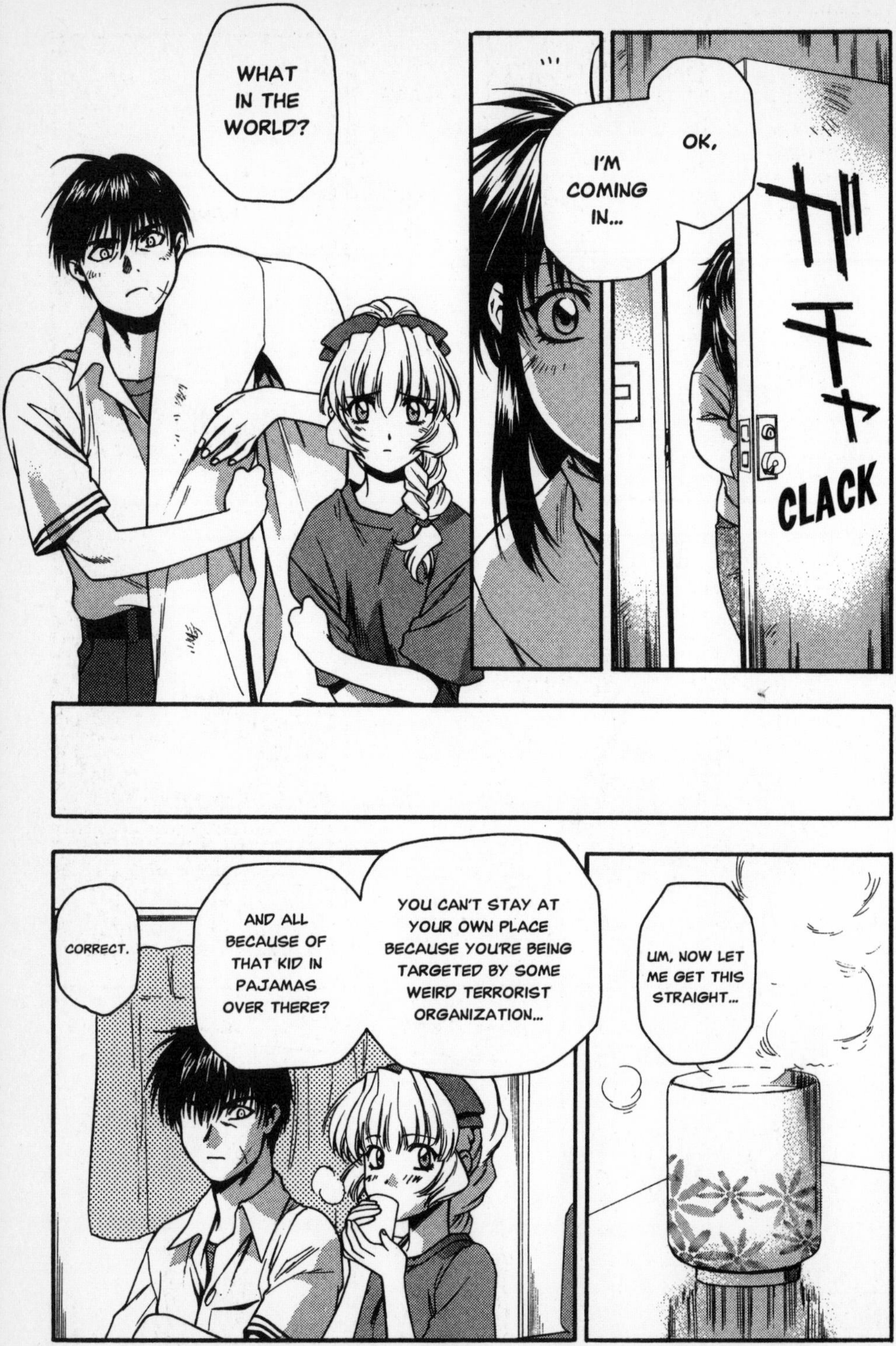
OK, I'M COMING IN...
ガチャ
CLACK
...
WHAT IN THE WORLD?
UM, NOW LET ME GET THIS STRAIGHT...
YOU CAN'T STAY AT YOUR OWN PLACE BECAUSE YOU'RE BEING TARGETED BY SOME WEIRD TERRORIST ORGANIZATION...
AND ALL BECAUSE OF THAT KID IN PAJAMAS OVER THERE?
CORRECT.

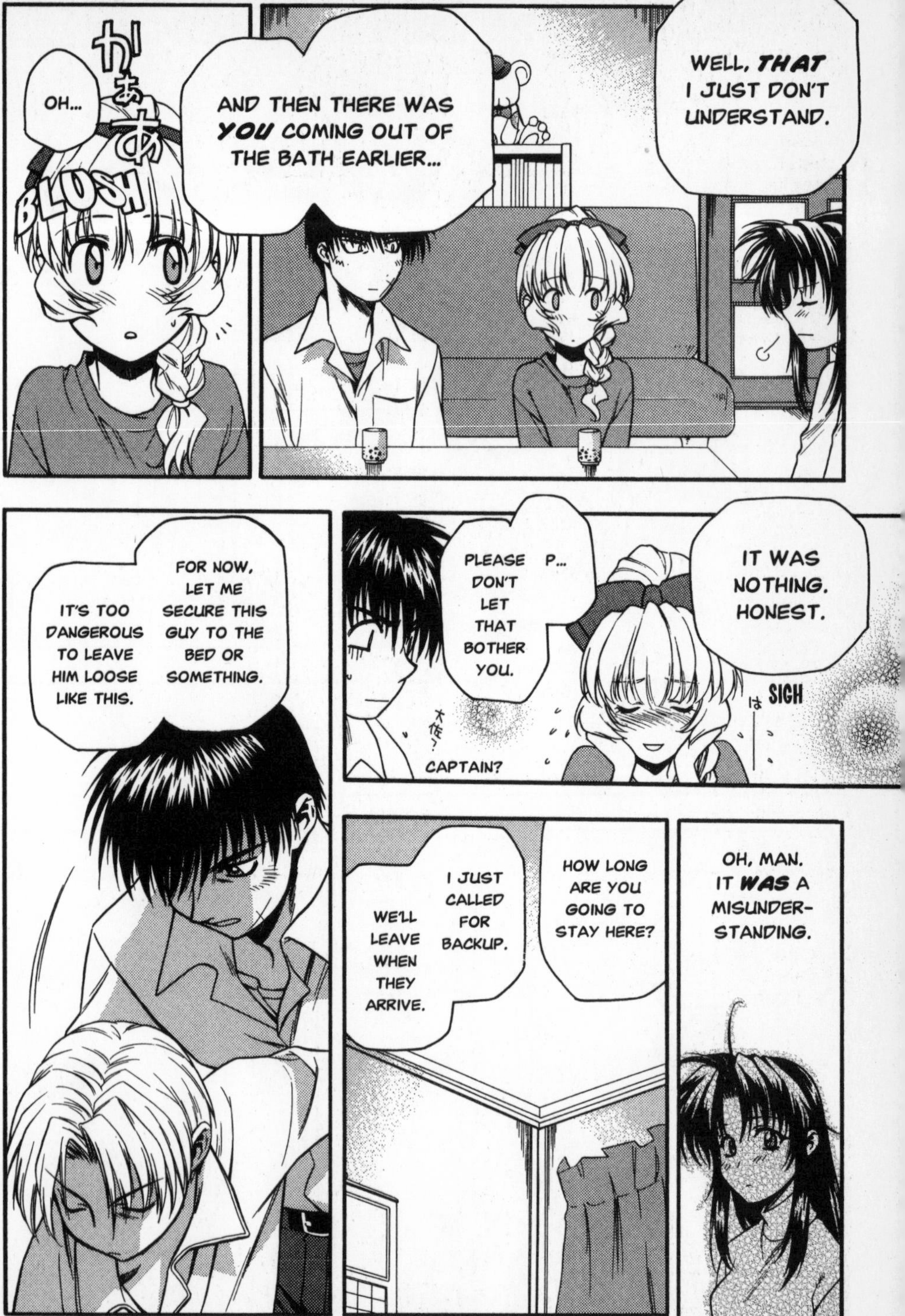
WELL, THAT I JUST DON'T UNDERSTAND.
AND THEN THERE WAS YOU COMING OUT OF THE BATH EARLIER...
かぁあ
BLUSH
OH...
IT WAS NOTHING. HONEST.
は…
SIGH
P... PLEASE DON'T LET THAT BOTHER YOU.
大佐？
CAPTAIN?
OH, MAN. IT WAS A MISUNDERSTANDING.
HOW LONG ARE YOU GOING TO STAY HERE?
I JUST CALLED FOR BACKUP. WE'LL LEAVE WHEN THEY ARRIVE.
FOR NOW, LET ME SECURE THIS GUY TO THE BED OR SOMETHING. IT'S TOO DANGEROUS TO LEAVE HIM LOOSE LIKE THIS.

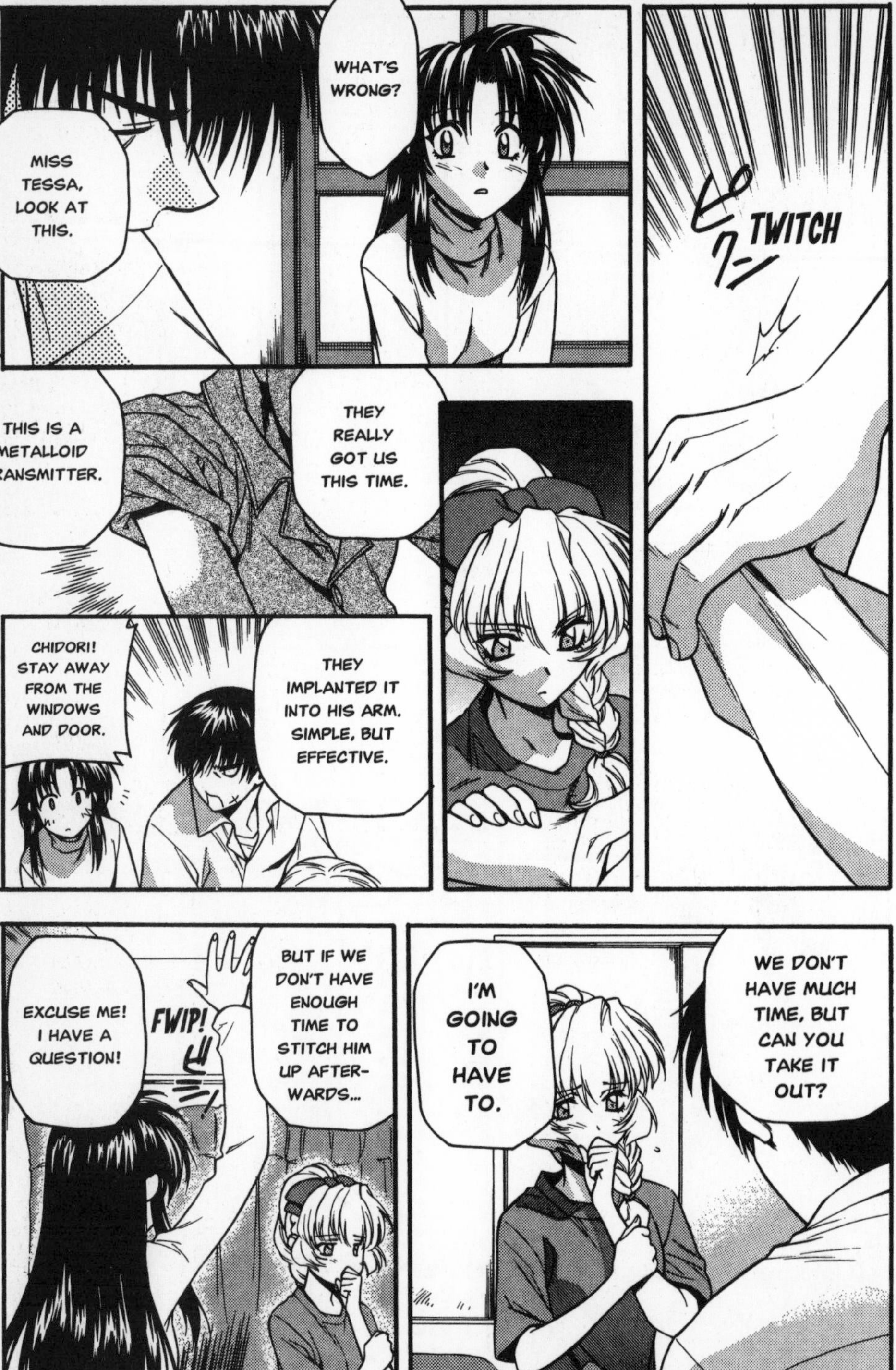

TWITCH
WHAT'S WRONG?
MISS TESSA, LOOK AT THIS.
THEY REALLY GOT US THIS TIME.
THIS IS A METALLOID TRANSMITTER.
THEY IMPLANTED IT INTO HIS ARM. SIMPLE, BUT EFFECTIVE.
CHIDORI! STAY AWAY FROM THE WINDOWS AND DOOR.
WE DON'T HAVE MUCH TIME, BUT CAN YOU TAKE IT OUT?
I'M GOING TO HAVE TO.
BUT IF WE DON'T HAVE ENOUGH TIME TO STITCH HIM UP AFTER-WARDS...
FWIP!
EXCUSE ME! I HAVE A QUESTION!

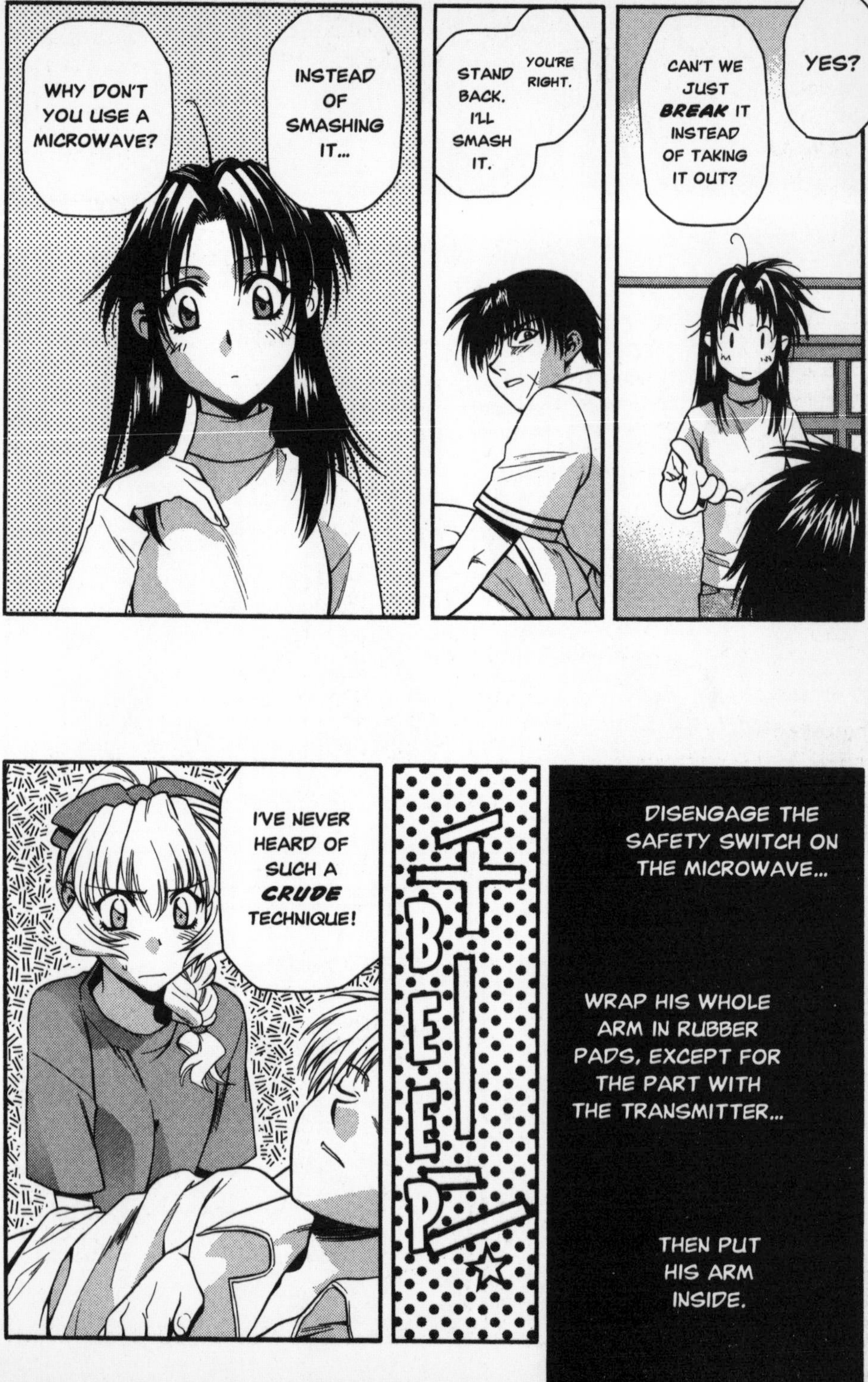
YES?
CAN'T WE JUST BREAK IT INSTEAD OF TAKING IT OUT?
YOU'RE RIGHT.
STAND BACK. I'LL SMASH IT.
INSTEAD OF SMASHING IT...
WHY DON'T YOU USE A MICROWAVE?
DISENGAGE THE SAFETY SWITCH ON THE MICROWAVE...
WRAP HIS WHOLE ARM IN RUBBER PADS, EXCEPT FOR THE PART WITH THE TRANSMITTER...
THEN PUT HIS ARM INSIDE.
BEEP
I'VE NEVER HEARD OF SUCH A CRUDE TECHNIQUE!

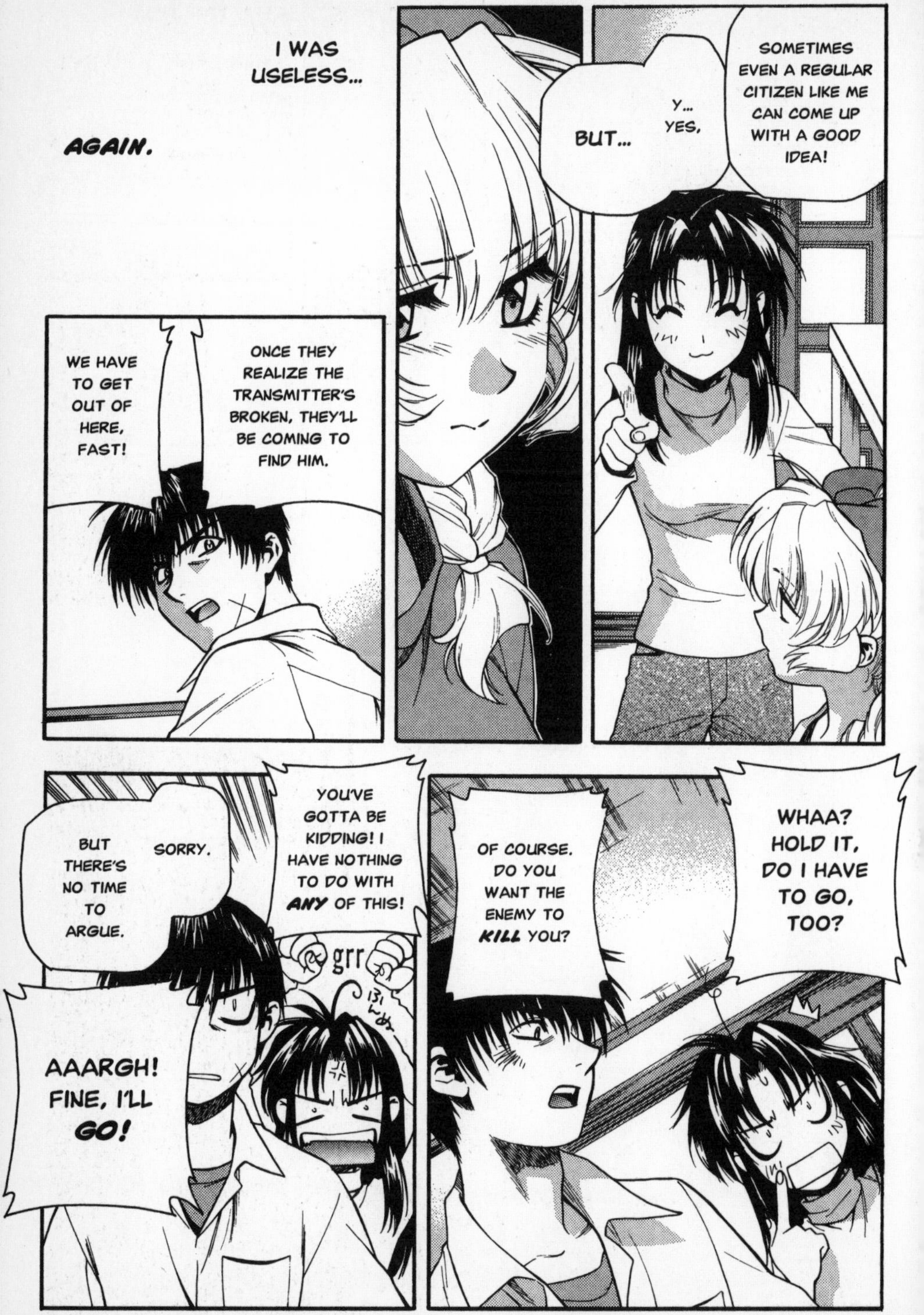
SOMETIMES EVEN A REGULAR CITIZEN LIKE ME CAN COME UP WITH A GOOD IDEA!
Y... YES,
BUT...
I WAS USELESS...
AGAIN.
ONCE THEY REALIZE THE TRANSMITTER'S BROKEN, THEY'LL BE COMING TO FIND HIM.
WE HAVE TO GET OUT OF HERE, FAST!
WHAA? HOLD IT, DO I HAVE TO GO, TOO?
OF COURSE. DO YOU WANT THE ENEMY TO KILL YOU?
YOU'VE GOTTA BE KIDDING! I HAVE NOTHING TO DO WITH ANY OF THIS!
SORRY.
BUT THERE'S NO TIME TO ARGUE.
grr
AAARGH! FINE, I'LL GO!

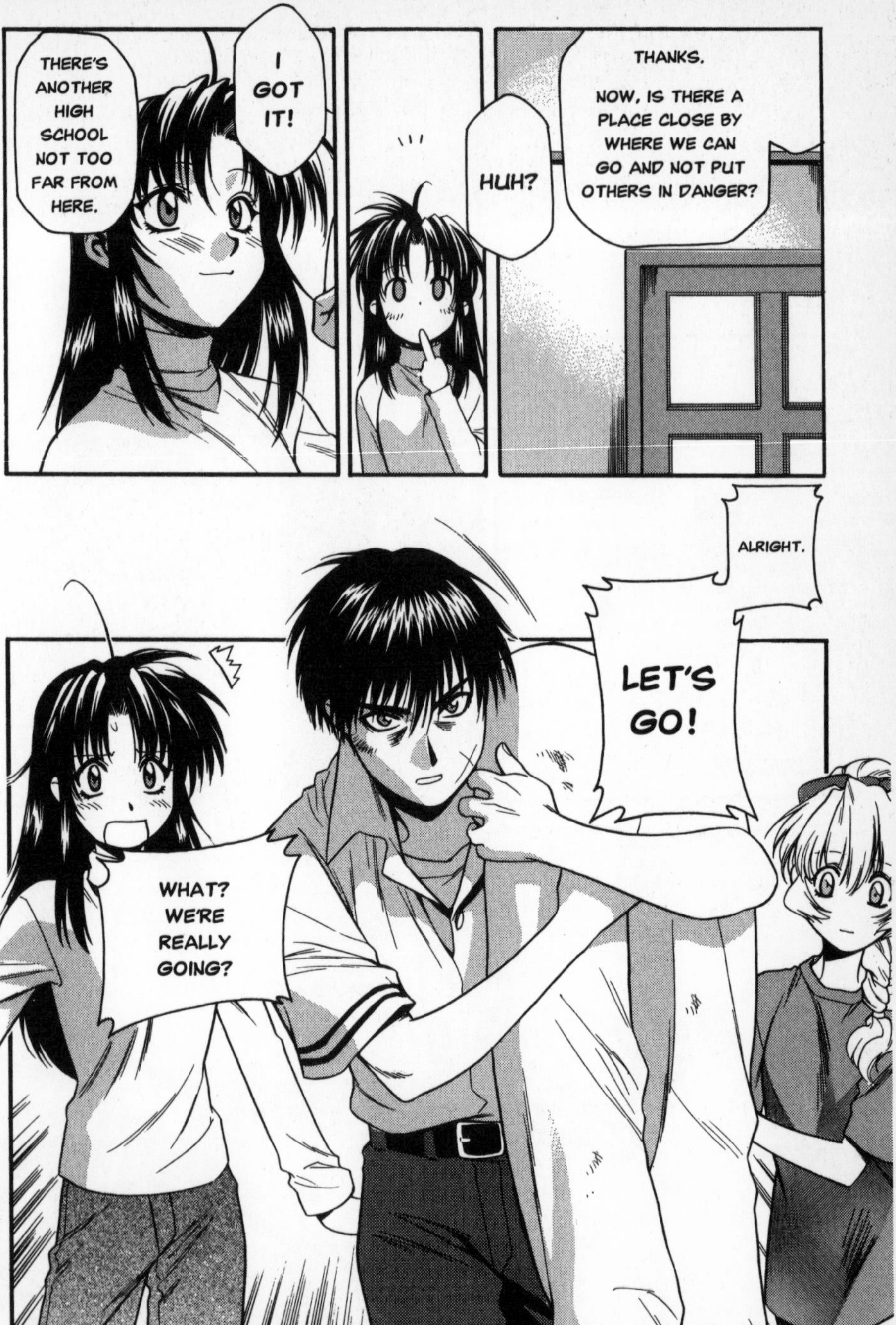
THANKS.
NOW, IS THERE A PLACE CLOSE BY WHERE WE CAN GO AND NOT PUT OTHERS IN DANGER?
HUH?
I GOT IT!
THERE'S ANOTHER HIGH SCHOOL NOT TOO FAR FROM HERE.
ALRIGHT.
LET'S GO!
WHAT? WE'RE REALLY GOING?

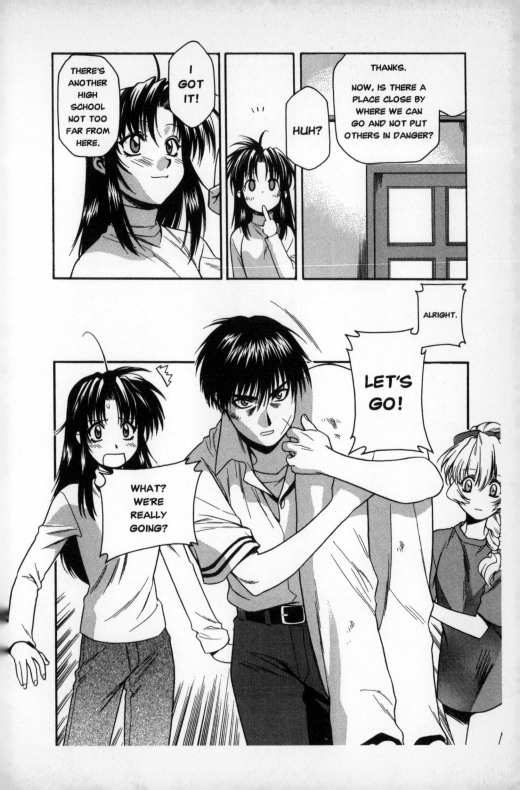

MISSION:25 Sagara's Decision

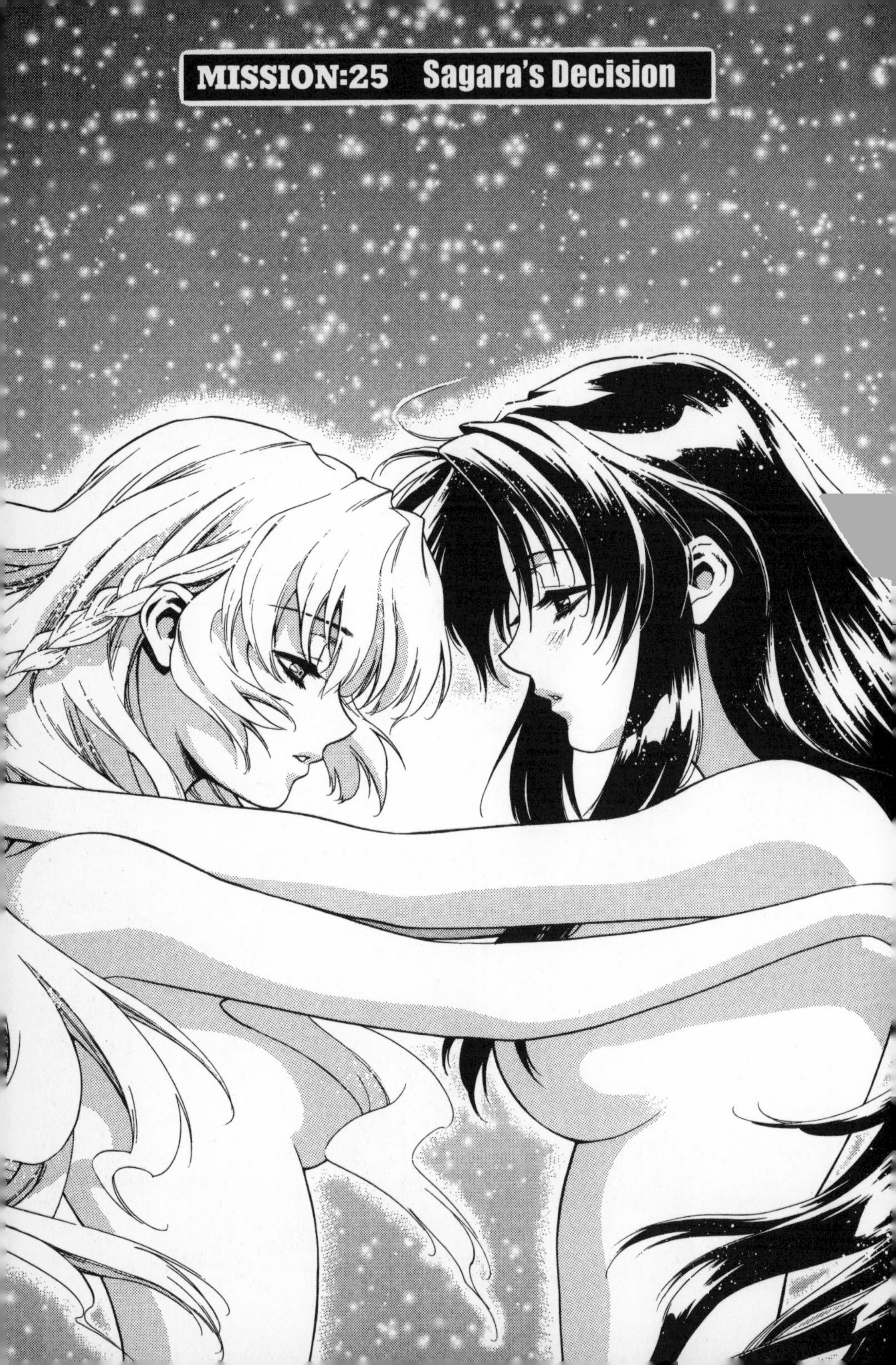

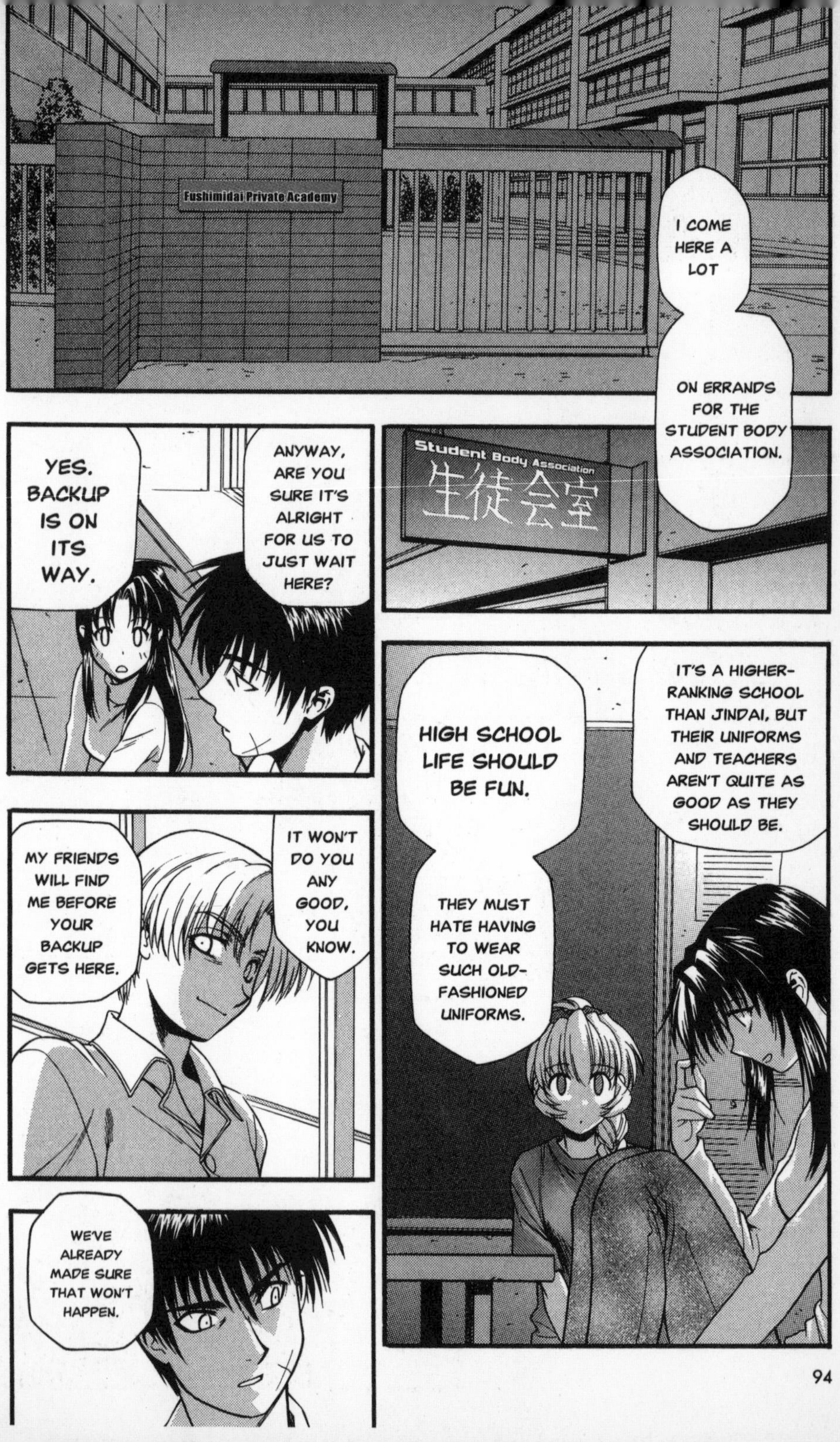
Fushimidai Private Academy
I COME HERE A LOT
ON ERRANDS FOR THE STUDENT BODY ASSOCIATION.
Student Body Association
生徒会室
ANYWAY, ARE YOU SURE IT'S ALRIGHT FOR US TO JUST WAIT HERE?
YES. BACKUP IS ON ITS WAY.
IT'S A HIGHER-RANKING SCHOOL THAN JINDAI, BUT THEIR UNIFORMS AND TEACHERS AREN'T QUITE AS GOOD AS THEY SHOULD BE.
HIGH SCHOOL LIFE SHOULD BE FUN.
THEY MUST HATE HAVING TO WEAR SUCH OLD-FASHIONED UNIFORMS.
IT WON'T DO YOU ANY GOOD, YOU KNOW.
MY FRIENDS WILL FIND ME BEFORE YOUR BACKUP GETS HERE.
WE'VE ALREADY MADE SURE THAT WON'T HAPPEN.

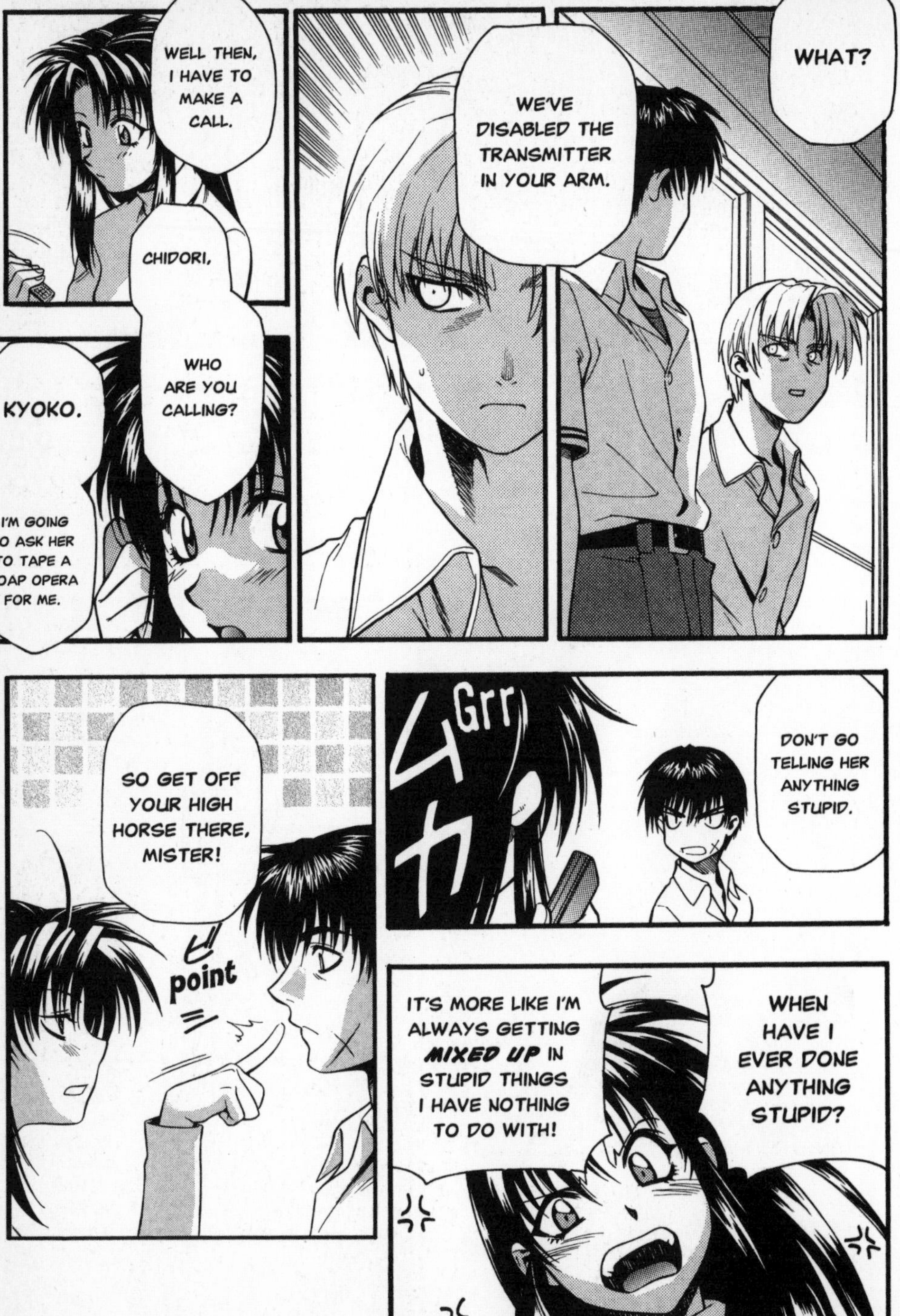

WHAT?
WE'VE DISABLED THE TRANSMITTER IN YOUR ARM.
WELL THEN, I HAVE TO MAKE A CALL.
CHIDORI,
WHO ARE YOU CALLING?
KYOKO.
I'M GOING TO ASK HER TO TAPE A SOAP OPERA FOR ME.
ムカ
Grr
DON'T GO TELLING HER ANYTHING STUPID.
WHEN HAVE I EVER DONE ANYTHING STUPID?
IT'S MORE LIKE I'M ALWAYS GETTING *MIXED UP* IN STUPID THINGS I HAVE NOTHING TO DO WITH!
SO GET OFF YOUR HIGH HORSE THERE, MISTER!
ビ
point

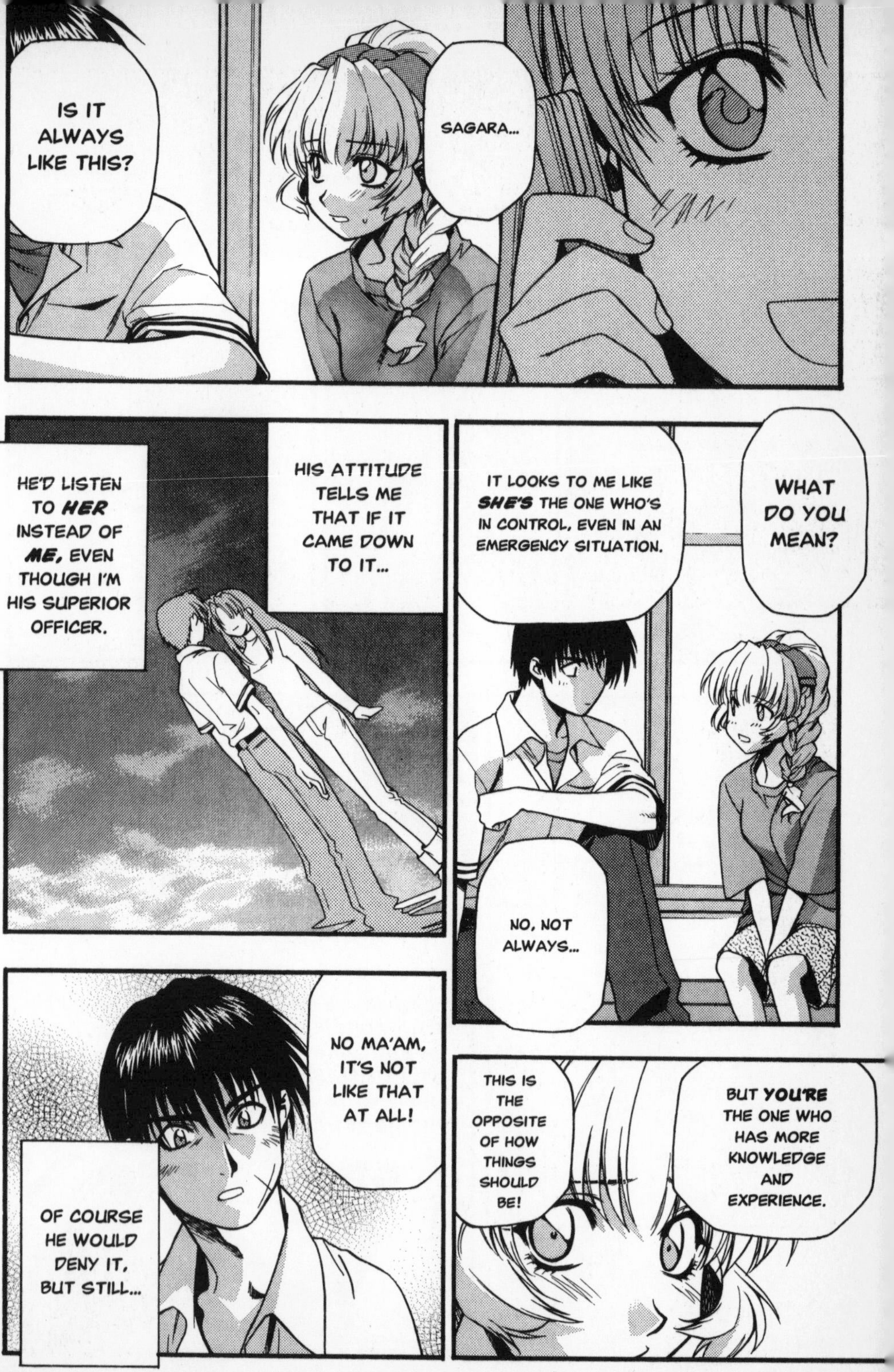
SAGARA...
IS IT ALWAYS LIKE THIS?
WHAT DO YOU MEAN?
IT LOOKS TO ME LIKE SHE'S THE ONE WHO'S IN CONTROL, EVEN IN AN EMERGENCY SITUATION.
NO, NOT ALWAYS...
HIS ATTITUDE TELLS ME THAT IF IT CAME DOWN TO IT...
HE'D LISTEN TO HER INSTEAD OF ME, EVEN THOUGH I'M HIS SUPERIOR OFFICER.
BUT YOU'RE THE ONE WHO HAS MORE KNOWLEDGE AND EXPERIENCE.
THIS IS THE OPPOSITE OF HOW THINGS SHOULD BE!
NO MA'AM, IT'S NOT LIKE THAT AT ALL!
OF COURSE HE WOULD DENY IT, BUT STILL...

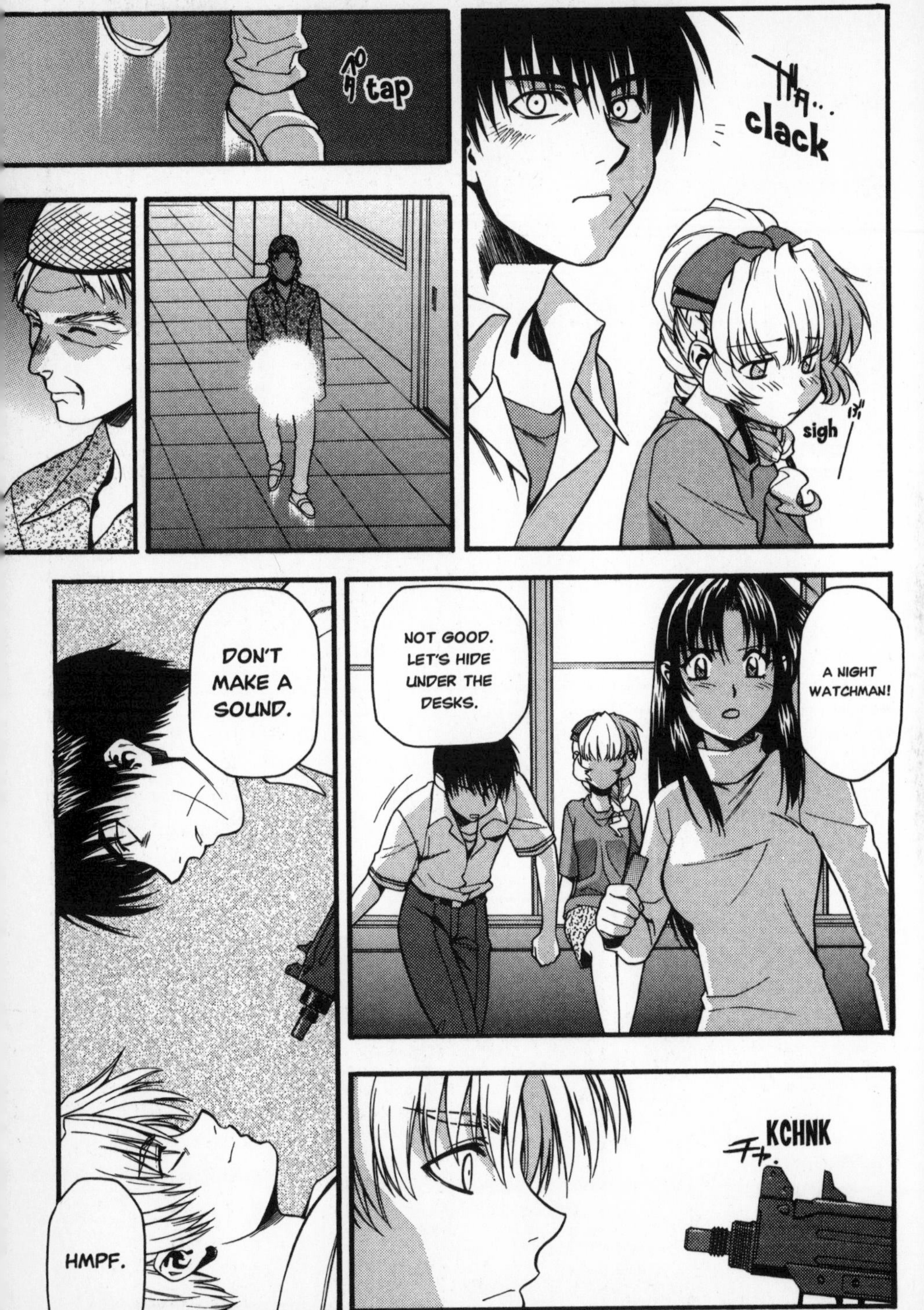
clack
sigh
tap
A NIGHT WATCHMAN!
NOT GOOD. LET'S HIDE UNDER THE DESKS.
KCHNK
DON'T MAKE A SOUND.
HMPF.

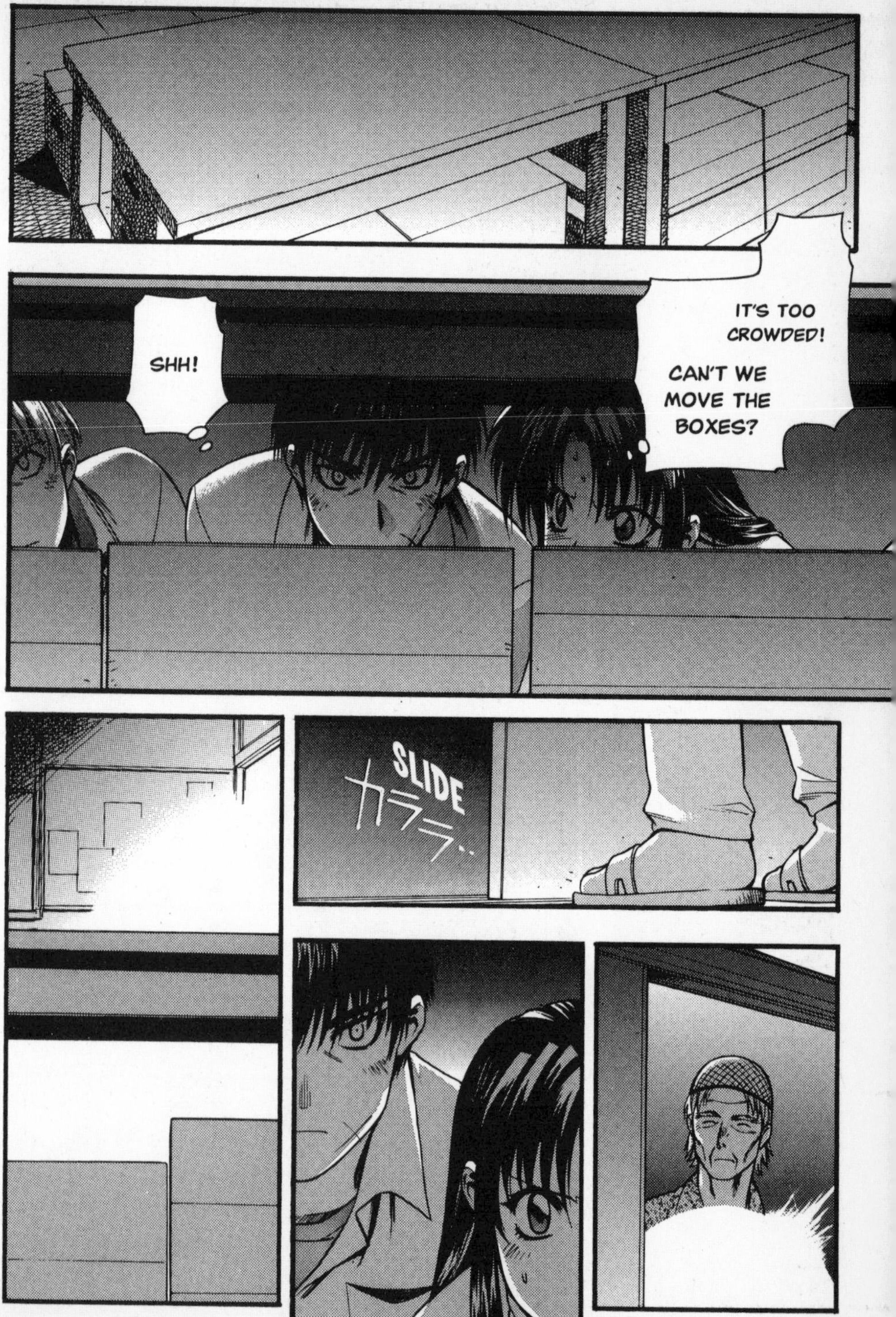
IT'S TOO CROWDED!
CAN'T WE MOVE THE BOXES?
SHH!
SLIDE
カララ‥

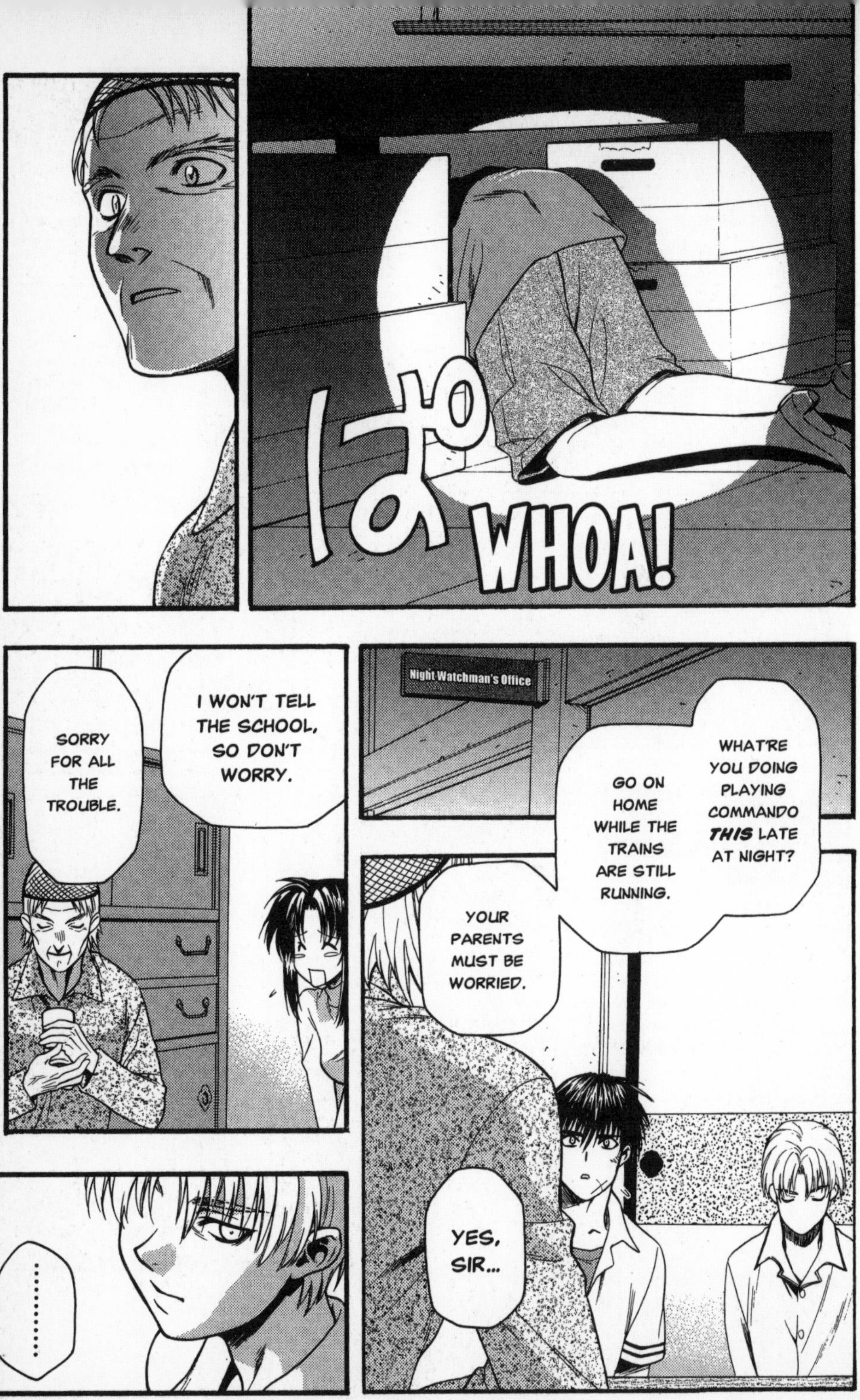
ぱ
WHOA!
Night Watchman's Office
WHAT'RE YOU DOING PLAYING COMMANDO *THIS* LATE AT NIGHT?
GO ON HOME WHILE THE TRAINS ARE STILL RUNNING.
YOUR PARENTS MUST BE WORRIED.
YES, SIR...
I WON'T TELL THE SCHOOL, SO DON'T WORRY.
SORRY FOR ALL THE TROUBLE.
....

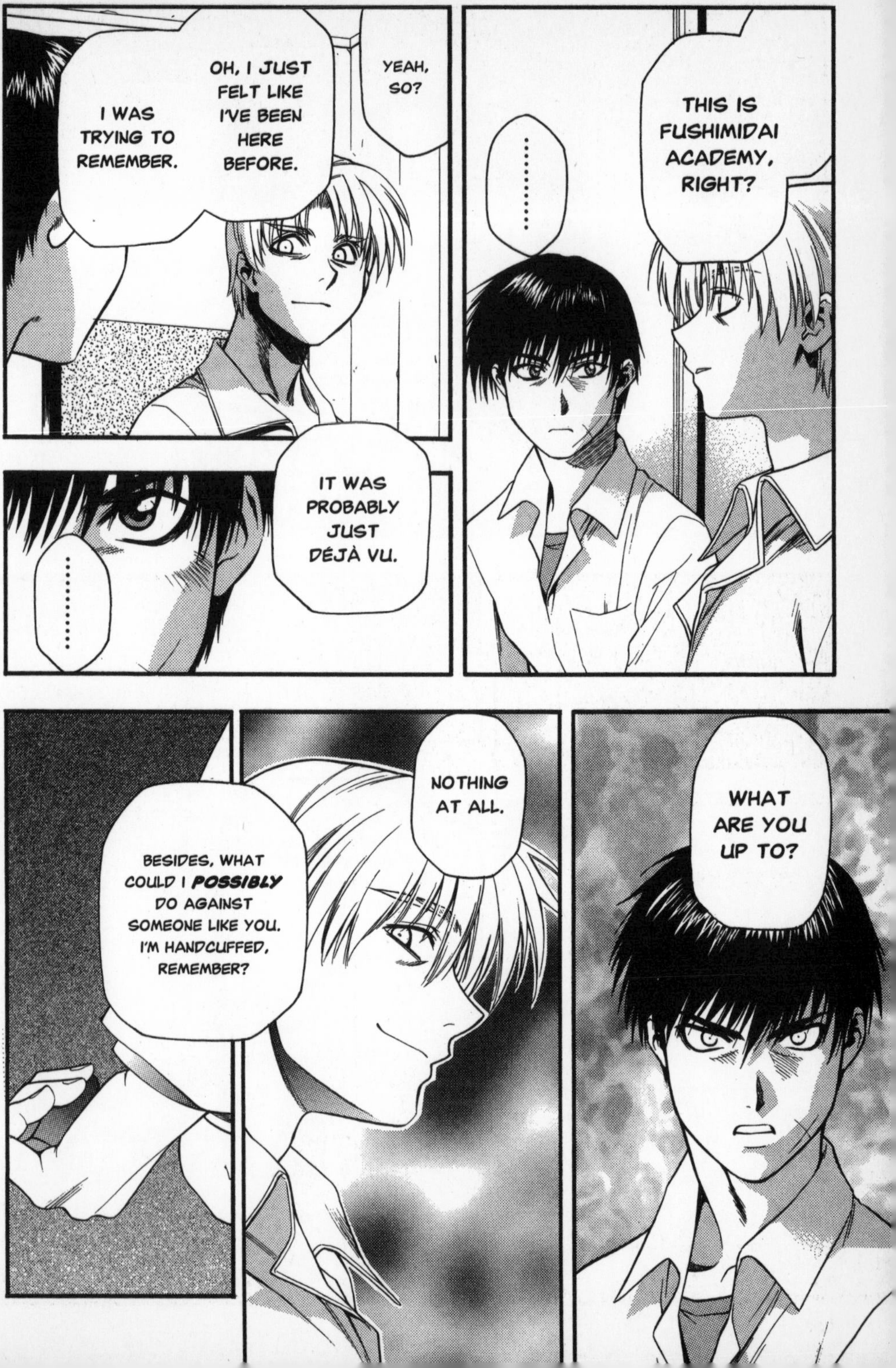
THIS IS FUSHIMIDAI ACADEMY, RIGHT?
……
YEAH, SO?
OH, I JUST FELT LIKE I'VE BEEN HERE BEFORE.
I WAS TRYING TO REMEMBER.
IT WAS PROBABLY JUST DÉJÀ VU.
……
WHAT ARE YOU UP TO?
NOTHING AT ALL.
BESIDES, WHAT COULD I ***POSSIBLY*** DO AGAINST SOMEONE LIKE YOU. I'M HANDCUFFED, REMEMBER?

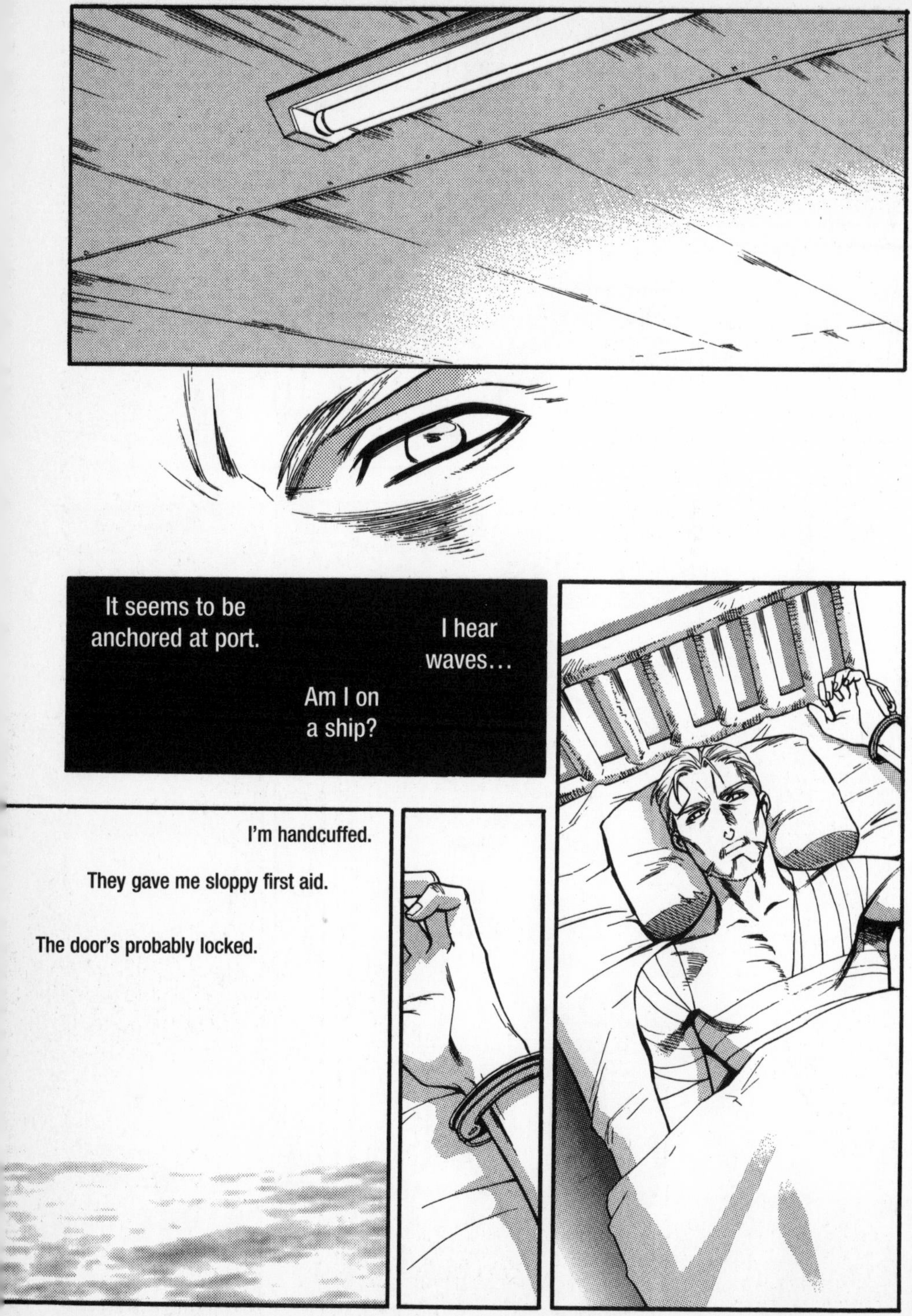
I hear waves…
Am I on a ship?
It seems to be anchored at port.
I'm handcuffed.
They gave me sloppy first aid.
The door's probably locked.

CLACK

TOK

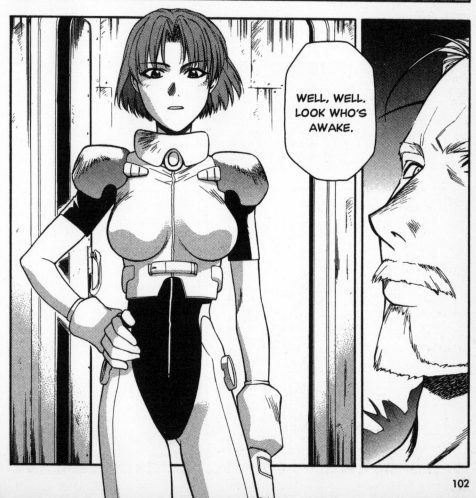

WELL, WELL. LOOK WHO'S AWAKE.

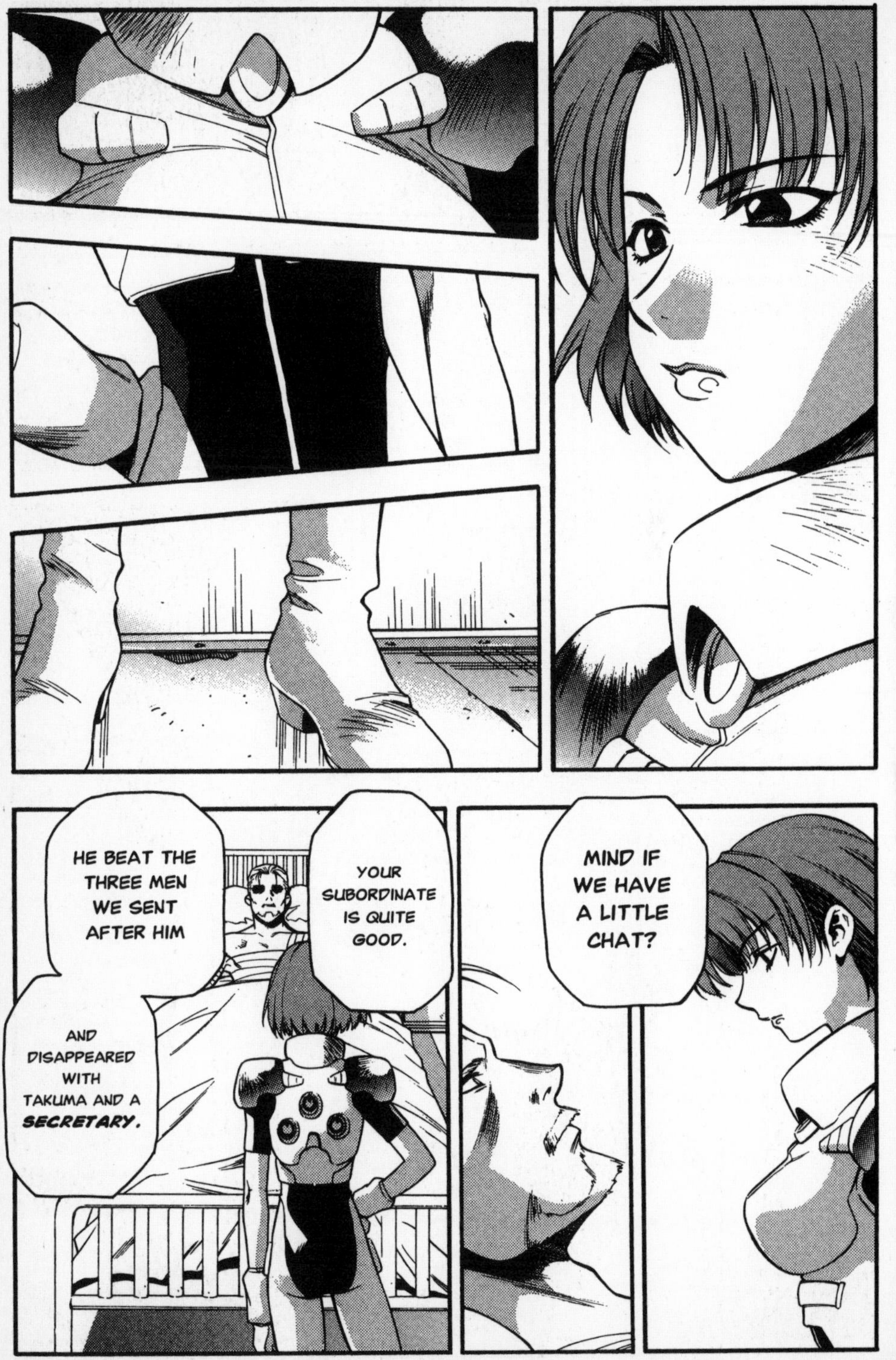
MIND IF WE HAVE A LITTLE CHAT?
YOUR SUBORDINATE IS QUITE GOOD.
HE BEAT THE THREE MEN WE SENT AFTER HIM
AND DISAPPEARED WITH TAKUMA AND A **SECRETARY.**

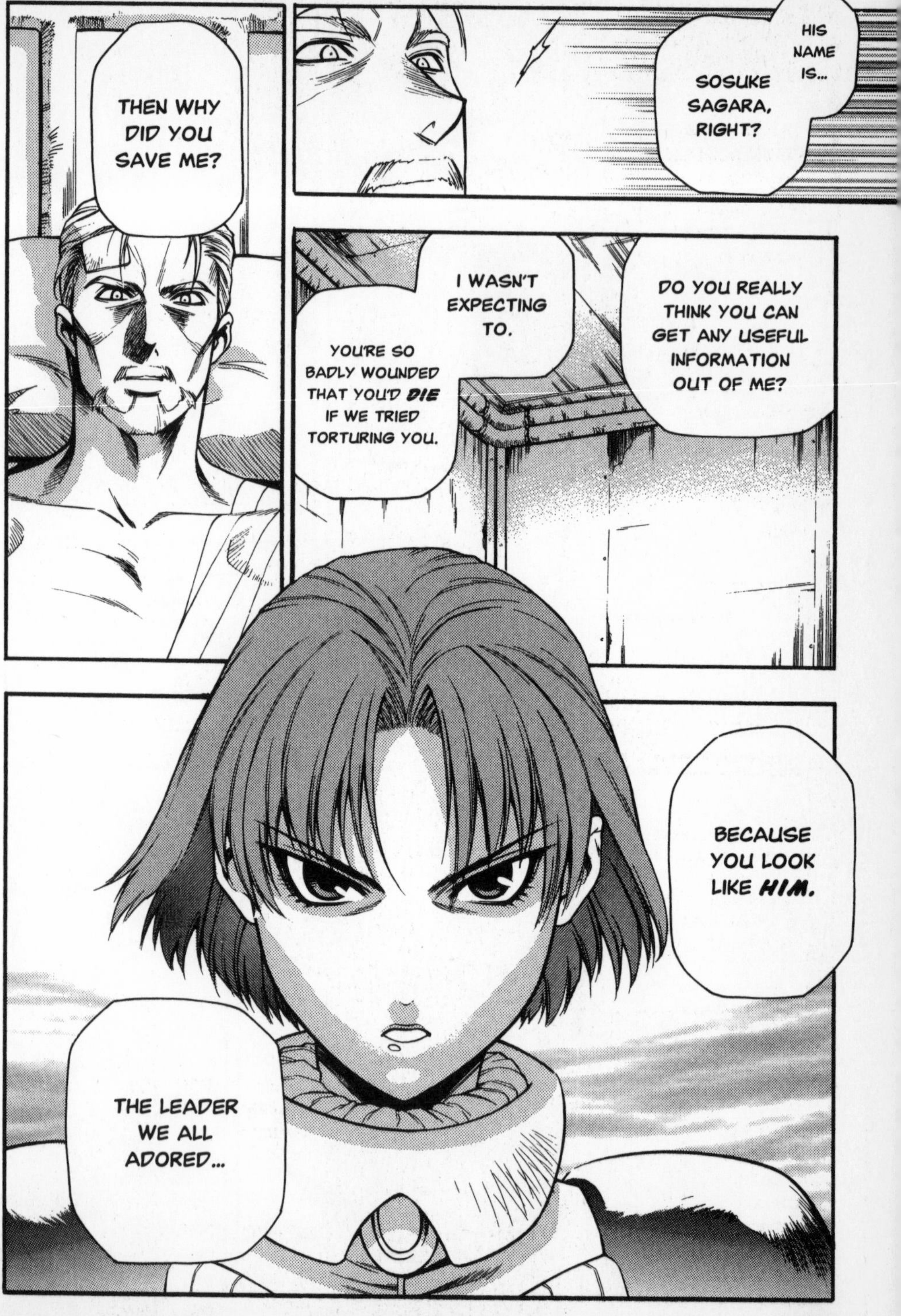
HIS NAME IS...
SOSUKE SAGARA, RIGHT?
DO YOU REALLY THINK YOU CAN GET ANY USEFUL INFORMATION OUT OF ME?
I WASN'T EXPECTING TO.
YOU'RE SO BADLY WOUNDED THAT YOU'D *DIE* IF WE TRIED TORTURING YOU.
THEN WHY DID YOU SAVE ME?
BECAUSE YOU LOOK LIKE *HIM.*
THE LEADER WE ALL ADORED...

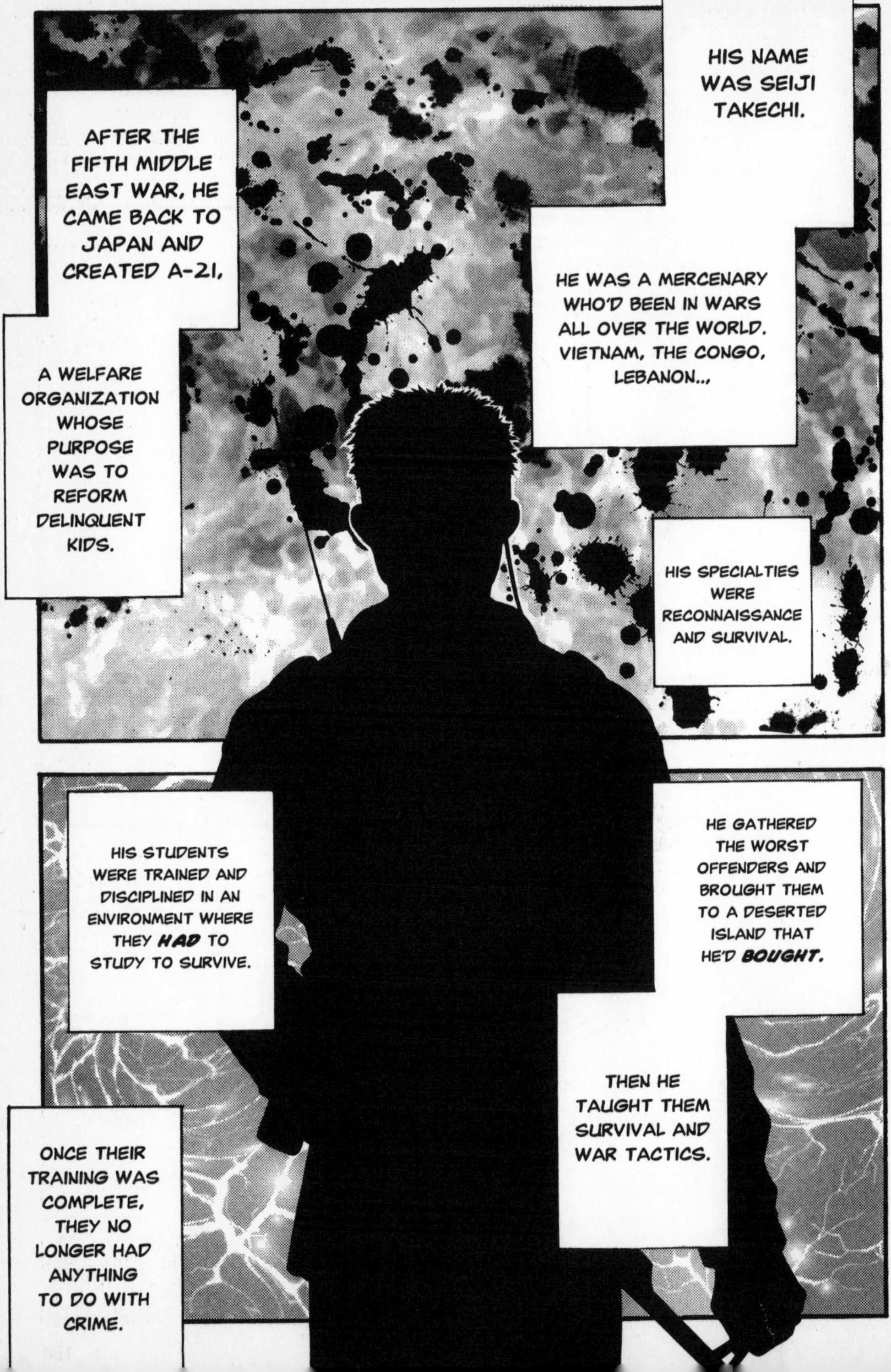
HIS NAME WAS SEIJI TAKECHI.
HE WAS A MERCENARY WHO'D BEEN IN WARS ALL OVER THE WORLD. VIETNAM, THE CONGO, LEBANON...
HIS SPECIALTIES WERE RECONNAISSANCE AND SURVIVAL.
AFTER THE FIFTH MIDDLE EAST WAR, HE CAME BACK TO JAPAN AND CREATED A-21,
A WELFARE ORGANIZATION WHOSE PURPOSE WAS TO REFORM DELINQUENT KIDS.
HE GATHERED THE WORST OFFENDERS AND BROUGHT THEM TO A DESERTED ISLAND THAT HE'D ***BOUGHT.***
THEN HE TAUGHT THEM SURVIVAL AND WAR TACTICS.
HIS STUDENTS WERE TRAINED AND DISCIPLINED IN AN ENVIRONMENT WHERE THEY ***HAD*** TO STUDY TO SURVIVE.
ONCE THEIR TRAINING WAS COMPLETE, THEY NO LONGER HAD ANYTHING TO DO WITH CRIME.

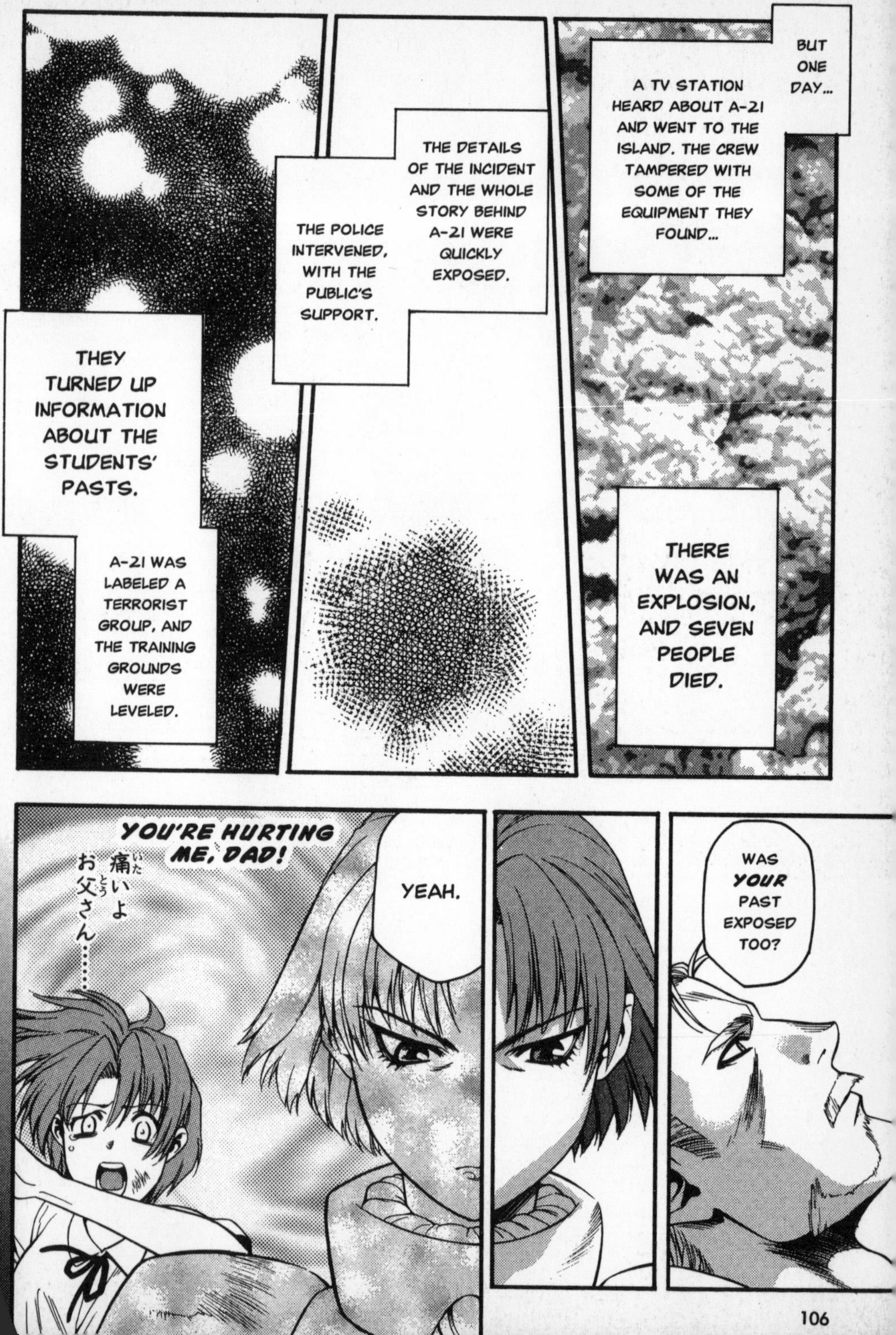

BUT ONE DAY...
A TV STATION HEARD ABOUT A-21 AND WENT TO THE ISLAND. THE CREW TAMPERED WITH SOME OF THE EQUIPMENT THEY FOUND...
THERE WAS AN EXPLOSION, AND SEVEN PEOPLE DIED.
THE DETAILS OF THE INCIDENT AND THE WHOLE STORY BEHIND A-21 WERE QUICKLY EXPOSED.
THE POLICE INTERVENED, WITH THE PUBLIC'S SUPPORT.
THEY TURNED UP INFORMATION ABOUT THE STUDENTS' PASTS.
A-21 WAS LABELED A TERRORIST GROUP, AND THE TRAINING GROUNDS WERE LEVELED.
WAS *YOUR* PAST EXPOSED TOO?
YEAH.
YOU'RE HURTING ME, DAD!
痛いよ お父さん……

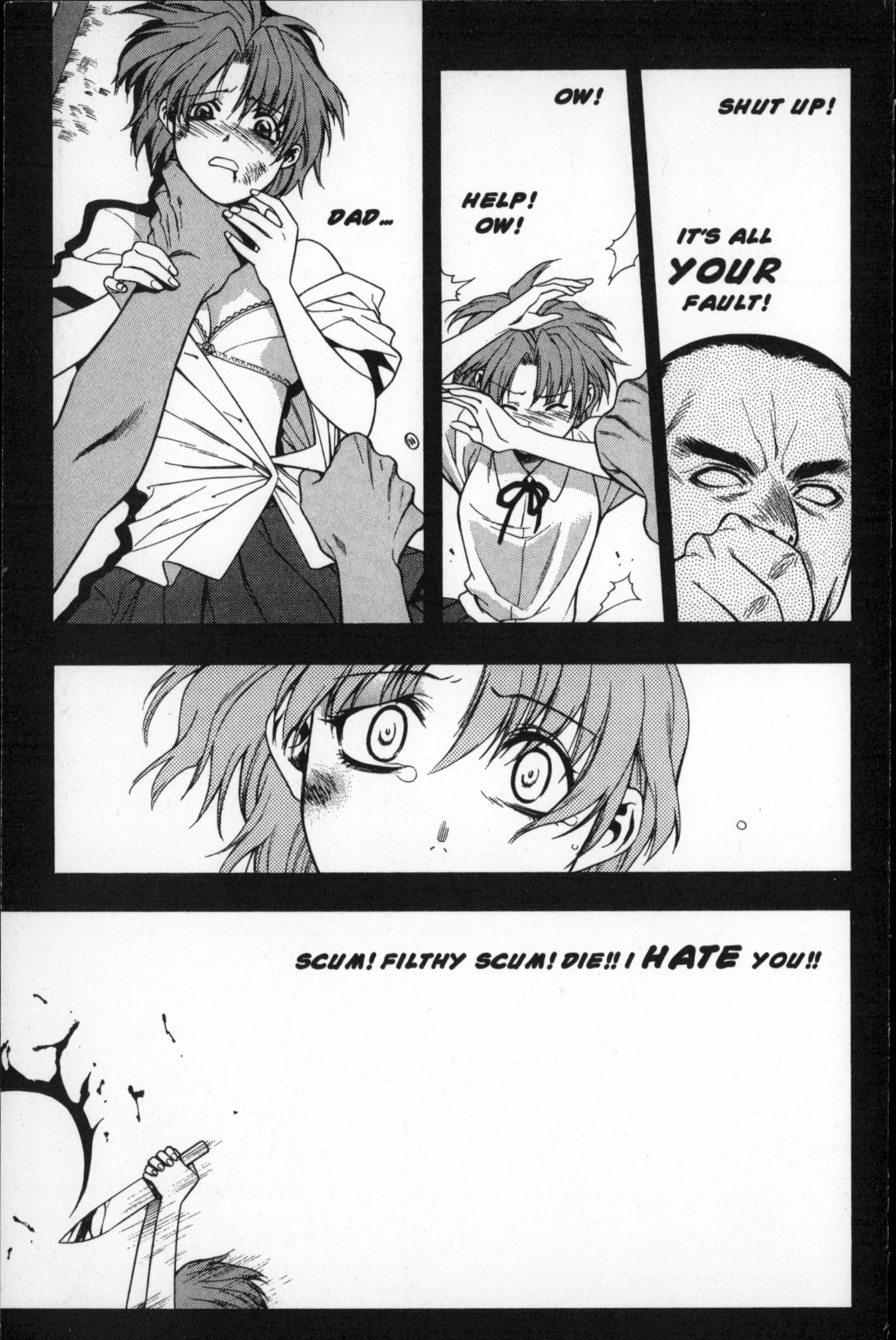
SHUT UP!
IT'S ALL YOUR FAULT!
OW!
HELP! OW!
DAD...
SCUM! FILTHY SCUM! DIE!! I HATE YOU!!

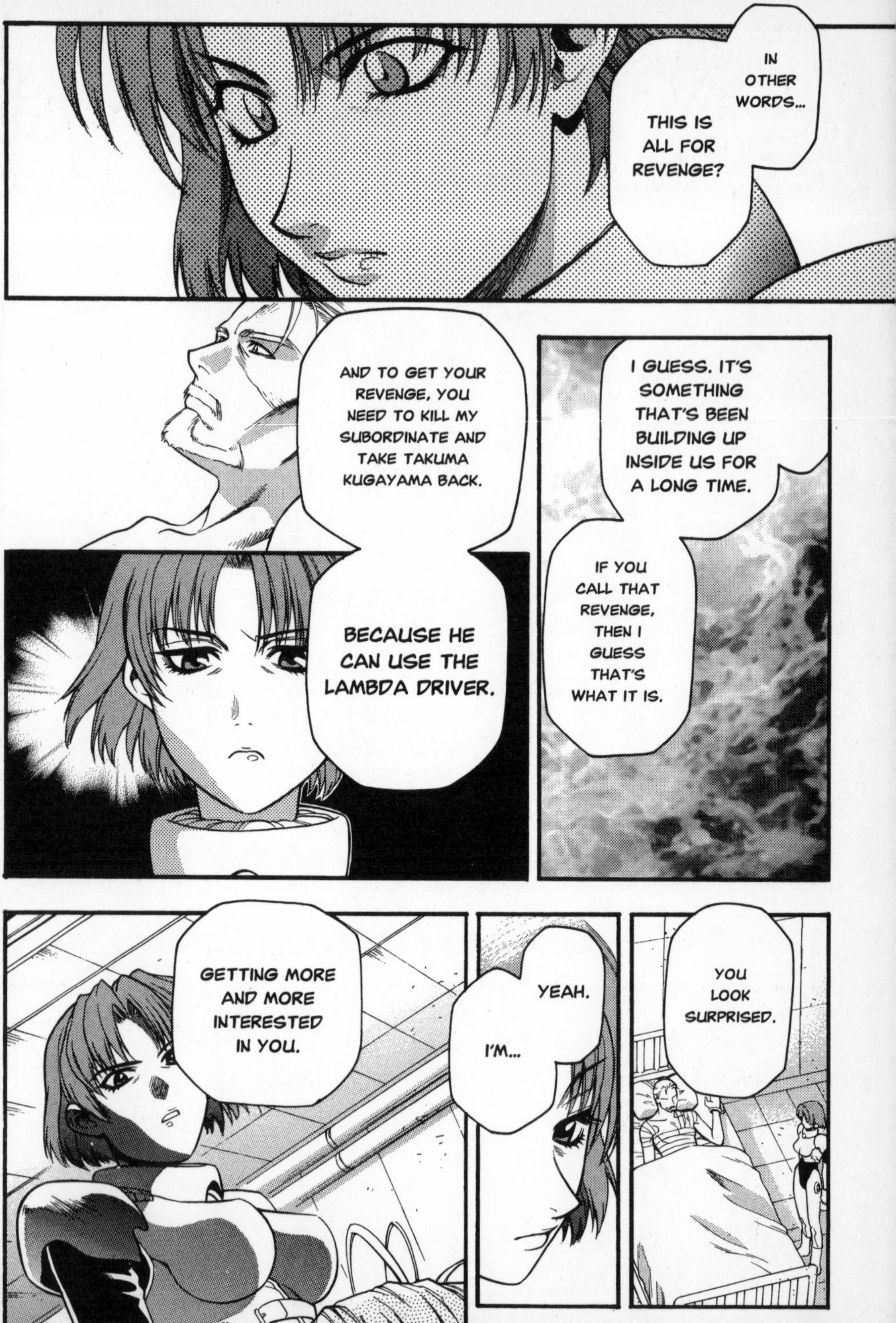
IN OTHER WORDS...
THIS IS ALL FOR REVENGE?
I GUESS. IT'S SOMETHING THAT'S BEEN BUILDING UP INSIDE US FOR A LONG TIME.
IF YOU CALL THAT REVENGE, THEN I GUESS THAT'S WHAT IT IS.
AND TO GET YOUR REVENGE, YOU NEED TO KILL MY SUBORDINATE AND TAKE TAKUMA KUGAYAMA BACK.
BECAUSE HE CAN USE THE LAMBDA DRIVER.
YOU LOOK SURPRISED.
YEAH.
I'M...
GETTING MORE AND MORE INTERESTED IN YOU.

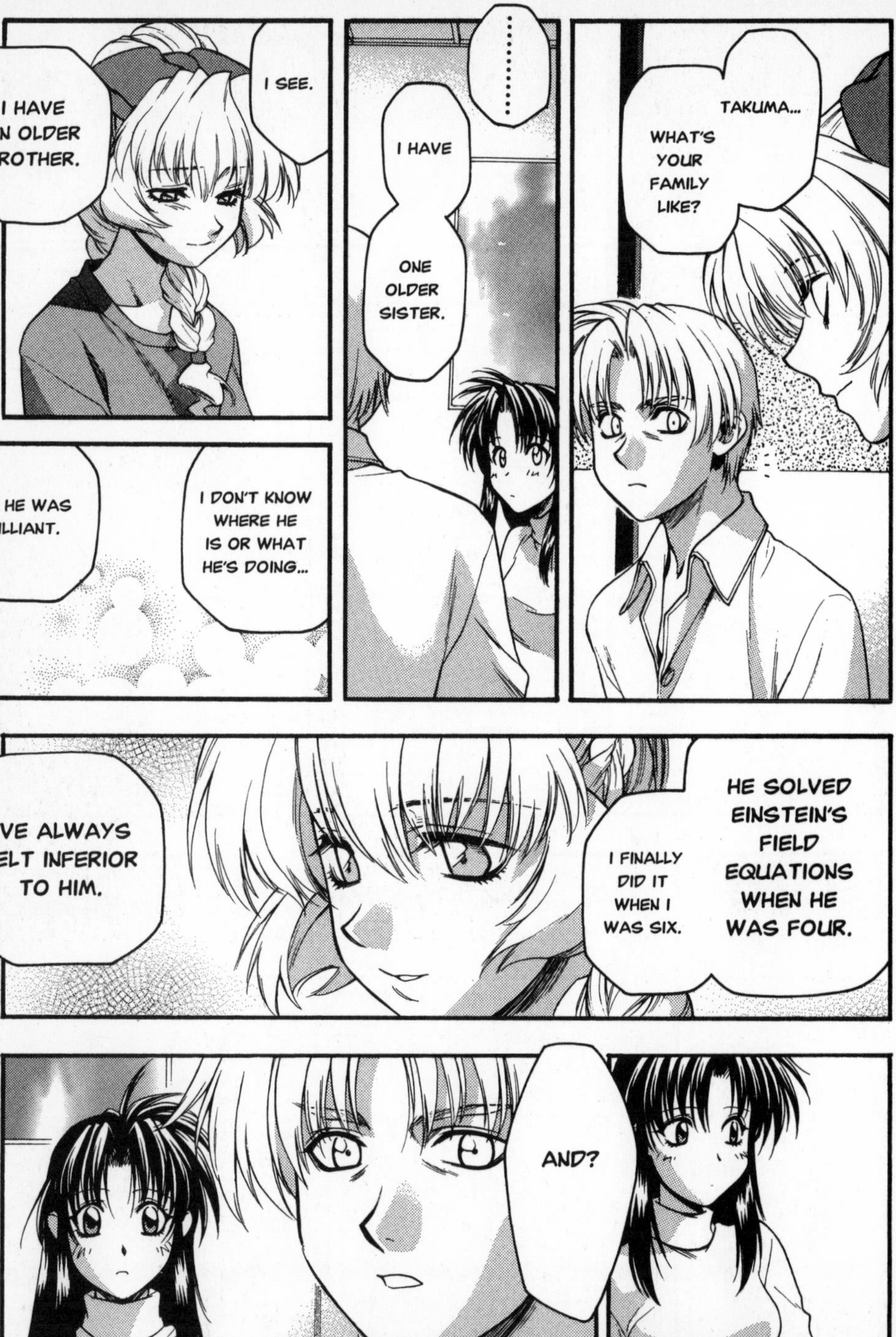
TAKUMA...
WHAT'S YOUR FAMILY LIKE?
......
I HAVE ONE OLDER SISTER.
I SEE.
I HAVE AN OLDER BROTHER.
I DON'T KNOW WHERE HE IS OR WHAT HE'S DOING...
BUT HE WAS BRILLIANT.
HE SOLVED EINSTEIN'S FIELD EQUATIONS WHEN HE WAS FOUR.
I FINALLY DID IT WHEN I WAS SIX.
I'VE ALWAYS FELT INFERIOR TO HIM.
AND?

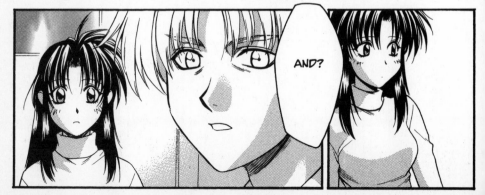

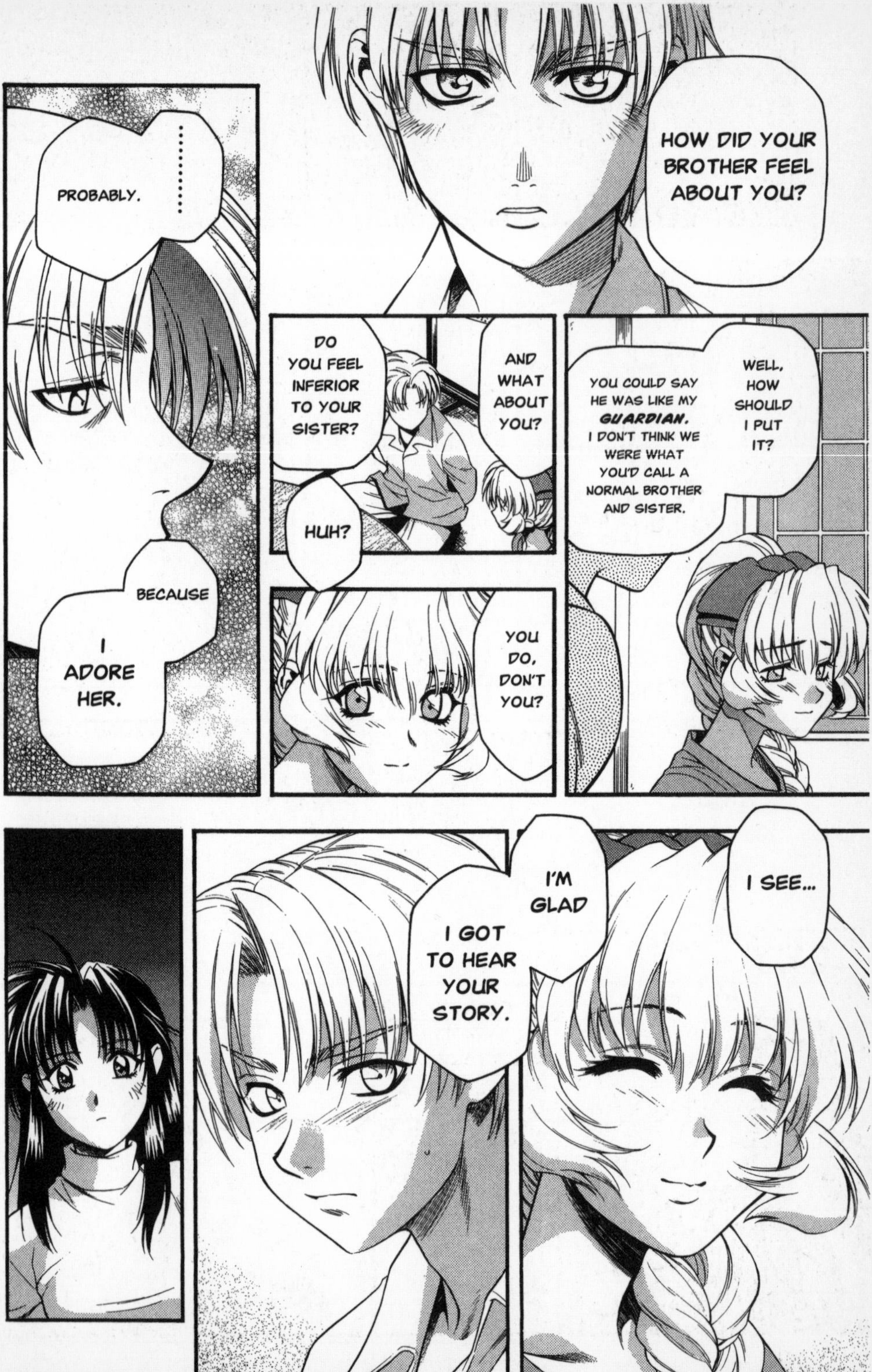
HOW DID YOUR BROTHER FEEL ABOUT YOU?
WELL, HOW SHOULD I PUT IT?
YOU COULD SAY HE WAS LIKE MY GUARDIAN. I DON'T THINK WE WERE WHAT YOU'D CALL A NORMAL BROTHER AND SISTER.
AND WHAT ABOUT YOU?
DO YOU FEEL INFERIOR TO YOUR SISTER?
HUH?
YOU DO, DON'T YOU?
......
PROBABLY.
BECAUSE
I ADORE HER.
I SEE...
I'M GLAD
I GOT TO HEAR YOUR STORY.

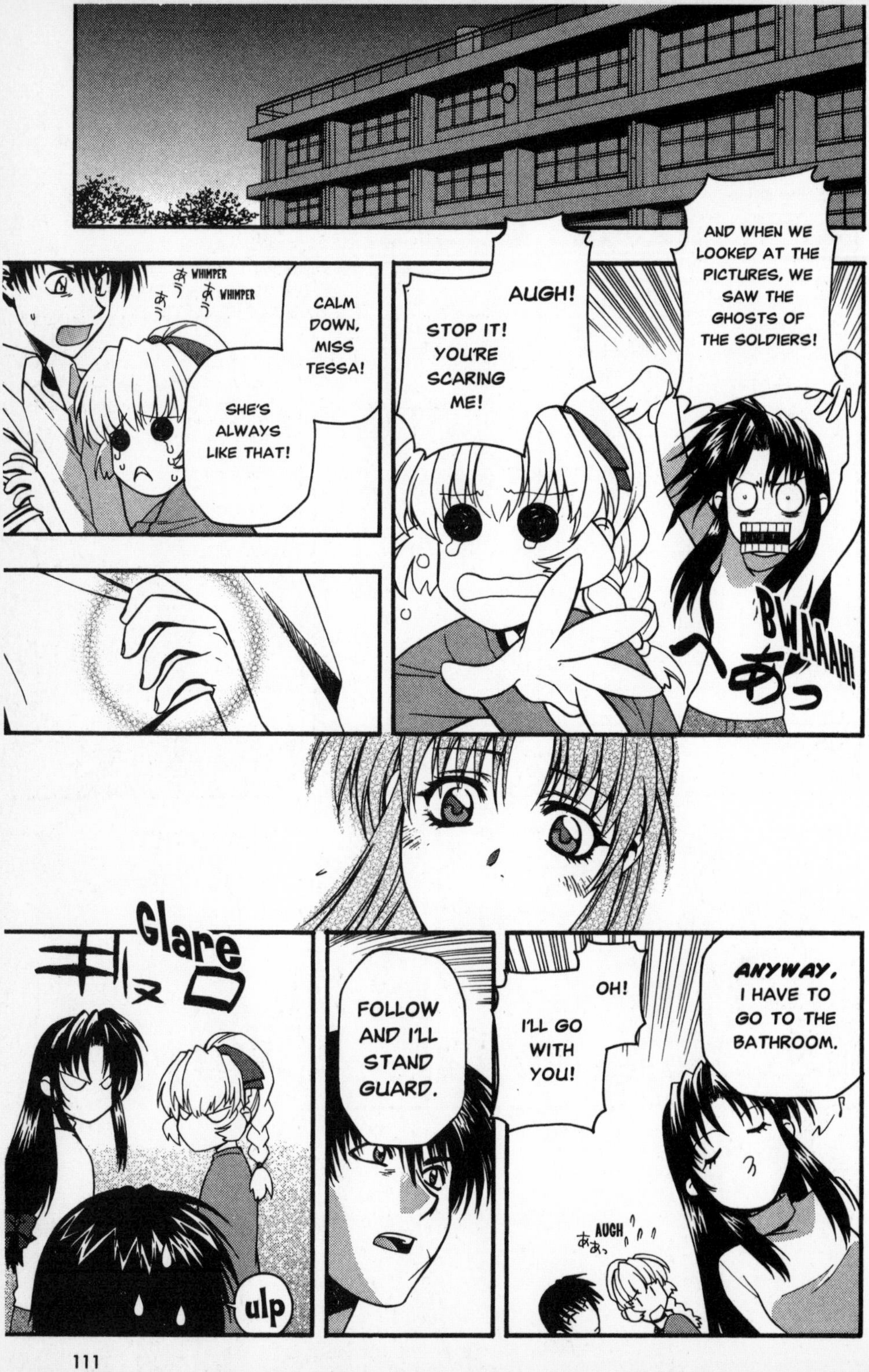

AND WHEN WE LOOKED AT THE PICTURES, WE SAW THE GHOSTS OF THE SOLDIERS!
AUGH!
STOP IT! YOU'RE SCARING ME!
BWAAAH!
CALM DOWN, MISS TESSA!
WHIMPER WHIMPER
SHE'S ALWAYS LIKE THAT!
ANYWAY, I HAVE TO GO TO THE BATHROOM.
OH!
I'LL GO WITH YOU!
AUGH
FOLLOW AND I'LL STAND GUARD.
Glare
ulp

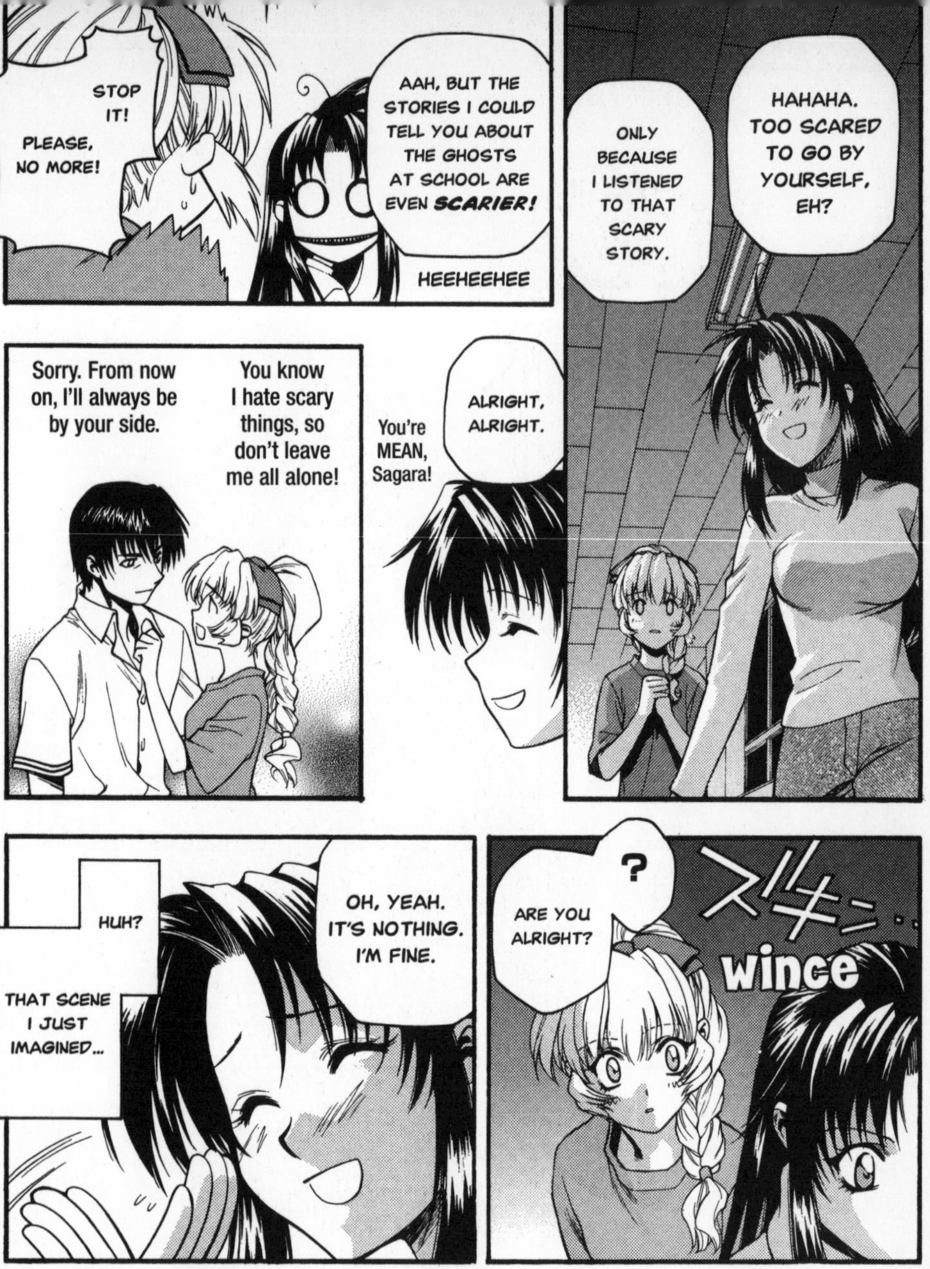
HAHAHA. TOO SCARED TO GO BY YOURSELF, EH?
ONLY BECAUSE I LISTENED TO THAT SCARY STORY.
AAH, BUT THE STORIES I COULD TELL YOU ABOUT THE GHOSTS AT SCHOOL ARE EVEN SCARIER!
HEEHEEHEE
STOP IT!
PLEASE, NO MORE!
ALRIGHT, ALRIGHT.
You're MEAN, Sagara!
You know I hate scary things, so don't leave me all alone!
Sorry. From now on, I'll always be by your side.
?
ARE YOU ALRIGHT?
wince
OH, YEAH. IT'S NOTHING. I'M FINE.
HUH?
THAT SCENE I JUST IMAGINED...

THEY SEEMED SO CLOSE AND PERFECT FOR EACH OTHER.

IT HURTS ME TO THINK LIKE THAT.

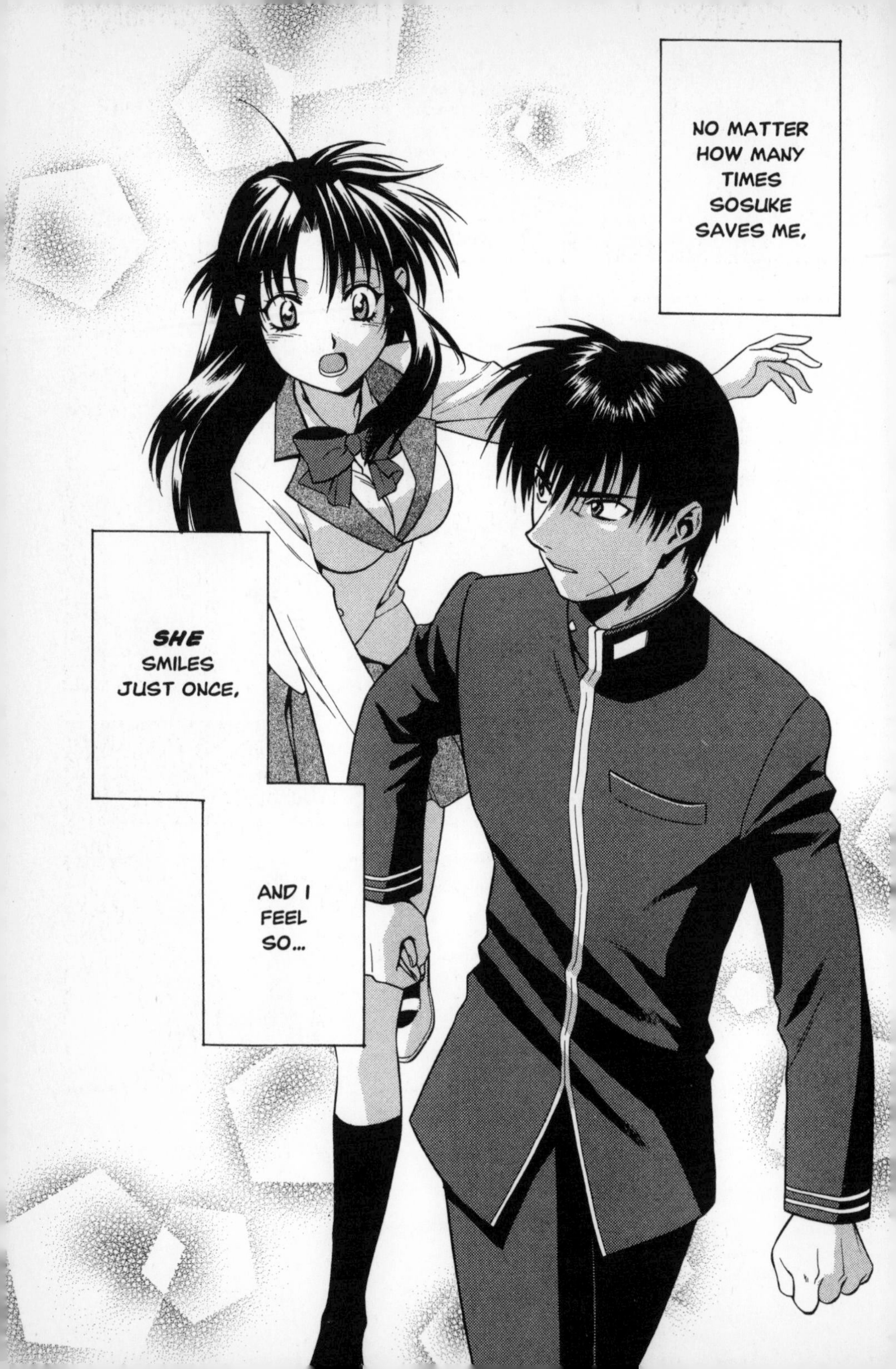
NO MATTER HOW MANY TIMES SOSUKE SAVES ME,
SHE SMILES JUST ONCE,
AND I FEEL SO...

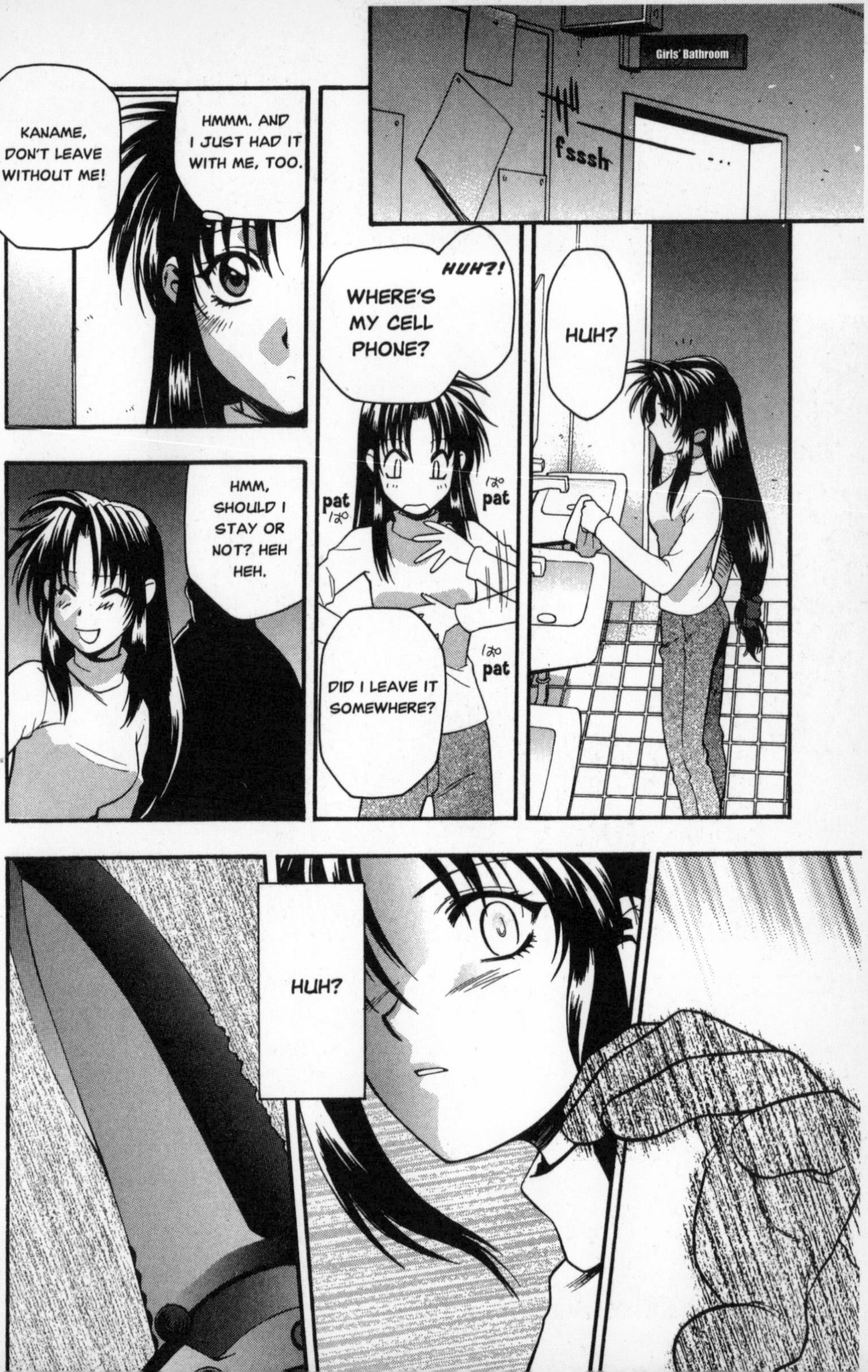
Girls' Bathroom
fsssh
...
HUH?
HUH?!
WHERE'S MY CELL PHONE?
pat
pat
pat
DID I LEAVE IT SOMEWHERE?
KANAME, DON'T LEAVE WITHOUT ME!
HMMM. AND I JUST HAD IT WITH ME, TOO.
HMM, SHOULD I STAY OR NOT? HEH HEH.
HUH?

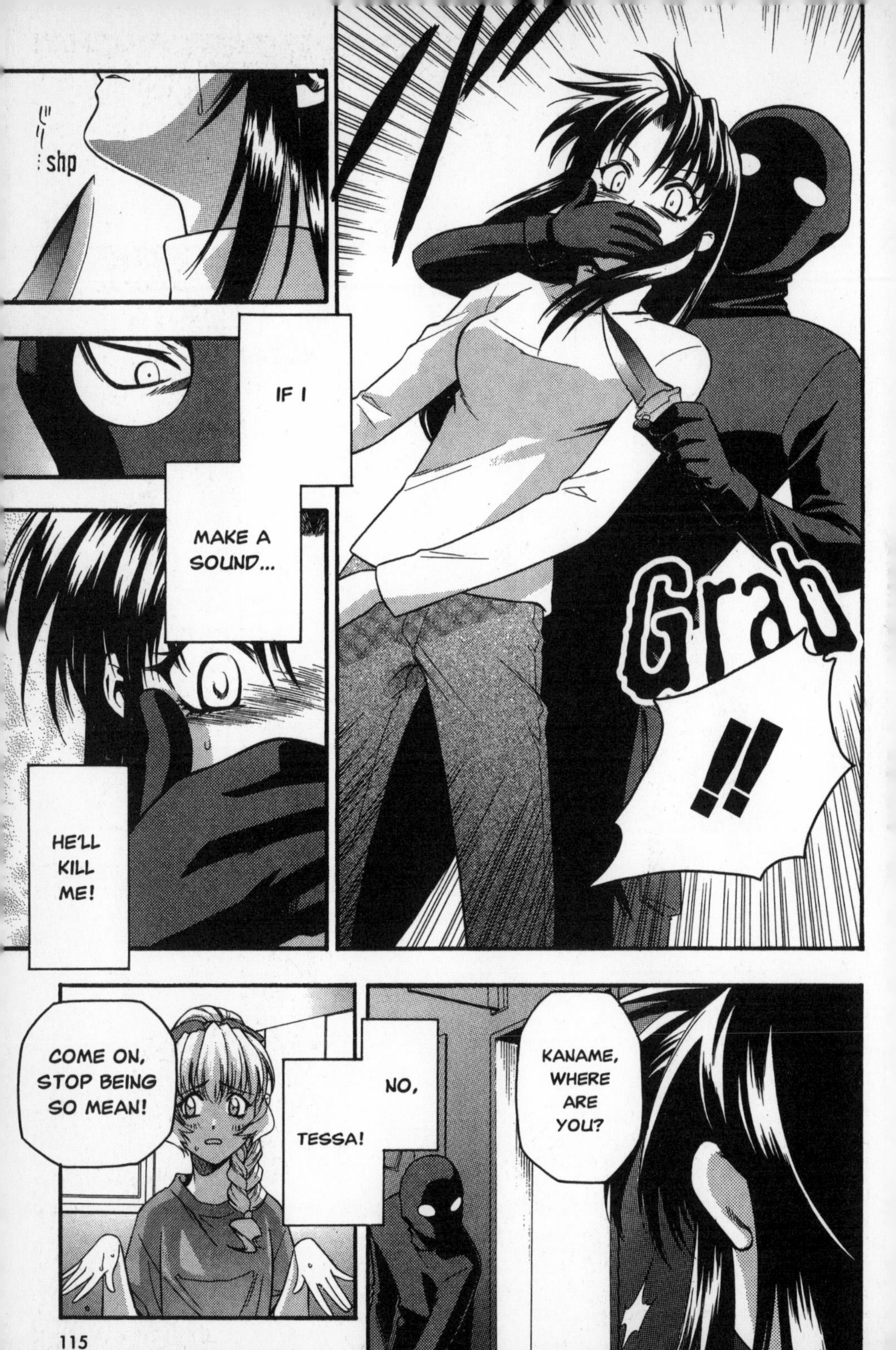
Grab
!!
shp
IF I
MAKE A SOUND...
HE'LL KILL ME!
KANAME, WHERE ARE YOU?
NO,
TESSA!
COME ON, STOP BEING SO MEAN!

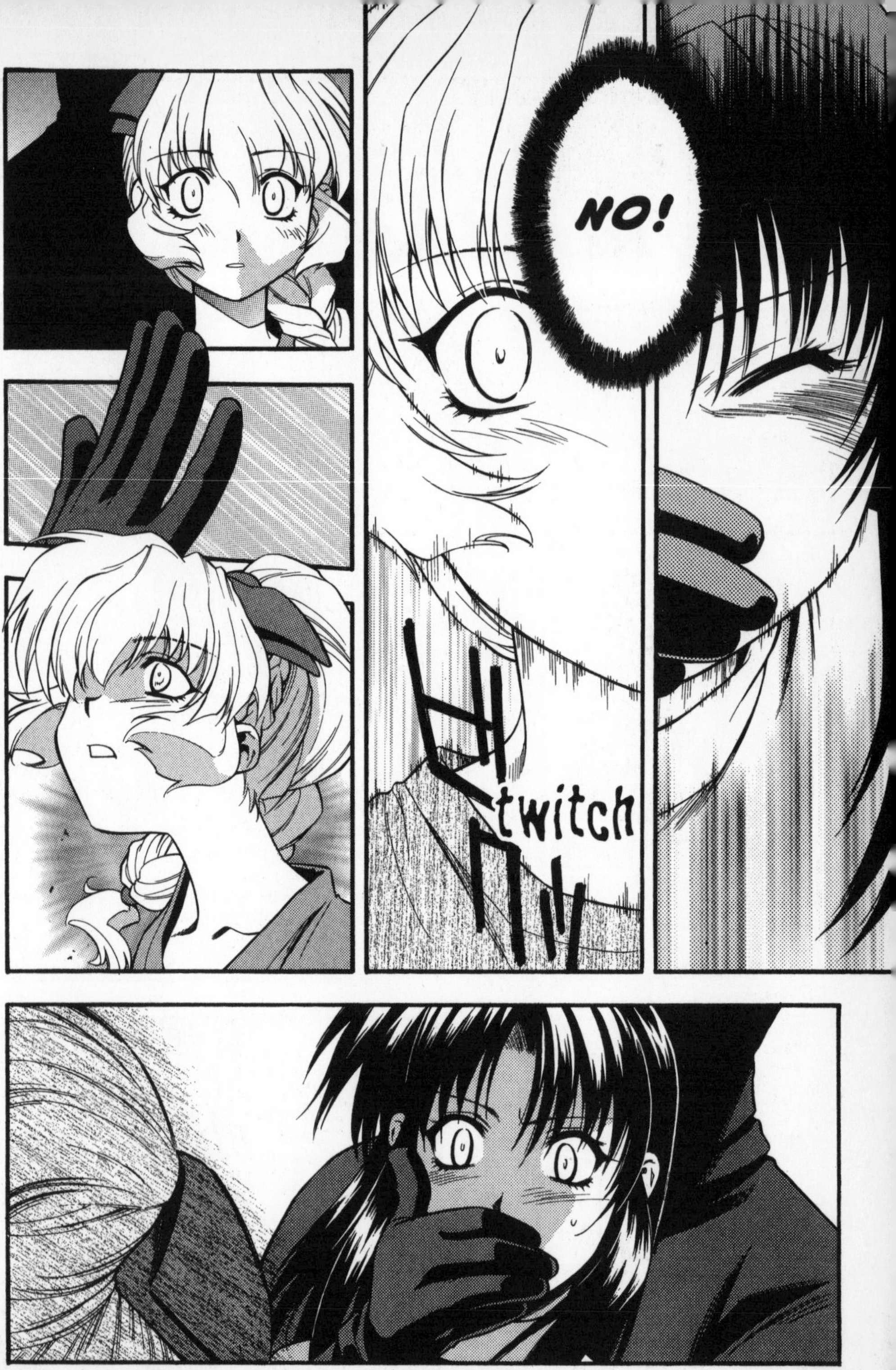
NO!
twitch

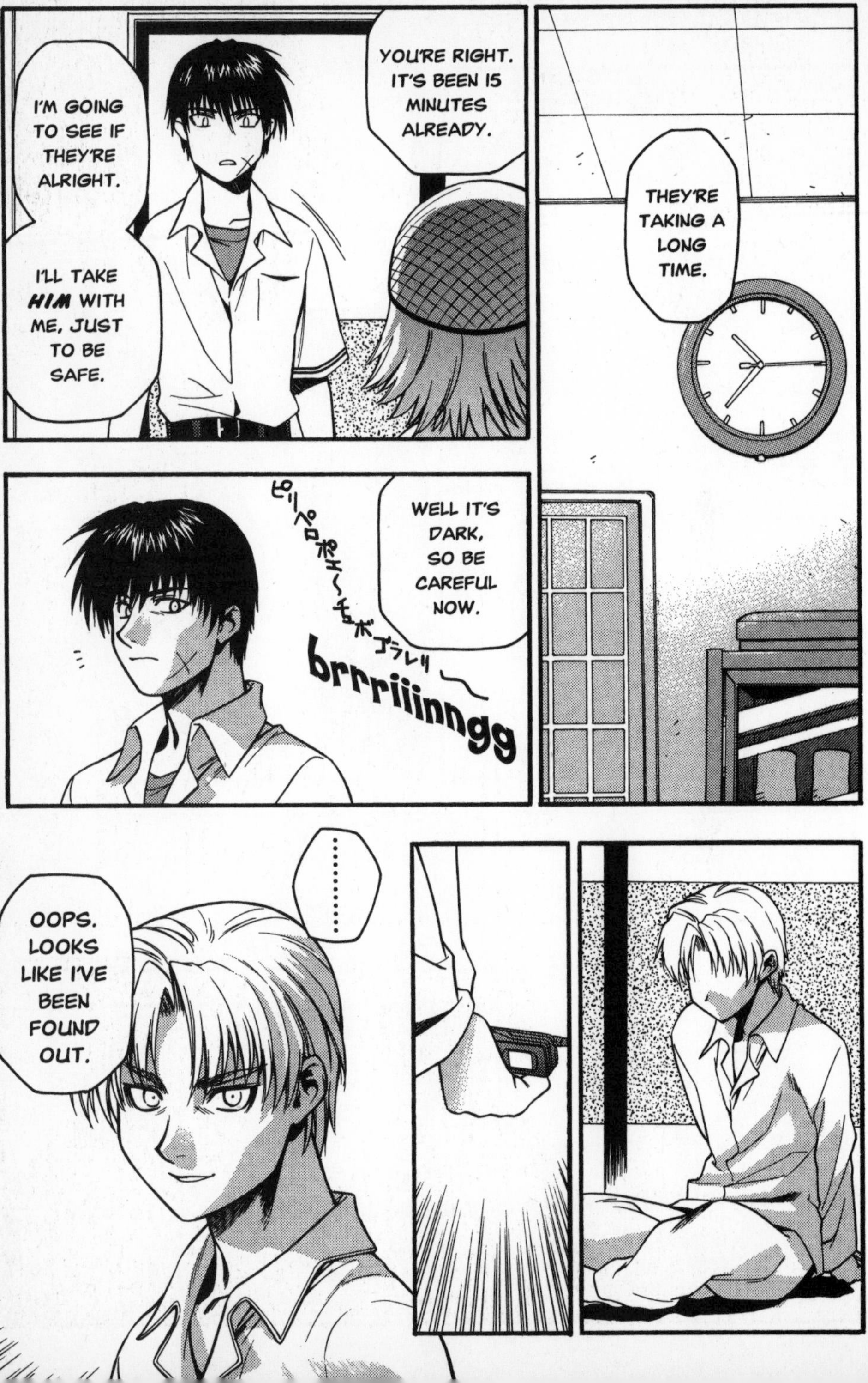
THEY'RE TAKING A LONG TIME.
YOU'RE RIGHT. IT'S BEEN 15 MINUTES ALREADY.
I'M GOING TO SEE IF THEY'RE ALRIGHT.
I'LL TAKE ***HIM*** WITH ME, JUST TO BE SAFE.
WELL IT'S DARK, SO BE CAREFUL NOW.
brrriiinnngg
……
OOPS. LOOKS LIKE I'VE BEEN FOUND OUT.

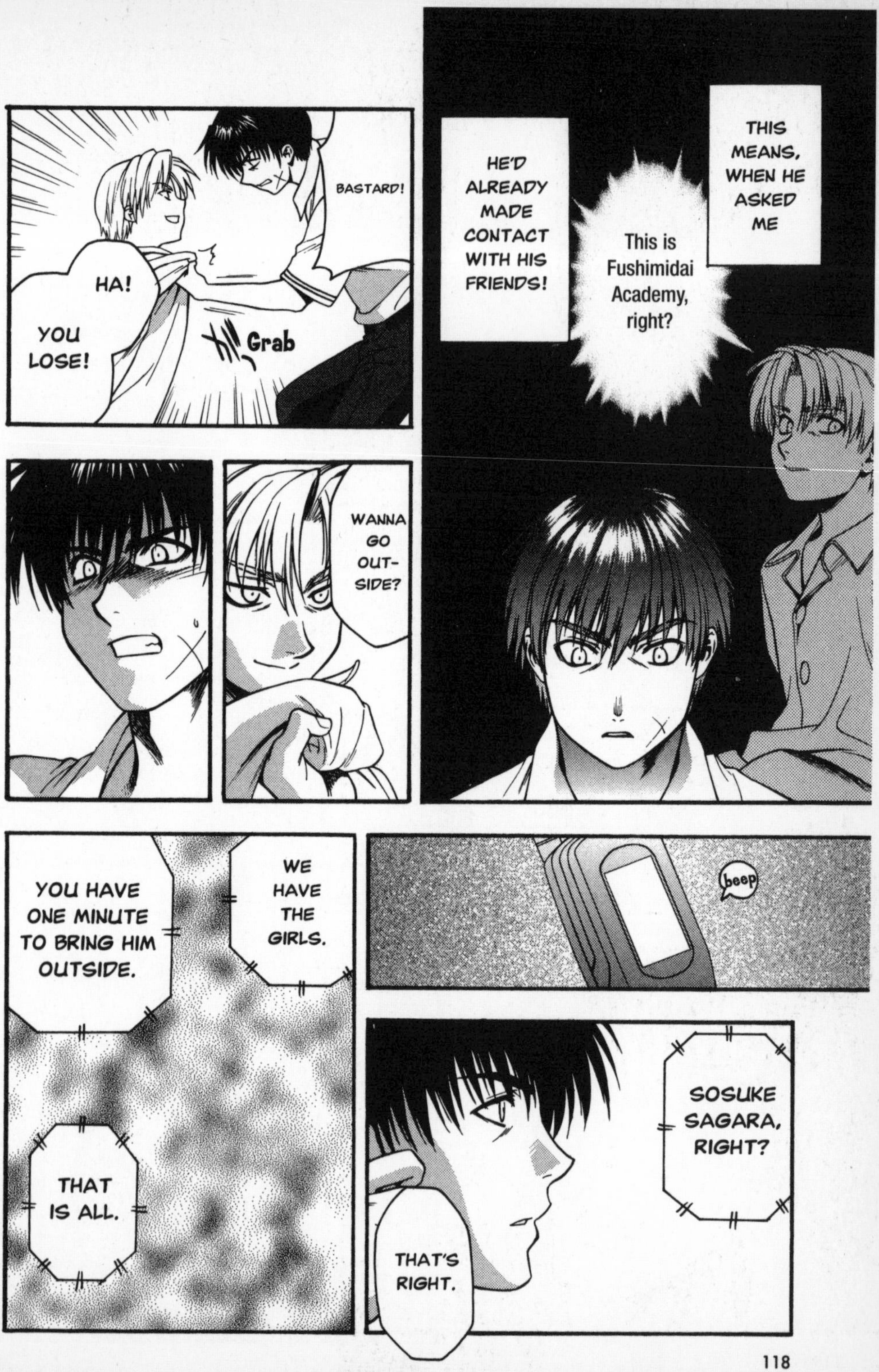
THIS MEANS, WHEN HE ASKED ME
This is Fushimidai Academy, right?
HE'D ALREADY MADE CONTACT WITH HIS FRIENDS!
BASTARD!
HA!
YOU LOSE!
Grab
WANNA GO OUT-SIDE?
beep
SOSUKE SAGARA, RIGHT?
THAT'S RIGHT.
WE HAVE THE GIRLS.
YOU HAVE ONE MINUTE TO BRING HIM OUTSIDE.
THAT IS ALL.

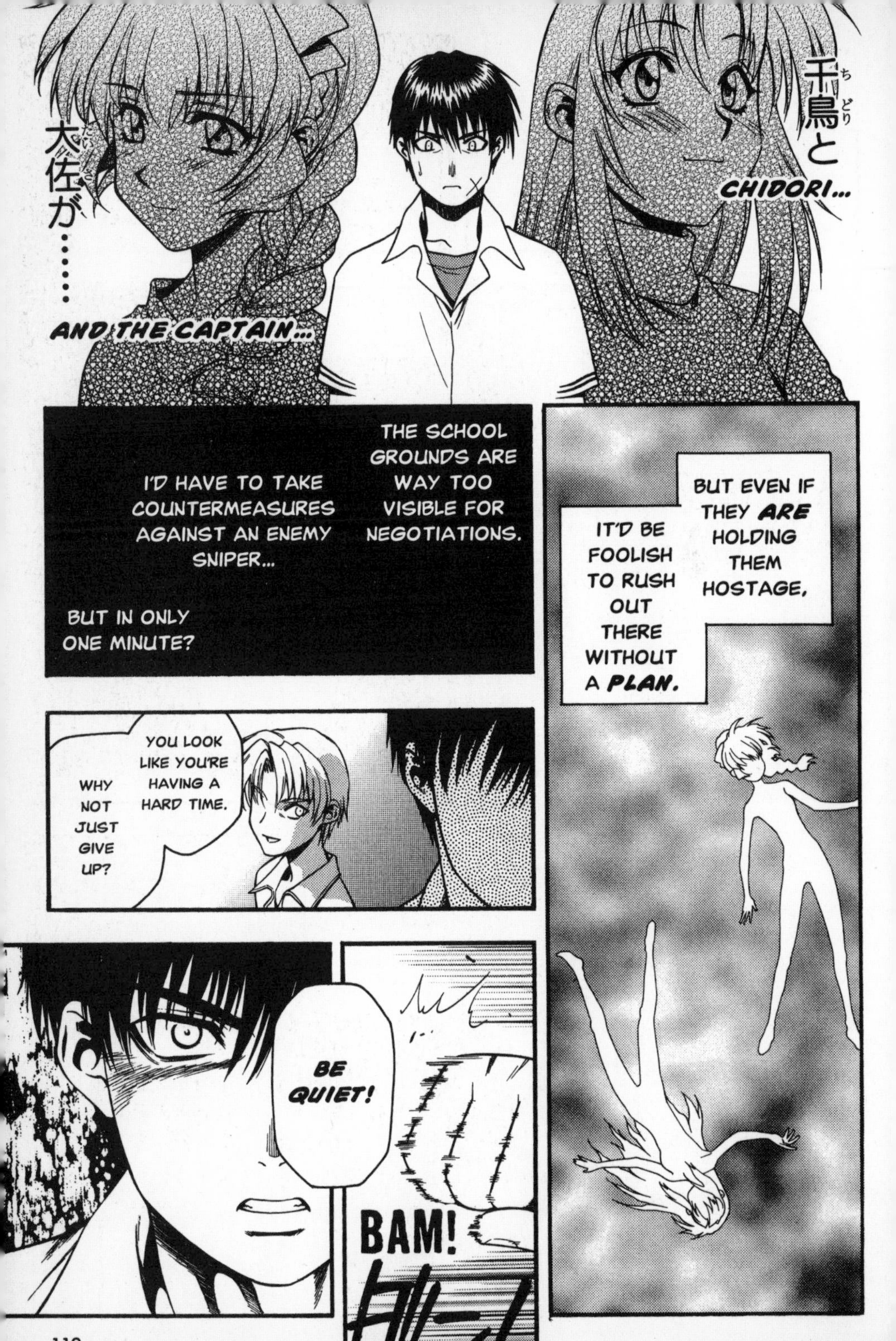
千鳥と
CHIDORI...
大佐が……
AND THE CAPTAIN...
BUT EVEN IF THEY ARE HOLDING THEM HOSTAGE,
IT'D BE FOOLISH TO RUSH OUT THERE WITHOUT A PLAN.
THE SCHOOL GROUNDS ARE WAY TOO VISIBLE FOR NEGOTIATIONS.
I'D HAVE TO TAKE COUNTERMEASURES AGAINST AN ENEMY SNIPER...
BUT IN ONLY ONE MINUTE?
YOU LOOK LIKE YOU'RE HAVING A HARD TIME.
WHY NOT JUST GIVE UP?
BE QUIET!
BAM!

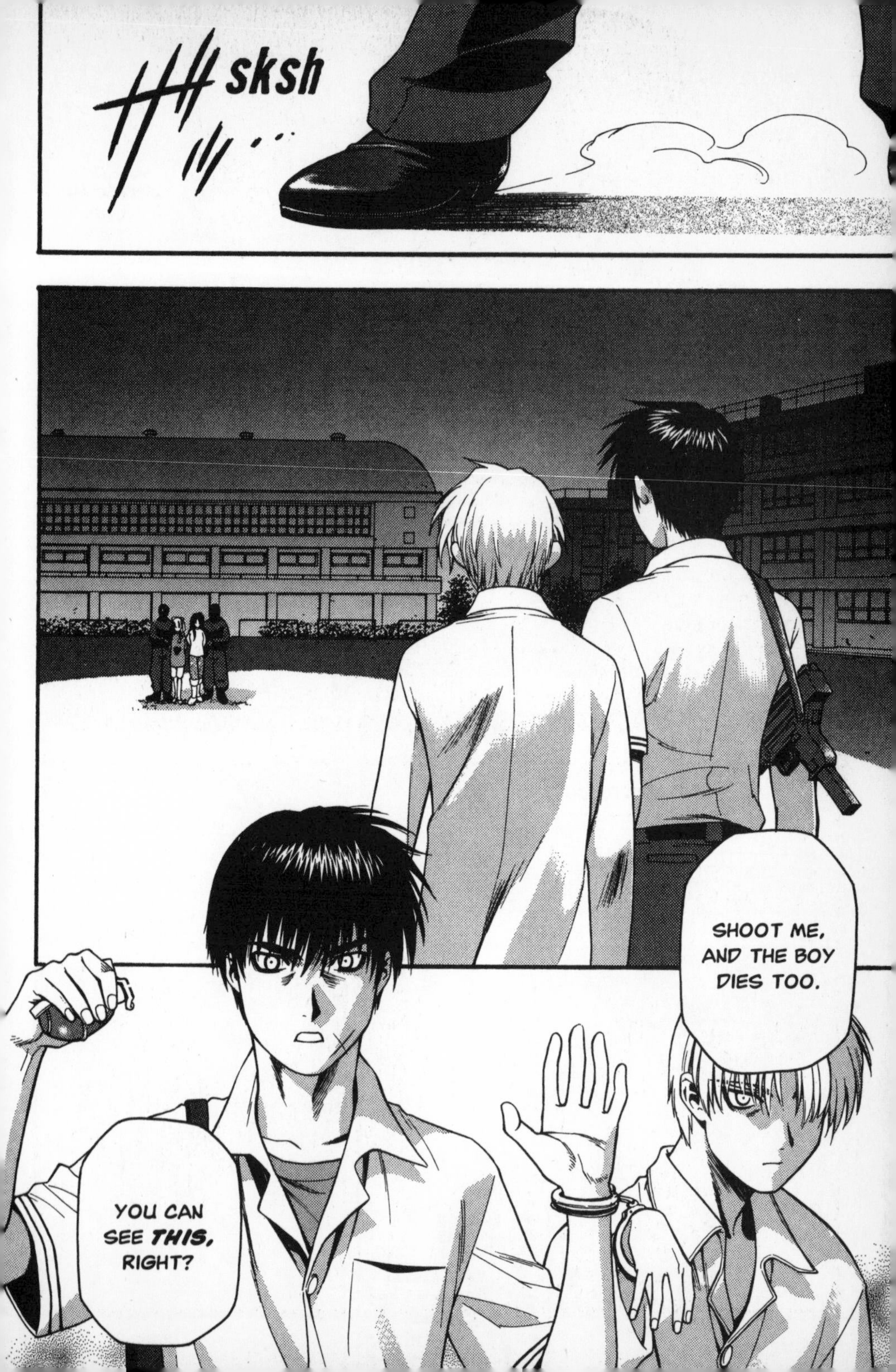
sksh
SHOOT ME, AND THE BOY DIES TOO.
YOU CAN SEE ***THIS,*** RIGHT?

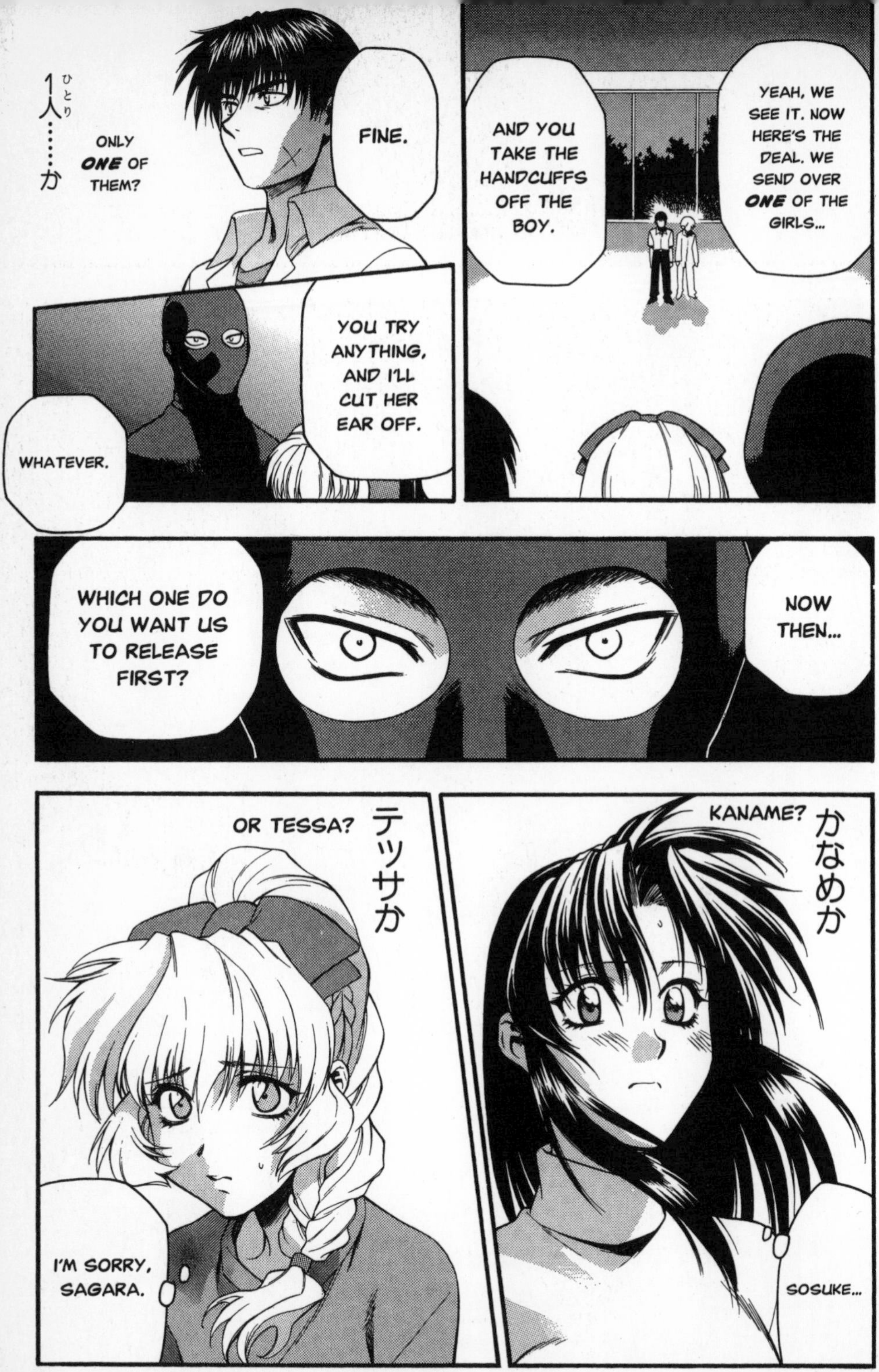
YEAH, WE SEE IT. NOW HERE'S THE DEAL. WE SEND OVER ONE OF THE GIRLS...
AND YOU TAKE THE HANDCUFFS OFF THE BOY.
FINE.
ONLY ONE OF THEM?
1人……か
YOU TRY ANYTHING, AND I'LL CUT HER EAR OFF.
WHATEVER.
NOW THEN...
WHICH ONE DO YOU WANT US TO RELEASE FIRST?
KANAME?
かなめか
SOSUKE...
OR TESSA?
テッサか
I'M SORRY, SAGARA.

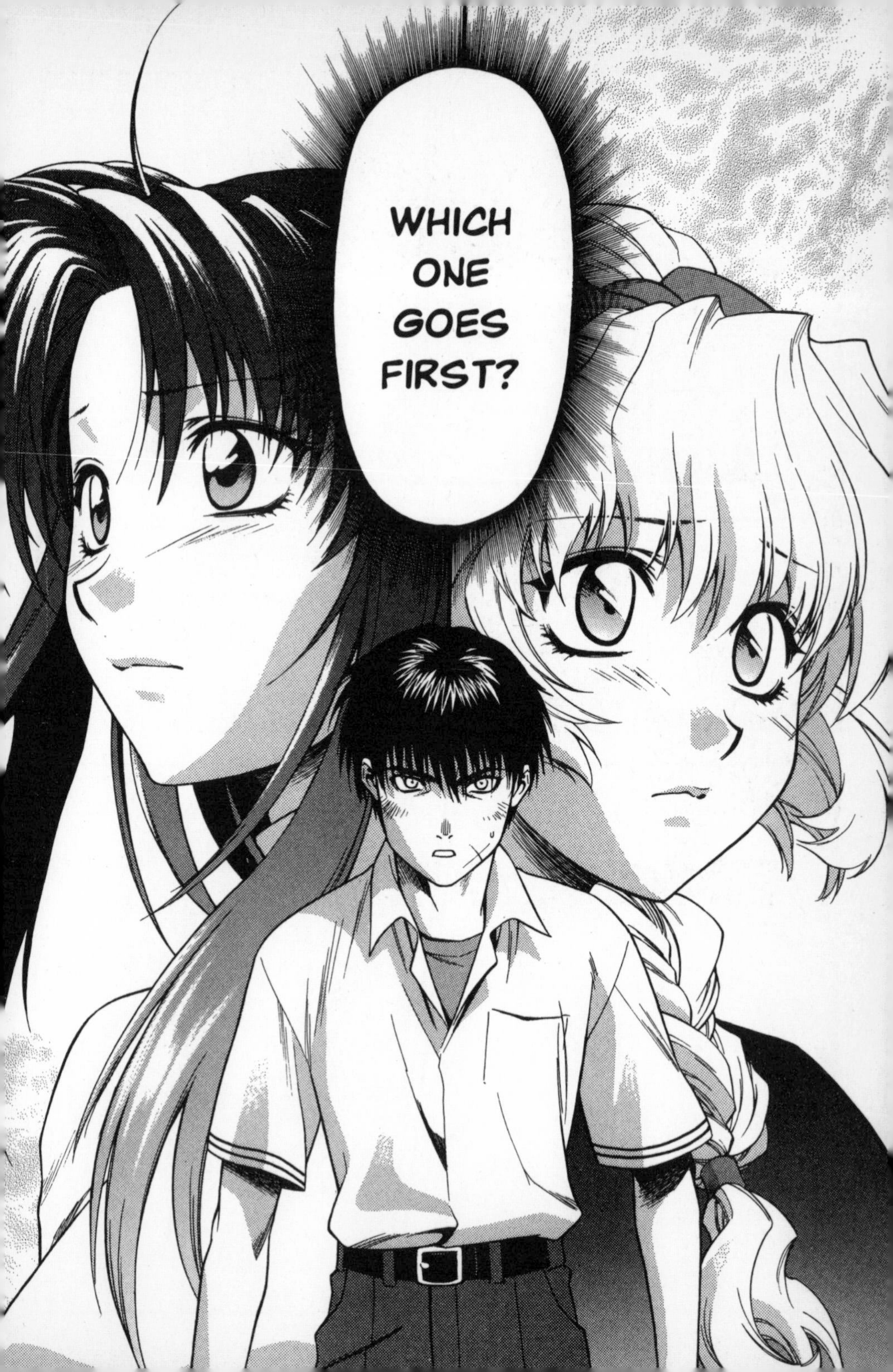
WHICH ONE GOES FIRST?

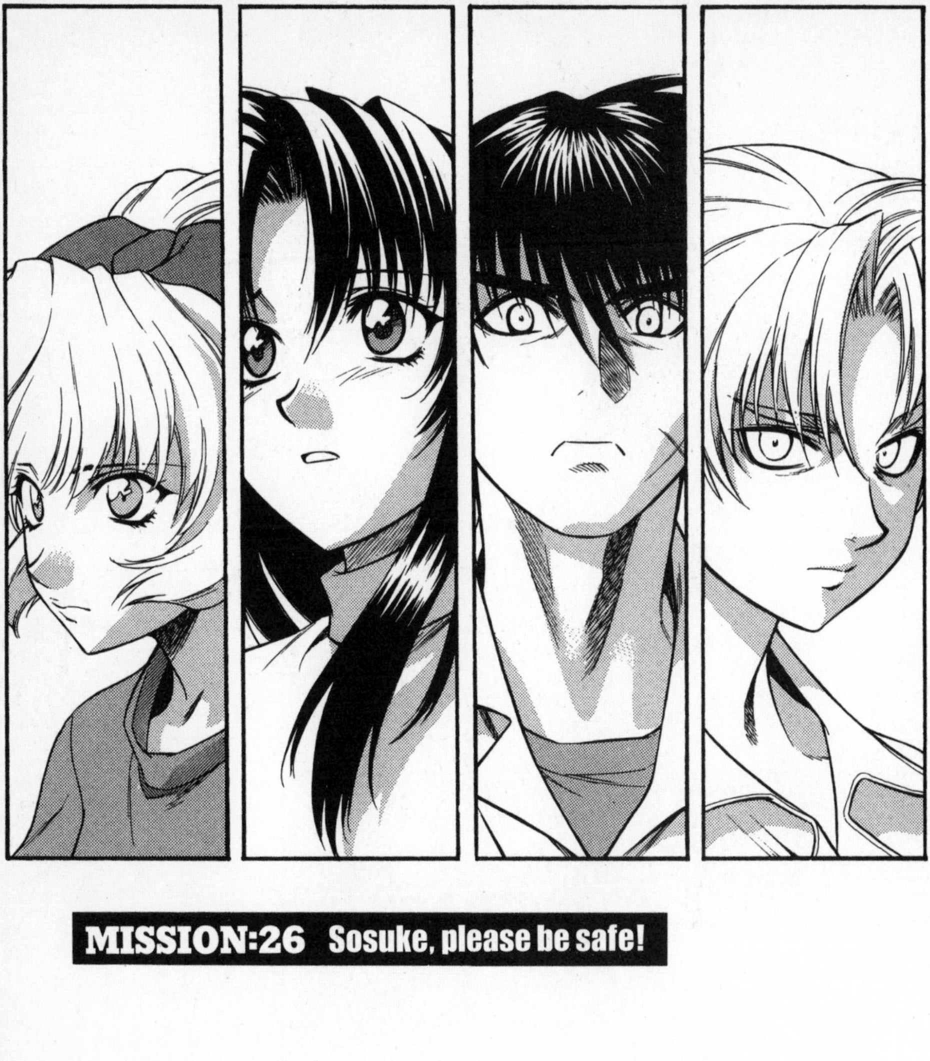

MISSION:26 Sosuke, please be safe!

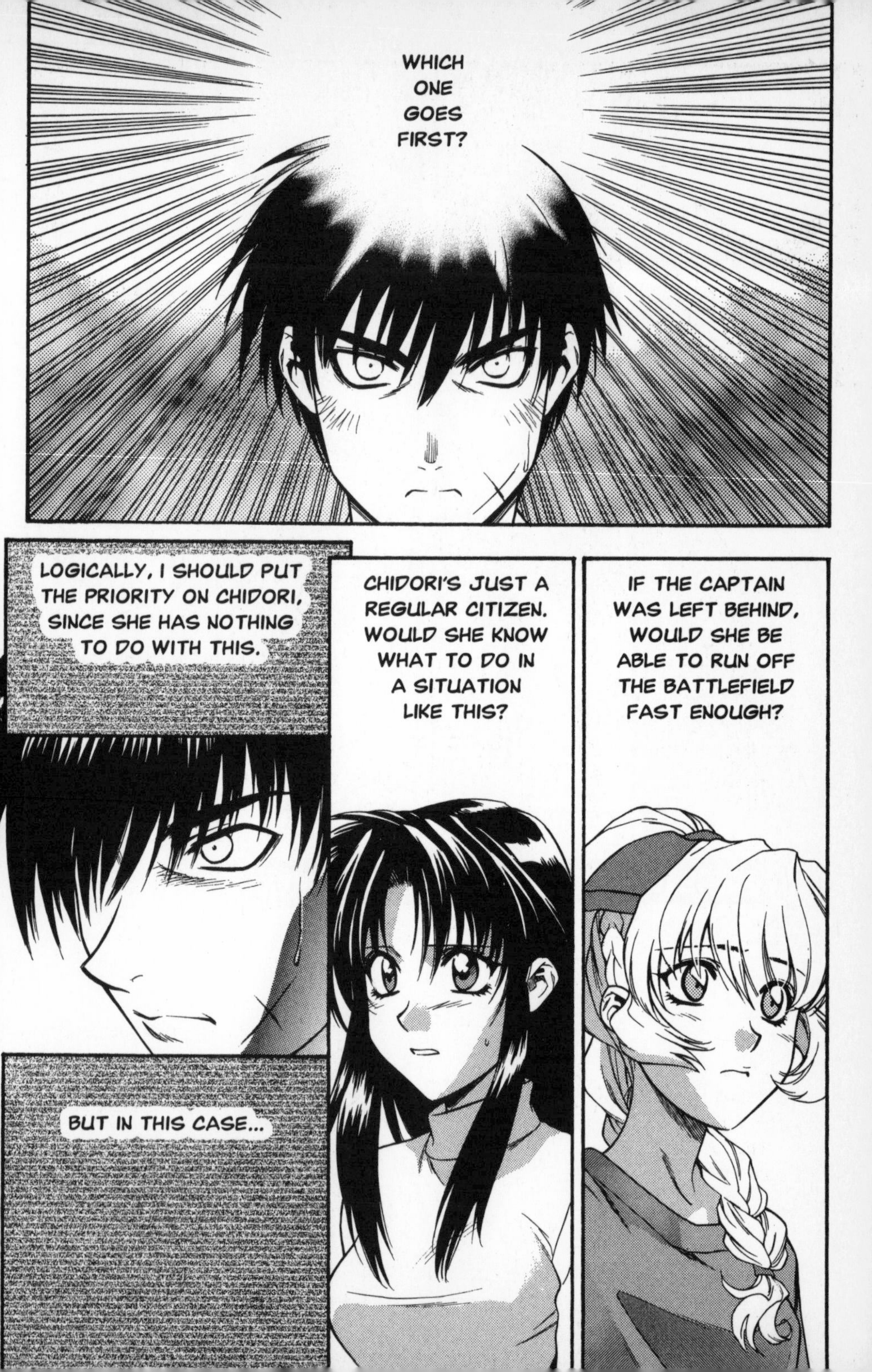
WHICH ONE GOES FIRST?
IF THE CAPTAIN WAS LEFT BEHIND, WOULD SHE BE ABLE TO RUN OFF THE BATTLEFIELD FAST ENOUGH?
CHIDORI'S JUST A REGULAR CITIZEN. WOULD SHE KNOW WHAT TO DO IN A SITUATION LIKE THIS?
LOGICALLY, I SHOULD PUT THE PRIORITY ON CHIDORI, SINCE SHE HAS NOTHING TO DO WITH THIS.
BUT IN THIS CASE...

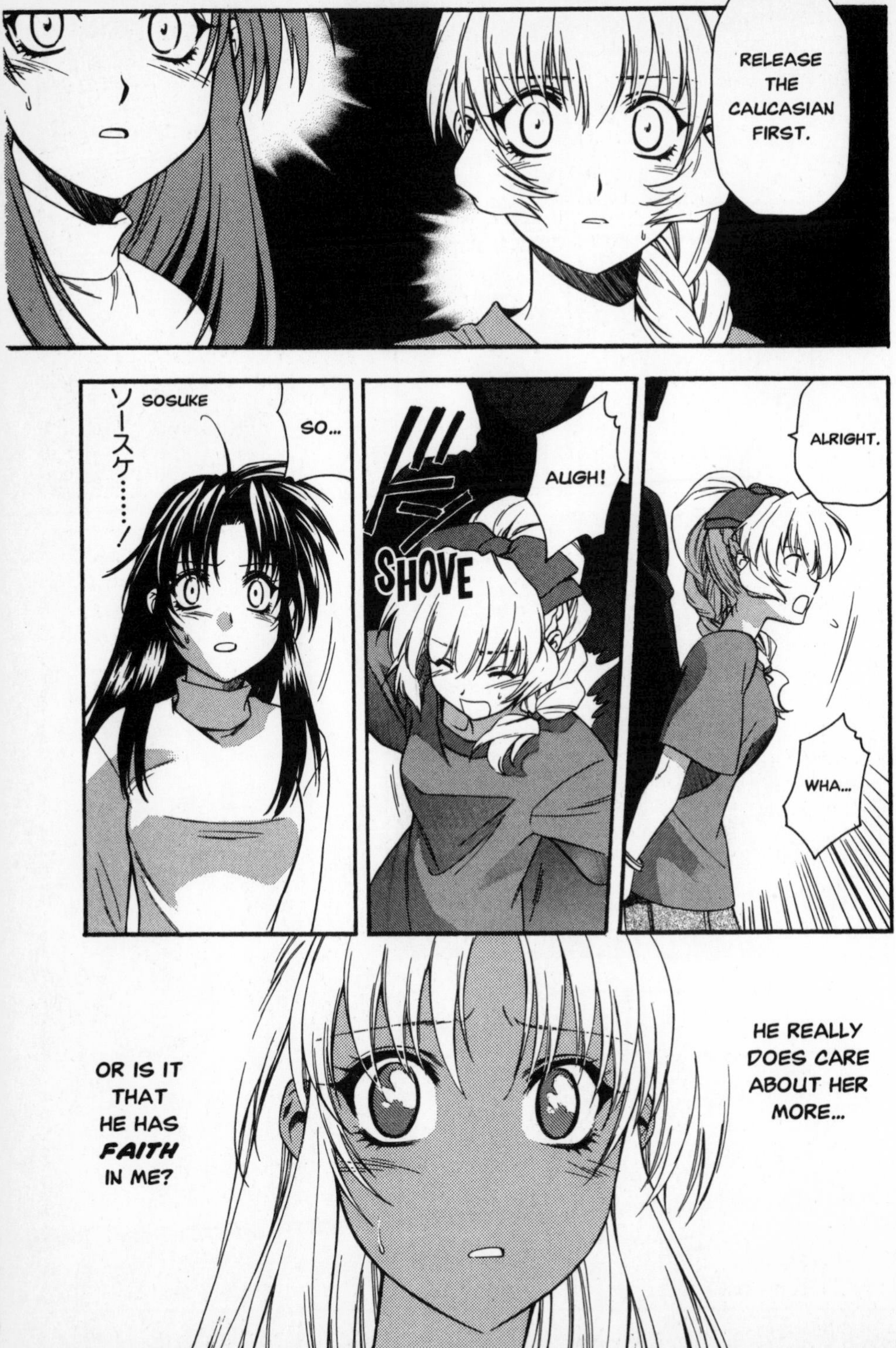
RELEASE THE CAUCASIAN FIRST.
ALRIGHT.
WHA...
AUGH!
SHOVE
SO...
SOSUKE
ソースケ……!
HE REALLY DOES CARE ABOUT HER MORE...
OR IS IT THAT HE HAS FAITH IN ME?

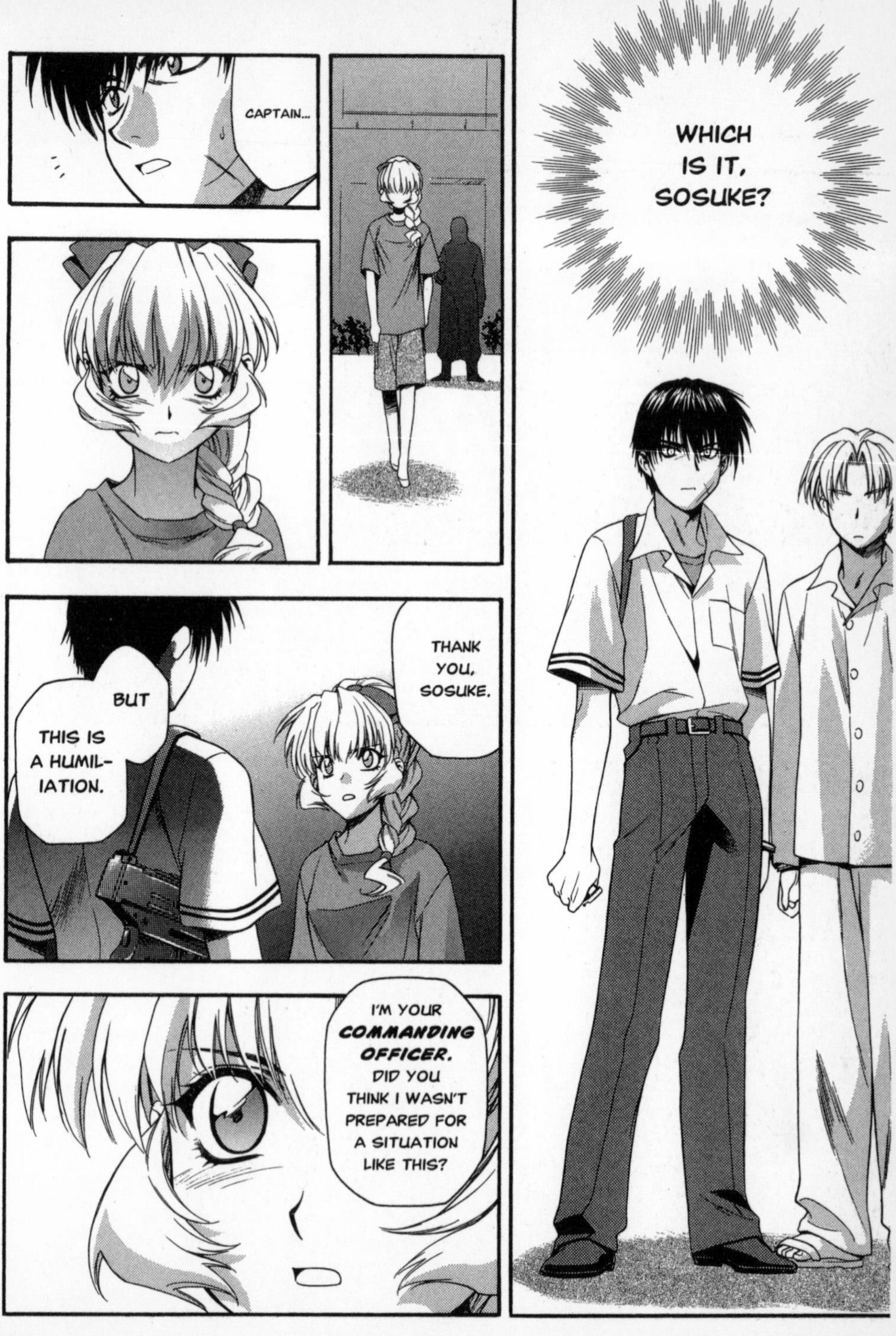
WHICH IS IT, SOSUKE?
CAPTAIN...
THANK YOU, SOSUKE.
BUT THIS IS A HUMIL- IATION.
I'M YOUR COMMANDING OFFICER. DID YOU THINK I WASN'T PREPARED FOR A SITUATION LIKE THIS?

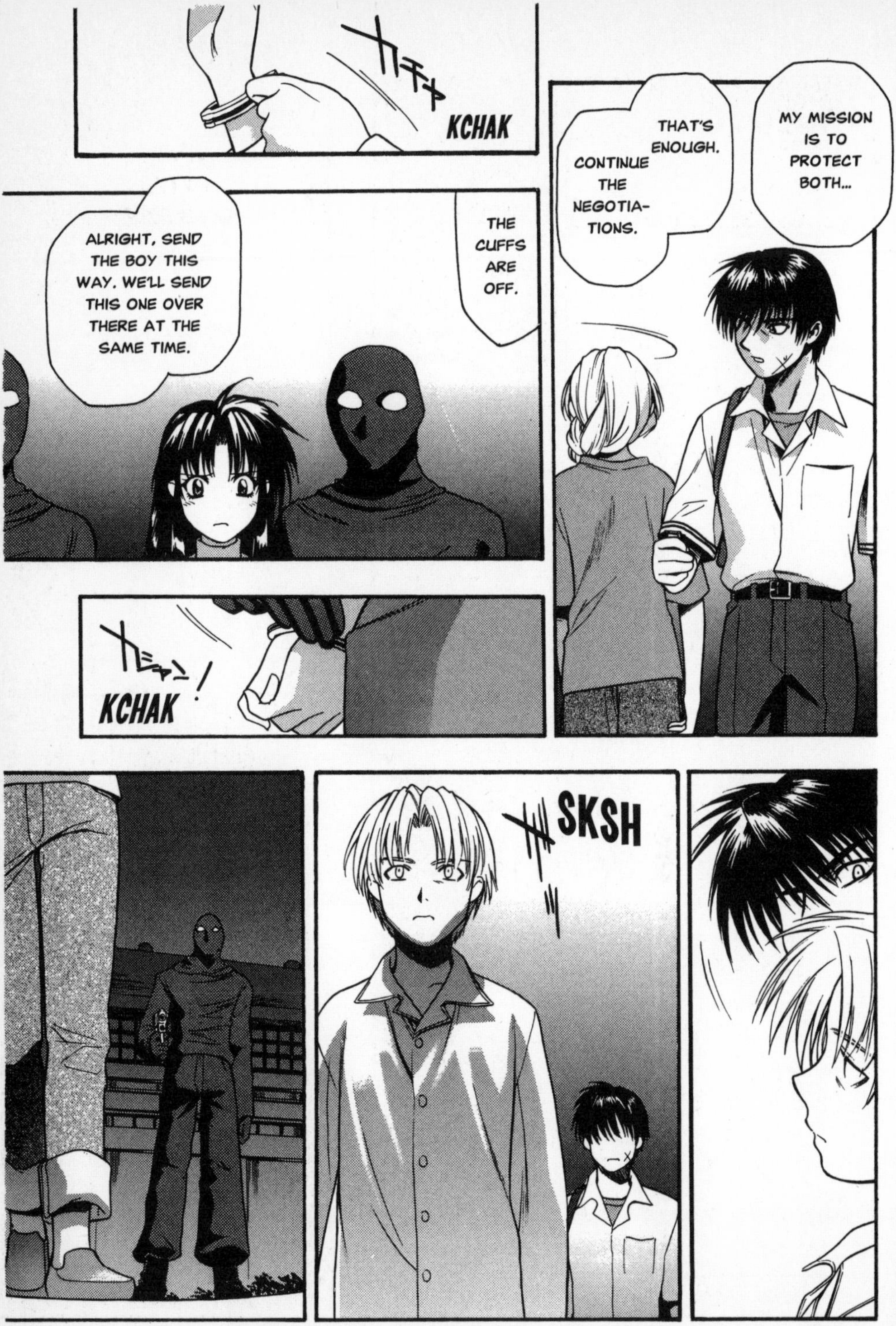
MY MISSION IS TO PROTECT BOTH...
THAT'S ENOUGH.
CONTINUE THE NEGOTIATIONS.
KCHAK
THE CUFFS ARE OFF.
ALRIGHT, SEND THE BOY THIS WAY. WE'LL SEND THIS ONE OVER THERE AT THE SAME TIME.
KCHAK
SKSH

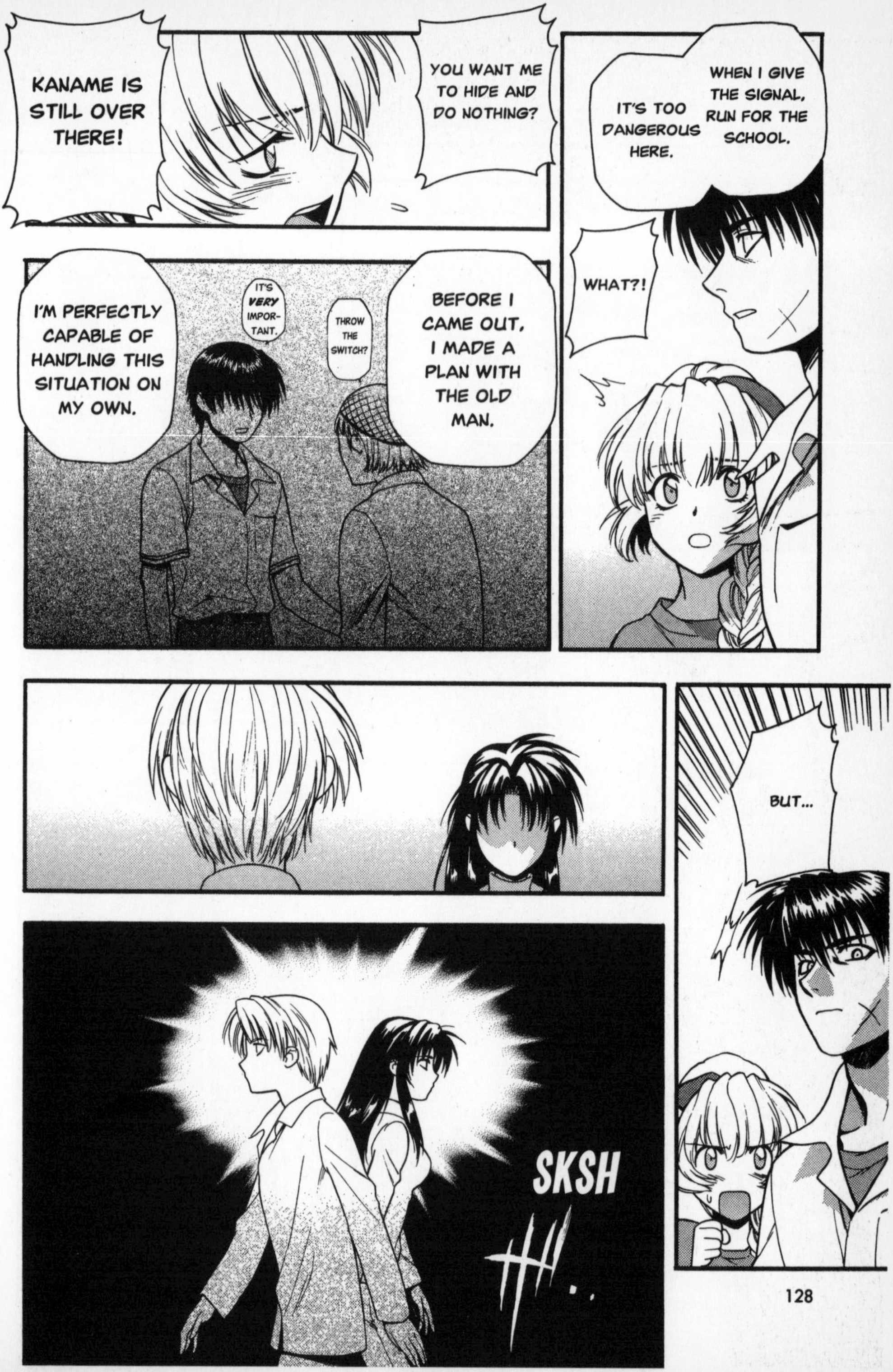
WHEN I GIVE THE SIGNAL, RUN FOR THE SCHOOL.
IT'S TOO DANGEROUS HERE.
WHAT?!
YOU WANT ME TO HIDE AND DO NOTHING?
KANAME IS STILL OVER THERE!
BEFORE I CAME OUT, I MADE A PLAN WITH THE OLD MAN.
THROW THE SWITCH?
IT'S *VERY* IMPORTANT.
I'M PERFECTLY CAPABLE OF HANDLING THIS SITUATION ON MY OWN.
BUT...
SKSH

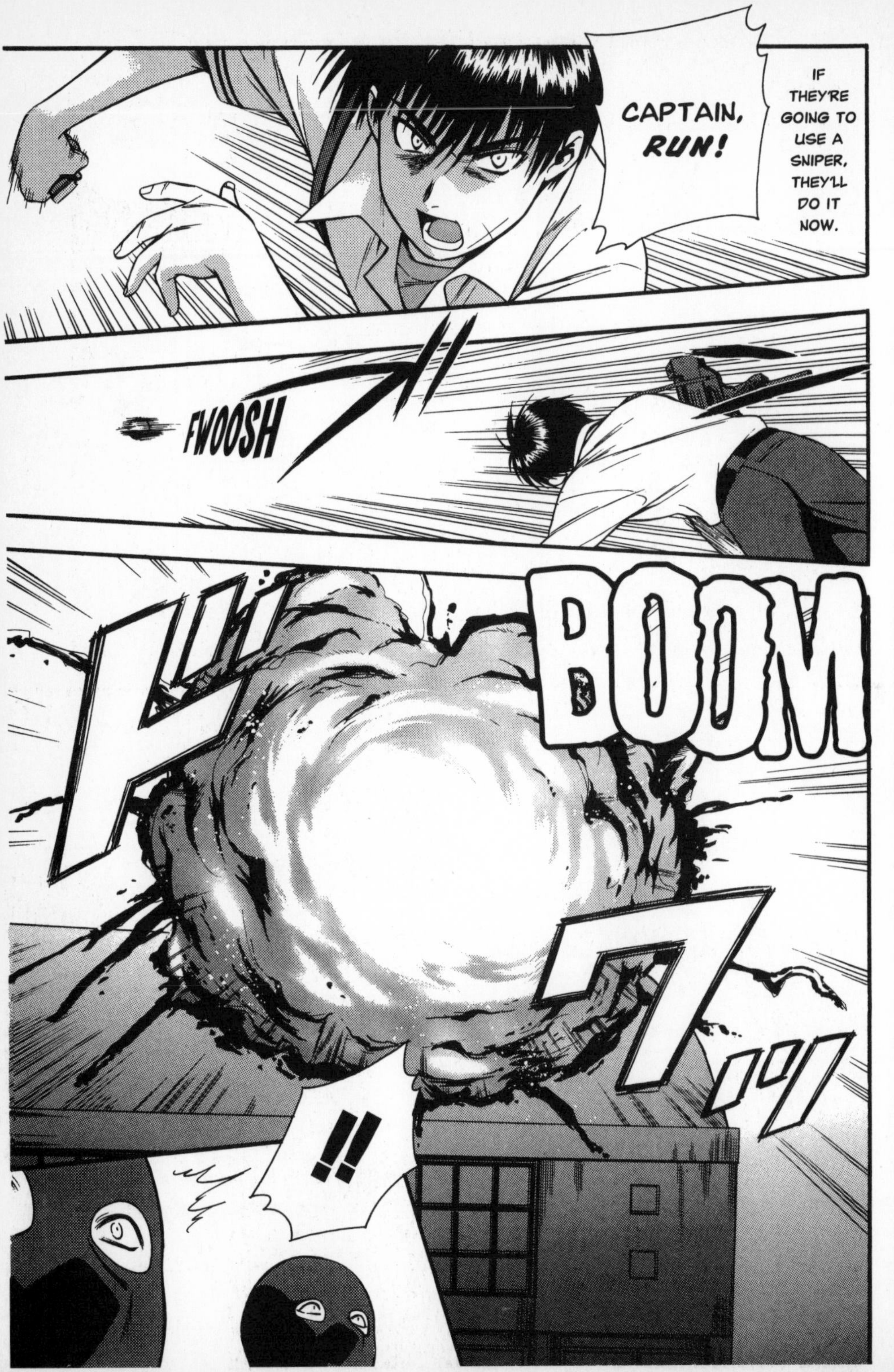
IF THEY'RE GOING TO USE A SNIPER, THEY'LL DO IT NOW.
CAPTAIN, RUN!
FWOOSH
BOOM
!!

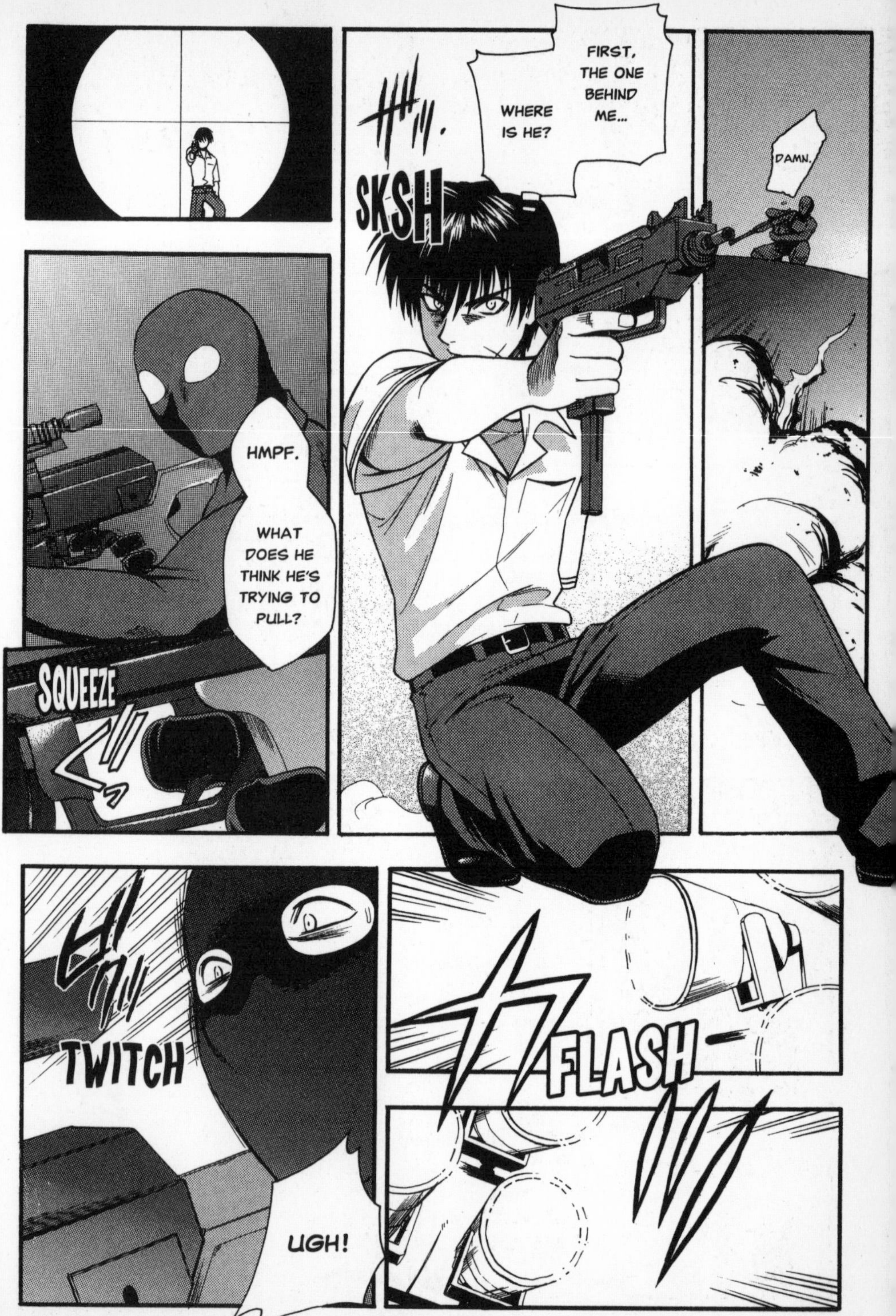
DAMN.
FIRST, THE ONE BEHIND ME...
WHERE IS HE?
SKSH
HMPF.
WHAT DOES HE THINK HE'S TRYING TO PULL?
SQUEEZE
FLASH
TWITCH
UGH!

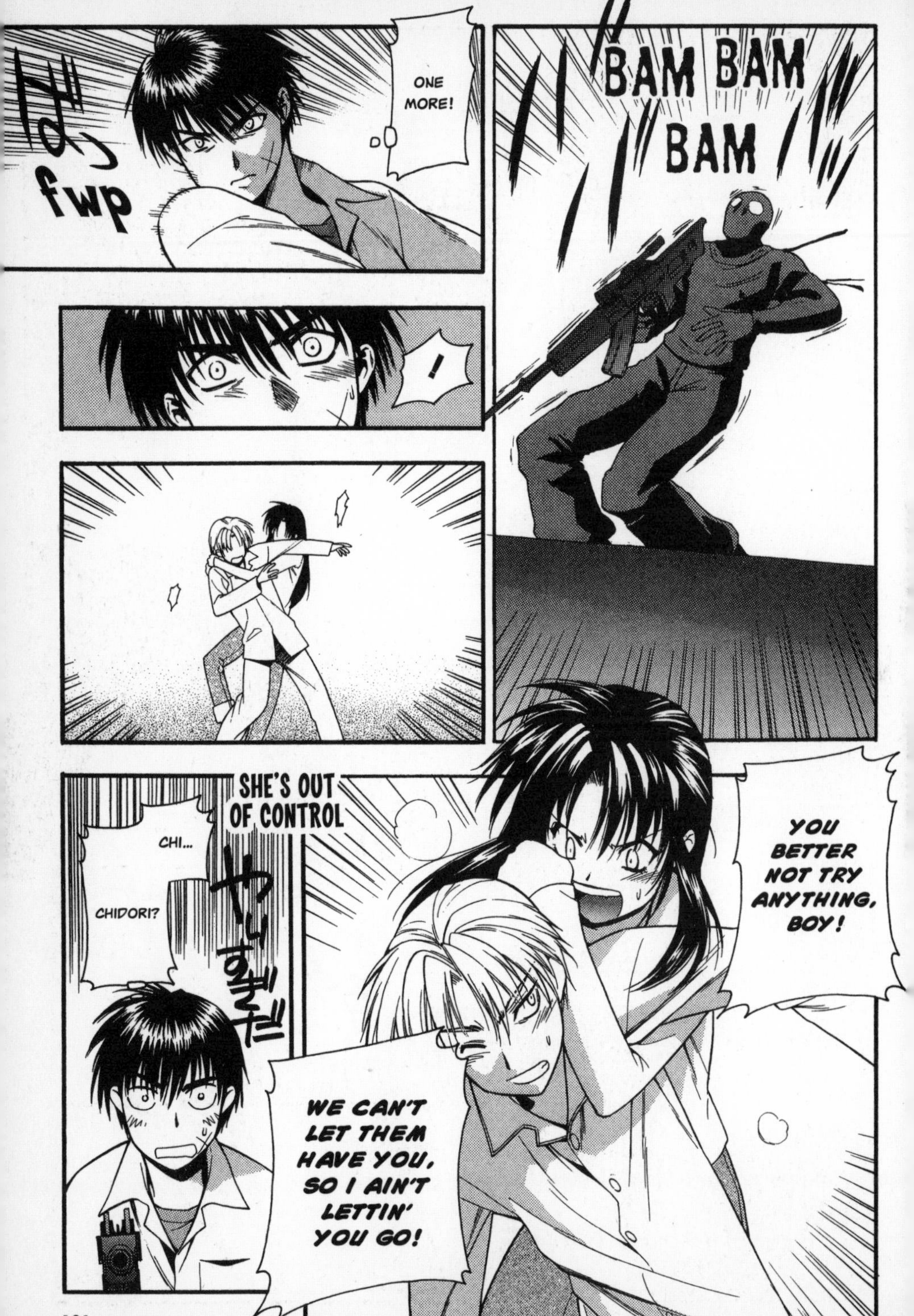
BAM BAM BAM
ばっ
fwp
ONE MORE!
!
YOU BETTER NOT TRY ANYTHING, BOY!
WE CAN'T LET THEM HAVE YOU, SO I AIN'T LETTIN' YOU GO!
SHE'S OUT OF CONTROL
やりすぎだ
CHI...
CHIDORI?

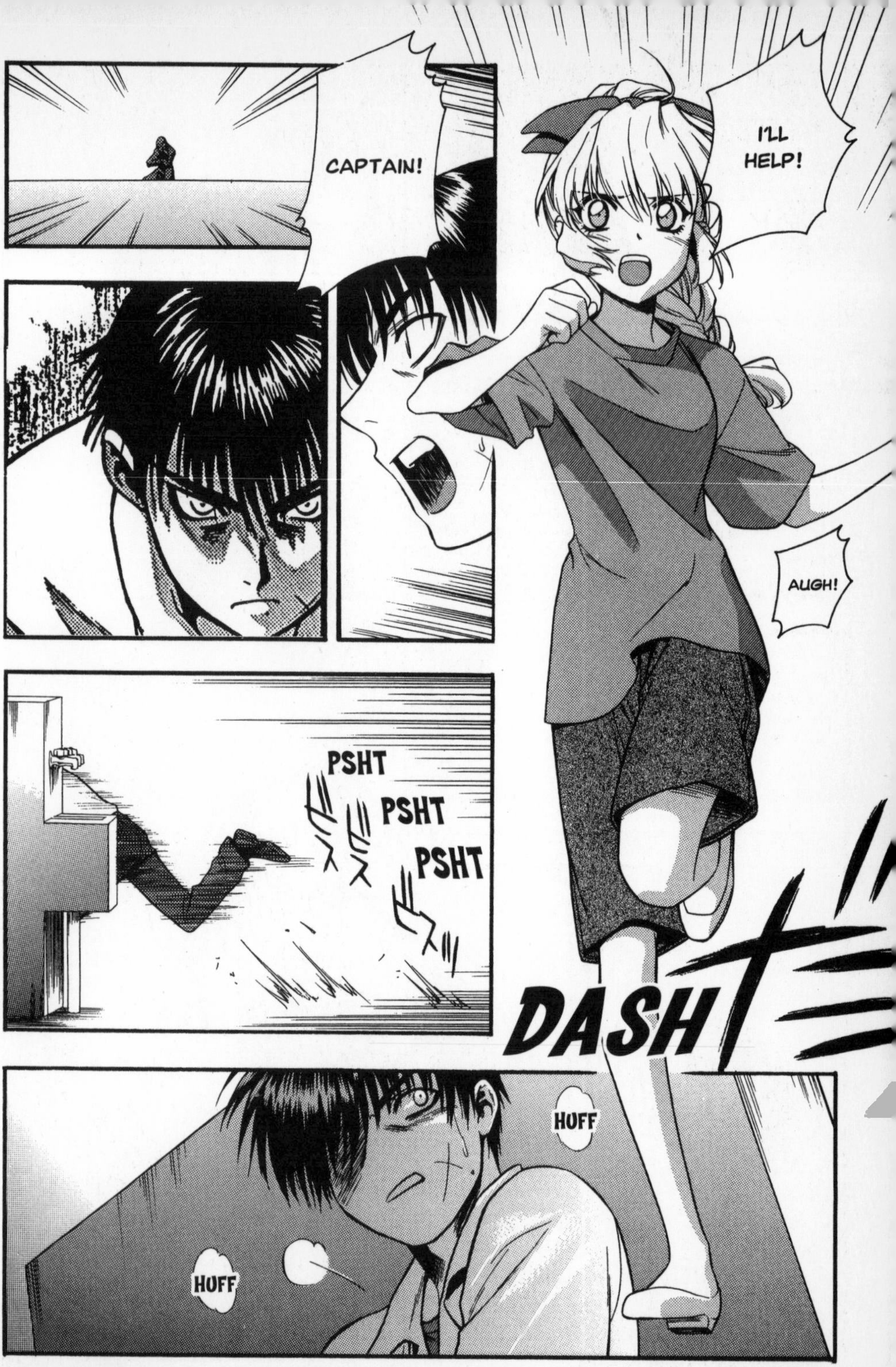

CAPTAIN!
I'LL HELP!
AUGH!
PSHT
PSHT
PSHT
DASH
HUFF
HUFF

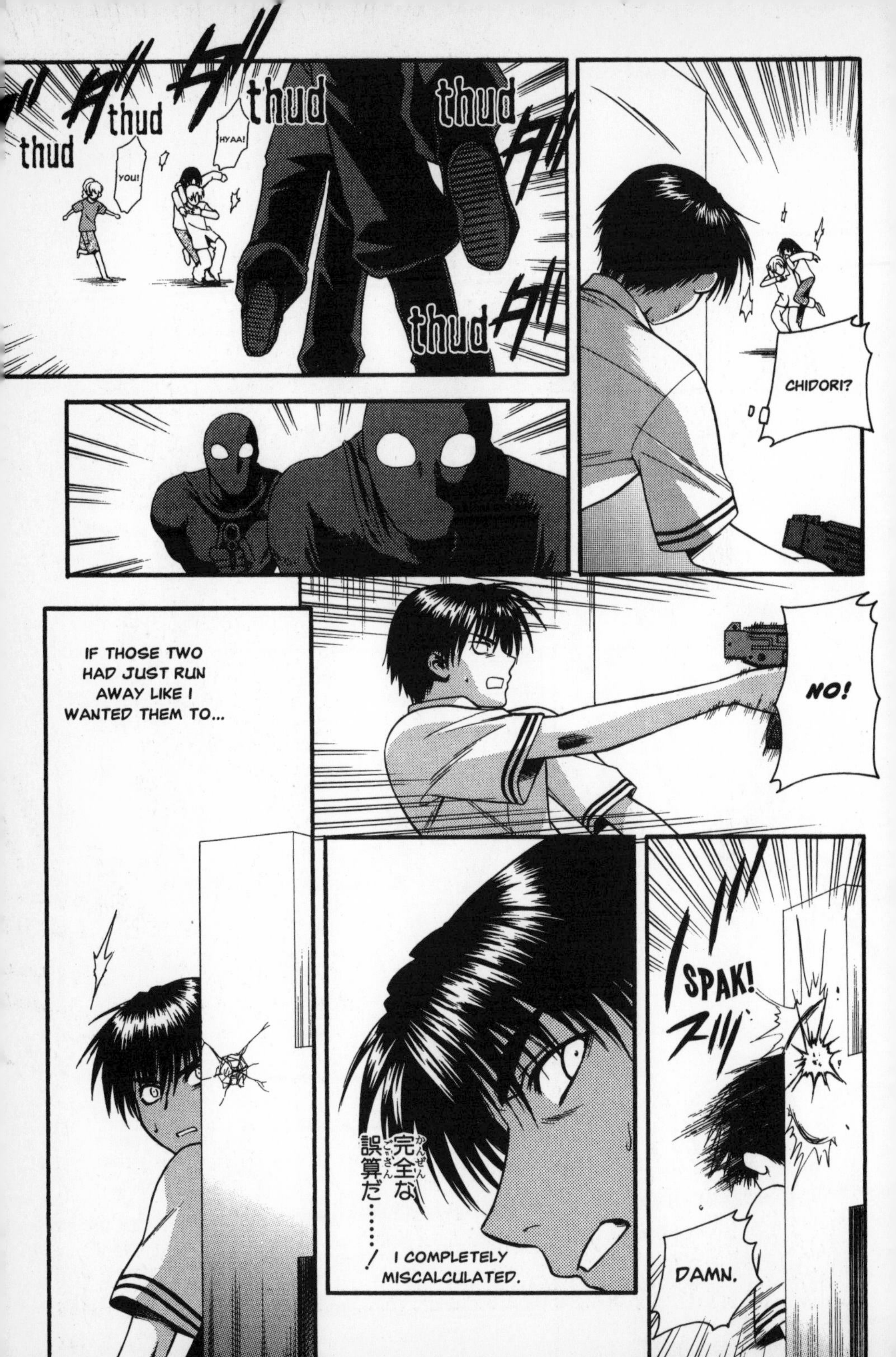
CHIDORI?
thud
thud
thud
HYAA!
YOU!
thud
thud
NO!
SPAK!
DAMN.
完全な誤算だ……!
I COMPLETELY MISCALCULATED.
IF THOSE TWO HAD JUST RUN AWAY LIKE I WANTED THEM TO...

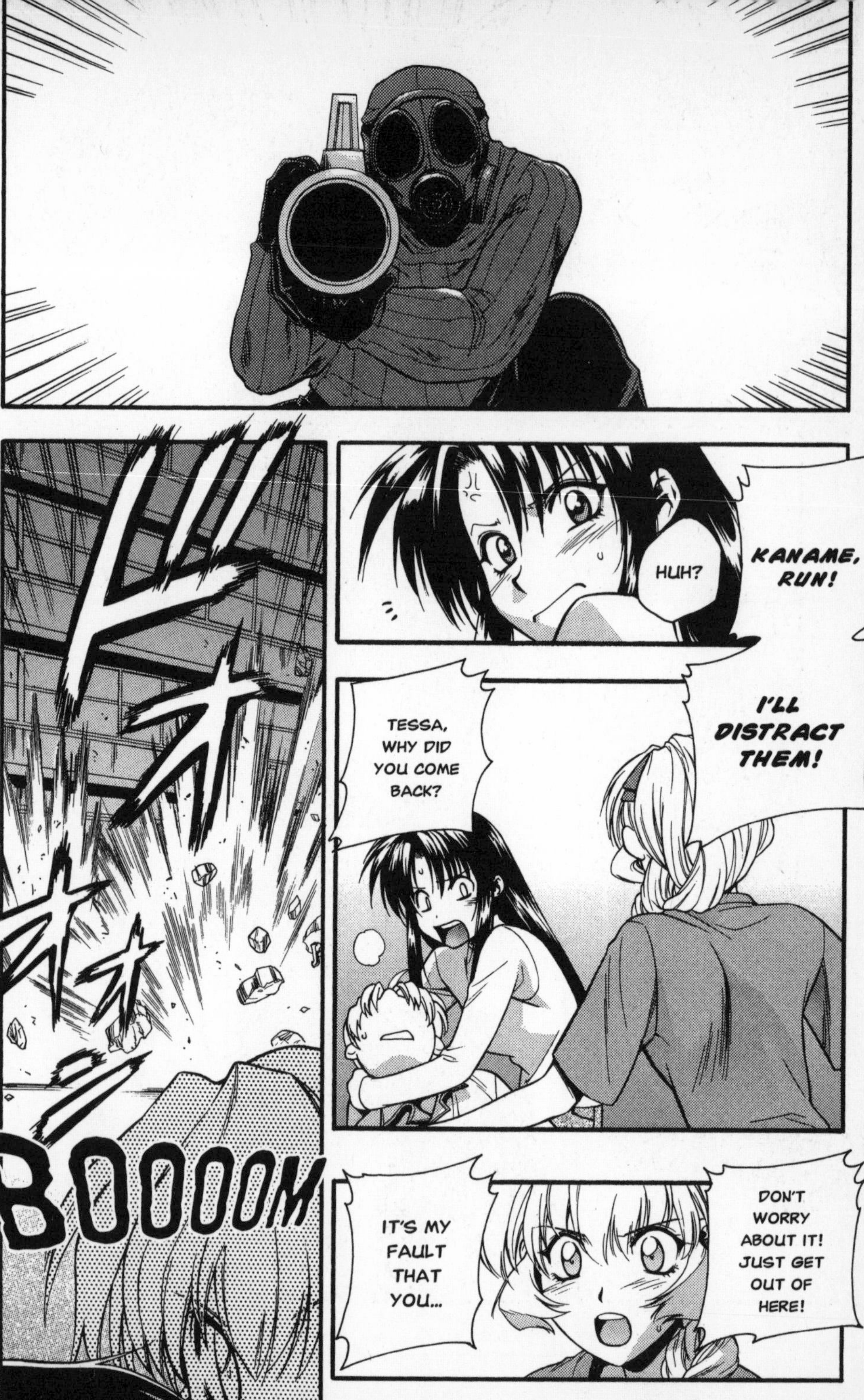
KANAME, RUN!
HUH?
I'LL DISTRACT THEM!
TESSA, WHY DID YOU COME BACK?
DON'T WORRY ABOUT IT! JUST GET OUT OF HERE!
IT'S MY FAULT THAT YOU...
BOOOOM

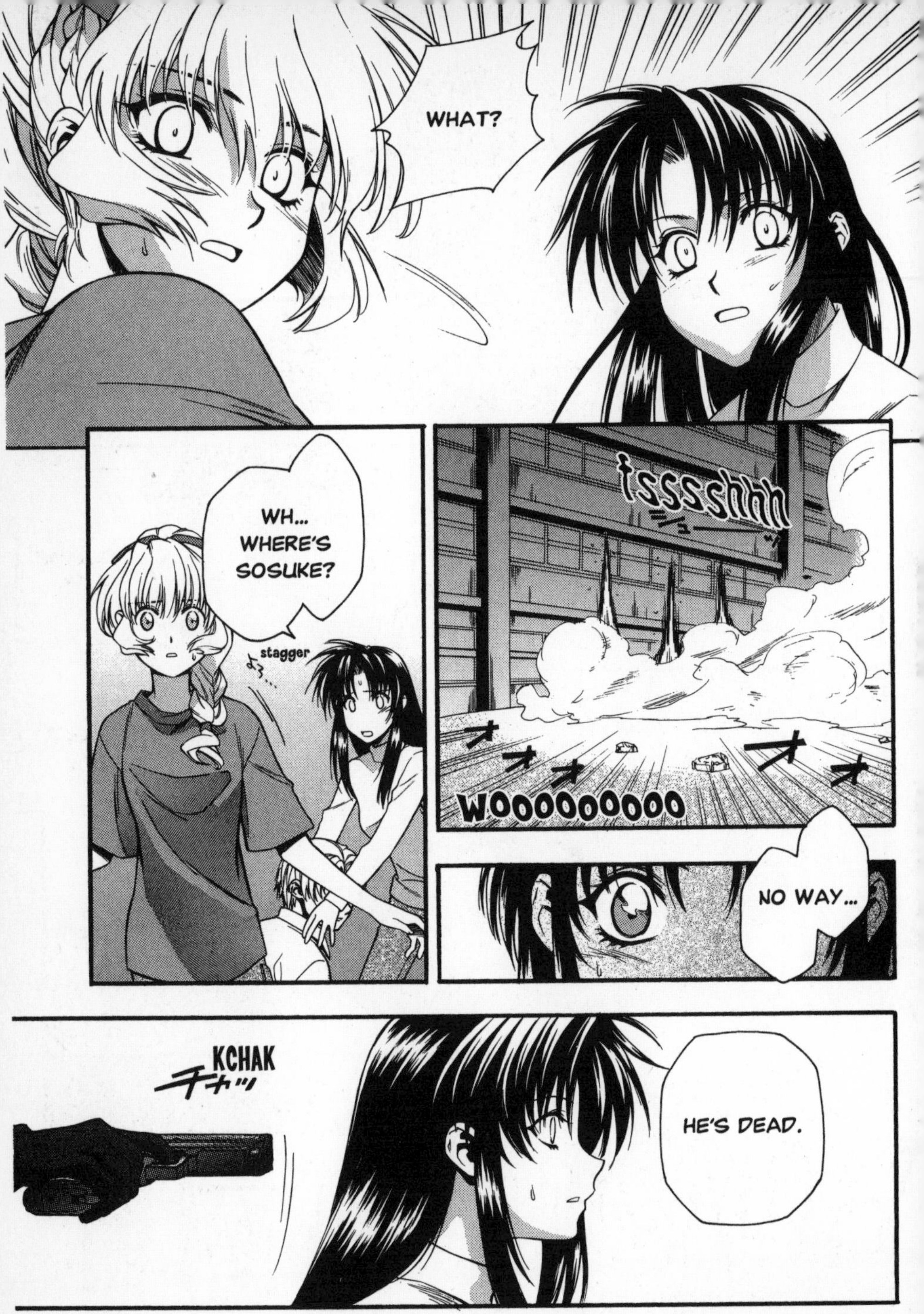
WHAT?
tssssHHH
WOOOOOOOOO
NO WAY...
WH... WHERE'S SOSUKE?
stagger
HE'S DEAD.
KCHAK

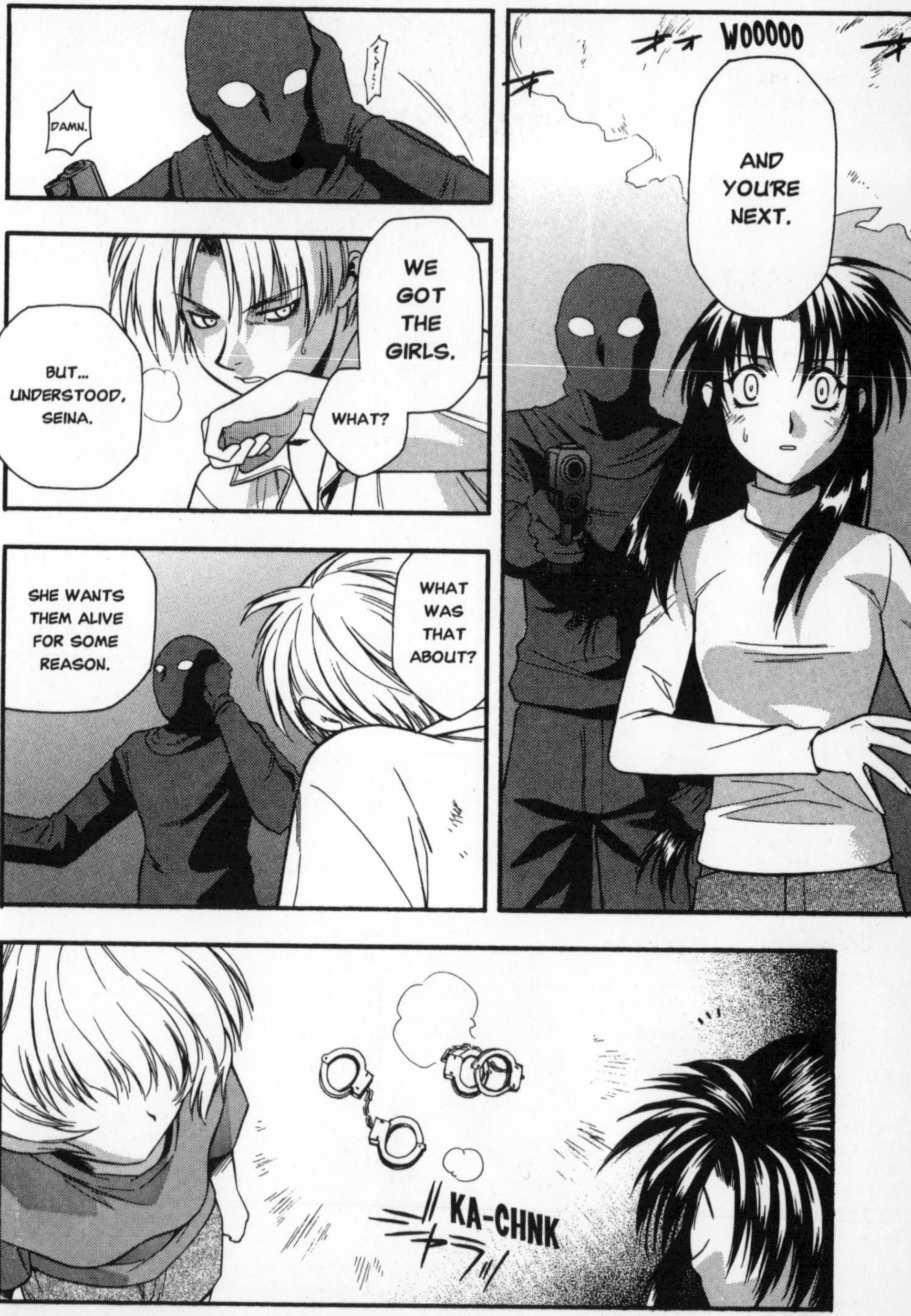
WOOOOO
AND YOU'RE NEXT.
DAMN.
WE GOT THE GIRLS.
WHAT?
BUT... UNDERSTOOD, SEINA.
WHAT WAS THAT ABOUT?
SHE WANTS THEM ALIVE FOR SOME REASON.
KA-CHNK

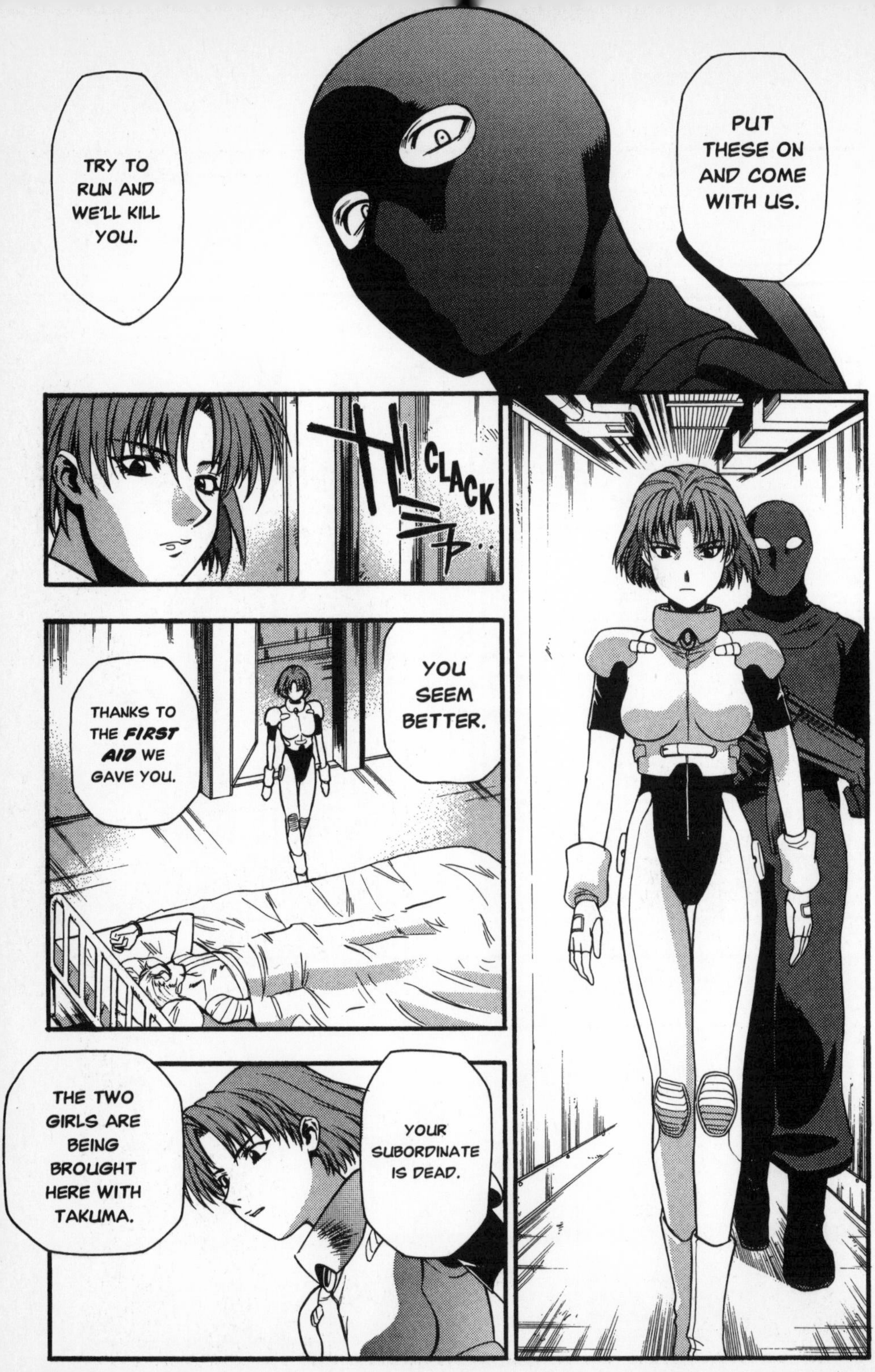
PUT THESE ON AND COME WITH US.
TRY TO RUN AND WE'LL KILL YOU.
CLACK
YOU SEEM BETTER.
THANKS TO THE ***FIRST AID*** WE GAVE YOU.
YOUR SUBORDINATE IS DEAD.
THE TWO GIRLS ARE BEING BROUGHT HERE WITH TAKUMA.

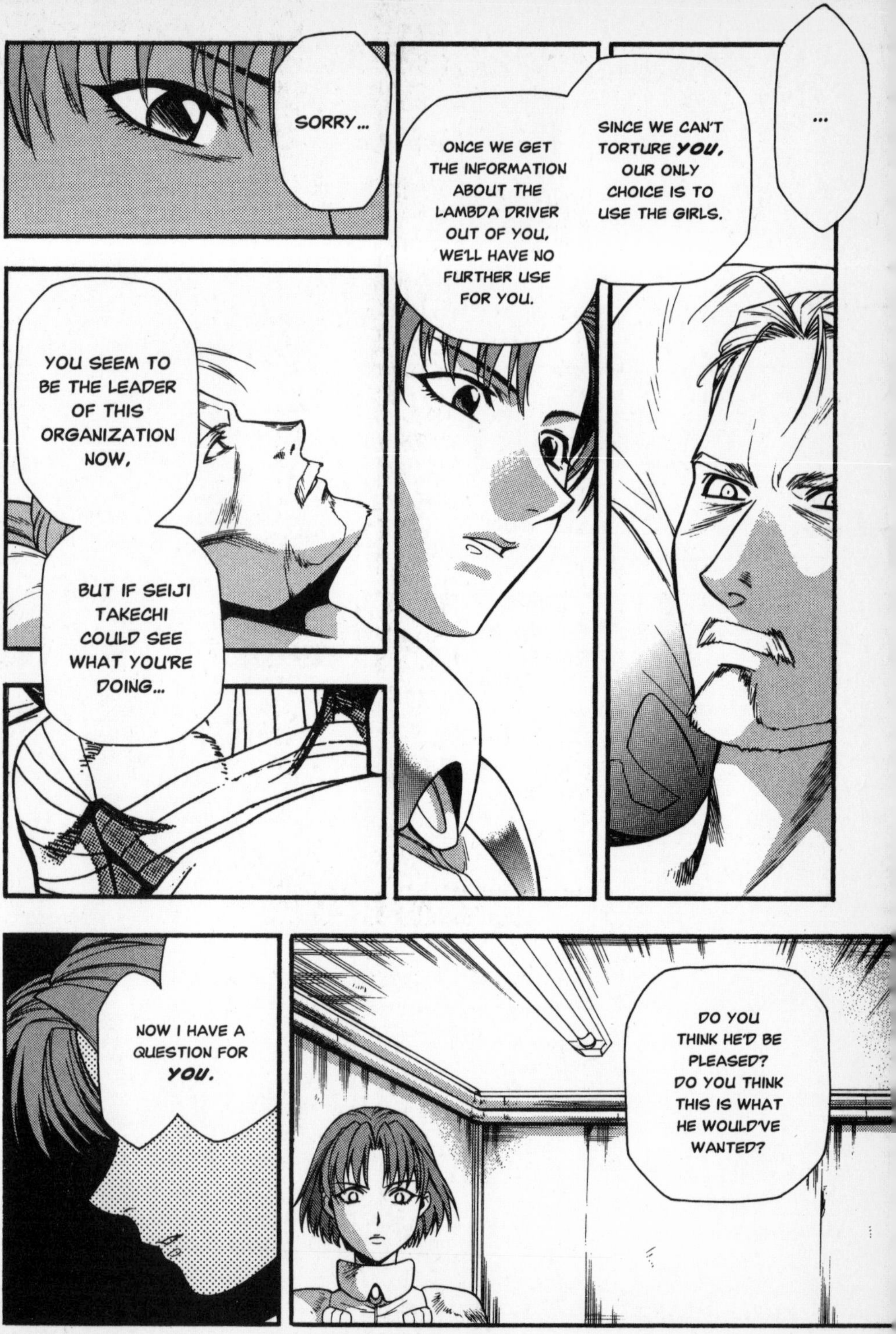
...
SINCE WE CAN'T TORTURE ***YOU,*** OUR ONLY CHOICE IS TO USE THE GIRLS.
ONCE WE GET THE INFORMATION ABOUT THE LAMBDA DRIVER OUT OF YOU, WE'LL HAVE NO FURTHER USE FOR YOU.
SORRY...
YOU SEEM TO BE THE LEADER OF THIS ORGANIZATION NOW,
BUT IF SEIJI TAKECHI COULD SEE WHAT YOU'RE DOING...
DO YOU THINK HE'D BE PLEASED? DO YOU THINK THIS IS WHAT HE WOULD'VE WANTED?
NOW I HAVE A QUESTION FOR ***YOU.***

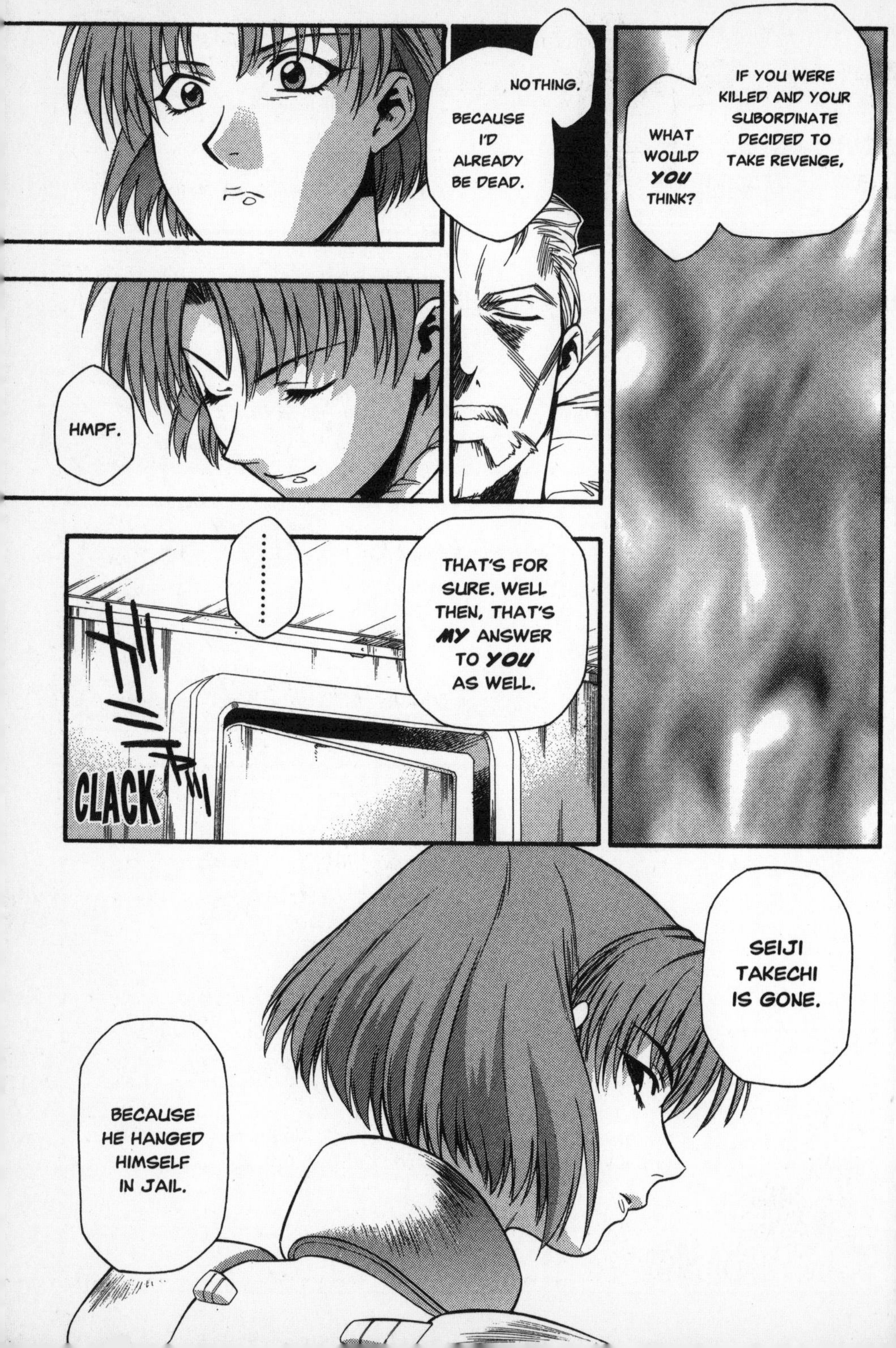
IF YOU WERE KILLED AND YOUR SUBORDINATE DECIDED TO TAKE REVENGE,
WHAT WOULD *YOU* THINK?
NOTHING.
BECAUSE I'D ALREADY BE DEAD.
HMPF.
THAT'S FOR SURE. WELL THEN, THAT'S *MY* ANSWER TO *YOU* AS WELL.
……
CLACK
SEIJI TAKECHI IS GONE.
BECAUSE HE HANGED HIMSELF IN JAIL.

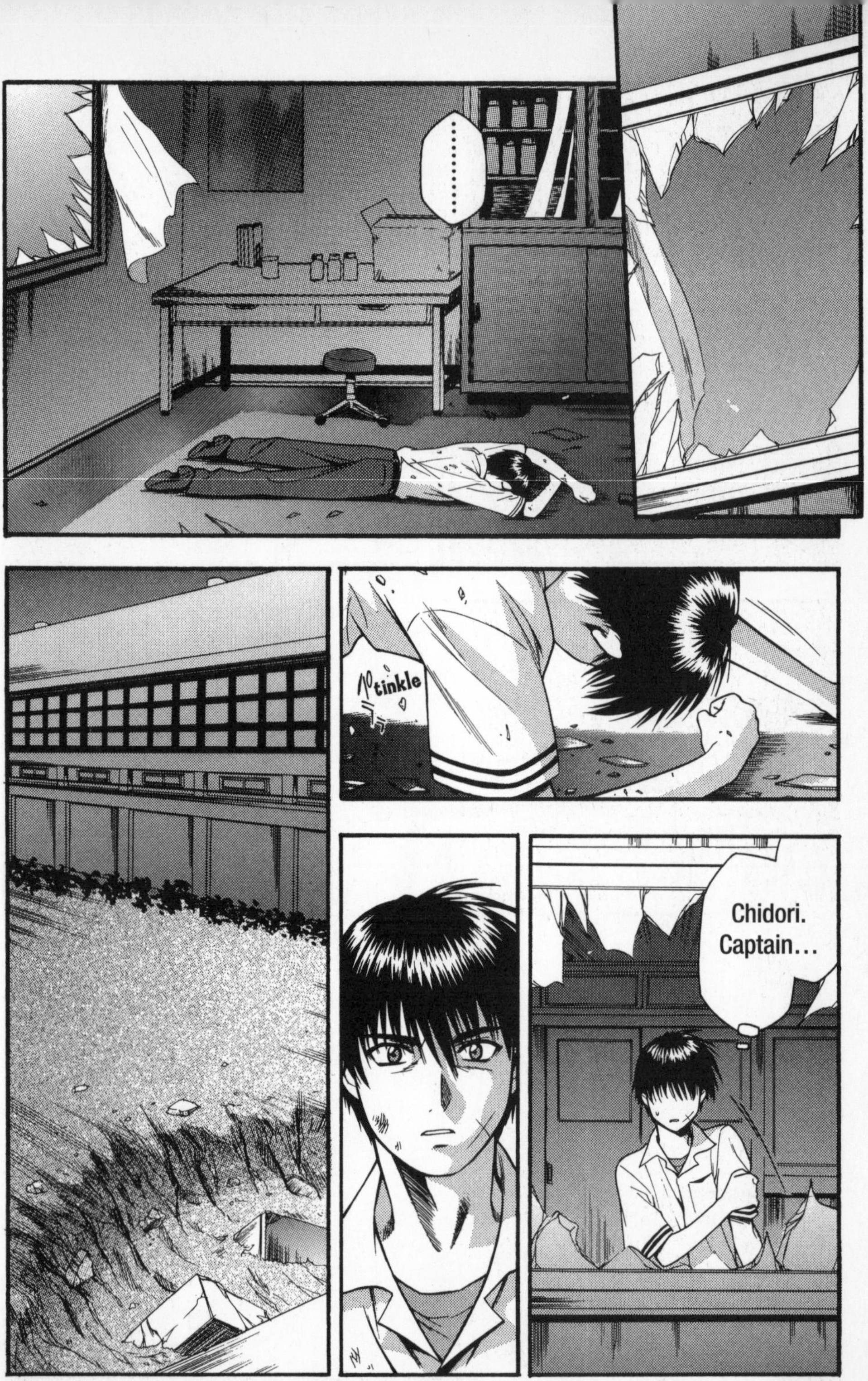
……
tinkle
Chidori. Captain…

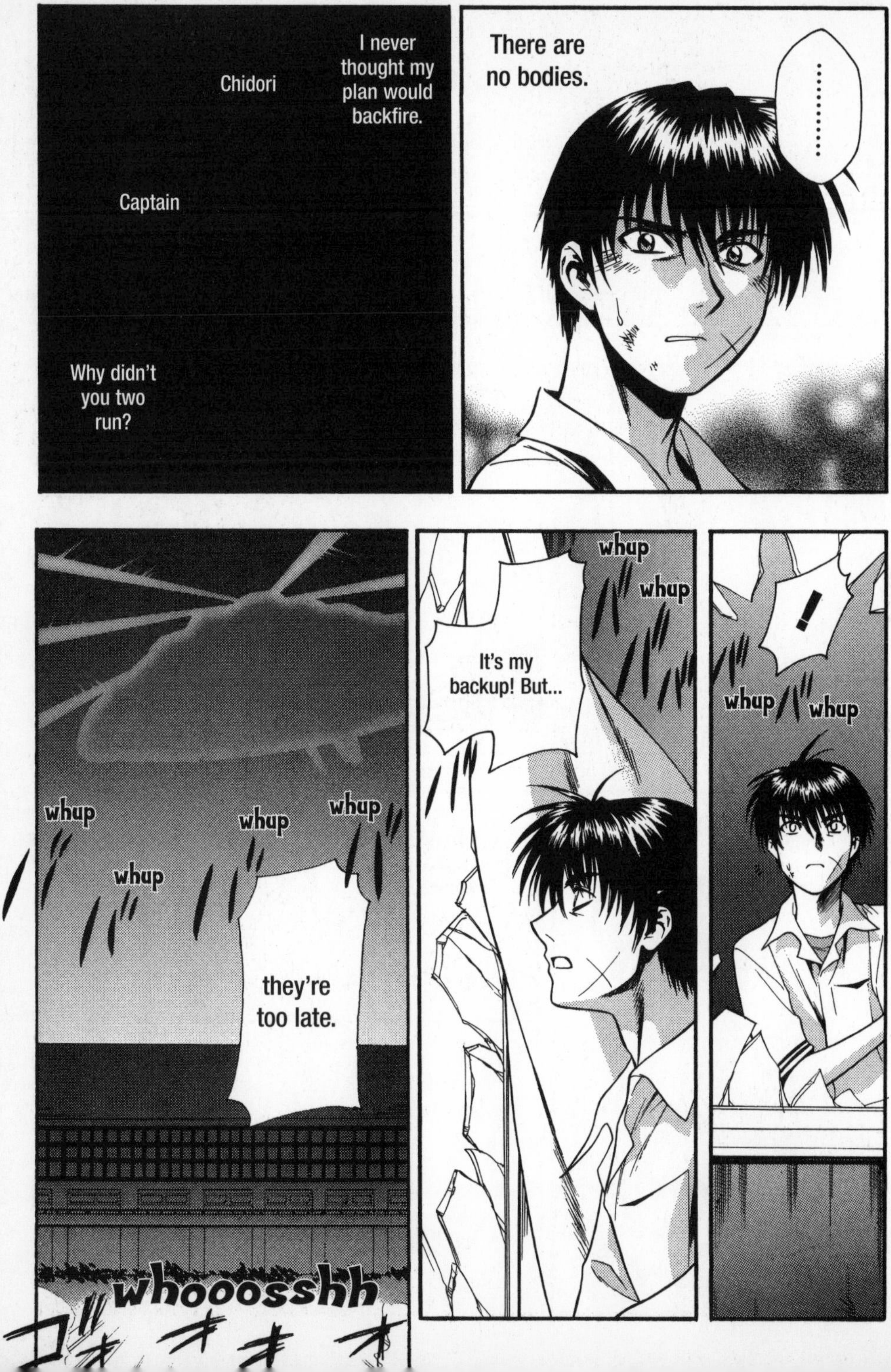
There are no bodies.
......
I never thought my plan would backfire.
Chidori
Captain
Why didn't you two run?
!
whup
whup
whup
whup
It's my backup! But...
whup
whup
whup
whup
they're too late.
whooosshh
ゴォオオオ

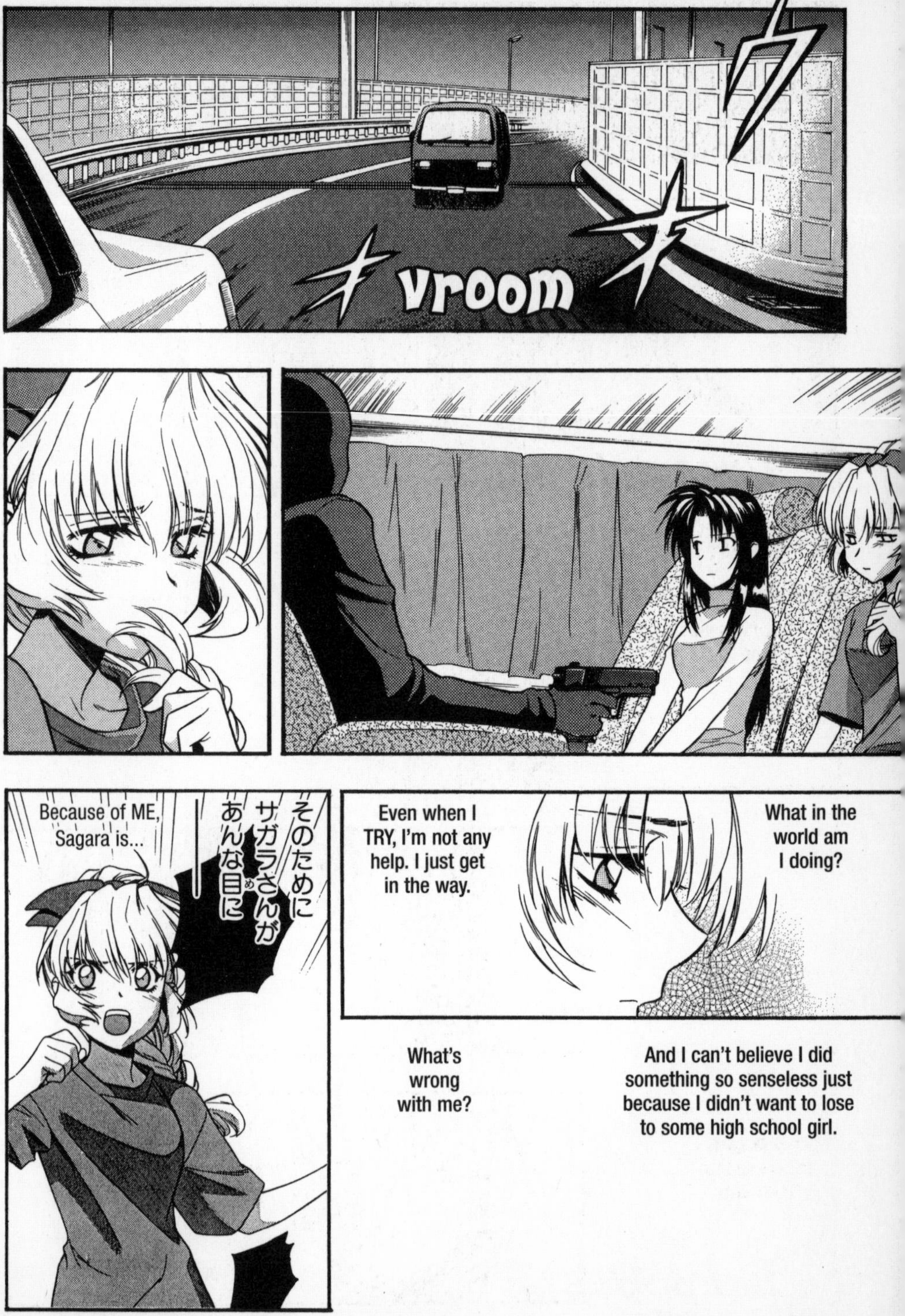
vroom
What in the world am I doing?
Even when I TRY, I'm not any help. I just get in the way.
Because of ME, Sagara is...
そのためにサガラさんがあんな目に——
And I can't believe I did something so senseless just because I didn't want to lose to some high school girl.
What's wrong with me?

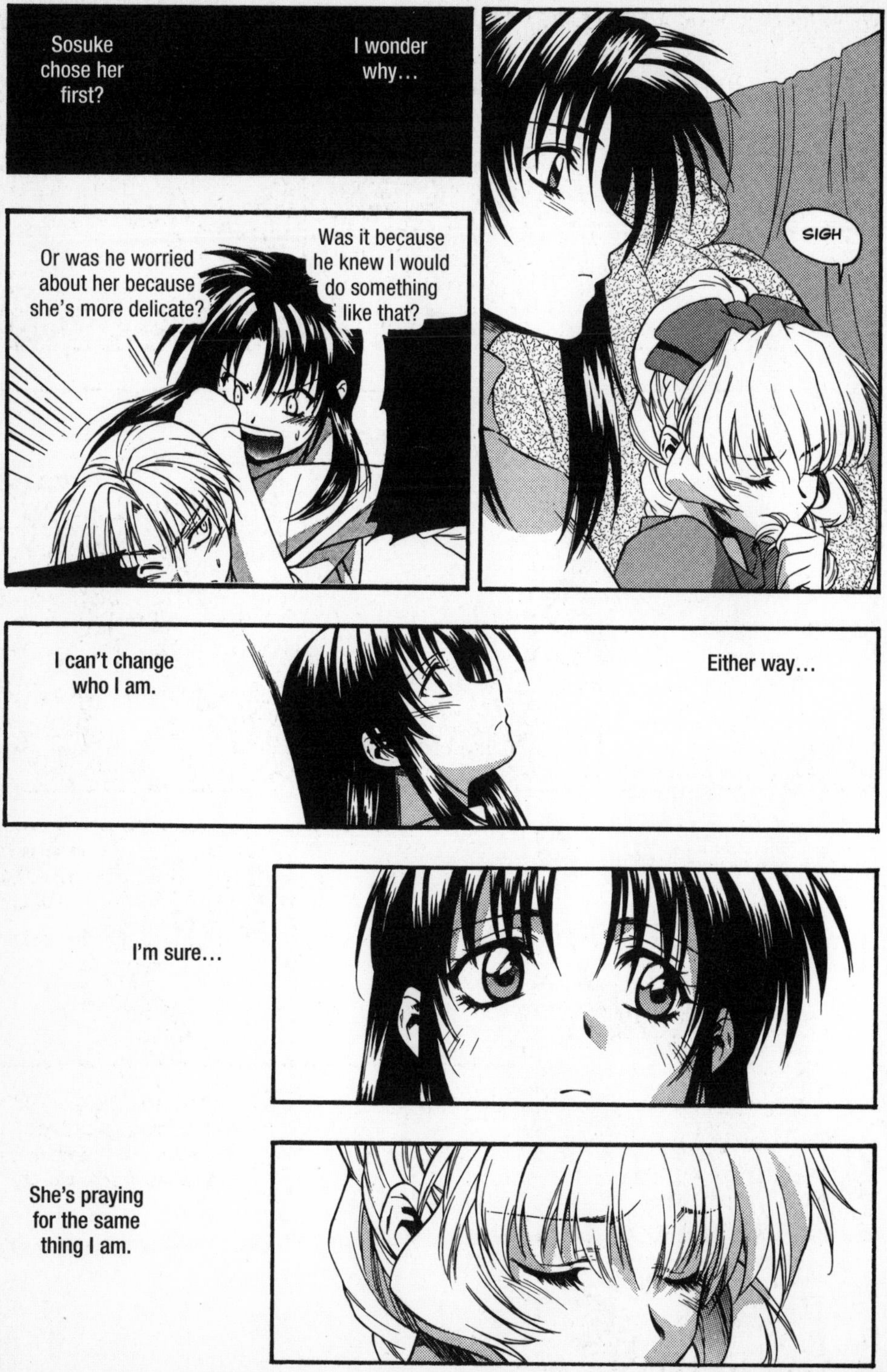
SIGH
I wonder why…
Sosuke chose her first?
Was it because he knew I would do something like that?
Or was he worried about her because she's more delicate?
Either way…
I can't change who I am.
I'm sure…
She's praying for the same thing I am.

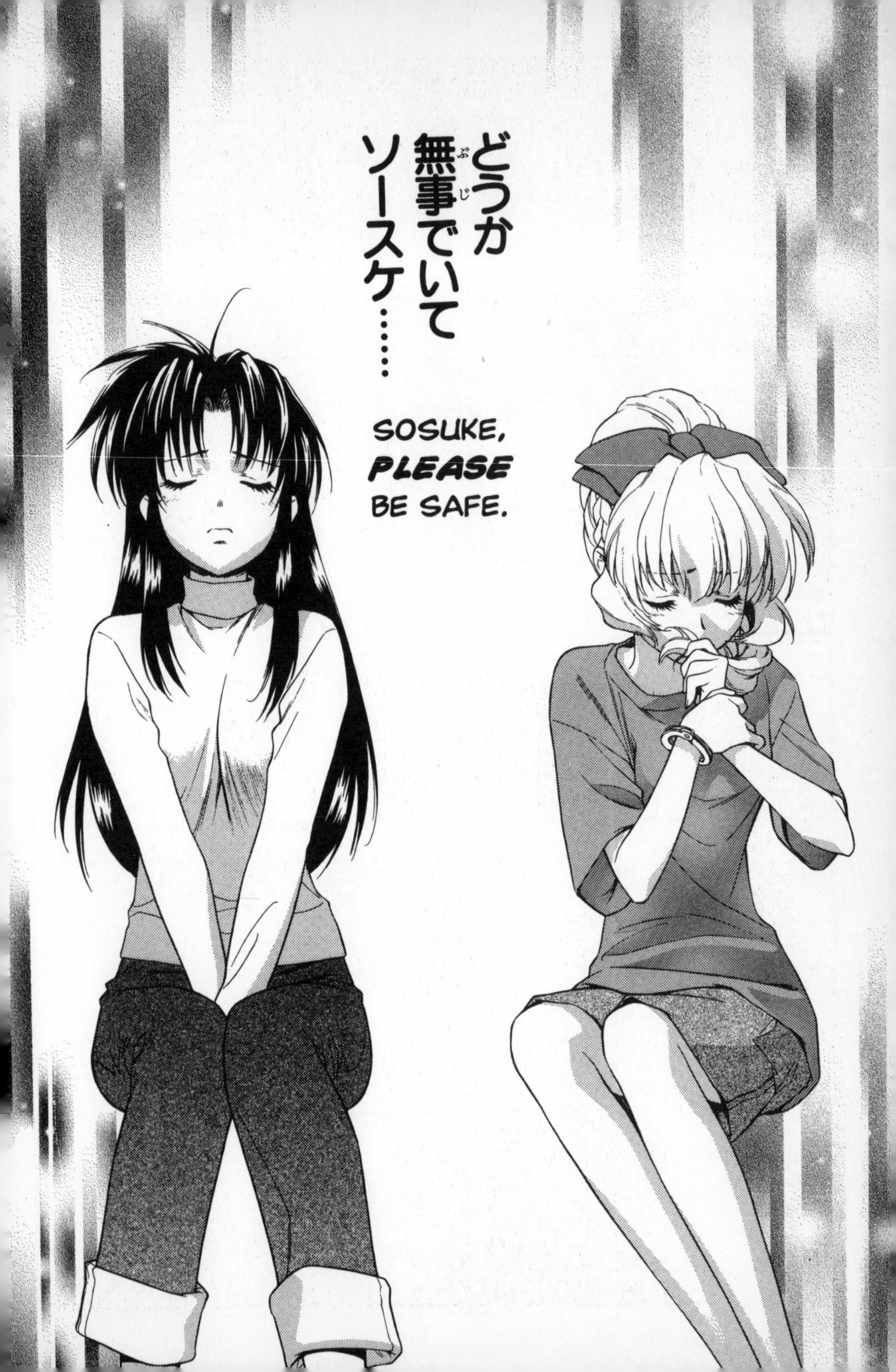
どうか無事でいてソースケ……
SOSUKE, **PLEASE** BE SAFE.

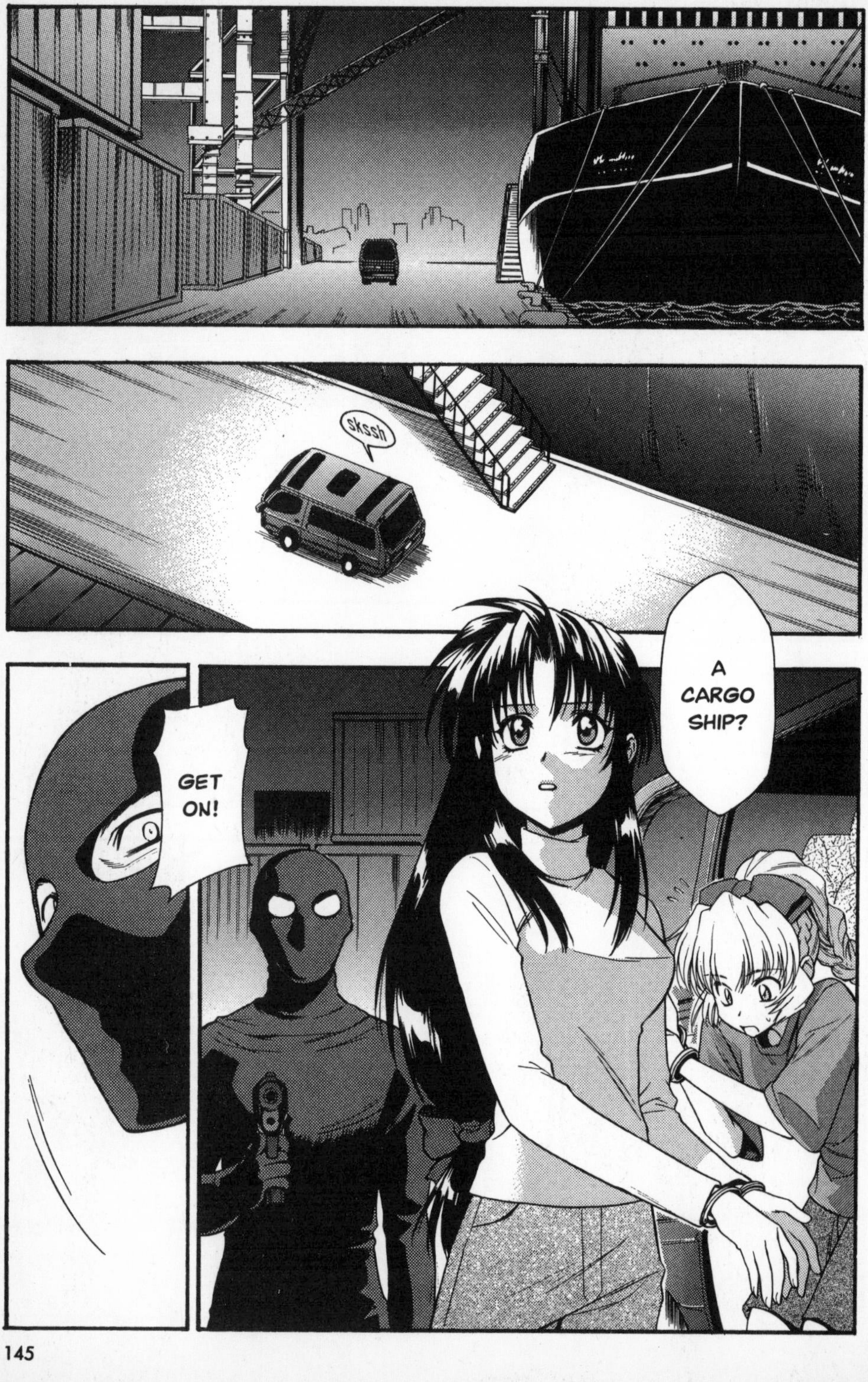
sksssh
A CARGO SHIP?
GET ON!

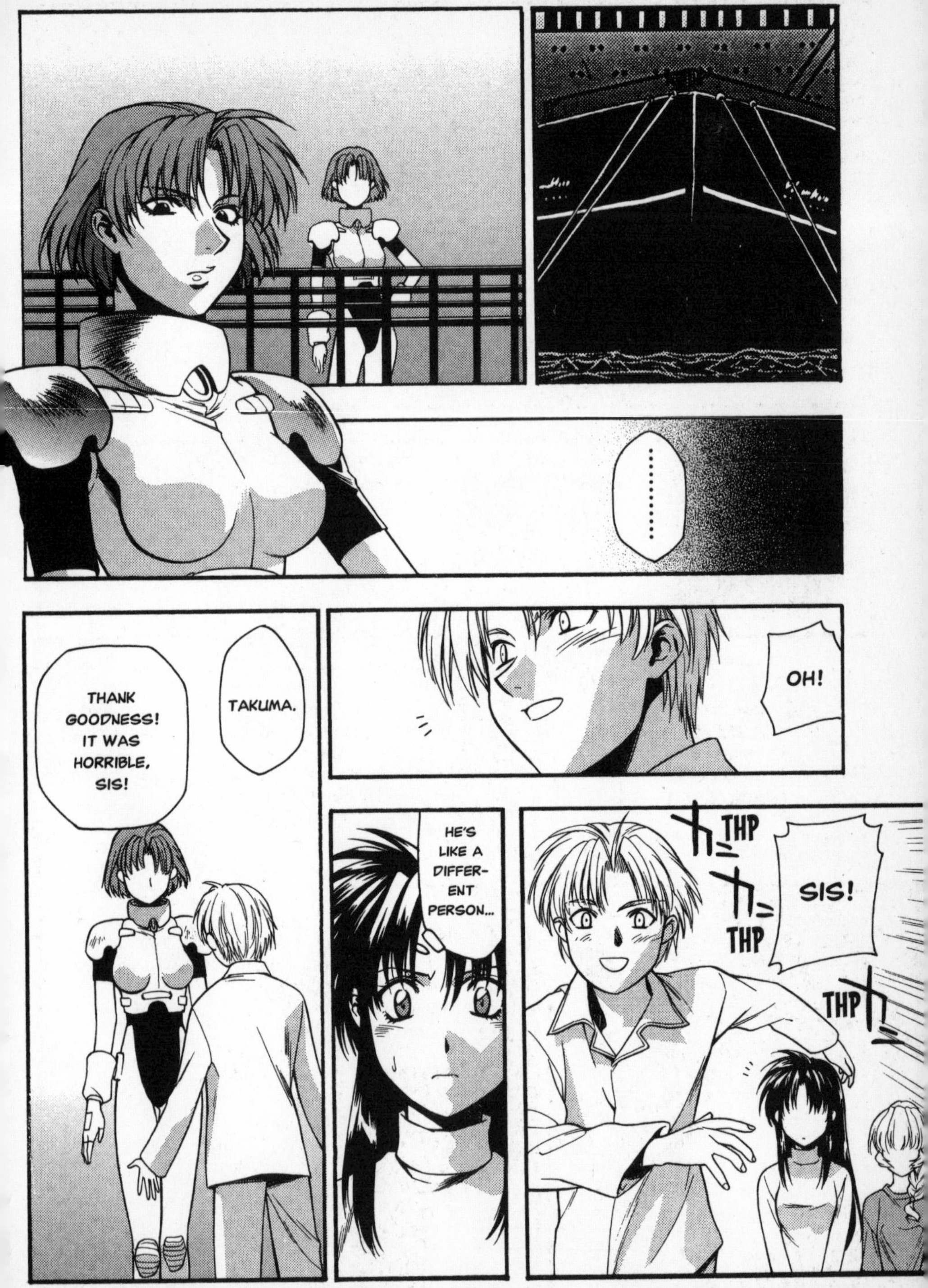
......
OH!
SIS!
THP
THP
THP
HE'S LIKE A DIFFER-ENT PERSON...
TAKUMA.
THANK GOODNESS! IT WAS HORRIBLE, SIS!

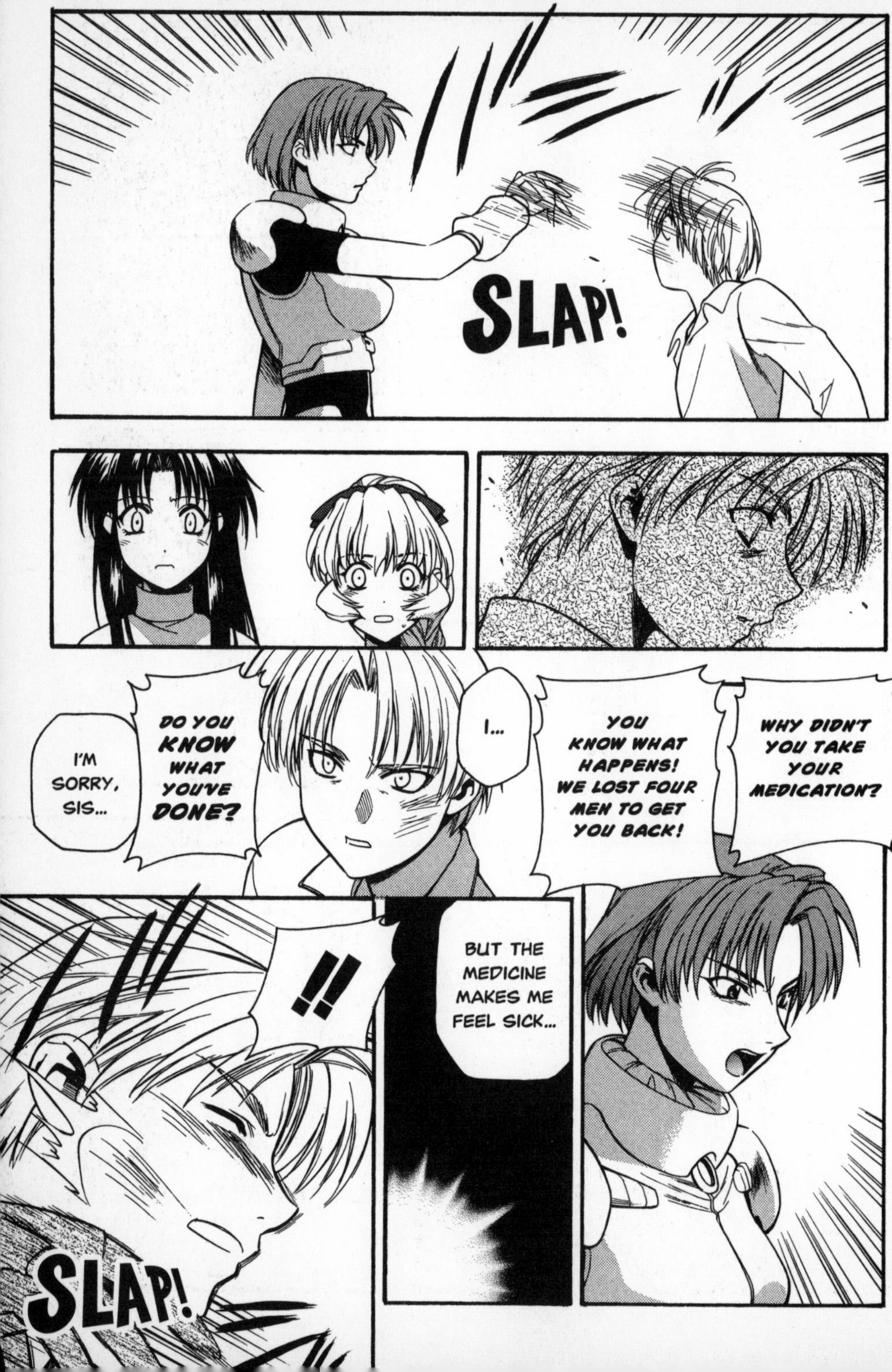
SLAP!
WHY DIDN'T YOU TAKE YOUR MEDICATION?
YOU KNOW WHAT HAPPENS! WE LOST FOUR MEN TO GET YOU BACK!
I...
DO YOU KNOW WHAT YOU'VE DONE?
I'M SORRY, SIS...
BUT THE MEDICINE MAKES ME FEEL SICK...
!!
SLAP!

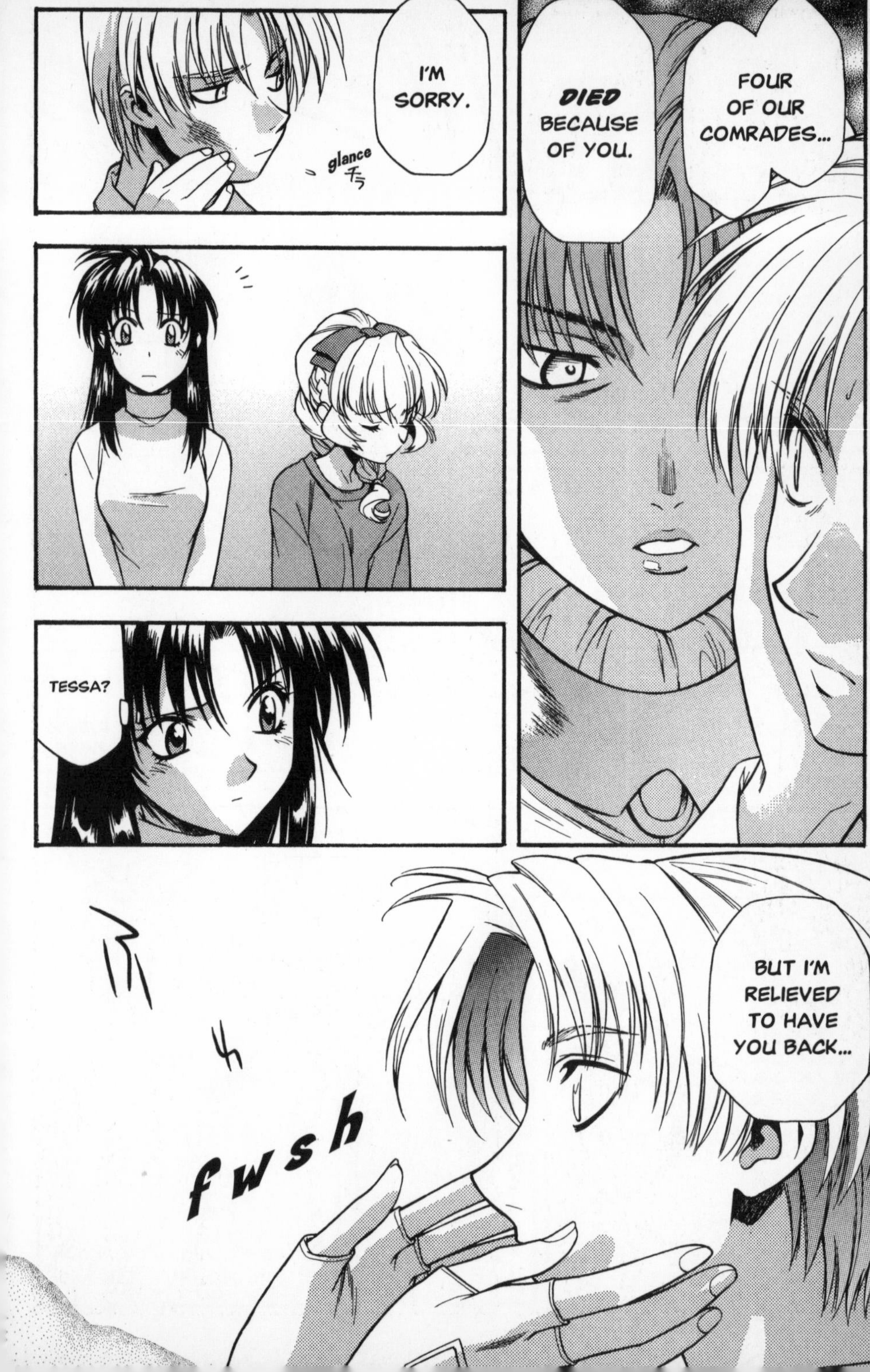
FOUR OF OUR COMRADES...
DIED BECAUSE OF YOU.
I'M SORRY.
glance
チラ
TESSA?
BUT I'M RELIEVED TO HAVE YOU BACK...
fwsh

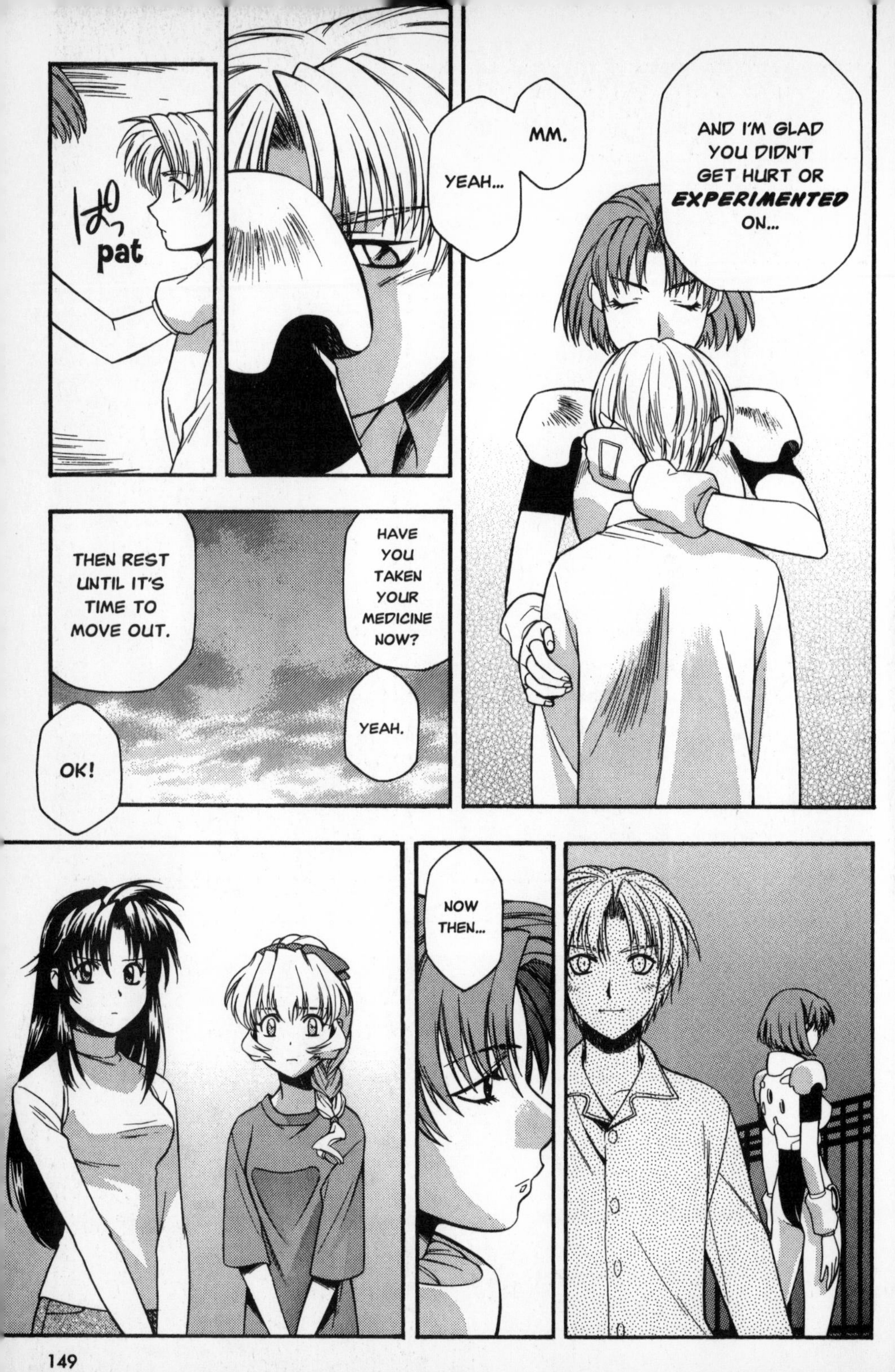
AND I'M GLAD YOU DIDN'T GET HURT OR EXPERIMENTED ON...
MM.
YEAH...
ぽっ
pat
HAVE YOU TAKEN YOUR MEDICINE NOW?
THEN REST UNTIL IT'S TIME TO MOVE OUT.
YEAH.
OK!
NOW THEN...

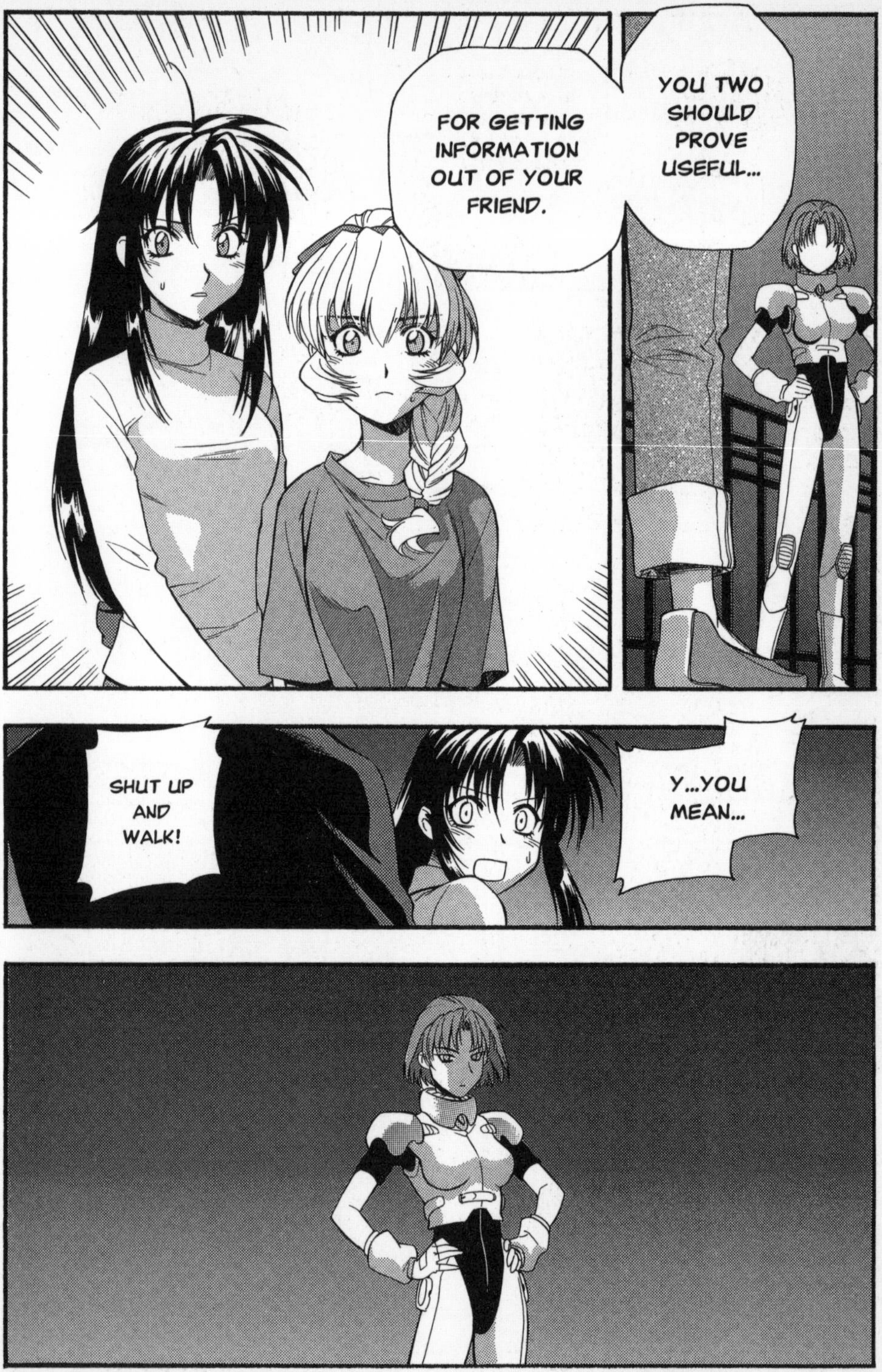
YOU TWO SHOULD PROVE USEFUL...
FOR GETTING INFORMATION OUT OF YOUR FRIEND.
Y...YOU MEAN...
SHUT UP AND WALK!

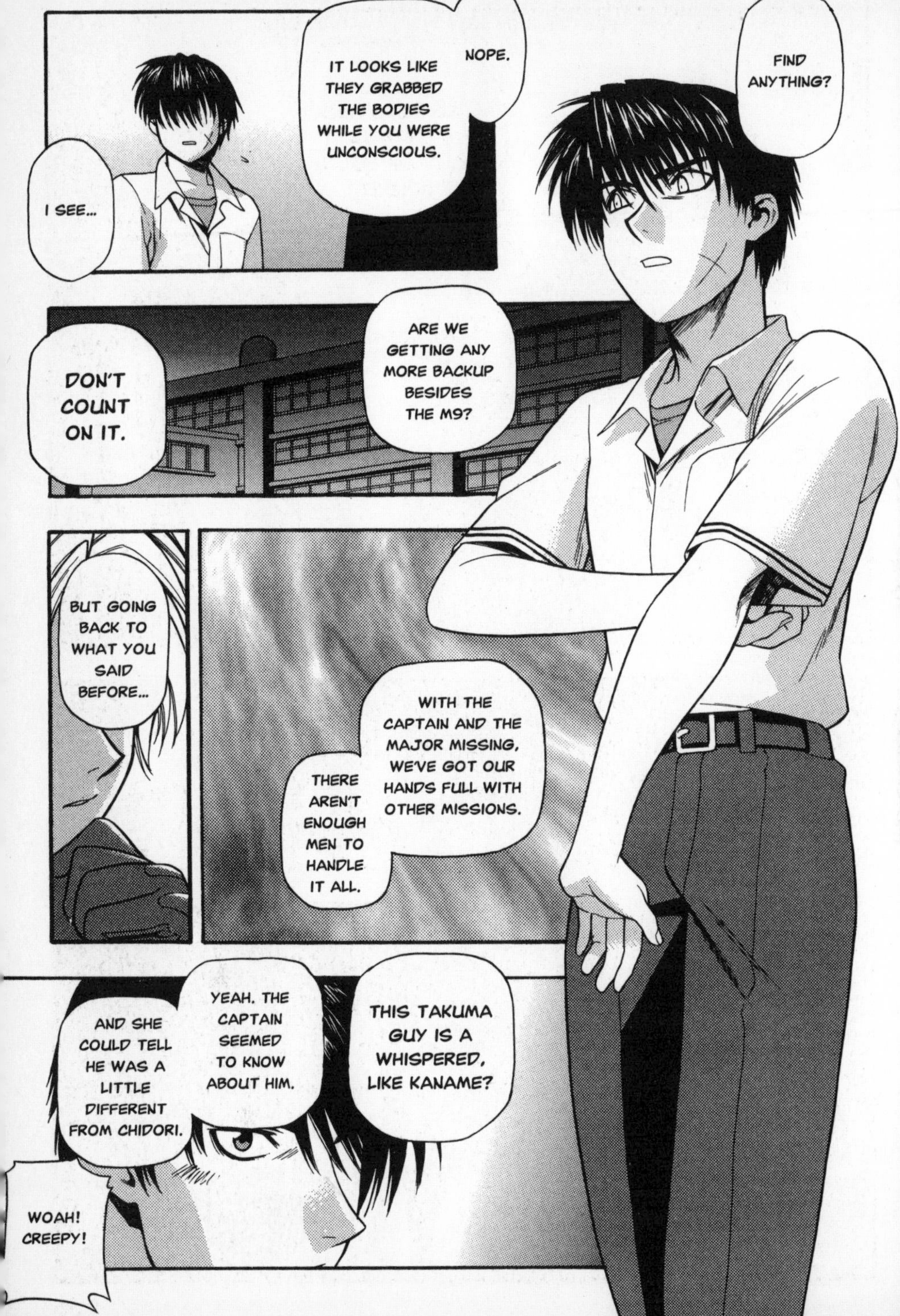
FIND ANYTHING?
NOPE.
IT LOOKS LIKE THEY GRABBED THE BODIES WHILE YOU WERE UNCONSCIOUS.
I SEE...
ARE WE GETTING ANY MORE BACKUP BESIDES THE M9?
DON'T COUNT ON IT.
WITH THE CAPTAIN AND THE MAJOR MISSING, WE'VE GOT OUR HANDS FULL WITH OTHER MISSIONS.
THERE AREN'T ENOUGH MEN TO HANDLE IT ALL.
BUT GOING BACK TO WHAT YOU SAID BEFORE...
THIS TAKUMA GUY IS A WHISPERED, LIKE KANAME?
YEAH. THE CAPTAIN SEEMED TO KNOW ABOUT HIM.
AND SHE COULD TELL HE WAS A LITTLE DIFFERENT FROM CHIDORI.
WOAH! CREEPY!

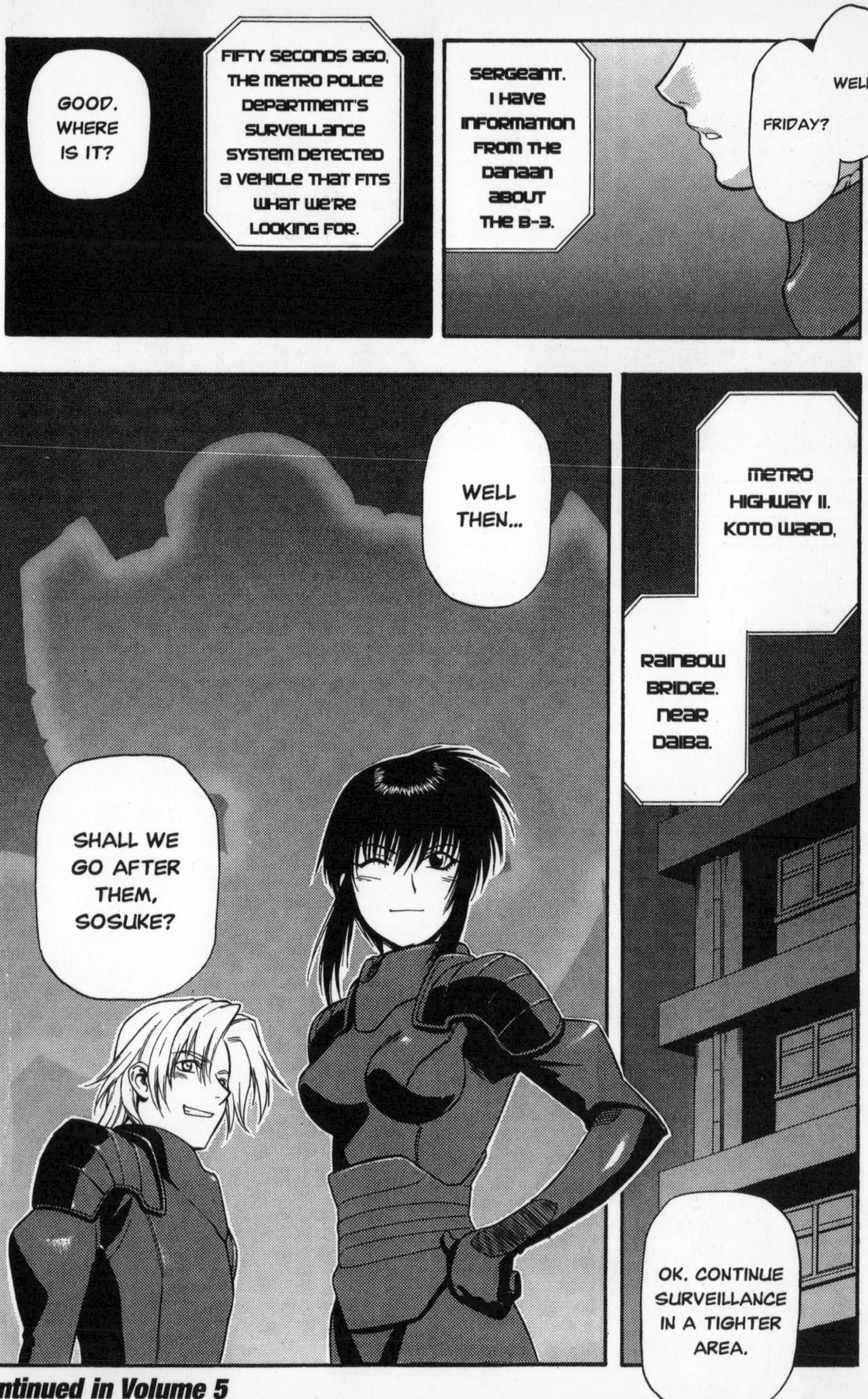
WELL, FRIDAY?
SERGEANT. I HAVE INFORMATION FROM THE DANAAN ABOUT THE B-3.
FIFTY SECONDS AGO, THE METRO POLICE DEPARTMENT'S SURVEILLANCE SYSTEM DETECTED A VEHICLE THAT FITS WHAT WE'RE LOOKING FOR.
GOOD. WHERE IS IT?
METRO HIGHWAY 11. KOTO WARD,
RAINBOW BRIDGE. NEAR DAIBA.
OK. CONTINUE SURVEILLANCE IN A TIGHTER AREA.
WELL THEN...
SHALL WE GO AFTER THEM, SOSUKE?

Continued in Volume 5

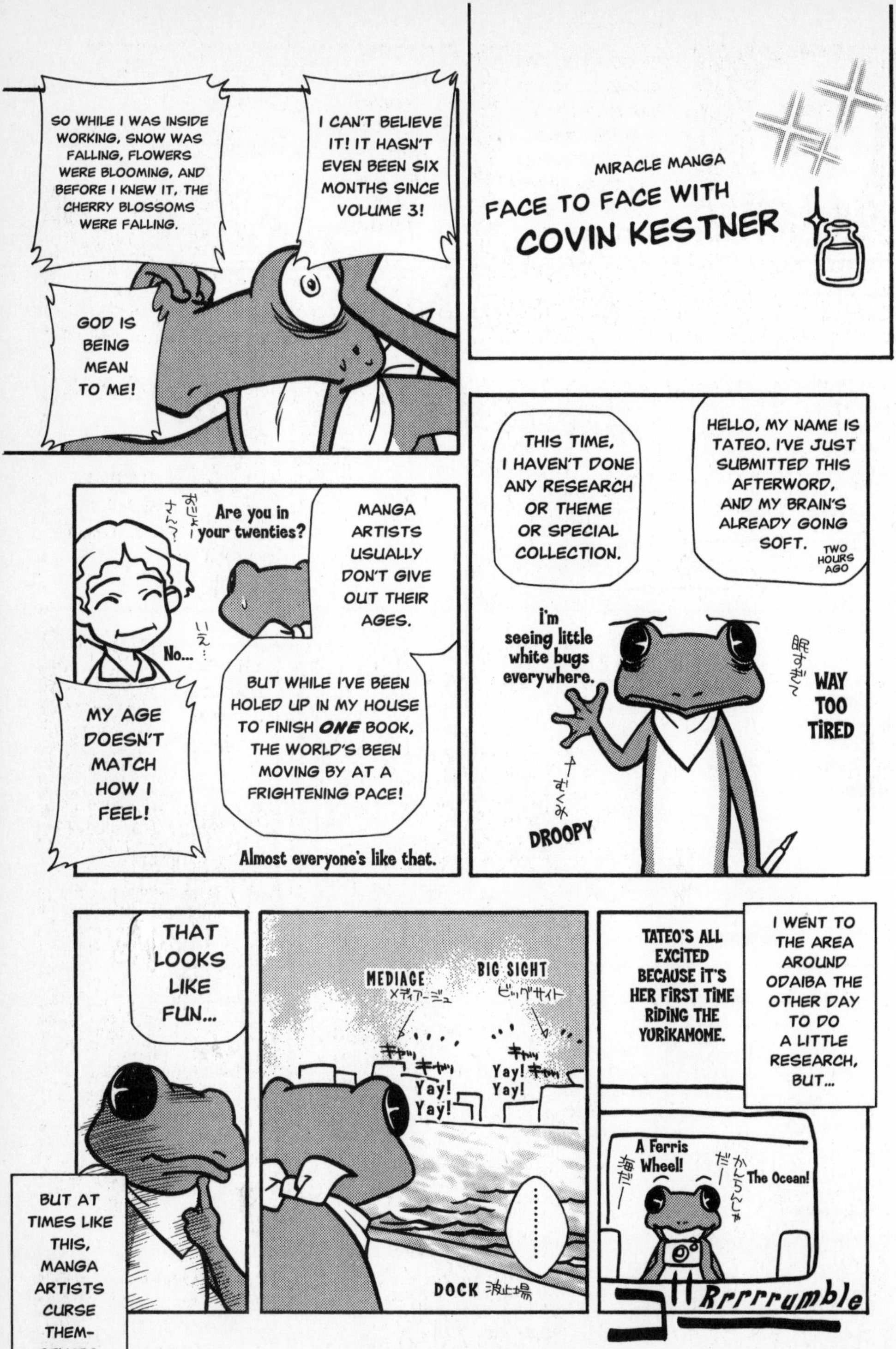
MIRACLE MANGA
FACE TO FACE WITH COVIN KESTNER
I CAN'T BELIEVE IT! IT HASN'T EVEN BEEN SIX MONTHS SINCE VOLUME 3!
SO WHILE I WAS INSIDE WORKING, SNOW WAS FALLING, FLOWERS WERE BLOOMING, AND BEFORE I KNEW IT, THE CHERRY BLOSSOMS WERE FALLING.
GOD IS BEING MEAN TO ME!
HELLO, MY NAME IS TATEO. I'VE JUST SUBMITTED THIS AFTERWORD, AND MY BRAIN'S ALREADY GOING SOFT.
TWO HOURS AGO
THIS TIME, I HAVEN'T DONE ANY RESEARCH OR THEME OR SPECIAL COLLECTION.
眠すぎて
WAY TOO TIRED
i'm seeing little white bugs everywhere.
すくみ
DROOPY
MANGA ARTISTS USUALLY DON'T GIVE OUT THEIR AGES.
Are you in your twenties?
おじょーさん？
BUT WHILE I'VE BEEN HOLED UP IN MY HOUSE TO FINISH ONE BOOK, THE WORLD'S BEEN MOVING BY AT A FRIGHTENING PACE!
いえ…
No...
MY AGE DOESN'T MATCH HOW I FEEL!
Almost everyone's like that.
I WENT TO THE AREA AROUND ODAIBA THE OTHER DAY TO DO A LITTLE RESEARCH, BUT...
TATEO'S ALL EXCITED BECAUSE iT'S HER FiRST TiME RiDiNG THE YURiKAMOME.
The Ocean!
かんらんしゃだー
A Ferris Wheel!
海だー
Rrrrrumble
BIG SIGHT
ビッグサイト
キャッ
Yay! キャッ
Yay!
MEDIAGE
メディアージュ
キャッ キャッ
Yay!
Yay!
......
DOCK 波止場
THAT LOOKS LIKE FUN...
BUT AT TIMES LIKE THIS, MANGA ARTISTS CURSE THEM-SELVES.

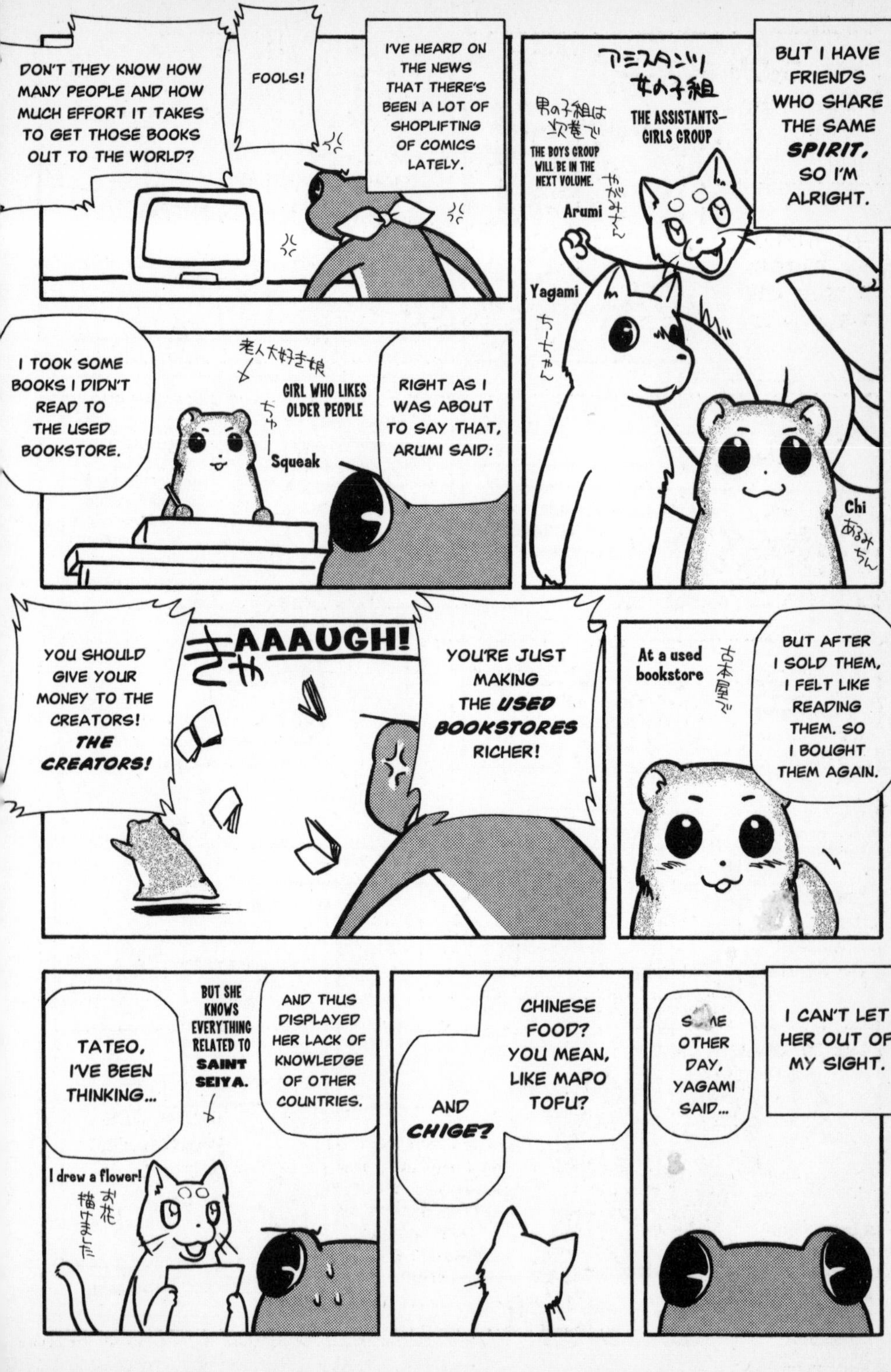
BUT I HAVE FRIENDS WHO SHARE THE SAME SPIRIT, SO I'M ALRIGHT.
アミスタンツ 女の子組
THE ASSISTANTS-GIRLS GROUP
男の子組は次巻で
THE BOYS GROUP WILL BE IN THE NEXT VOLUME.
やがみさん
Arumi
Yagami
ちーちゃん
Chi
あるみちん
I'VE HEARD ON THE NEWS THAT THERE'S BEEN A LOT OF SHOPLIFTING OF COMICS LATELY.
FOOLS!
DON'T THEY KNOW HOW MANY PEOPLE AND HOW MUCH EFFORT IT TAKES TO GET THOSE BOOKS OUT TO THE WORLD?
RIGHT AS I WAS ABOUT TO SAY THAT, ARUMI SAID:
老人大好き娘
GIRL WHO LIKES OLDER PEOPLE
ちゃー
Squeak
I TOOK SOME BOOKS I DIDN'T READ TO THE USED BOOKSTORE.
At a used bookstore
古本屋で
BUT AFTER I SOLD THEM, I FELT LIKE READING THEM. SO I BOUGHT THEM AGAIN.
YOU'RE JUST MAKING THE USED BOOKSTORES RICHER!
きゃ
AAAUGH!
YOU SHOULD GIVE YOUR MONEY TO THE CREATORS! THE CREATORS!
I CAN'T LET HER OUT OF MY SIGHT.
SOME OTHER DAY, YAGAMI SAID...
CHINESE FOOD? YOU MEAN, LIKE MAPO TOFU?
AND CHIGE?
AND THUS DISPLAYED HER LACK OF KNOWLEDGE OF OTHER COUNTRIES.
BUT SHE KNOWS EVERYTHING RELATED TO SAINT SEIYA.
TATEO, I'VE BEEN THINKING...
I drew a flower!
お花描けました

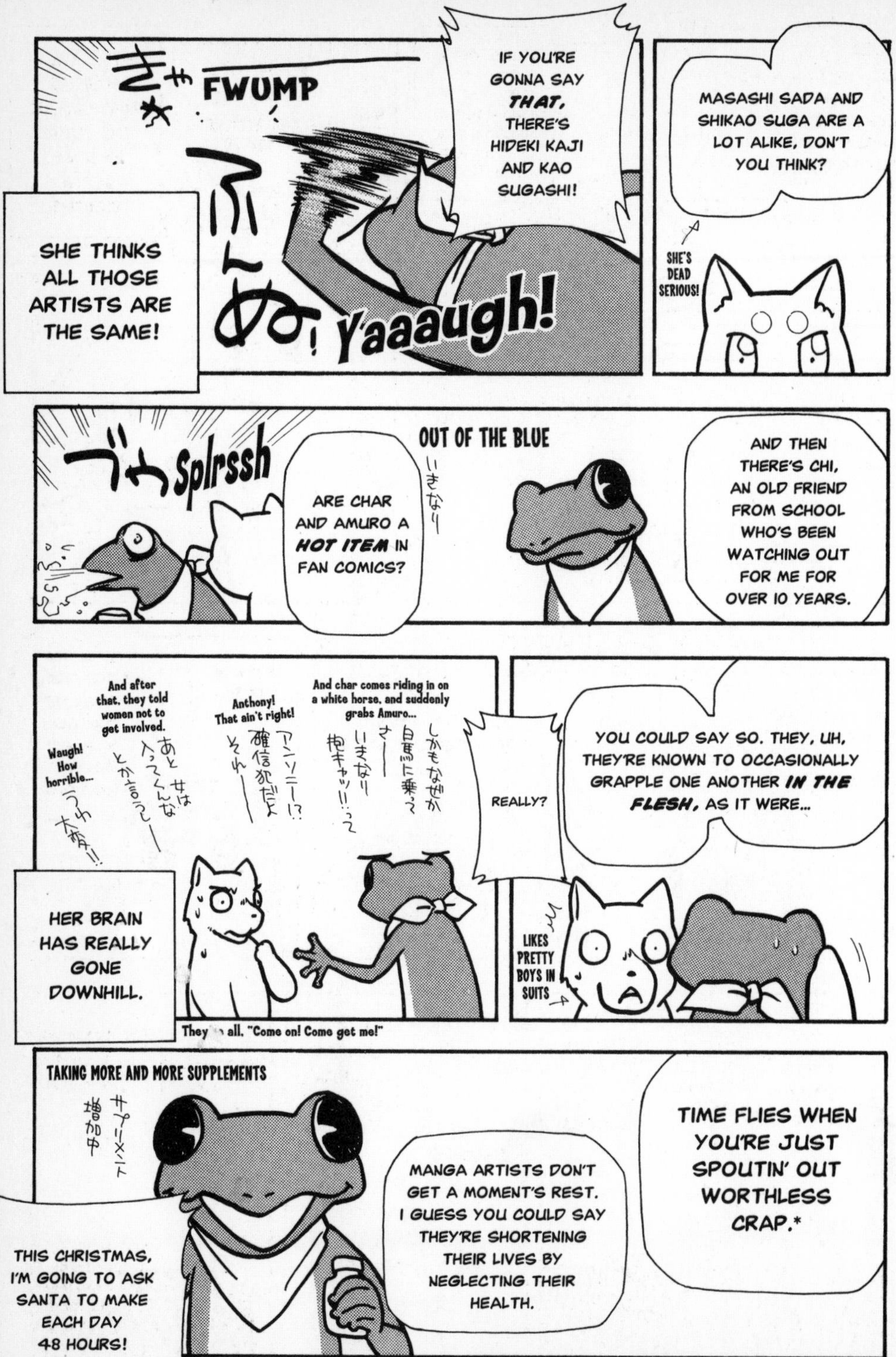
MASASHI SADA AND SHIKAO SUGA ARE A LOT ALIKE, DON'T YOU THINK?
SHE'S DEAD SERIOUS!
IF YOU'RE GONNA SAY *THAT*, THERE'S HIDEKI KAJI AND KAO SUGASHI!
FWUMP
Yaaaugh!
SHE THINKS ALL THOSE ARTISTS ARE THE SAME!
AND THEN THERE'S CHI, AN OLD FRIEND FROM SCHOOL WHO'S BEEN WATCHING OUT FOR ME FOR OVER 10 YEARS.
OUT OF THE BLUE
いきなり
ARE CHAR AND AMURO A *HOT ITEM* IN FAN COMICS?
splrssh
YOU COULD SAY SO. THEY, UH, THEY'RE KNOWN TO OCCASIONALLY GRAPPLE ONE ANOTHER *IN THE FLESH*, AS IT WERE...
REALLY?
LIKES PRETTY BOYS IN SUITS
And char comes riding in on a white horse, and suddenly grabs Amuro...
しかもなぜか白馬に乗ってさー いきなり抱キャッ!!って
Anthony! That ain't right!
アンソニー!? 確信犯だよそれー
And after that, they told women not to get involved.
あと女は入ってくんなとか言うしー
Waugh! How horrible...
うわ大変!!
HER BRAIN HAS REALLY GONE DOWNHILL.
They're all, "Come on! Come get me!"
TIME FLIES WHEN YOU'RE JUST SPOUTIN' OUT WORTHLESS CRAP.*
MANGA ARTISTS DON'T GET A MOMENT'S REST. I GUESS YOU COULD SAY THEY'RE SHORTENING THEIR LIVES BY NEGLECTING THEIR HEALTH.
TAKING MORE AND MORE SUPPLEMENTS
サプリメント増加中
THIS CHRISTMAS, I'M GOING TO ASK SANTA TO MAKE EACH DAY 48 HOURS!

* AND BY THAT I MEAN, THE KIND OF STUFF THAT COMES OUT OF AN OTAKU'S MOUTH WHEN THEY'RE TALKING WITH OTHER OTAKU.

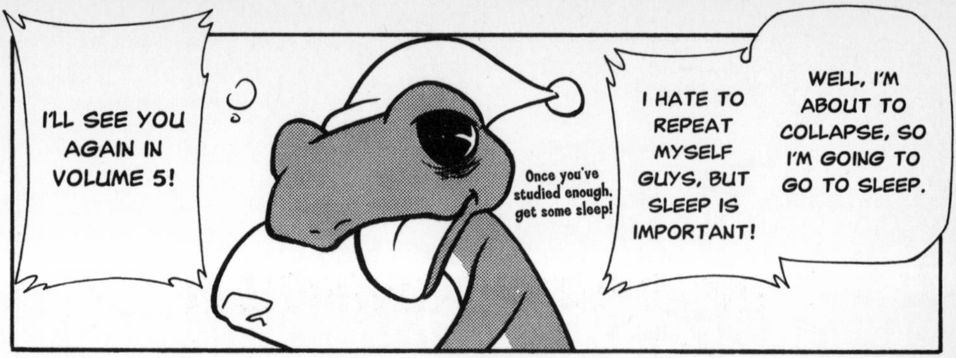

WELL, I'M ABOUT TO COLLAPSE, SO I'M GOING TO GO TO SLEEP.
I HATE TO REPEAT MYSELF GUYS, BUT SLEEP IS IMPORTANT!
Once you've studied enough, get some sleep!
I'LL SEE YOU AGAIN IN VOLUME 5!

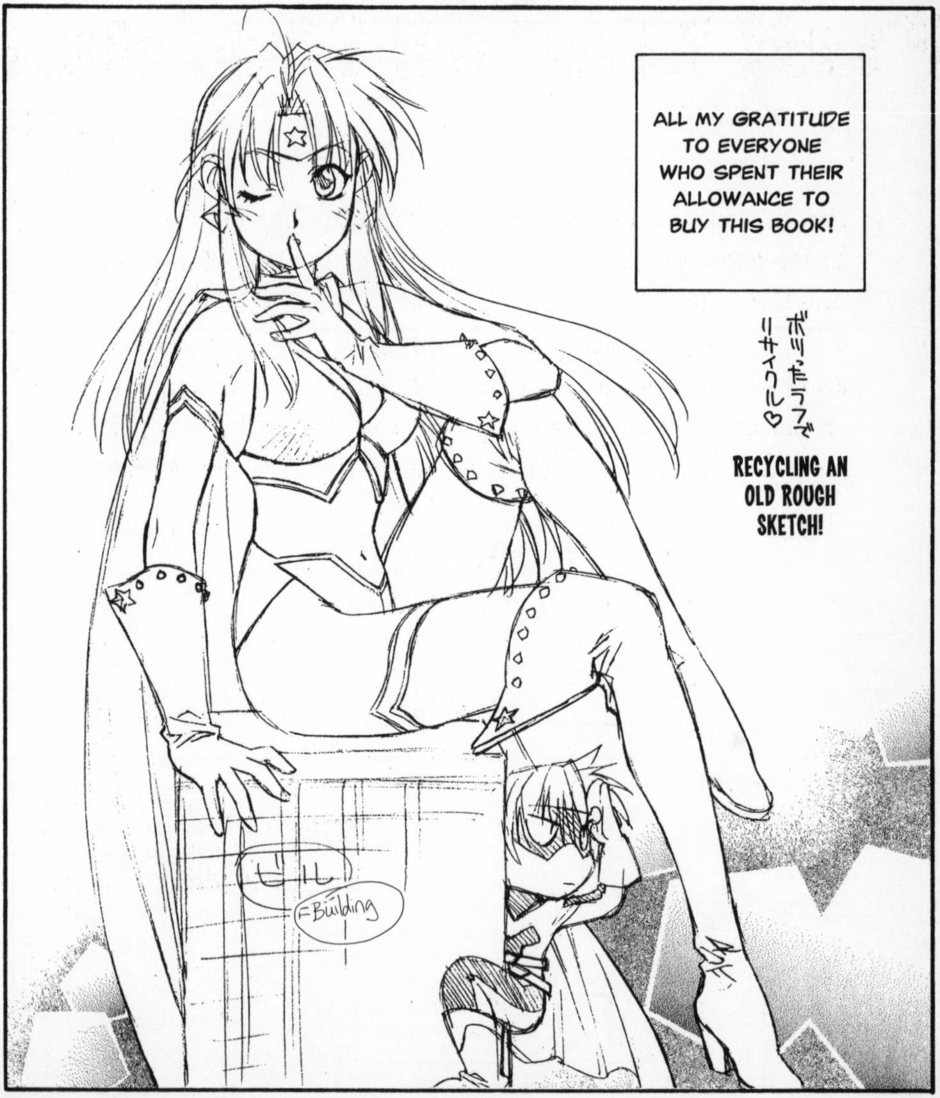

ALL MY GRATITUDE TO EVERYONE WHO SPENT THEIR ALLOWANCE TO BUY THIS BOOK!
ボツったラフでリサイクル♡
RECYCLING AN OLD ROUGH SKETCH!
ビル
Building

THE ADVENTURE CONTINUES IN

Full Metal Panic!
Vol. 05

Kaname and Tessa have been captured! The terrorist group A-21 is desperate for information and attempts to use the girls to get data out of Kalinin. Escape looks bleak, unless they can destroy a massive weapon held by the terrorists. If A-21 manages to activate it, the result could prove to be catastrophic. Only one man has the power to get the huge machine moving. Will he succeed, or will Kaname and Tessa be able to stop him in time? See firsthand if they can escape their captors in the thrilling fifth volume of *Full Metal Panic!*

COMING JUNE 2004 FROM ADV MANGA!

www.adv-manga.com

Full Metal Panic! Volume Four

Author **SHOUJI GATOU**
Illustrator **RETSU TATEO**
Character Creation **SHIKIDOUJI**

© 2002 RETSU TATEO • SHOUJI GATOU • SHIKIDOUJI
Originally published in Japan in 2002 by KADOKAWA SHOTEN PUBLISHING CO., LTD., Tokyo.
English translation rights arranged with KADOKAWA SHOTEN PUBLISHING CO., LTD., Tokyo.

Translator **AMY FORSYTH**
Lead Translator/Translation Supervisor **JAVIER LOPEZ**
ADV Manga Translation Staff **KAY BERTRAND, BRENDAN FRAYNE AND EIKO MCGREGOR**

Print Production/Art Studio Manager **LISA PUCKETT**
Art Production Manager **RYAN MASON**
Sr. Designer/Creative Manager **JORGE ALVARADO**
Graphic Designer/Group Leader **SHANNON RASBERRY**
Graphic Designer **GEORGE REYNOLDS**
Graphic Artists **HEATHER GARY, SHANNA JENSCHKE, WINDI MARTIN,**
KRISTINA MILESKI, NATALIA MORALES, SCOTT SAVAGE, LANCE SWARTOUT,
LISA RAPER, CHRIS LAPP AND NANAKO TSUKIHASHI
Graphic Intern **IVAN CURIEL**

International Coordinator **TORU IWAKAMI**
International Coordinator **ATSUSHI KANBAYASHI**

Publishing Editor **SUSAN ITIN**
Assistant Editor **MARGARET SCHAROLD**
Editorial Assistant **VARSHA BHUCHAR**
Proofreader **SHERIDAN JACOBS**

Research/ Traffic Coordinator **MARSHA ARNOLD**

President, C.E.O. & Publisher **JOHN LEDFORD**

Email: editor@adv-manga.com
www.adv-manga.com
www.advfilms.com

For sales and distribution inquiries please call 1.800.282.7202

is a division of A.D. Vision, Inc.
10114 W. Sam Houston Parkway, Suite 200, Houston, Texas 77099

ISBN: 1-4139-0039-9
First printing, April 2004
10 9 8 7 6 5 4 3 2 1
Printed in Canada

LETTTER FROM THE EDITOR

Dear Reader,

Thank you for purchasing an ADV Manga book. We hope you enjoyed the romantic and thrilling adventures of Kaname and Sosuke in this volume of the *Full Metal Panic!* series.

It is our sincere commitment in reproducing Asian comics and graphic novels to retain as much of the character of the original book as possible. From the right-to-left format of the Japanese books to the meaning of the story in the original language, the ADV Manga team is working hard to publish a quality book for our fans and readers. Write to us with your questions or comments, and tell us how you liked this and other ADV books. Be sure to visit our website at www.adv-manga.com and view the list of upcoming titles, sign up for special announcements, and fill out our survey.

The ADV Manga team of translators, designers, graphic artists, production managers, traffic managers, and editors hope you will buy more ADV books – there's a lot more in store from ADV Manga!

www.adv-manga.com

Publishing Editor	Assistant Editor	Editorial Assistant
Susan B. Itin	Margaret Scharold	Varsha Bhuchar

LETTER FROM THE ADV MANGA TRANSLATION STAFF

Dear Reader,

On behalf of the ADV Manga translation team, thank you for purchasing an ADV book. We are enthusiastic and committed to our work, and strive to carry our enthusiasm over into the book you hold in your hands.

Our goal is to retain the true spirit of the original Japanese book. While great care has been taken to render a true and accurate translation, some cultural or readability issues may require a line to be adapted for greater accessibility to our readers. At times, manga titles that include culturally-specific concepts will feature a "Translator's Notes" section, which explains noteworthy references to the original text.

We hope our commitment to a faithful translation is evident in every ADV book you purchase.

Sincerely,

Javier Lopez
Lead Translator

Eiko McGregor

Kay Bertrand

Brendan Frayne

Amy Forsyth

www.adv-manga.com

Full Metal Panic Vol 04

PG. 22 Bonta-kun
Bonta-kun is modeled after Gonta-kun, a character from **Dekiru kana**, the long-running program that taught children the fun of craft-making.

PG. 46 Boiled and seasoned daikon
The Japanese name for this dish is *daikon no nimono*. While not a particularly extravagant dish, it is considered a quintessential part of home cooking, hence Kaname's surprise. Kyoko's surprise, on the other hand, is at how much Kaname appears to want to cook for Sosuke (a gesture which has quite a romantic feel to it).

PG. 94 Old-fashioned uniforms
In Japan, students tend to place some importance on the style of a school's uniform, to the extent that it can influence their choice of schools.

PG. 109 Einstein's field equations
The "field equations" is the set of 10 second-order partial differential equations which Einstein used to describe his General Theory of Relativity. Solving these equations gives the strength of the gravitational field at any location in space-time.

$\mathcal{C}$ontinued...

PG. 163 (1) Yurikamome
Yurikamome is the name of a train that runs near Odaiba.

(2) Big Sight and Mediage
Big Sight is Japan's largest exhibition and convention center. One of the many events held there is Comiket, Japan's biggest comic market. Mediage is an amusement complex which includes a cinema.

PG. 164 Mapo tofu and chige
Mapo tofu is a Chinese dish consisting of tofu and ground beef (or sometimes pork) in a spicy sauce. Chige, however, is Korean. It's a kind of "hot pot" whose ingredients include kimchee, meat or fish, vegetables, mushrooms and tofu. The fact that Yagami thought both of these dishes were Chinese displayed her "lack of knowledge of other countries."

PG. 165 (1) The artists
The joke here has to do with the names of the artists—when written in Japanese, all their names contain five characters. Thus, Ayumi thought that this similarity in their names meant that the artists themselves were similar.

(2) Likes pretty boys in suits
The topic of discussion here is *dojinshi*, the so-called "fan comics" whose contents tend to get rather explicit. "Pretty boys in suits" is actually *riman* (a contraction of "salaryman"), here used as a genre of homoerotic fan comics where the principal actors are dressed in business suits.

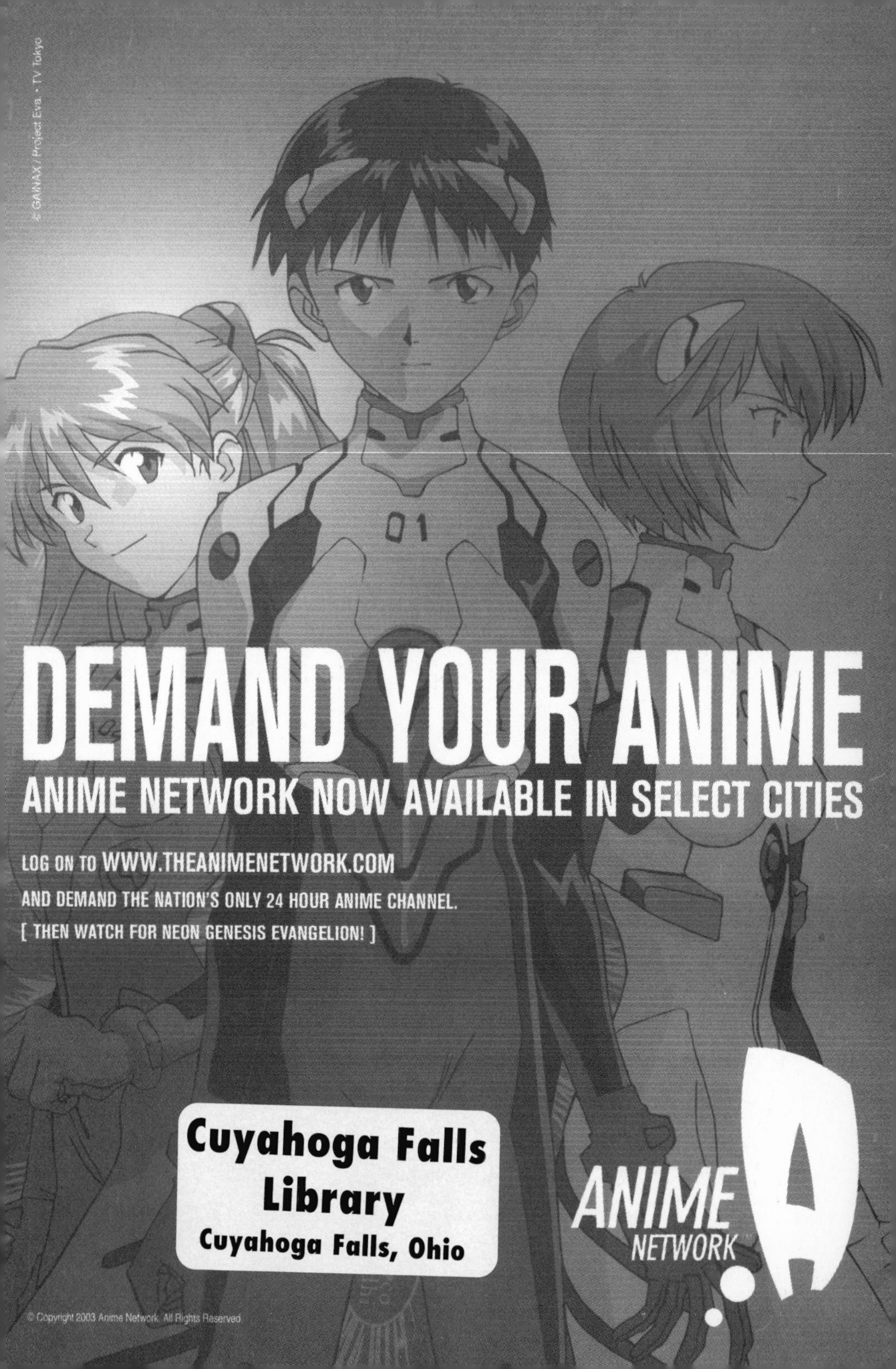
© GAINAX / Project Eva • TV Tokyo
01
DEMAND YOUR ANIME
ANIME NETWORK NOW AVAILABLE IN SELECT CITIES
LOG ON TO WWW.THEANIMENETWORK.COM
AND DEMAND THE NATION'S ONLY 24 HOUR ANIME CHANNEL.
[THEN WATCH FOR NEON GENESIS EVANGELION!]
ANIME NETWORK
© Copyright 2003 Anime Network. All Rights Reserved.

ALSO AVAILABLE FROM

Manga

- Louie the Rune Soldier
- Azumanga Daioh
- Demon City Hunter
- Demon City Shinjuku
- Demon Palace Babylon
- Seven of Seven
- Gunslinger Girl
- Steel Angel Kurumi
- Those Who Hunt Elves
- Happy Lesson
- Darkside Blues

Illustration Books

Rahxephon Bible
●

Full Metal Panic!
●

It's a thin line between love and hate...

A LINE THAT'S ABOUT TO BE SMASHED!

So you want to meet someone, fall in love and get married? Think again!

Love is on the run as the deliciously wicked Lady Raindevila conspires to rid the world of romance and love. With the help of her henchman, Pluie, the world is turned upside down, as lovers stab each other in the back, mothers attack daughters, and best friends try to rip each other's throats out.

Armed with a mysterious ruby ring left by her mother, the unsuspecting Momoko finds herself caught in the middle of this cosmic battle. She's cute, she's sassy, and she's full of love! But will it be enough? Hold on to your corsages! Who knew love could be quite like this???

Volume one available as a single disc as well as a **SPECIAL COLLECTOR'S EDITION** which contains:

Wedding Peach : Volume 1, Love Rain

PLUS A SPECIAL BONUS DISC featuring exclusive extra material not sold separately!

Collector's box set to house all five volumes **PLUS** an inflatable Wedding Peach beach ball!

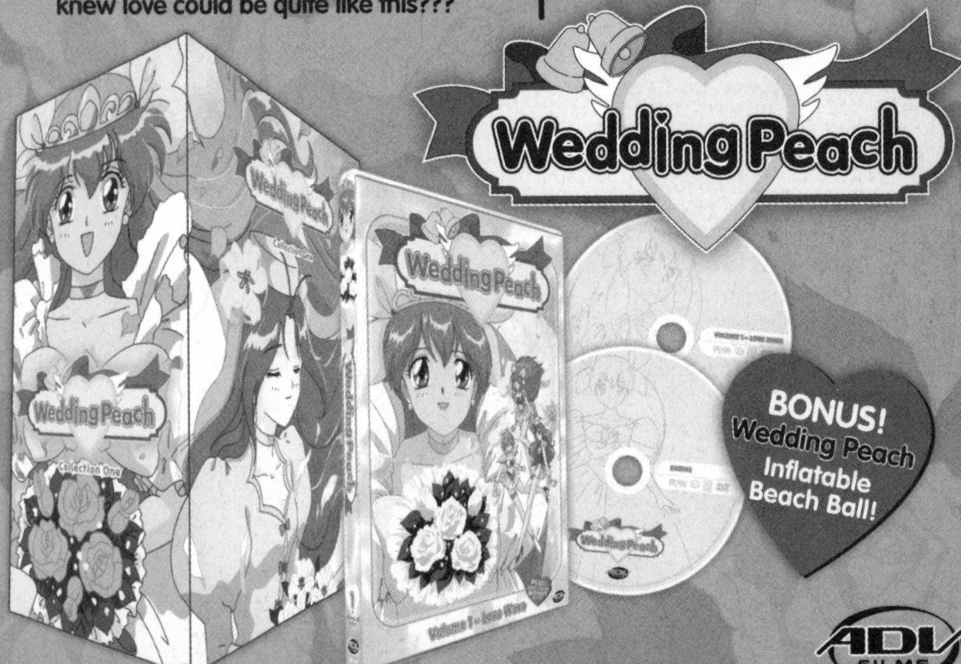

Wedding Peach
Wedding Peach
Collection One
Wedding Peach
BONUS! Wedding Peach Inflatable Beach Ball!

ADV FILMS

www.advfilms.com

Don't Panic!

FULL METAL PANIC!

Volumes 1-3 Available NOW!

Full Metal Panic! vol.1, ISBN 1-4139-0001-1, $9.99
Full Metal Panic! vol.2, ISBN 1-4139-0006-2, $9.99
Full Metal Panic! vol.3, ISBN 1-4139-0007-0, $9.99

www.adv-manga.com

JAPAN'S LEADING MANGA AND ANIME MONTHLY IS AVAILABLE IN ENGLISH!

Packed with exclusive insider information, features and reviews, plus a manga insert, free DVDs, posters, postcards and much, much more! Available at bookstores, specialty shops and newsstands everywhere, or subscribe online today for huge savings off the cover price!

Newtype
THE MOVING PICTURES MAGAZINE. USA 米国版
www.newtype-usa.com

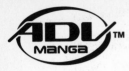

MANGA SURVEY

PLEASE MAIL THE COMPLETED FORM TO: EDITOR – ADV MANGA
c/o A.D. Vision, Inc. 10114 W. Sam Houston Pkwy., Suite 200 Houston, TX 77099

Name: ______________________________
Address: ______________________________
City, State, Zip: ______________________________
____
E-Mail: ______________________________
Male ☐ Female ☐ Age: ______________________________

☐ ***CHECK HERE IF YOU WOULD LIKE TO RECEIVE OTHER INFORMATION OR FUTURE OFFERS FROM ADV.***

All information provided will be used for internal purposes only. We promise not to sell or otherwise divulge your information.

1. Annual Household Income (*Check only one*)

- ☐ Under $25,000
- ☐ $25,000 to $50,000
- ☐ $50,000 to $75,000
- ☐ Over $75,000

2. How do you hear about new Manga releases? (*Check all that apply*)

- ☐ Browsing in Store
- ☐ Internet Reviews
- ☐ Anime News Websites
- ☐ Direct Email Campaigns
- ☐ Magazine Ad
- ☐ Online Advertising
- ☐ Conventions
- ☐ TV Advertising
- ☐ Online forums (message boards and chat rooms)
- ☐ Carrier pigeon
- ☐ Other: ______________________________

3. Which magazines do you read? (*Check all that apply*)

- ☐ Wizard
- ☐ SPIN
- ☐ Animerica
- ☐ Rolling Stone
- ☐ Maxim
- ☐ DC Comics
- ☐ URB
- ☐ Polygon
- ☐ Original Play Station Magazine
- ☐ Entertainment Weekly
- ☐ YRB
- ☐ EGM
- ☐ Newtype USA
- ☐ SciFi
- ☐ Starlog
- ☐ Wired
- ☐ Vice
- ☐ BPM
- ☐ I hate reading
- ☐ Other: ____________________